"*The heart and soul of football in all its glory*" - Henry Winter

FA C

150

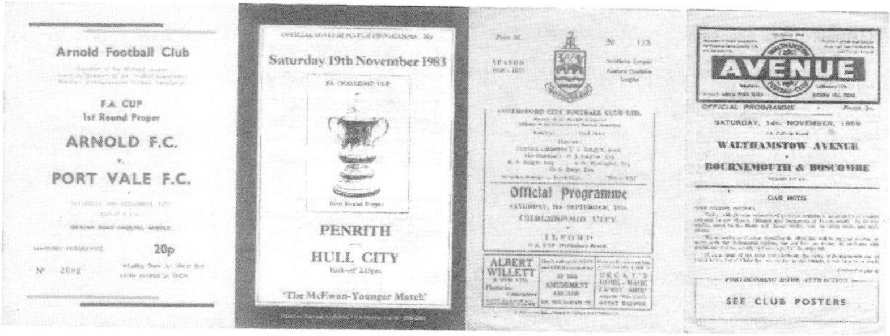

An unofficial compendium of FA Cup facts and stats from FACupFactfile celebrating **150 years** of the original and best knock-out competition

Phil Annets

ISBN 978-1-5272-9564-3 First published in 2021

FA Cup 150

Contents

EVERY CLUB. EVERY SEASON. EVERY MATCH.

Preface

"For every single round of the FA Cup that I cover, I can happily guarantee that Phil from FACupFactfile will come up with a nugget or two that I will make a note of and use in my match commentaries"

John Murray – BBC Football Correspondent – May 2021

The FACupFactfile database contains every single result across 150 years of FA Cup history, involving more than 3,240 clubs playing over 73,300 matches between them and collectively scoring greater than a quarter of a million goals. The premise of FACupFactfile is to provide FA Cup facts and stats covering the whole competition from August to May each season, providing as much prominence to the hundreds of small town and village clubs that participate in it each year as it does to those in the Premier League.

Principally, FACupFactfile has focused on sharing club based FA Cup facts and stats via Twitter, Facebook and on-line blogs since 2015, and has been included in five of the last six FA Cup Final programmes. This includes traditional facts such as top goal-scorers, record wins, most titles etc. that one would expect from a stats provider, but also incorporates a heavy focus on more peculiar facts and stats such as longest combined named ties, most continuous matches requiring replays, and most disqualifications to name but three.

It has always been the case that a book of football statistics is out of date the moment it is published, and this has never been more true than in the current digital age where updated facts and records are posted on-line almost continuously twenty-four seven. However, it is appropriate to produce books of facts and records at key milestone periods such as this, the 150th anniversary of the FA Cup, providing a 'stake in the ground' picture from which future stats and records can be built.

This FACupFactfile *FA Cup 150* book is designed to do just that, but its intention is not necessarily to be the definitive account of the competition's 150 year history, rather it is to provide interesting, significant and many quirky FA Cup facts and records that can be referenced alongside other books published to celebrate this key anniversary. A complete and vast FACupFactfile record of the competition has also been produced, of course, and snapshots from that will be shared via social media throughout the 2021/22 FA Cup campaign.

"As it celebrates its 150th anniversary, it's only right that the unique history of FA Cup is celebrated with this remarkable labour of love by the man who probably knows more than anyone alive about the world's oldest cup competition. Simply a fact-finder's delight."

Steve Wilson – Football Commentator – May 2021

Introduction

Dedicated to everyone the world over who loves the FA Cup.

The FA Cup was the brainchild of Charles W. Alcock, Secretary of the Football Association, who proposed the idea of a knockout competition for all member clubs of the fledgling FA to its committee members on 20 July 1871. One hundred and fifty years later the competition remains a highlight of the English domestic football calendar and is loved, watched and adored by millions of fans worldwide.

Just 15 clubs entered that inaugural 1871/72 competition, with only a dozen of those actually participating in it. A century and a half later the competition now comprises of more than 730 clubs spanning the professionals of the Premier League and the Football League, right down to a plethora of village and small town clubs the length and breadth of the country. Whilst those involved at either ends of the FA Cup's timespan would not recognise the game and competition at their respective opposing ends, the structure of the competition has remained more or less the same throughout; a series of rounds pitting teams together in each round resulting in half continuing on to the next round whilst the other half end their interest in that season's competition. This process continues until the last two clubs meet in the FA Cup Final and the winner of that match is declared the champion. Well, there was one exception to that process.

The competition's actual full name is '*The FA Challenge Cup*' and the original concept was that the holders of the Trophy would be challenged by the club that won through the knock-out process, to play out a Final to determine that season's winner. This approach was only used in the 1872/73 season, the second to be contested, and never used again, although the official name of the competition, '*The FA Challenge Cup*', remains to this day. There have been over 73,000 matches played in the FA Cup since eight clubs kicked the whole thing off on 11 November 1871, with more than 250,000 goals scored since Jarvis Kenrick registered the competition's first ever one playing for Clapham Rovers in their 3-0 win over Upton Park.

This 'FA Cup 150' book pulls together disparate rankings and lists containing, where possible, the top 150 or most notable 150 entries within each of those lists. Some lists are what would be expected to be found in any publication covering the history of the FA Cup, such as a list of winning teams or a ranking of top goal-scorers. However, this book also provides some less familiar lists and rankings, and mixes them all together to provide a cornucopia of facts and stats about the FA Cup designed to delight and surprise even the most ardent football statistician. But first, a little bit about why I love the FA Cup and why I spend an inordinate amount of time analysing the competition and producing facts and stats all about it.

Love of the FA Cup

Why does the FA Cup have such a hold on me? Why do I have a passion for covering the exploits of teams that have a snowball's chance in hell of ever lifting the famous trophy? Why have I been obsessed with capturing the records of every club that has ever entered the competition? Well, it's not because the club I have supported for 50 years has had real FA Cup pedigree during my conscious lifetime, anyway, that's for sure.

I've been a fan of Leeds United since the very early nineteen-seventies, but I only have a vague recollection of watching their 1972 FA Cup triumph 'live' on TV as a seven year-old, even though I know I did. I have a much clearer memory of watching the Cup Final the following year, which also involved Leeds United, although that might be because it is replayed on TV ad nauseum every time Sunderland are involved in an FA Cup game, or any time the TV wants to show an example of a great FA Cup upset, or any time they want to show an example of outstanding goalkeeping. You get the picture. And since then, just two semi-finals and a smattering of quarter-finals is all that Leeds United has to show for 50 more years of effort in the competition. Given that only 16 different clubs have won the FA Cup since 1972, there must be millions of football fans in the same boat as me. That's one of the reasons the competition is so special to so many; a great FA Cup run for most fans is a rare beast, so it is to be savoured when it does actually come along. Just ask Leicester City fans.

Personally, I've not even been to Wembley (or elsewhere) to watch an FA Cup Final, only wanting to go to the Final if Leeds United were involved, which seems more unlikely every passing year. I have actually seen Leeds United play at Wembley, but in the Charity Shield against Liverpool, and have seen them play at The Millennium Stadium in Cardiff for what proved to be a dismal play-off Final against Watford. I have also experienced Wembley, old and new, through attending the first FA Vase final (my home town team Epsom & Ewell were in it – they lost), the FA Trophy final with Southport (a former home town team – they lost), and watching several England Internationals. I've even seen an American Football match there and watched Madonna's *'Blond Ambition'* show from the stands. But never an FA Cup Final.

Of course, I have witnessed all the FA Cup finals over the last 50 years 'live' on TV, and I have watched on in dismay as what was once treated as the crowning glory to the end of the domestic season, has been eroded by a combination of TV scheduling, Premier League dominance and Champions League finals, to become almost a footnote to it. Or, in other words, the increasing investment of money elsewhere adversely impacting on this famous annual day. The FA Cup's standing has suffered as a consequence of top-flight club owners' financial objectives influencing team selection decisions resulting in managers opting to field less regular first team players and reserves in early rounds of the FA Cup. This approach is taken not just by those clubs at the top of the Premier League, but by almost all clubs in that division, as well as many EFL Championship teams and lower level Football League clubs. As a consequence the FA Cup's supposed lustre and magic can often feel to be lacking in the early 'Proper' Rounds, although clubs do appear to take the competition more seriously the closer they get to Wembley.

For me the FA Cup remains the optimum football competition for three reasons. As it was the first knock-out competition, the FA Cup is the only one that links the modern game with its formative years. Secondly, because the competition is open-entry to all clubs across the top nine levels of the football pyramid, it is the only one that directly links the top clubs in the Premier League with the community clubs the length and breadth of the country. Finally, the FA Cup is the only competition where every game really matters. One loss and you're out. No second chances. No second legs. No future group games to put things right. Get it wrong on the day and you will come a cropper, maybe on the wrong end of a potentially embarrassing giant-killing, and will have to sit it out and watch others advance until the chance comes around to play in it again the next season. Added to those three reasons you will find that, at earlier stages of the competition, away from the Final and the later rounds, the FA Cup continues to thrive, the magic is very much alive, and the love for it is almost on a par with my own.

In the late 1990s I moved to South Oxfordshire, not an area known for being a hotbed of football and FA Cup success. I began to watch local games as the cost involved in physically supporting Leeds United became prohibitive, opting to spread my attendance across many teams within the County and in the surrounding area rather than focusing on just one team. The early stages of the FA Cup were the perfect platform to get to experience as many local clubs as possible. And through attending these matches, I saw a side to football that wasn't evident in what was being served up on TV or at the top end of the game, a difference that would become more and more pronounced in line with the increasing financial support for the game at the top level. This was football by the people and for the people. Those that played the game knew those that watched the game. Those that invested in the game did so because the club, and the town it represented, meant something to them. There was a community feel, people were giving their precious time for the club, and everyone was 'in it together'. A far cry from the ivory tower of the Premier League.

As I experienced these local clubs and the people involved with them, I became exposed to similar clubs and people from across neighbouring counties and beyond. I wanted to know more about those clubs that took part in the early stages of the FA Cup, hundreds and hundreds of clubs in the competition that the mainstream media ignore and about which the general football watching public are oblivious. I had always been as interested in the statistical side of football as much as I was in the game itself, and had already collated comprehensive FA Cup records for the 'Proper' Rounds of the competition, as well as for all other aspects of English and European football. However, I had not really delved into the world of non-league football, only covering those clubs when they appeared in the 'Proper' Rounds of the FA Cup, but weekly exposure to that level of football triggered a desire to complete my records of the FA Cup by incorporating the qualifying rounds, too.

I discovered Tony Brown's excellent *Complete FA Cup Results* book, the magnificent '*The Football Club History Database*' wonderfully maintained by Richard Rundle on the internet, and the '*Godfather of FA Cup Stats*' Mike Collett's *FA Cup Complete Records* book. Being the completer-finisher that I am, and because it didn't already exist, I determined that I wanted to be the one to collate every possible result to identify every club's record, no matter how insignificant, and to be able to produce insight and interesting information about those performances in the competition. It's not possible to get that deep into anything without it becoming etched on to your heart. I already had a passion for football stats at the top level, and now I had transferred that passion to the records of thousands of lesser known clubs, current and long gone, with a particular focus on how they have performed in the FA Cup.

And now I have completed my task, although just as the Forth Bridge once needed to be continuously painted, my FA Cup database needs continually updating every season. I now have a record of all 3,240 plus clubs that have ever participated in the FA Cup, their individual performances, games played, and bespoke achievements. And thanks to my inherent penchant for statistical analysis, I have been able to produce unique new insights into those performances, which I now share via Twitter (@FACupFactfile). Sometimes they are stats that only one person would be interested in, other times they are surprising facts that a wider audience wants to know about. I love finding new nuggets of information, I love sharing that information with those with a similar passion for the competition, and I love watching clubs in those early round matches and seeing their delight at progressing to the next round. My approach is one of treating all clubs involved in the FA Cup as equal, producing stats and facts for local village clubs as much as are produced for Premier League sides.

I now get as much pleasure in following those clubs' exploits as I do from Leeds United's own performance (although, of course, I'd still prefer to one day see Leeds United walk out in an FA Cup Final at Wembley). I particularly enjoy those clubs quoting my stats on Twitter or using them in their match-day programmes. However, I have never been as proud as the day my stats were first incorporated into the FA Cup Final programme itself.

In short, it's fair to say, I just love the FA Cup!

Extract from the first set of FACupFactfile Stats to appear in an FA Cup Final programme

The Challenges of Compiling FA Cup Records

It might seem strange in a book about facts and stats that I include a section explaining how there may well be errors and mistakes within it. However, I am fully aware that it is highly likely that there will be. And knowing how damning it can be for any statistician's reputation - regardless of the fact that 99% of what is produced could be accurate it is the 1% of errors that people want to shout about - I wanted to address it upfront. No matter how thoroughly the data is researched, there are always going to be mistakes made in record-collating, publishing records and providing detailed analysis.

There are four main types of potential errors that may occur in a reference book such as this, as detailed below, and I welcome feedback and supportive evidence of any facts and stats that I include that may not be considered as being correct. I will more than happily include the names of people who have helped address errors in future versions of FA Cup facts books I write. My sole aim is to do whatever is necessary to ensure that what I produce is as completely accurate a reflection of every club's FA Cup history as it can be. Any accidental errors contained within this book are exactly that; accidental errors.

Lack of Record Keeping in the Past

Today's world of super-fast, vast internet database searches is a far cry from the pen and ink recordings of the latter half of the nineteenth century when organised football first saw the light of day. Newspapers and magazines were the only media reporting football matches in its formative years, sporadically for much of the early years, and naturally they never presented information in such a way knowing that over 100 years later there would be an army of statisticians, reporters, bloggers and journalists all keen to read and report on what happened. As a consequence there are always going to be discrepancies in the records of match results from football's infancy. Some newspaper reports just recorded the score, some just wrote about the action or just named the winner, other results simply did not get published, and many were incorrectly printed either with the wrong scoreline or with wrong team names. Those who have undertaken the momentous task of siphoning through often illegible newspaper cuttings on fiche machines have my utmost respect and admiration.

Human Error

With all the best intentions in the world, with the vast amount of data to be collated, analysed and converted into presentable charts and graphs, there is always going to be an element of human error. I know from occasions when I've tweeted facts and stats how easy it is to mistype or misread some information when transferring it into a Tweet (I quickly get informed of my error). However, when recording data and creating charts on a large scale, errors are bound to creep in, no matter how much proof-reading is undertaken. Those errors could be mine, or they could have been made in the source material, taken as fact and incorporated into my analysis.

Deliberate Incorrect Data (Mountweasels)

Gathering information such as the complete FA Cup scores takes years to compile, and those that first undertook the task quite rightly would want recompense for their data being duplicated in other publications. Often, researched information will get printed without quoting the source (overtly or covertly claiming the data as their own). As a form of protection and to help identify the perpetrators, owners of the original data would often incorporate deliberate errors that if reprinted could legally be shown to be their source data. Obviously the data I have collated comes from a combination of my own extensive research, speaking with people and searching the internet and public libraries, as well as via already existing publications. To that end I will never just duplicate information sourced from other researchers, rather I take that data and re-present it in my own unique style. I earlier quoted three major contributing sources that I have used when researching my FA Cup facts, all of which through my own research were found to contain errors and omissions. There could be more erroneous facts I have not yet identified as being so, which I have then re-presented in this book. Some may have been intentionally included by the authors. Often, these kind of 'errors' are small in number and usually have little impact on the FA Cup statistics I present.

Unclarified Club Histories

Tracing the history of any football club can be fraught with problems, not least due to inaccurate record keeping and reporting. However, different individuals and different sources may provide different interpretations of historical events. Again, when momentous events occur such as a club closing down and re-forming, it is not always obvious whether the 'new' club is just a continuation of the previous club (and thereby owns its history), or is indeed a brand new entity. Even when there are clear records that the 'new' club is different from the previous club, many fans and those involved in the clubs will consider the two as one.

There are too many instances of unclarified club histories to be listed here, but some examples are Chesterfield (presented as one continuous club despite at least re-forming three times), Ilford (the 1987 formed club is considered to be separate from the one formed in 1881 despite fans' view that they the same), and Nelson (recorded as one continuous club despite the club's own website stating that the original club folded and a 'new' Nelson Town was formed). Whatever choices I've made I've done so to the best of my knowledge of what is the right way to report club histories. I've made changes to my position upon presentation of hard facts to the contrary, and am always happy to do so again. The final table of this *FA Cup 150* book shows the complete list of when 2020/21 competing clubs first entered the FA Cup. From this list it is possible to deduce how I treat each club whatever their considered history.

Summary of Potential Errors

As I stated earlier, it might seem strange that a book all about FA Cup facts and stats should include a disclaimer that some of the facts and stats it contains might not necessarily be accurate. But I'm sure you will agree that in a work that sources data over 140 seasons, for 3,240 plus clubs and for over 73,300 matches, the odd error creeping in is often inconsequential. Best of all, you can always bring any errors you spot to my attention, and I will incorporate the corrections into future work.

The Seven Ages of the FA Cup

Across the FA Cup's illustrious 150 year history, only seven clubs have ever been able to make the claim that they are the 'Greatest FA Cup Club of All Time'. This claim can only be made by the club with the best FA Cup record at any point in time, and is based on which one has lifted the Trophy the most often since the competition's first season. If two or more clubs had lifted the Trophy the same number of times at any point in history, then it is the club from that tied list that has appeared in the most finals. If that still couldn't separate them, then the most number of semi-final appearances comes into play, then the most quarter-finals etc. etc. until there is a difference.

Obviously, after just one season, the first ever winners, The Wanderers, were able to make that claim, and now after 150 years it is Arsenal, with their record of 14 FA Cup triumphs, who are regarded as the 'Greatest FA Cup Club of All time'. The other five clubs to have held the title are Blackburn Rovers, Aston Villa (for two separate periods), Newcastle United, Manchester United (for two separate periods) and Tottenham Hotspur. Tracking the time periods when these clubs occupied the position of 'Greatest FA Cup Club of All Time' brings focus on how the FA Cup, and football as a whole, has developed over these past 150 years, creating the 'Seven Ages of the FA Cup'.

Old Boys Network – The Age of the Southern Amateurs

Competitive football was originally a sport participated in by 'southern amateur gentlemen' who predominantly had either been educated at a public school such as Eton and Harrow, or were officer class in the army (or both). This amateur status was one of the core values of the fledgling Football Association and the early seasons of the FA Cup were pretty much exclusive to teams made up of players from this old boys' network with a strong amateur ethos. In fact, many of the players involved were also key individuals at the Football Association. Even provincial clubs such as Maidenhead and Marlow, and Queen's Park from Scotland, were populated by individuals with the same ethos.

The first FA Cup Final in 1872 saw The Wanderers defeat Royal Engineers and in doing so they became the first club to be able to lay claim to the title 'the Greatest FA Cup Club of All time'. This would be a claim the club could make for almost 20 years, as they supplemented their first FA Cup victory with four other triumphs across the next six seasons. The Wanderers are still one of only two clubs to have won a hat-trick of FA Cup finals in successive seasons, and are also one of only two clubs to have participated in multiple finals and win them all. Their FA Cup record is so strong that it wasn't until almost 140 years later that they would not be regarded as one of the ten best clubs in the FA Cup.

1871-72 to 1878-79	w	f	sf	qf	5	4	3	2	1	Rank
Wanderers, The	5			2					1	1
Royal Engineers	1	3		2			1	1		2
Oxford University	1	2	2	2						3
Old Etonians	1	2							2	4

The Top Four Clubs in FA Cup at End of 1870s

Nb. All charts used in this section show number of exits per Round

But, as with the amateur ethos that founded competitive football, their dominance of the game and the FA Cup was short-lived. By the time The Wanderers won their fifth FA Cup in 1877/78 the competition witnessed that season the arrival of northern based 'professional' clubs in the shape of Notts County and Darwen.

The Age of the Professionals

There was considerable resistance by the FA to clubs paying players to participate in the FA Cup, and for the next ten years there would be a battle between the two sides, both on and off the field. Several clubs were ejected from the competition after being accused of, and being found guilty of paying their players, and many (usually northern based) clubs tried to disguise the fact players were being paid, by club owners 'employing' them in the factories also owned by the club's chairmen. But gradually, professionalism won the day, and just ten years after The Wanderers' last FA Cup triumph, the Football League was launched involving a dozen northern and midlands based professional clubs only, including Accrington, one of the first clubs to be disqualified from the FA Cup for paying their players.

And it wasn't long after The Wanderers' last FA Cup win that northern professional clubs would go on to dominate the competition as well. Blackburn Olympic are famously known for being the first such club to lift the Trophy in 1883, but it would be another club from the same town who would go on to become the second 'Greatest FA Cup Club of All Time'. Blackburn Rovers actually reached the FA Cup Final one year earlier than their local rivals (the first professional club to do so), and it would be this runners-up appearance that would enable them to jump ahead of the Wanderers when winning the FA Cup for a fifth time in 1891. A position they would retain right up until the outbreak of World War I.

1871-72 to 1890-91	w	f	sf	qf	5	4	3	2	1	Rank
Blackburn Rovers	5	1	1	1			1	3		1
Wanderers, The	5			2			1		3	2

The Top Two Clubs in FA Cup after Blackburn Rovers' Fifth Triumph

War and Peace – The Age of the Working Man's Game

For 45 years after Blackburn Rovers first FA Cup Final appearance in 1882, only one southern based club lifted the FA Cup, Tottenham Hotspur in 1901. However, the 'north' did not have it all its own way, as another hotbed of high quality football emerged in the West Midlands with Aston Villa, West Bromwich Albion and Wolverhampton Wanderers being victorious in ten FA Cup finals during that time, with Villa being the most dominant. Aston Villa first lifted the FA Cup in 1887 against West Bromwich Albion and won it for the fifth time in 1913 against league champions Sunderland in what was their sixth Final. However, because Blackburn Rovers had appeared in 11 semi-finals by then as opposed to Villa's nine last four appearances, it was they who retained the title of 'Greatest FA Cup Club of All Time'.

1871-72 to 1919-20	w	f	sf	qf	5	4	3	2	1	Rank
Aston Villa	6	1	3	4	1	3	5	8	6	1
Blackburn Rovers	5	1	5	4			4	8	10	2
Wanderers, The	5			2			1		3	3

The Top three Clubs in FA Cup after Aston Villa's Sixth Triumph

But this all changed in the first competition after the Great War, won 1-0 by Aston Villa against Huddersfield Town at Stamford Bridge. Villa became the first club to lift the Trophy six times, and claimed the title of 'Greatest FA Cup Club of All Time', a title they would hold for all but two seasons over the next 70 years.

The Golden Age

Football, and the FA Cup, first sealed its position as the nation's number one sport immediately after the Great War, and then again after the end of the Second World War, with the 1950s regarded by many as the Golden Age of the game. A national home for the game was built at Wembley Stadium in 1923 where the FA Cup Final would also find a permanent home, bestowing the venue with mythical-like status and a desire for fans to see their club play there in the showpiece finale of the season.

Aston Villa failed to add to their FA Cup winning tally for nigh on 40 years, opening the door to other clubs to challenge them for their 'Greatest FA Cup Club of All time' status. Blackburn Rovers did match Villa's sixth triumph in 1928, but by then Aston Villa had been runners-up once more and so held a slight advantage over their Lancastrian rivals. However, it was the club that had defeated Aston Villa in 1924 which would go on to claim to be the next 'Greatest FA Cup Club of All Time', namely Newcastle United, albeit briefly. Newcastle United had dominated English football at the start of the 20th Century and, but for what seemed like a curse with the name Crystal Palace, would have been regarded as the 'Greatest FA Cup Club of All time' much sooner.

In five FA Cup finals across seven seasons at Crystal Palace, Newcastle United were successful just the once. They even managed to be knocked out of the competition in one of the other two seasons by Crystal Palace FC, then a Southern League club. But they would finally claim the 'Greatest Club' title thanks to three wins in five seasons the 1950s. Victories in 1951 and 1952 were added to by beating Manchester City in 1955 to match the six FA Cup triumphs of Aston Villa and Blackburn Rovers.

1871-72 to 1954-55	w	f	sf	qf	5	4	3	2	1	Rank
Newcastle United	6	4	2	4	5	4	10	9	9	1
Aston Villa	6	2	6	9	3	9	16	8	7	2
Blackburn Rovers	6	1	7	6	4	6	15	9	12	3

The Top three Clubs in FA Cup after Newcastle United's Sixth Triumph

As it turned out, though, all those near misses at the start of the Century meant that Newcastle United had had more FA Cup Final appearances than their rivals and so were able to claim the title of 'Greatest FA Cup Club of All Time'. However, with Aston Villa becoming the first club to win the FA Cup seven times when defeating Manchester United just two years later, it meant that Newcastle United's claim was limited to just two seasons. Villa would retain the 'Greatest Club' title right up until 1990 to be the club that has held it the longest, but bizarrely neither they nor Newcastle United have won the FA Cup again since.

1871-72 to 1956-57	w	f	sf	qf	5	4	3	2	1	Rank
Aston Villa	7	2	6	9	3	10	16	8	7	1
Newcastle United	6	4	2	5	5	5	10	9	9	2
Blackburn Rovers	6	1	7	6	5	6	16	9	12	3

Aston Villa Regain the Title 'Greatest FA Cup Club of All Time'

The TV Age

Football gained another surge in popularity thanks to the advent of TV coverage which firmly came into its own from the mid-1960s onward. And its introduction also had an effect on the future of which clubs would go on to dominate the FA Cup, bringing visibility and support of clubs outside of their local area. There wasn't an immediate impact as for eleven seasons from 1962/63 to 1972/73 eleven different clubs lifted the FA Cup, but from then Liverpool began to dominate the League and Manchester United would emerge along with Tottenham Hotspur as the FA Cup specialists. Tottenham had actually set an FA Cup record in 1982 of winning their first seven FA Cup finals, but they were still behind Aston Villa in the FA Cup rankings because of not having appeared in any more than those seven finals.

By the time the 1989/90 season came along an FA Cup triumph for any one of Aston Villa, Tottenham Hotspur, Manchester United or Newcastle United, would see that club be crowned the 'Greatest FA Cup Club of All Time' at the end of that season. Spurs lost their opportunity by exiting the competition in the 3rd Round, whilst Newcastle United were defeated by Manchester United in the 5th Round. Villa lost to Oldham Athletic in the quarter-finals who were then narrowly beaten by Manchester United in the semi-finals. A replay victory for the Red Devils against Crystal Palace meant they tied with Villa and Spurs on seven FA Cup victories. However, because it was their 11th FA Cup Final, more than their rivals, Manchester United also claimed the title of 'Greatest FA Cup Club of All time'. But they would lose that title almost as soon as they'd claimed it.

1871-72 to 1989-90	w	f	sf	qf	5	4	3	2	1	Rank
Manchester United	7	4	7	10	5	14	19	8	13	1
Aston Villa	7	2	8	14	9	16	28	8	9	2
Tottenham Hotspur	7	1	4	15	12	11	22	5	6	3
Newcastle United	6	5	2	7	9	16	25	9	9	4

Manchester United Win the Four-Horse Race to 'Greatest FA Cup Club of All-Time' in 1990.

The Coin Age

Tottenham Hotspur would become the first club to lift the FA Cup eight times just one season later with a comeback victory over Nottingham Forest and take the 'Greatest FA Cup Club of All Time' crown from Manchester United in the process.

1871-72 to 1990-91	w	f	sf	qf	5	4	3	2	1	Rank
Tottenham Hotspur	8	1	4	15	12	11	22	5	6	1
Manchester United	7	4	7	10	6	14	19	8	13	2
Aston Villa	7	2	8	14	9	16	29	8	9	3

Tottenham Hotspur Become the First Club to Win FA Cup Eight Times.

However, when the Premier League came into being two seasons later, it was the Manchester club who would become the main beneficiary of a significant influx of money into the game, dominating both the League and Cup over the next decade or so. By 1994, thanks to a 4-0 win over Chelsea, they had regained their title as the 'Greatest FA Cup Club of All time' and would go on to become the first club to win the FA Cup nine, ten and eleven times, including a trio of League and Cup Doubles in the 1990s, to cement that status. They would retain that particular crown for the next 20 years.

1871-72 to 1993-94	w	f	sf	qf	5	4	3	2	1	Rank
Manchester United	8	4	7	10	7	15	19	8	13	1
Tottenham Hotspur	8	1	5	15	12	12	23	5	6	2

Manchester United Quickly Regain the 'Greatest FA Cup Club of All-Time' Title.

The Doomed Age?

Premature reports of the death of the FA Cup have been made on several occasions as top clubs focus more on achieving a top four position in the League to qualify for the lucrative Champions League. This desire has also coincided with a vast wealth opportunity for all clubs in the Premier League by virtue of the multi-billion pound TV deals that have been forged. This has meant that winning the FA Cup has moved down the priority list for all Premier League Club owners as even those not likely to reach the Champions League will focus more on avoiding losing their Premier League membership. And this has a knock on effect to those clubs in the Championship wanting to have access to all that wealth, who forego FA Cup runs for the opportunity to reach the play-offs and beyond.

However, during this period the FA Cup has primarily been won by one of only five teams (plus Portsmouth, Wigan Athletic and Leicester City) all of which have challenged for Champions League places at the same time. This apparent dichotomy has come about because these much wealthier clubs can field second teams for the FA Cup earlier rounds that contain arguably better players than all eleven first teamers put out by their opponents. And two clubs out of those five have been the most dominant since the turn of the 21st Century, Arsenal and Chelsea. They've even met each other three times in FA Cup finals this Century (all won by Arsenal) and because they've won 13 of the FA Cup finals since 1999 between them, it is no surprise to see that they both occupy a top three position in the current overall FA Cup rankings.

However, by the end of the 20th Century Chelsea had only been FA Cup champions twice, thereby currently ruling them out with a challenge for 'Greatest FA Cup Club of All Time', whereas Arsenal already had seven FA Cup triumphs under their belt. And when they lifted the Trophy once again in 2014 following a terrific comeback win over Hull City, the Gunners matched Manchester United's record of 11 FA Cup victories. The overall FA Cup record of the two clubs at that time was remarkably similar.

1871-72 to 2013-14	w	f	sf	qf	5	4	3	2	1	Rank
Arsenal	11	7	9	13	14	14	18	9	17	1
Manchester United	11	7	9	12	10	19	21	8	13	2

Arsenal Claim the 'Greatest FA Cup Club of All-Time' Title by the Narrowest of Margins.

They had both won the Cup 11 times and had both been runners-up on a further seven occasions. They'd even both lost nine of their twenty-seven FA Cup semi-finals. However, Arsenal had had one more quarter-final appearance than Manchester United, and by virtue of that fact would lay claim to being the 'Greatest FA Cup Club of All Time', a title they have retained to this day thanks to three further FA Cup triumphs, although Manchester United have remained hot on their heels.

1871-72 to 2020-21	w	f	sf	qf	5	4	3	2	1	Rank
Arsenal	14	7	9	14	14	16	19	9	17	1
Manchester United	12	8	10	16	10	19	21	8	13	2

Arsenal are the current 'Greatest FA Cup Club of All-Time'.

The Next Age?

So Arsenal are the current 'Greatest FA Cup Club of All Time' having now won the FA Cup 14 times, and they or Manchester United will hold that title for the foreseeable future. But what of the FA Cup's future? Is its long announced death truly imminent? Well it was already struggling, and then the covid_19 pandemic came along which has had an impact on the competition, as it has had on every part of life and sport. Prior to that the Emirates had extended their contract to sponsor the FA Cup which had resulted in early round prize money being doubled, but rewards reverted to previous levels for the pandemic hit 2020/21 season.

However, the demand for clubs to participate in the FA Cup has never been higher, with far more non-league clubs than the 644 that are currently accepted into the FA Cup wishing to be involved with it. And the fans and players of clubs across the whole football pyramid still love the FA Cup, just ask those involved with Wigan Athletic for example. And with the attention of the world's eyes as the FA Cup celebrates its 150th anniversary, interest in the competition has never been higher. Interestingly, the FA Cup games played by top clubs during the pandemic-hit season has seen a marked change in the number of regular first team players being selected in the early rounds. Maybe, one positive to come out of this awful situation is that the FA Cup has regained its respect across the whole footballing community and now has its future secured.

The 150 Years of FA Cup Finals

Any FA Cup history book worth its salt would be remiss not to include a basic list of FA Cup finals, even though their details are easy to find on the World Wide Web, and so all the cup finals contested up to the 2020/21 season are listed below, along with facts and stats associated with each Final, many as they would have read at the time of each Final, and some of which might not be so easy to find on the Internet.

Overview of FA Cup Finals

There have been 44 different clubs that have lifted one of three FA Cup Trophies over its 150 years of history, with a further 13 clubs appearing in finals but finishing as runners-up only. Just over 400 goals have been scored by more than 300 different players in 154 Cup Final matches, played at 13 different venues, and witnessed by over 11 million paying spectators. Arsenal have lifted the Trophy the most often (14 times) and appeared in most FA Cup finals (21 in total). Manchester United and Everton have been runners-up the most times (eight each), whilst Queen's Park, Birmingham City, Crystal Palace and Watford FC jointly hold the record for most FA Cup Final appearances without lifting the Trophy (twice each). The Wanderers and Bury FC are the only two clubs to have appeared in more than one Final and remain undefeated. Bury FC is also the only club to have contested more than one FA Cup Final and not conceded a goal in any appearance. Conversely, Watford FC is the only club to have appeared in more than one FA Cup Final and failed to score. Arsene Wenger has won the FA Cup a record seven times as a manager (all with Arsenal), and Ashley Cole has won the Cup a record seven times as a player (three with Arsenal and four with Chelsea). Ian Rush has scored the most FA Cup Final goals (five, all for Liverpool), whilst Didier Drogba has scored in the most different number of FA Cup finals (four, all for Chelsea). Three players have scored FA Cup Final hat-tricks: William Townley for Blackburn Rovers in 1890, Jimmy Logan for Notts County in 1894, and Stan Mortenson for Blackpool in 1953.

All FA Cup Final Programmes including replays, 1948–2021 (*courtesy of Chris Wathen*)

Facts and Feats of 150 Years of FA Cup Finals (by Season)

(Including summaries of FA Cup Final Achievements at the time of the Finals themselves)

1872 Kennington Oval The Wanderers [1] 1-0 Royal Engineers 2,000

The Wanderers become the first club to lift the FA Cup.
Charles W. Alcock 'scores' the first disallowed goal in an FA Cup Final.
Morton P. Betts (AKA A. H. Chequer) scores the first ever FA Cup Final goal.
Kennington Oval becomes first venue to host an FA Cup Final.

1873 Lillie Bridge The Wanderers [2] 2-0 Oxford University 3,000

The only season when the competition was run as a true 'Challenge' Cup.
The Wanderers become the first club to appear in two FA Cup finals.
The Wanderers become the first club to win the FA Cup twice.
The Wanderers become the first club to retain the FA Cup.
The Wanderers become the first club to lift the Trophy without conceding at all.
The Wanderers become the first club to score twice in an FA Cup Final.
Lillie Bridge becomes the second venue to host a Final, chosen by The Wanderers.
Edward Bowen (Wands.) is oldest player, at the time, in a Cup Final (36 yrs 364 days).

1874 Kennington Oval Oxford University [1] 2-0 Royal Engineers 2,000

Oxford University become the first previous season's runners-up to win FA Cup.
Both clubs equal the most number of FA Cup Final appearances (two).
Royal Engineers become first club to lose in two FA Cup finals.
Kennington Oval becomes the first venue to host more than one FA Cup Final.
This was the earliest in the year the FA Cup has ever been won (14th March).

1875 Kennington Oval Royal Engineers 1-1* Old Etonians 2,000
Replay Kennington Oval Royal Engineers [1] 2-0 Old Etonians 3,000

First FA Cup Final to require extra time and the first to require a replay.
Royal Engineers become the first club to appear in three FA Cup finals.
Royal Engineers become the first club to finally lift the FA Cup at their third attempt.
Royal Engineers become the second previous season's runners-up to lift the Trophy.
Henry Renny-Tailyour becomes first player to score two FA Cup Final goals.
William Merriman becomes the first goalkeeper to captain an FA Cup winning side.
Old Etonians become the first club to score in an FA Cup Final and not lift the Trophy.
William Stafford (RE) is youngest player, at the time, to score in Cup Final (20y 87d).

The first ten FA Cup Finals were contested by just six different clubs.

1876	Kennington Oval	The Wanderers	1-1*	Old Etonians	3,500
Replay	**Kennington Oval**	**The Wanderers [3]**	**3-0**	**Old Etonians**	**1,500**

George Bonsor reportedly becomes the first player to score in consecutive finals?
Old Etonians equal the record for most times as FA Cup Final runners-up (two).
Old Etonians become the first club to be runners-up in successive FA Cup Finals.
The Wanderers equal the record for most FA Cup Final appearances (three).
The Wanderers become the first club to win three FA Cup finals.
Thomas Hughes (The Wanderers) becomes first player to score twice in one Final.
The Wanderers become the first club to score three goals in an FA Cup Final.
The first game was the earliest the Cup Final has ever been contested (11th March).

1877	**Kennington Oval**	**The Wanderers [4]**	**2-1***	**Oxford University**	**3,000**

First time the same two clubs contested two separate FA Cup finals.
The Wanderers become first club to defeat same Final opponents more than once.
Lord Kinnaird (The Wanderers) becomes first player to score an own goal in a Final.
The Wanderers become the first club to appear in four FA Cup finals.
The Wanderers become the first club to lift the FA Cup four times.
Oxford University equal the record for most times as Cup Final runners-up (two).
Oxford University become first club to score in a Cup Final and lose in just one game.
This was the first FA Cup Final to be settled in extra time.

1878	**Kennington Oval**	**The Wanderers [5]**	**3-1**	**Royal Engineers**	**4,500**

The Wanderers become the first club to win a hat-trick of successive FA Cup finals.
The Wanderers become the first club to appear in five FA Cup finals.
The Wanderers become the first club to lift the Trophy five times.
The Wanderers become the first club to score ten or more FA Cup Final goals.
Jarvis Kenrick becomes the first player to score three FA Cup Final goals.
Royal Engineers become the first club to be runners-up three times.
The identity of the Royal Engineers goal-scorer has never been confirmed.
James Kirkpatrick (Wands.) is oldest player, at the time, in a Cup Final (37 yrs 1 day).

1879	**Kennington Oval**	**Old Etonians [1]**	**1-0**	**Clapham Rovers**	**5,000**

Old Etonians become the second club to win FA Cup for first time in their third Final.
James Prinsep (Clapham) is youngest player, at the time, in a Cup Final (17y 245d).

1880	**Kennington Oval**	**Clapham Rovers [1]**	**1-0**	**Oxford University**	**6,000**

Clapham Rovers become the third previous season's runners-up to lift the Trophy.
Oxford University reached at least the quarter-finals in all eight of their campaigns.
Oxford University equal the record for most times as Cup Final runners-up (three).
Oxford University are first club with a Final appearance as their last FA Cup game.
This was the first FA Cup Final to be played in April (10th).

1881 Kennington Oval Old Carthusians [1] 3-0 Old Etonians 4,000

Old Carthusians would go on to become first club to win FA Cup & FA Amateur Cup.
Old Carthusians equal the highest margin of FA Cup victory.
Old Etonians equal the record for most times as Cup Final runners-up (three).
Old Etonians become the first club to concede ten or more FA Cup Final goals.
Edward Wynyard is youngest player, at the time, to score in Cup Final (20y 8d).
First FA Cup Final contested by clubs starting with the same letter of the alphabet.

1882 Kennington Oval Old Etonians [2] 1-0 Blackburn Rovers 6,500

Old Etonians equal the record for most FA Cup Final appearances (five).
Old Etonians become first club to lift the FA Cup in two separate decades.
Old Etonians become the fourth previous season's runners-up to lift the Trophy.
Old Etonians become only the second club to lift the Trophy more than once.
Blackburn Rovers become first northern professional club to appear in a Cup Final.
Blackburn Rovers were the first future Football League club to appear in a Cup Final.

1883 Kennington Oval Blackburn Olympic [1] 2-1* Old Etonians 8,000

Blackburn Olympic become the first northern professional club to win the FA Cup.
Old Etonians become the first club to appear in six FA Cup finals.
Old Etonians become the first holders to be runners-up the following season.
Old Etonians become first club in three successive cup finals not to win them all.
Old Etonians become the first club to be runners-up four times.
Old Etonians become the first club to appear in four finals over five successive years.
Lord Arthur Kinnaird (Old Etonians) participates in a record ninth FA Cup Final.

1884 Kennington Oval Blackburn Rovers [1] 2-1 Queen's Park 4,000

Blackburn becomes the first town to have two successive different FA Cup winners.
Blackburn Rovers were the first future Football League club to win the FA Cup.
Queen's Park become the first Scottish and first non-English side in a Cup Final.
Queen's Park scored a record, at the time, of 44 goals in one FA Cup campaign.
James Forrest (BRFC) is youngest player, at the time, to score in Cup Final (19y 277d).

1885 Kennington Oval Blackburn Rovers [2] 2-0 Queen's Park 12,500

First and only time to date same two clubs have contested two successive cup finals.
Blackburn Rovers become only the second club to retain the FA Cup.
Blackburn Rovers become only the third club to lift the Trophy more than once.
First FA Cup Final to attract a crowd greater than 10,000.
Queen's Park become the second club to be runners-up in successive FA Cup finals.
Queen's Park are the last Amateur club to appear in an FA Cup Final.

1886	Kennington Oval	Blackburn Rovers	0-0	West Bromwich Alb.	15,000
Replay	**Racecourse Ground**	**Blackburn Rovers [3]**	**2-0**	**West Bromwich Alb.**	**12,000**

First time an FA Cup Final has ended goal-less.
First time FA Cup Final (replay) has been contested outside of London (in Derby).
Blackburn Rovers become second club to lift the Trophy in three successive years.
Blackburn Rovers become 2nd club to appear in four finals over five successive years.
The first FA Cup Final to involve a club with a name that is not just two words.
West Bromwich Albion become first club to fail to score in both Final and Replay.
The first FA Cup Final to feature two future Football League clubs.

1887	**Kennington Oval**	**Aston Villa [1]**	**2-0**	**West Bromwich Alb.**	**15,500**

Archie Hunter becomes first player to score in every round played. (A 'bye' in 4th Rd).
Aston Villa become first and only FA Cup winners to date to score 40 goals in total.
West Brom become the third club to be runners-up in successive FA Cup finals.

1888	**Kennington Oval**	**West Bromwich Alb. [1]**	**2-1**	**Preston North End**	**19,000**

West Bromwich Albion become the first club to win FA Cup with an all-English team.
West Brom become the third club to win FA Cup for first time in their third final.
West Bromwich Albion are first club to win just the third of three successive finals.
West Brom become the fifth previous season's runners-up to lift the Trophy.
The first FA Cup Final between two clubs each with three words in their name.
Preston North End scored a record, to date, of 50 goals in one FA Cup campaign.

1889	**Kennington Oval**	**Preston North End [1]**	**3-0**	**Wolverhampton W.**	**22,000**

Preston North End become the first club to win the League and FA Cup Double.
Preston North End become first club to lift Trophy without conceding in all rounds.
Preston North End become the sixth previous season's runners-up to lift the Trophy.
Preston North End equal the highest margin of FA Cup Final victory.
The first FA Cup Final to attract a crowd greater than 20,000.
This was the first FA Cup competition to involve qualifying rounds.

1890	**Kennington Oval**	**Blackburn Rovers [4]**	**6-1**	**The Wednesday**	**20,000**

Blackburn Rovers become the first club to score six goals in an FA Cup Final.
Blackburn Rovers become the third club to appear in five FA Cup finals.
Blackburn Rovers become the second club to lift the Trophy as many as four times.
Bill Townley becomes the first player to score an FA Cup Final hat-trick.
The Wednesday become the first non-league side to appear in an FA Cup Final.
This was the first FA Cup Final with five different players on the scoresheet.

1891 Kennington Oval Blackburn Rovers [5] 3-1 Notts County 23,000

Blackburn Rovers officially become the 'best FA Cup side to date' with fifth win.
(Same number of FA Cup wins as The Wanderers, but with one runners-up, too.)
Blackburn Rovers equal the record for most appearances in an FA Cup Final (six).

1892 Kennington Oval West Bromwich Alb.[2] 3-0 Aston Villa 32,810

West Bromwich Albion become first club to avenge a previous FA Cup Final defeat.
The first FA Cup Final to attract a crowd greater than 30,000.
The first FA Cup Final to utilise goal nets.
This was the last of 22 FA Cup Final matches to be contested at Kennington Oval.
Billy Evans (AVFC) becomes oldest player, at the time, in a Cup Final (38 yrs 31 days).

1893 Fallowfield Wolverhampton W. [1] 1-0 Everton 45,000

First FA Cup Final to be scheduled to take place outside of London (Manchester).
The first FA Cup Final to attract a crowd greater than 40,000.
Everton become the first single word named club to appear in an FA Cup Final.

1894 Goodison Park Notts County [1] 4-1 Bolton Wanderers 37,000

Notts County become the first club from the second tier to appear in a Cup Final.
Notts County become the first club from the second tier to lift the FA Cup.
Jimmy Logan becomes the second player to score an FA Cup Final hat-trick.
First FA Cup Final to be played in the city of Liverpool.

1895 Crystal Palace Aston Villa [2] 1-0 West Bromwich Alb. 42,560

Aston Villa and West Bromwich Albion are first pair of clubs to contest three finals.
West Bromwich Albion become the fourth club to appear in five FA Cup finals.
The first time the FA Cup Final was played at its second home, Crystal Palace.
Bob Chatt scores the fastest ever FA Cup Final goal, at the time, 40 seconds.

1896 Crystal Palace The Wednesday [1] 2-1 Wolverhampton W. 48,836

Crystal Palace becomes only the second ground to host more than one Cup Final.
The Wednesday become the first to appear in finals as a League & non-league club.
The Wednesday become the first club from the city of Sheffield to lift the FA Cup.

1897 Crystal Palace Aston Villa [3] 3-2 Everton 65,891

Aston Villa become only the second club to win the League and Cup Double.
Everton become first club to score twice in one Cup Final game and lose the match.
The first FA Cup Final to attract a crowd greater than both 50,000 and 60,000.

1898 Crystal Palace Nottingham Forest [1] 3-1 Derby County 62,017

First FA Cup Final since 1872 to involve two clubs both competing in their first Final.

1899	**Crystal Palace**	**Sheffield United** [1]	**4-1**	**Derby County**	**73,833**

Sheffield United become first club to score four goals in their debut FA Cup Final.
Derby County become the fourth club to be runners-up in successive FA Cup finals.
The first FA Cup Final to attract a crowd greater than 70,000.

1900	**Crystal Palace**	**Bury** [1]	**4-0**	**Southampton**	**68,945**

Bury became the first club to score four goals without reply in a Cup Final.
Southampton are only the second non-league club to appear in an FA Cup Final.
Only the third ever FA Cup Final to be contested by two debutant Cup Final clubs.
Bury become the first single named club to win the FA Cup.

1901	Crystal Palace	Tottenham Hotspur	2-2	Sheffield United	110,820
Replay	**Burnden Park**	**Tottenham Hotspur** [1]	**3-1**	**Sheffield United**	**20,470**

Tottenham Hotspur are only the third non-league club to appear in an FA Cup Final.
First and only FA Cup Final so far won by a non-league side, Tottenham Hotspur.
The first FA Cup Final to attract a crowd greater than both 100,000 and 110,000.
Sandy Brown becomes first player to score in every possible round of the FA Cup.
Sandy Brown also scored 15 of Tottenham Hotspur's twenty FA Cup goals.
John Cameron becomes the first player-manager to lift the FA Cup.
Sheffield United become first club to score a total of three Cup Final goals and lose.
Fred Priest is first player to score two FA Cup Final goals and be on losing side.
Only FA Cup Final to be played in Bolton, but second in Greater Manchester.

1902	Crystal Palace	Sheffield United	1-1	Southampton	76,914
Replay	**Crystal Palace**	**Sheffield United** [2]	**2-1**	**Southampton**	**33,068**

Sheffield United become the seventh previous season's runners-up to lift the Trophy.
Billy Barnes (Sheffield United) scores the 100th FA Cup Final goal in the replay.
Southampton become only club so far to play in two cup finals as a non-league club.

1903	**Crystal Palace**	**Bury** [2]	**6-0**	**Derby County**	**63,102**

Bury become the first club to score six goals in a Cup Final without reply.
Bury's goal aggregate in FA Cup finals is scored ten, conceded nil.
Bury become second club to lift Trophy without conceding & playing in all rounds.
Bury become only second club to lift the Trophy in both first two FA Cup finals.
The only time to date five different players scored for the same club in the Final.
Derby County become the first club to lose in their first three FA Cup finals.
George Ross (Bury) is oldest player, at the time, to score in Cup Final (32y 67d).

1904	**Crystal Palace**	**Manchester City** [1]	**1-0**	**Bolton Wanderers**	**61,374**

Manchester City become the first club from that city to lift the FA Cup.
Bolton Wanderers become the first club from second tier to be runners-up.

1905 Crystal Palace — Aston Villa [4] — 2-0 — Newcastle United — 101,117

Harry Hampton becomes the third player to score in every round.
Aston Villa become the third club to lift the FA Cup four times.
Aston Villa become the fifth club to appear in five FA Cup finals.
Aston Villa become the first club to lift FA Cup in three different decades.

1906 Crystal Palace — Everton [1] — 1-0 — Newcastle United — 75,609

Everton become the first club from the city of Liverpool to lift the FA Cup.
Everton become the fourth club to win FA Cup for first time in their third Final.
Newcastle United become the fifth club to be runners-up in successive FA Cup finals.

1907 Crystal Palace — The Wednesday [2] — 2-1 — Everton — 84,594

Everton become first previous season's winners to return to a Crystal Palace Final.
Everton become the second FA Cup holders to be runners-up the following season.

1908 Crystal Palace — Wolverhampton W. [2] — 3-1 — Newcastle United — 74,697

Wolverhampton Wanderers become lowest ranked second tier club to lift Cup (9th).
Newcastle United are first club to play in three finals in four years and lose them all.
Newcastle United become the second club to lose their first three FA Cup finals.
The four goals were scored by the only 4 players whose names began with letter 'H'.

1909 Crystal Palace — Manchester United [1] — 1-0 — Bristol City — 71,401

Only the fourth ever FA Cup Final to be contested by two debutant Cup Final clubs.

1910 Crystal Palace — Newcastle United — 1-1 — Barnsley — 77,747
Replay Goodison Park — Newcastle United [1] — 2-0 — Barnsley — 69,000

Albert Shephard becomes the first player to take and score a penalty in a Cup Final.
Newcastle United become the first club to finally win FA Cup at the fourth attempt.
Goodison Park becomes the first ground outside of London to host two cup finals.

1911 Crystal Palace — Bradford City — 0-0 — Newcastle United — 69,068
Replay Old Trafford — Bradford City [1] — 1-0 — Newcastle United — 58,000

Bradford City become first team to lift the new Trophy which was made in Bradford.
Newcastle United become the sixth club to appear in five FA Cup finals.
Newcastle United equal the record for most times as Cup Final runners-up (four).
Newcastle Utd become third FA Cup holders to be runners-up the following season.
Manchester becomes first city outside London to host two cup finals at two venues.

First 12 FA Cup Finals of 20th Century saw 12 different winners.

1912	Crystal Palace	Barnsley	0-0	West Bromwich Alb.	54,556
Replay	**Bramall Lane**	**Barnsley [1]**	**1-0***	**West Bromwich Alb.**	**38,555**

This was the first time three successive FA Cup finals required replays.
First time no goals have been scored in normal time in both first match and replay.
Barnsley become the only team to date to play 12 games en route to lifting Trophy.
Barnsley become only FA Cup winners to score fewer goals (11) than games played.
Barnsley become the first club to appear in two FA Cup finals as a second tier club.
West Bromwich Albion equal the record for most FA Cup Final appearances (six).
West Bromwich Albion equal the record for being Cup Final runners-up (four).
George Baddeley (WBA) is oldest player, at the time, in a Cup Final (38 yrs 11 mths.).

1913 Crystal Palace Aston Villa [5] 1-0 Sunderland 121,919

First time the top two in the League contested an FA Cup Final (second beat first).
Aston Villa equal the record for most times lifting the FA Cup Trophy (five).
Aston Villa equal the record for most FA Cup Final appearances (six).
Aston Villa become the first club to lift the FA Cup in four different decades.
The first FA Cup Final to attract a crowd greater than 120,000.
Charlie Wallace (Aston Villa) becomes the first player to miss a penalty in a Cup Final.

1914 Crystal Palace Burnley [1] 1-0 Liverpool 72,778

First reigning monarch (George V) to attend an FA Cup Final and present Trophy.
Last FA Cup Final to date to involve two clubs both appearing in their first Final.
Last of 21 FA Cup Final matches to be played at Crystal Palace.

1915 Old Trafford Sheffield United [3] 3-0 Chelsea 49,557

Manchester becomes the first city outside London to host three FA Cup finals.

1920 Stamford Bridge Aston Villa [6] 1-0* Huddersfield Town 50,018

Aston Villa become first club to lift FA Cup six times and become 'best FA Cup club'.
Aston Villa became the first club to appear in seven FA Cup finals.
First of three successive FA Cup finals held at Stamford Bridge.

1921 Stamford Bridge Tottenham Hotspur [2] 1-0 Wolverhampton W. 72,805

Tottenham Hotspur are only club to lift FA Cup as a non-league and a League side.
Tottenham Hotspur become third club to lift Trophy in both first two FA Cup finals.
Wolverhampton Wanderers become the seventh club to appear in five FA Cup finals.

1922 Stamford Bridge Huddersfield Town [1] 1-0 Preston North End 53,000

The first FA Cup Final to be settled by a single penalty scored by Billy Smith.
Huddersfield Town become the only club to appear in two finals at Stamford Bridge.
All three FA Cup finals held at Stamford Bridge ended in a 1-0 scoreline.

1923 Wembley (Orig.) Bolton Wanderers [1] 2-0 West Ham United 126,047
First FA Cup Final played at the original Wembley (known as the Empire Stadium).
Known as the 'White Horse' final thanks to PC George Scorey and his mount 'Billy'.
Highest crowd at an FA Cup Final, 126,047, although unofficially more than 200,000.

1924 Wembley (Orig.) Newcastle United [2] 2-0 Aston Villa 91,695
Second club to avenge previous FA Cup Final defeat, both times against Aston Villa.
Newcastle United become fifth club to appear in six FA Cup finals.
Aston Villa become the first club to appear in eight FA Cup finals.
Walter Hampson (NUFC) becomes oldest player in an FA Cup Final (41 yrs, 257 days).

1925 Wembley (Orig.) Sheffield United [4] 1-0 Cardiff City 91,763
Cardiff City become the first and so far only Welsh club to appear in an FA Cup Final.
Sheffield United become the fourth club to lift the FA Cup four times.
Sheffield United become the eighth club to appear in five FA Cup finals.

1926 Wembley (Orig.) Bolton Wanderers [2] 1-0 Manchester City 91,447
Bolton Wanderers become the third club to avenge a previous FA Cup Final defeat.
Bolton Wanderers become the first club to lift the FA Cup twice at Wembley.
Manchester City become first club to appear in an FA Cup Final and be relegated.

1927 Wembley (Orig.) Cardiff City [1] 1-0 Arsenal 91,206
Cardiff City become the first Welsh, and first non-English, club to lift FA Cup.
Cardiff City become the first club to both win and lose a Cup Final at Wembley.
First of a record 21 FA Cup Final appearances for Arsenal.
First FA Cup Final to be broadcast 'live' (on the radio).

1928 Wembley (Orig.) Blackburn Rovers [6] 3-1 Huddersfield Town 92,041
Blackburn Rovers equal the record for most times lifting the FA Cup Trophy (six).
Blackburn Rovers become the first club to win six finals in six successive appearances.
Blackburn Rovers become the second club to appear in seven FA Cup finals.
Huddersfield Town become first club to be runners-up in both League and FA Cup.
Huddersfield Town become first club to score in a Wembley Cup Final and lose.

1929 Wembley (Orig.) Bolton Wanderers [3] 2-0 Portsmouth 92,576
Bolton Wanderers become the first club to win FA Cup three times at Wembley.
Bolton Wanderers become the ninth club to appear in five FA Cup finals.
Harold Blackmore becomes the fourth player to score in every round.

1930 Wembley (Orig.) Arsenal [1] 2-0 Huddersfield Town 92,488
The first time Arsenal lift the FA Cup in what was the competition's 55th season.
Huddersfield Town become the first club to lose two Wembley FA Cup finals.

1931 Wembley (Orig.) West Bromwich Alb.[3] 2-1 Birmingham 92,406
West Bromwich Albion become first club to win FA Cup and be promoted.
West Bromwich Albion become the third club to appear in seven FA Cup finals.

1932 Wembley (Orig.) Newcastle United [3] 2-1 Arsenal 92,298
Arsenal become first team to score first in a Wembley Cup Final and not lift Trophy.
Newcastle United become the fourth club to appear in seven FA Cup finals.
Bob John (Arsenal) is oldest player, at the time, to score in Cup Final (32y 80d).

1933 Wembley (Orig.) Everton [2] 3-0 Manchester City 92,950
First use of numbered shirts in an FA Cup final: Everton 1-11, Manchester City 12-22.
Everton become the tenth club to appear in five FA Cup finals.
Jimmy Dunn (Everton) is oldest player, at the time, to score in Cup Final (32y 155d).

1934 Wembley (Orig.) Manchester City [2] 2-1 Portsmouth 93,258
Manchester City become the eighth previous season's runners-up to lift the Trophy.
Manchester City become first previous season's Wembley runners-up to win Cup.
This Cup Final involved two future Knights: player Matt Busby and ref. Stanley Rous.

1935 Wembley (Orig.) Sheff. Wednesday [3] 4-2 West Bromwich Alb. 93,204
Sheffield Wednesday become first club to win FA Cup under two different names.
Ellis Rimmer becomes first player to score in every round and in every game played.
West Bromwich Albion become the first club to be FA Cup runners-up five times.
West Bromwich Albion equal the record for most FA Cup Final appearances (eight).

1936 Wembley (Orig.) Arsenal [2] 1-0 Sheffield United 93,384
Arsenal became the first club to appear in four Wembley FA Cup finals.
This is last time to date that 4-time winners Sheffield United appeared in a cup final.
Sheffield United become the sixth club to appear in six FA Cup finals.

1937 Wembley (Orig.) Sunderland [1] 3-1 Preston North End 93,495
First FA Cup Final to be partially broadcast on television.
First FA Cup Final to be played in the now traditional month of May (1st).
Frank O'Donnell becomes first player to score in every round, but not lift the Cup.

1938 Wembley (Orig.) Preston North End [2] 1-0* Huddersfield Town 93,497

Preston North End set record at the time of longest gap between Cup wins, 49 years.
Preston North End become the ninth previous season's runners-up to lift the Trophy.
First FA Cup Final broadcast 'live' on television in its entirety.
Second FA Cup Final settled by a solitary penalty, mirroring the result of the first one.
Huddersfield Town become the first club to lose three Wembley FA Cup finals.
The two teams become the 11th and 12th clubs to appear in five FA Cup finals.

1939 Wembley (Orig.) Portsmouth [1] 4-1 Wolverhampton W. 99,370

The last occasion successive cup finals were won by different clubs with same initial.
Wolverhampton Wanderers become the seventh club to appear in six FA Cup finals.
Dickey Dorsett (Wolves) is youngest player at time, to score in Cup Final (19y 147d).

1946 Wembley (Orig.) Derby County [1] 4-1* Charlton Athletic 98,000

The first time three goals have been scored in extra time in a Cup Final.
Derby County finally win FA Cup at fourth attempt, 48 years after their first Final.
Bert Turner (Charlton Athletic) becomes first player to score for both teams in Final.
Bert Turner becomes oldest player, to date, to score in Cup Final, and o.g. (36y 312d).
First instance of the ball bursting during the FA Cup Final.
Charlton Athletic became first club to reach Final after legally losing an earlier match.

1947 Wembley (Orig.) Charlton Athletic [1] 1-0* Burnley 99,000

Charlton Athletic become the tenth previous season's runners-up to lift the Trophy.
The winning goal was scored by Chris Duffy, the only non-English player involved.
For the second successive season the ball burst during play.

1948 Wembley (Orig.) Manchester United [2] 4-2 Blackpool 99,000

Manchester United become fourth club to lift Trophy in both first two FA Cup finals.
Stan Mortenson becomes second player to score in every round, but not lift the Cup.
Eddie Shimwell becomes first player to score a penalty in a Final and not win Cup.

1949 Wembley (Orig.) Wolverhampton W. [3] 3-1 Leicester City 99,500

Leicester City are lowest ranked League club to contest a Final (19th in second tier).
Wolverhampton Wanderers become the fifth club to appear in seven FA Cup finals.

1950 Wembley (Orig.) Arsenal [3] 2-0 Liverpool 100,000

Arsenal become the second club to lift the FA Cup three times at Wembley.
Arsenal become the 13th club to appear in five FA Cup finals, the first all at Wembley.

1951 Wembley (Orig.) Newcastle United [4] 2-0 Blackpool 100,000
Newcastle United become the third club to lift the FA Cup three times at Wembley.
Newcastle United equal the record for most FA Cup Final appearances (eight).
Jackie Milburn becomes the eighth player to score in every round.

1952 Wembley (Orig.) Newcastle United [5] 1-0 Arsenal 100,000
Newcastle United become only the fourth club to lift the Trophy five times.
Newcastle United become the first club to lift the FA Cup four times at Wembley.
Newcastle United become first club to retain the FA Cup at Wembley.
Newcastle United become first club in 61 years, and only third club to retain Trophy.
Newcastle United become the first club to appear in nine FA Cup finals.
Arsenal become the eighth club to appear in six FA Cup finals.
George Robledo becomes the first Chilean to score in an FA Cup Final.

1953 Wembley (Orig.) Blackpool [1] 4-3 Bolton Wanderers 100,000
Stan Mortenson becomes first & only player to score a Wembley Cup Final hat-trick.
Blackpool become first club to lift FA Cup after being two goals behind.
Bolton Wanderers become first club to score three goals and lose in FA Cup Final.
Bolton Wanderers become the ninth club to appear in six FA Cup finals.
Nat Lofthouse becomes the third player to score in every round, but not lift the Cup.
Willie Moir (Bolton Wanderers) scores the 200th FA Cup Final goal.

1954 Wembley (Orig.) West Bromwich Alb.[4] 3-2 Preston North End 100,000
West Bromwich Albion equal the record for most FA Cup Final appearances (nine).
Preston North End become the tenth club to appear in six FA Cup finals.
Charlie Wayman becomes second PNE player to score in every round and not win.

1955 Wembley (Orig.) Newcastle United [6] 3-1 Manchester City 100,000
Newcastle United lift FA Cup for sixth time to become 'best FA Cup club'.
(Same number of FA Cup wins as Aston villa and Blackburn Rovers, but more finals).
Newcastle United become first club to win FA Cup five times at Wembley.
Newcastle United become first club to appear in ten FA Cup finals.
Manchester City become the 14th club to appear in five FA Cup finals.

1956 Wembley (Orig.) Manchester City [3] 3-1 Birmingham City 100,000
Manchester City become the 11th previous season's runners-up to lift the Trophy.
(Manchester City become the first club to achieve this feat twice).
Birmingham City are only club to lose both their cup finals under different names.
Manchester City become the 11th club to appear in six FA Cup finals.
Bobby Johnstone becomes first player to score in successive Wembley cup finals.

1957 Wembley (Orig.) Aston Villa [7] 2-1 Manchester United 100,000
Aston Villa become first club to lift FA Cup seven times & regain 'best FA Cup club'.
Aston Villa become the first club to lift the FA Cup at four different venues.
Aston Villa are only club to date to lift the FA Cup after conceding in every round.
Aston Villa become the third club to appear in nine FA Cup finals.

1958 Wembley (Orig.) Bolton Wanderers [4] 2-0 Manchester United 100,000
Manchester United become sixth club to be runners-up in successive FA Cup finals.
(Becoming the first club to do so in Wembley FA Cup finals.)
Bolton Wanderers become the sixth club to appear in seven FA Cup finals.

1959 Wembley (Orig.) Nottingham Forest [2] 2-1 Luton Town 100,000
Nottingham Forest become fifth club to lift Trophy in both first two FA Cup finals.
Nottingham Forest post longest ever gap between first two FA Cup finals; 61 years.

1960 Wembley (Orig.) Wolverhampton W. [4] 3-0 Blackburn Rovers 100,000
Wolverhampton Wanderers become first club to qualify for Europe by winning Cup.
The two teams become the fourth and fifth clubs to appear in eight FA Cup finals.

1961 Wembley (Orig.) Tottenham Hotspur [3] 2-0 Leicester City 100,000
Tottenham Hotspur become first club in 20th Century to win FA Cup/League Double.
Tottenham Hotspur become second club to lift Trophy in all first three FA Cup finals.

1962 Wembley (Orig.) Tottenham Hotspur [4] 3-1 Burnley 100,000
Tottenham Hotspur become fourth overall, and second at Wembley, to retain FA Cup.
Tottenham Hotspur become second club to lift Trophy in all first four FA Cup finals.

1963 Wembley (Orig.) Manchester United [3] 3-1 Leicester City 100,000
Manchester United become the 15th club to appear in five FA Cup finals.
Leicester City become third club to be runners-up in all first three FA Cup finals.

1964 Wembley (Orig.) West Ham United [1] 3-2 Preston North End 100,000
West Ham post second longest wait, at time, from first Final to win Cup, 41 years.
Preston North End equal the record for most times as FA Cup runners-up (five).
Preston North End become the seventh club to appear in seven FA Cup finals.
Johnny Sissons (WHU) is youngest player at the time, to score in Cup Final (18y 216d).

1965 Wembley (Orig.) Liverpool [1] 2-1* Leeds United 100,000
Liverpool post longest wait, at time, from first Final to lifting Trophy, 51 years.
This was second to last Final to be contested by clubs, at the time, yet to win FA Cup.

1966 Wembley (Orig.) Everton [3] 3-2 Sheffield Wednesday 100,000
Everton become the first club to win FA Cup after being 2-0 down in the Final.
Everton become the 12th club to appear in six FA Cup finals.
Sheffield Wednesday become the 16th club to appear in five FA Cup finals.
Sheffield Wednesday become 2nd club to lose two finals under two different names.

1967 Wembley (Orig.) Tottenham Hotspur [5] 2-1 Chelsea 100,000
The first all-London FA Cup Final.
Tottenham Hotspur become the fifth club to lift the Trophy five times.
Tottenham Hotspur become second club to lift Trophy in all first five FA Cup finals.
Tottenham Hotspur become the 17th club to appear in five FA Cup finals.
Cliff Jones (Spurs) & Joe Kirkup (Chelsea) become first substitutes listed in Cup Final.

1968 Wembley (Orig.) West Bromwich Alb.[5] 1-0* Everton 100,000
West Bromwich Albion become the sixth club to lift the Trophy five times.
West Bromwich Albion equal the record for most FA Cup Final appearances (ten).
Jeff Astle scores a goal in every round including the only goal of the Final.
Dennis Clarke (West Bromwich Albion) becomes first substitute to play in Cup Final.
Everton become the eighth club to appear in seven FA Cup finals.

1969 Wembley (Orig.) Manchester City [4] 1-0 Leicester City 100,000
Leicester City become the first club to be runners-up in their first four FA Cup finals.
Leicester City become second club to be runners-up and be relegated in same season.
Manchester City become the ninth club to appear in seven FA Cup finals.

1970 Wembley (Orig.) Chelsea 2-2* Leeds United 100,000
Replay Old Trafford Chelsea [1] 2-1* Leeds United 62,078
First Wembley FA Cup Final to require a replay.
Chelsea become first club to win FA Cup after being behind three times.
Peter Osgood scores a goal in every round, including the Cup Final replay.
Old Trafford becomes the first ground outside London to host three FA Cup finals.
Manchester becomes the first city outside London to host four FA Cup finals.
This is last FA Cup Final to date contested by both teams who were yet to lift Trophy.
This is the last FA Cup Final to date played in the month of April (11th and 29th).

1971 Wembley (Orig.) Arsenal [4] 2-1* Liverpool 100,000
Arsenal become second club of the 20th Century to achieve League and Cup Double.
Arsenal become the tenth club to appear in seven FA Cup finals.
Eddie Kelly (Arsenal) becomes the first substitute to score in an FA Cup Final.

1972 Wembley (Orig.) Leeds United [1] 1-0 Arsenal 100,000
The Centenary FA Cup Final.
Arsenal become the fourth FA Cup holders to be runners-up the following season.
(Becoming the first FA Cup holders at Wembley to be runners-up the next year.)
Arsenal become the sixth club to appear in eight FA Cup finals.

1973 Wembley (Orig.) Sunderland [2] 1-0 Leeds United 100,000
Sunderland become the first club from second tier to lift FA Cup in 42 years.
Leeds United become the fifth FA Cup holders to be runners-up the following season.
Regarded by many as the greatest FA Cup Final shock of all time.

1974 Wembley (Orig.) Liverpool [2] 3-0 Newcastle United 100,000
Newcastle United become the first club to appear in 11 FA Cup finals.
Newcastle United equal the record for most times as FA Cup runners-up (five).
Liverpool become the 18th club to appear in five FA Cup finals.

1975 Wembley (Orig.) West Ham United [2] 2-0 Fulham 100,000
The second all-London FA Cup Final.
Third FA Cup Final involving West Ham United, all three including a second tier club.
Alan Taylor scores a brace in each of quarter-final, semi-final and final.

1976 Wembley (Orig.) Southampton [1] 1-0 Manchester United 100,000
Southampton set longest gap between first FA Cup Final and first win; 76 years.
Manchester United become the 13th club to appear in six FA Cup finals.
Shortest gap between FA Cup victories for second tier clubs, just three years.

1977 Wembley (Orig.) Manchester United [4] 2-1 Liverpool 100,000
Manchester United become the 12th previous season's runners-up to lift the Trophy.
Manchester United become the 11th club to appear in seven FA Cup finals.
Liverpool become the 14th club to appear in six FA Cup finals.
Jimmy and Brian Greenhoff become first brothers to win FA Cup for 25 years.

1978 Wembley (Orig.) Ipswich Town [1] 1-0 Arsenal 100,000
Ipswich Town become the 40th different club to lift the FA Cup.
Arsenal become the first club to be FA Cup runners-up at Wembley five times.
Arsenal equal the record for most times as FA Cup runners-up (five).
Arsenal become the fourth club to appear in nine FA Cup finals.

1979	**Wembley (Orig.)**	**Arsenal [5]**	**3-2**	**Manchester United**	**100,000**

Arsenal become the 13th previous season's runners-up to lift the Trophy.
Arsenal become the seventh club to lift the FA Cup five times.
Arsenal become the third club to appear in ten FA Cup finals.
Manchester United become the seventh club to appear in eight FA Cup finals.

1980	**Wembley (Orig.)**	**West Ham United [3]**	**1-0**	**Arsenal**	**100,000**

The third all-London FA Cup Final.
West Ham United become the last non- top-flight club to date to lift FA Cup.
West Ham United become joint lowest finishing League club to win FA Cup (29th).
Fourth FA Cup Final involving West Ham United, all four including a second tier club.
Arsenal equal the record for most FA Cup Final appearances (11).
Arsenal become the first club to be FA Cup runners-up six times.
Arsenal become first club in three successive FA Cup finals for 92 years.
Arsenal become the sixth FA Cup holders to be runners-up the following season.
(Becoming the first holders to be runners-up the following season twice.)
Paul Allen (WHU) becomes youngest player to date to be FA Cup winner (17y 256d).

1981	Wembley (Orig.)	Tottenham Hotspur	1-1*	Manchester City	100,000
Replay	**Wembley (Orig.)**	**Tottenham Hotspur [6]**	**3-2**	**Manchester City**	**92,000**

The 100th FA Cup Final.
Tottenham Hotspur become the first club to win all their first six FA Cup finals.
Tottenham Hotspur become fourth club to win FA Cup six times.
Tottenham Hotspur become the 15th club to appear in six FA Cup finals.
Manchester City become the eighth club to appear in eight FA Cup finals.
Tommy Hutchison becomes the second player to score Cup Final goals for both clubs.
The first FA Cup Final replay to be played at Wembley.

1982	Wembley (Orig.)	Tottenham Hotspur	1-1*	Queens Park Rangers	100,000
Replay	**Wembley (Orig.)**	**Tottenham Hotspur [7]**	**1-0**	**Queens Park Rangers**	**90,000**

The fourth all-London FA Cup Final.
Tottenham Hotspur become the first club to win all their first seven FA Cup finals.
Tottenham Hotspur equal the record for most times lifting the FA Cup Trophy (seven).
Tottenham Hotspur become the third club to retain the FA Cup more than once.
Tottenham Hotspur become the 12th club to appear in seven FA Cup finals.

Three consecutive FA Cup Finals required replays from 1981-1983 for only the second time since the Finals of 1910-1912.

1983 Wembley (Orig.) Manchester United 2-2* Brighton & Hove Alb. 100,000
Replay Wembley (Orig.) Manchester United [5] 4-0 Brighton & Hove Alb. 100,000

Manchester United post the biggest ever win in an FA Cup Final replay.
Manchester United become third club to score six FA Cup Final goals in one season.
Manchester United become the eighth club to lift the FA Cup five times.
Manchester United become the fourth club to appear in nine FA Cup finals.
Norman Whiteside (Manchester United) scores the 300th FA Cup Final goal, in replay.
Norman Whiteside becomes youngest player to date to score in Cup Final (18y 18d).
Brighton & Hove Albion become third runners-up to be relegated in same season.
Highest official attendance for an FA Cup Final replay.

1984 Wembley (Orig.) Everton [4] 2-0 Watford 100,000

Everton become the ninth club to appear in eight FA Cup finals.
The first FA Cup Final where players wore sponsors' names on their shirts.

1985 Wembley (Orig.) Manchester United [6] 1-0 Everton 100,000

Kevin Moran (Manchester Utd) becomes the first player sent off in an FA Cup Final.
Manchester United become first club to win FA Cup after having a player sent off.
Manchester United become the fifth club to lift the FA Cup Trophy six times.
Manchester United become the fourth club to appear in ten FA Cup finals.
Everton become the seventh FA Cup holders to be runners-up the following season.
(Becoming the second holders to be runners-up the following season twice.)
Everton become the fifth club to be FA Cup runners-up five times.
Everton become the fifth club to appear in nine FA Cup finals.

1986 Wembley (Orig.) Liverpool [3] 3-1 Everton 98,000

First ever all-Merseyside derby in FA Cup Final.
Liverpool become first club to win FA Cup with no players eligible to play for England.
Liverpool become the fifth club to win the League and Cup Double.
Kenny Dalglish becomes the second player-manager to lift the FA Cup.
First time the League winners beat League runners-up in FA Cup Final.
Liverpool become the 13th club to appear in seven FA Cup finals.
Everton become first club to be in three successive finals to win only the first game.
Everton become the seventh club to be runners-up in successive FA Cup finals.
Everton equal the record for most times as FA Cup runners-up (six).
Everton become the fifth club to appear in ten FA Cup finals.

1987 Wembley (Orig.) Coventry City [1] 3-2* Tottenham Hotspur 98,000

Tottenham Hotspur become the tenth club to appear in eight FA Cup finals.
Gary Mabbutt becomes the third player to score goals for both teams in the Final.
Coventry City become first team to beat Tottenham Hotspur in Spurs' eighth final.
Coventry City become the 41st different club to win the FA Cup.

1988 Wembley (Orig.) Wimbledon [1] 1-0 Liverpool 98,203

Dave Beasant (Wimbledon) becomes the first keeper to save a penalty at Wembley.
Dave Beasant becomes first goalkeeper to captain a Wembley FA Cup winning side.
Wimbledon become the 42nd different club to win the FA Cup.
Liverpool become the 11th club to appear in eight FA Cup Finals.
Liverpool become the sixth club to be FA Cup runners-up five times.

1989 Wembley (Orig.) Liverpool [4] 3-2* Everton 82,500

The second all-Merseyside derby FA Cup Final.
Stewart McCall (Everton) becomes first substitute to score twice in a Cup Final.
Ian Rush (Liverpool) becomes second substitute to score twice in a Cup Final.
Liverpool become the 14th previous season's runners-up to lift the Trophy.
Liverpool become the seventh club to appear in nine FA Cup finals.
Everton equal the record for most FA Cup Final appearances (11).
Everton become the first club to be FA Cup runners-up on seven occasions.

1990 Wembley (Orig.) Manchester United 3-3* Crystal Palace 80,000
Replay Wembley (Orig.) Manchester United [7] 1-0 Crystal Palace 80,000

Manchester United become 'best FA Cup club of all time' with seventh win.
(Same number of wins as Aston Villa and Spurs but with more Final appearances.)
Manchester United equal the record for most FA Cup Final appearances (11).
Crystal Palace become only second club to score 3 times in Final and not lift Trophy.

1991 Wembley (Orig.) Tottenham Hotspur [8] 2-1* Nottingham Forest 80,000

Tottenham Hotspur become first club to lift the FA Cup eight times.
Tottenham Hotspur become sixth club to claim to be 'best FA Cup club of all time'.
Tottenham Hotspur become the eighth club to appear in nine FA Cup finals.

1992 Wembley (Orig.) Liverpool [5] 2-0 Sunderland 80,000

Liverpool become the ninth club to lift the FA Cup five times.
Liverpool become the sixth club to appear in ten FA Cup finals.
Ian Rush scores his 5th FA Cup Final goal to set a record for the competition.
Sunderland are the last FA Cup Finalists to date to field a totally British born team.

For 13 consecutive FA Cup Finals from 1966 to 1978 there were 13 different FA Cup winners. There have only been 13 different winners in the 43 FA Cup Finals since then.

1993	Wembley (Orig.)	Arsenal	1-1*	Sheffield Wednesday	79,347
Replay	**Wembley (Orig.)**	**Arsenal [6]**	**2-1***	**Sheffield Wednesday**	**62,627**

The first time the FA Cup Final was contested by same clubs as the League Cup Final.
Arsenal become the first club win the FA Cup and League Cup in same season.
The first FA Cup Final where players had their names on backs of their shirts.
The last FA Cup Final to go to a replay.
Arsenal become the sixth club to lift the FA Cup six times.
Arsenal become the first club to appear in 12 FA Cup finals.
Ian Wright is the last player to score double figures in a single FA Cup campaign.
Sheffield Wednesday become the 16th club to appear in six FA Cup finals.
This was the first season both FA Cup semi-finals were played at Wembley Stadium.

1994 Wembley (Orig.) Manchester United [8] 4-0 Chelsea 79,634

Eric Cantona becomes the first player to score two penalties in one FA Cup Final.
Manchester United regain the title of 'best FA Cup club of all time' with eighth win.
Manchester United become the sixth club to win the League and Cup Double.
Manchester United equal the record for most FA Cup Final appearances (12).

1995 Wembley (Orig.) Everton [5] 1-0 Manchester United 79,592

Manchester United become the first club to appear in 13 FA Cup finals.
Everton become the tenth club to lift the FA Cup five times.
Everton become the third club to appear in 12 FA Cup finals.
Manchester United become seventh club to be FA Cup runners-up five times.
Manchester Utd become eighth FA Cup holders to be runners-up the next season.

1996 Wembley (Orig.) Manchester United [9] 1-0 Liverpool 79,007

Manchester United become the first club to lift the FA Cup nine times.
Manchester United become the 15th previous season's runners-up to lift the Trophy.
Manchester United become the first club to win the Double for a second time.
Manchester United become the first club to appear in 14 FA Cup finals.
Liverpool become the third club to be FA Cup runners-up six times.
Liverpool become the sixth club to appear in 11 FA Cup finals.

1997 Wembley (Orig.) Chelsea [2] 2-0 Middlesbrough 79,160

Ruud Gullit becomes the first non-British manager of an FA Cup winning team.
Roberto di Matteo scores the fastest Cup Final goal at Wembley yet, at 42 seconds.
Chelsea become the 19th club to appear in five FA Cup finals.
Middlesbrough become 4th club to be runners-up and be relegated in same season.

1998 Wembley (Orig.) Arsenal [7] 2-0 Newcastle United 79,183

Arsenal become the second club to win the League and Cup Double twice.
Arsenal become the fourth club to lift the FA Cup seven times.
Arsenal become the second club to appear in 13 FA Cup finals.
Newcastle United become the fourth club to appear in 12 FA Cup finals.
Newcastle United become the fifth club to be FA Cup runners-up six times.

1999 Wembley (Orig.) Manchester United[10] 2-0 Newcastle United 79,101

Manchester Utd become first club to win 'treble'; League, FA Cup & Champions Lge.
Manchester Utd become the first club to win the League and Cup Double three times.
Manchester United become the first club to lift the FA Cup ten times.
Manchester United become the first club to appear in 15 FA Cup finals.
Newcastle United become the third club to appear in 13 FA Cup finals.
Newcastle United equal the record for most times as FA Cup runners-up (seven).
Newcastle United become the eighth club to lose two consecutive FA Cup finals.
Newcastle United become first club to lose successive FA Cup finals twice.

2000 Wembley (Orig.) Chelsea [3] 1-0 Aston Villa 78,217

This was the last of 77 FA Cup Final matches played at original Wembley Stadium.
Chelsea become the 17th club to appear in six FA Cup finals.
Aston Villa become the seventh club to appear in ten FA Cup finals.
Nb. Manchester United become only club to date not to defend their FA Cup title.

2001 Millennium Stadium Liverpool [6] 2-1 Arsenal 72,500

First FA Cup Final played outside of England (at Millennium Stadium, Cardiff).
Liverpool become the seventh club to lift the FA Cup six times.
Liverpool become the fifth club to appear in 12 FA Cup finals.
Arsenal become the second club to appear in 14 FA Cup finals.
Arsenal equal the record for most times as FA Cup runners-up (seven).

2002 Millennium Stadium Arsenal [8] 2-0 Chelsea 73,963

The fifth all-London FA Cup Final.
Arsenal become the second club to win the League and Cup Double three times.
Arsenal become first club to win the Double three times in three separate decades.
Arsenal become the third club to lift the FA Cup eight times.
Arsenal become the 16th previous season's runners-up to lift the Trophy.
Arsenal equal the record for most FA Cup Final appearances (15).
Chelsea become the 14th club to appear in seven FA Cup finals.
Highest attendance of the six FA Cup finals played at the Millennium Stadium.

2003 Millennium Stadium Arsenal [9] 1-0 Southampton 73,726

Arsenal become the first club to appear in 16 FA Cup finals.
Arsenal become the second club to lift the FA Cup nine times.
Arsenal become only the fifth different club to retain the FA Cup.
Arsenal become the first club to appear in three successive finals for a second time.
First FA Cup Final to be played indoors (Millennium Stadium roof closed).
Paul Jones (Southampton) becomes the first substitute goalkeeper to play in Final.

2004 Millennium Stadium Manchester United [11] 3-0 Millwall 71,350

Manchester United become the first club to lift the FA Cup 11 times.
Manchester United equal the record for most FA Cup Final appearances (16).
Curtis Weston (Millwall) becomes youngest player to date in a Cup Final (17y 119d).
Millennium Stadium becomes first venue outside London to host more than 3 finals.

2005 Millennium Stadium Arsenal [10] 0-0 Manchester United 71,876**
(Arsenal won 5-4 on Penalty kicks)

First FA Cup Final to be decided on penalties (Arsenal first to win on penalties).
Arsenal become first club to win FA Cup without scoring a goal in the Final.
The two teams both become the first two clubs to appear in 17 FA Cup finals.
Arsenal become the second club to lift the FA Cup ten times.
Arsenal become the third club to appear in four finals over five successive years.
Manchester Utd become ninth FA Cup holders to be runners-up the next season.
Manchester United become the sixth club to be FA Cup runners-up six times.

2006 Millennium Stadium Liverpool [7] 3-3 West Ham United 71,140**
(Liverpool won 3-1 on Penalty kicks)

Second FA Cup Final to be decided by penalties.
West Ham United become only third club to score three goals in Cup Final and lose.
Liverpool become the fifth club to lift the FA Cup seven times.
Liverpool become the fourth club to appear in 13 FA Cup finals.
West Ham United become the 20th club to appear in five FA Cup finals.
This is the only one of West Ham's five FA Cup finals involving two top-flight clubs.

2007 Wembley (New) Chelsea [4] 1-0* Manchester United 89,826

First FA Cup Final played at the New Wembley.
Chelsea lift FA Cup in both last Final at old Wembley and first Final at new Wembley.
Manchester United become the first club to appear in 18 FA Cup finals.
Manchester United equal the record for most times as FA Cup runners-up (seven).
Chelsea become the 12th club to appear in eight FA Cup finals.

2008 Wembley (New) Portsmouth [2] 1-0 Cardiff City 89,874

Portsmouth set record gap between FA Cup Final wins; 69 years.
Portsmouth score seven goals en route to lifting Cup, the lowest in current format.
Cardiff City become the first Welsh and first non-English side in three FA Cup finals.
Cardiff City set the record for longest gap between FA Cup finals; 81 years.
Cardiff City are the last non-top-flight club in FA Cup Final to date.
The highest Cup Final attendance at the new Wembley Stadium to date.

2009 Wembley (New) Chelsea [5] 2-1 Everton 89,391

Chelsea become 11th club to lift FA Cup five times.
Chelsea become ninth club to appear in nine FA Cup finals.
Everton become the first club to be FA Cup runners-up eight times.
Everton become the fifth club to appear in 13 FA Cup finals.
Louis Saha (Everton) scores the fastest FA Cup Final goal to date, 25 seconds.

2010 Wembley (New) Chelsea [6] 1-0 Portsmouth 88,335

Chelsea become the eighth club to lift the FA Cup six times.
Chelsea become the seventh club to win the League and Cup Double.
Chelsea become the sixth different club to retain the FA Cup.
Chelsea become the eighth club to appear in ten FA Cup finals.
Portsmouth become the 21st club to appear in five FA Cup finals.
Portsmouth become the fifth club to be runners-up and relegated in the same season.

2011 Wembley (New) Manchester City [5] 1-0 Stoke City 88,634

Manchester City become the 12th club to lift the FA Cup five times.
Manchester City become the tenth club to appear in nine FA Cup finals.
Stoke City set record for longest gap between forming and first Cup Final; 143 years.

2012 Wembley (New) Chelsea [7] 2-1 Liverpool 89,041

Chelsea become the sixth club to lift the FA Cup seven times.
Chelsea become the sixth club to appear in 11 FA Cup finals.
Chelsea become only the second club to win FA Cup four times across six seasons.
Liverpool become the fifth club to be FA Cup runners-up seven times.
Liverpool become the third club to appear in 14 FA Cup finals.
Didier Drogba (Chelsea) becomes first player to score in four different FA Cup finals.

2013	**Wembley (New)**	**Wigan Athletic** [1]	**1-0**	**Manchester City**	**86,254**

Wigan Athletic become the first club to win FA Cup and be relegated.
Wigan Athletic become the 43rd different club to win the FA Cup.
Wigan Athletic become first new name on Trophy for 25 years, the longest such gap.
Manchester City become the ninth club to appear in ten FA Cup finals.
Manchester City become the eighth club to be FA Cup runners-up five times.

2014	**Wembley (New)**	**Arsenal** [11]	**3-2***	**Hull City**	**89,345**

Arsenal become 'the best FA Cup club of all time' with their eleventh win.
(Courtesy of having more quarter-Final appearances than Manchester United.)
Arsenal equal the record for most FA Cup Final appearances (18).
Arsenal become the second club to win the FA Cup after having been 2-0 down.

2015	**Wembley (New)**	**Arsenal** [12]	**4-0**	**Aston Villa**	**89,283**

Arsenal become the first club to lift the FA Cup 12 times.
Arsenal become the first club to appear in 19 FA Cup finals.
Arsenal become the fourth club to retain the FA Cup more than once.
Aston Villa become the seventh club to appear in 11 FA Cup finals.
The last FA Cup Final to date to involve two clubs beginning with the same letter.

2016	**Wembley (New)**	**Manchester United** [12]	**2-1***	**Crystal Palace**	**88,619**

Manchester United equal the record for most times lifting the FA Cup Trophy (12).
Manchester United equal the record for most FA Cup Final appearances (19).
Crystal Palace become second club to lose to same opponents in both their finals.

2017	**Wembley (New)**	**Arsenal** [13]	**2-1**	**Chelsea**	**89,472**

The sixth all-London FA Cup Final.
Arsenal become the first club to lift the FA Cup 13 times.
Arsenal become the first club to appear in 20 FA Cup finals.
Chelsea become the sixth club to appear in 12 FA Cup finals.
Chelsea become the ninth club to be FA Cup runners-up five times.

2018	**Wembley (New)**	**Chelsea** [8]	**1-0**	**Manchester United**	**87,647**

First time three consecutive FA Cup finals involved clubs that had met in finals before.
Chelsea become the fourth club to lift the FA Cup eight times.
Chelsea become the sixth club to appear in 13 FA Cup finals.
Chelsea become the 17th previous season's runners-up to lift the Trophy.
Manchester United equal the record for most FA Cup Final appearances (20).
Manchester United equal the record for most times as FA Cup runners-up (eight).

2019 Wembley (New) Manchester City [6] 6-0 Watford 85,854

Manchester City equal the biggest margin of FA Cup victory.
Manchester City become the eighth club to lift the FA Cup six times.
Manchester City become the first club to win the domestic 'Treble'.
Manchester City become the eighth club to win League and Cup Double.
Gabriel Jesus & Raheem Sterling are first to both score twice for same club in Final.
Watford become the first club to play in more than one Final and not score a goal.

2020 Wembley (New) Arsenal [14] 2-1 Chelsea 0

The seventh all-London FA Cup Final.
Arsenal become the first club to lift the FA Cup 14 times (10% of Winners).
Arsenal become the first club to appear in 21 FA Cup finals (15% of finals).
Pierre-Emerick Aubameyang (Arsenal) scores the 400th FA Cup Final goal.
Arsenal become the first club to beat the same opponents in three separate finals.
Arsenal become second club to win seven finals in seven successive appearances.
First ever FA Cup Final played behind closed doors with official attendance of zero.
First FA Cup Final to be contested in the month of August.
Chelsea become the fourth club to appear in 14 FA Cup finals.
Chelsea become the sixth club to be FA Cup runners-up six times.

2021 Wembley (New) Leicester City[1] 1-0 Chelsea 20,000

Leicester City become the 44th different club to lift the FA Cup.
Leicester City set record for longest time since forming to win FA Cup – 137 years.
Leicester City become the first club to win FA Cup for the first time at the 5th attempt.
Leicester City become the 22nd club to appear in five FA Cup finals.
Leicester City record 2nd longest wait between first FA Cup Final and lifting Trophy.
Chelsea become the third club to appear in 15 FA Cup finals.
Chelsea become the fourth club to appear in four finals over five successive years.
Chelsea become the ninth club to lose two consecutive FA Cup finals.
Chelsea become the sixth club to lose seven FA Cup finals.

Rank	Premier League	W	Fin	SF	QF	R5	R4	R3
1	Arsenal	9	1	3	2	4	7	3
2	Chelsea	7	5	3	4	5	3	2
3	Manchester United	5	4	3	6	4	4	2
4	Liverpool	2	2	1	1	4	11	8
5	Manchester City	2	1	3	4	7	3	4
6	Everton	1	1	2	6	2	7	10

Top Six FA Cup Clubs whilst Members of Premier League.

Nb. Chart shows number of exits per Round

FA Cup Rankings by Club

Identifying the best club in FA Cup history is easy, right? It's simply the club that has lifted the Trophy the most times, surely? And that definition would certainly be accepted by any logical person. Arsenal have lifted the FA Cup 14 times, more than any other club, and so they are by rights considered to be the best FA Cup club in history. But it has not always been so obvious which club should be regarded as the best ever, especially when in the past two or more clubs have jointly lifted the Trophy the most times. And the waters are muddied even further when it comes to ranking clubs. Who's the second best? The third best? The 100th best? Identifying the ranked positions by clubs is fraught with challenges and many different ways exist to determine them.

The situation is complicated because the structure of the FA Cup has not remained consistent over time. It has been affected by many factors including the FA having to learn as it went along due to it being the first competition of its kind, the number of entries each season, and how football has evolved over the years. Prior to the Football League being formed in 1888 there were no qualifying rounds and during the fledgling years of the competition the Final fluctuated from being the equivalent of the fifth round through to being the eighth round. Once qualifying rounds were introduced a delineation occurred between qualifying rounds and 'proper' rounds. This initially resulted in the Final being the ninth round overall but only the fifth 'proper' round. Over the next 35 years the number of 'proper' rounds increased to six (including the Final) and the number of qualifying rounds fluctuated between four and nine. The FA Cup Final had variously been the 9th, the 10th, the 11th, the 12th, the 13th and the 14th round of the competition.

With the expansion of the Football League to four divisions soon after the end of World War One a structural change to the FA Cup was made to reflect the difference between the professional clubs of the League and the amateur clubs outside of it. In 1925 the format we recognise to this day was first implemented, although it still took several years before the clear distinction between the two codes was finally established. Ostensibly, all non-league clubs try to qualify for the 'proper' rounds and all Football League clubs are exempted until then. This has created a fixed situation since 1925/26 season whereby there has constantly been eight 'proper' rounds (including the Final). However, this has not been the case within the qualifying rounds. Originally there were six qualifying rounds, but due to changes in FA criteria for accepting clubs into the competition, this was reduced to five in 1951, and reduced further to four in 1962, before growing back to five in 1967 and returning to six in 2000.

The following table shows how the structure of the FA Cup has fluctuated over its 150 year existence highlighting the challenge that exists of comparing performances from across the years in order to determine a ranked listing of clubs achievements.

Key to all FA Cup Ranking Tables

Fin=Finals, W=Winners, RU=Runners-up, SF=Semi-Finals, QF=Quarter-Finals, R6=6th Round, R5=5th Round, R4=4th Round, R3=3rd Round, R2=2nd Round, R1=1st Round, ir=Intermediate Round, q6=6th qualifying round, q5=5th qualifying round, q4=4th qualifying round, q3=3rd qualifying round, q2=2nd qualifying round, q1=1st qualifying round, Pr=preliminary, EP=extra preliminary round

How the FA Cup Structure has Changes over 150 Years

Years	EP	Pr	q1	q2	q3	q4	q5	q6	ir	R1	R2	R3	R4	R5	R6	SF	Fin.
1871-72										x	x	x				x	X
1872-73										x	x	x	x				X
1873-76										x	x	x				x	X
1876-79										x	x	x	x			x	X
1879-84										x	x	x	x	x		x	X
1884-88										x	x	x	x	x	x	x	X
1888-90			x	x	x	x				x	x	x				x	X
1890-91		x	x	x	x	x				x	x	x				x	X
1891-92			x	x	x	x				x	x	x				x	X
1892-93		x	x	x	x	x				x	x	x				x	X
1893-94			x	x	x	x				x	x	x				x	X
1895-96		x	x	x	x	x				x	x	x				x	X
1897-00		x	x	x	x	x	x			x	x	x				x	X
1900-03		x	x	x	x	x	x		x	x	x	x				x	X
1903-04	x	x	x	x	x	x	x		x	x	x	x				x	X
1904-05	x	x	x	x	x	x	x	x	x	x	x	x				x	X
1905-06		x	x	x	x	x				x	x	x	x			x	X
1906-08		x	x	x	x	x	x			x	x	x	x			x	X
1908-14	x	x	x	x	x	x	x			x	x	x	x			x	X
1914-25	x	x	x	x	x	x	x	x		x	x	x	x			x	X
1925-51	x	x	x	x	x	x				x	x	x	x	x	x	x	X
1951-62		x	x	x	x	x				x	x	x	x	x	x	x	X
1962-67			x	x	x	x				x	x	x	x	x	x	x	X
1967-00		x	x	x	x	x				x	x	x	x	x	x	x	X
2000-21	x	x	x	x	x	x				x	x	x	x	x	x	x	x

'x' indicates the rounds utilised in each period of the FA Cup

Invariably, the top ranked clubs will all have achieved FA Cup runs to the latter stages of the competition, so in theory only the 'Proper' rounds need to be compared and contrasted. Two challenges still exist, though. Firstly, should the rounds reached be the considered factor for determining rankings or should number of teams remaining be the determining factor? The 3rd Round in the 19th century could now be labelled the quarter-finals (last eight) whereas in modern times the last eight is traditionally the 6th Round. Secondly, in the seasons immediately prior to 1925, the 5th and 6th qualifying rounds appear to be the equivalent of modern day 1st and 2nd 'proper' rounds. Many would argue that reaching the 6th qualifying round in 1924/25 is the same as reaching the 2nd round 'proper' today.

Other alternative ranking solutions include allocating a points system to each round and either using the cumulative points tally to determine positions, or use an average to identify them. Notwithstanding the fact that determining how points are allocated to each round is an arbitrary decision, the former of the two methods favours those clubs that have participated in the FA Cup the longest (Aston Villa, Blackburn Rovers and Nottingham Forest would likely be the one-two-three), whilst the latter method favours clubs that have participated during the seasons when there have been 14 rounds in total (Chelsea, Liverpool and Everton would be the most likely top three).

At the end of the day, no matter what method is used to determine overall club rankings in the FA Cup, it can never be infallible, and so to that end a method has to be selected and then adhered to as best as possible. For the rankings of clubs in this book, the following process has been adopted. The principle that one FA Cup win in one Final appearance (e.g. Wigan Athletic) is better than two FA Cup runners-up in two Final appearances (e.g. Watford) has been applied to all levels of the competition. A solitary fifth round appearance is better than best runs ending in multiple fourth round exits. Reaching the 1st Round 'proper' just once is better than at best being knocked out many times in the last qualifying round. So Wigan Athletic is ranked above Watford because FA Cup Winners have to be placed above a club that has at best been runners-up. The same goes for Queens Park Rangers who are ranked above Norwich City because the London club has one Cup Final appearance despite reaching the semi-finals fewer times than the Norfolk club.

So the criteria for determining rankings is as follows: first the number of times a club has lifted the Trophy, second the number of finals contested, third the number of semi-finals appeared in, and so on down to the number of Preliminary Round and Extra Preliminary Round knockouts experienced. If two or more clubs have lifted the Cup the same number of times, then their total number of finals is used to separate them, then their number of semi-finals and then quarter-finals etc. This method proved critical when determining which of Arsenal or Manchester United should be regarded as the 'best FA Cup club of all time back' back in 2016 when the Red Devils won the FA Cup for the 12th time to match the Gunners' tally. The two clubs' comparative achievements at the time are detailed in the table below.

Club	Winners	Finalists	Semi-Finals	Quarter-Finals
Arsenal	12	19	28	42
Manchester United	12	19	28	41

The two teams were matched on number of times lifting the Trophy, their number of Final appearances, and the number of times they'd reached the last four. Arsenal were confirmed as the 'best FA Cup club of all time' by virtue of appearing in one more quarter-final than their rivals. As stated previously, the methodology is not perfect (quarter-finals have been variously the 3rd, 4th, 5th or 6th round), but it is applied consistently across the years for all clubs.

Now with 14 titles, Arsenal are clearly the number one club as the FA Cup celebrates its 150th anniversary. However, the competition had already been running for 55 years before the Gunners' first Final appearance and by ranking clubs at different times throughout the competition's history it can be shown how it has evolved over time and which clubs dominated during which periods. Scattered throughout this book are the rankings for the Top 150 clubs across five different time periods: prior to the foundation of the Football League, from then until the outbreak of WWI, between the Wars, after WWII until the end of the 20th Century, and in the 21st Century. Additionally there is a ranking of the overall Top 150 clubs to commemorate the competition's 150th anniversary, and a ranking of those teams that have participated in the FA Cup since 1888 that have always done so as non-league clubs.

Top 150 FA Cup Clubs Prior to Formation of Football League (1871/72 to 1887/88)

Two hundred and eighty-six different clubs entered the FA Cup during its fledgling years, a period that witnessed the game transition in dominance from the amateur clubs predominantly from the south of England to the working class, professional clubs of the north. The competition structure underwent a myriad of changes as the FA tried to accommodate the surge of interest across the early years, but one constant throughout these 17 seasons was that each campaign always began with the 1st Round. By 1888/89, when owners of some professional clubs needed more certainty of fixtures and founded the Football League, the FA also recognised the need to exempt the better clubs until later rounds of the FA Cup to avoid a repeat of the embarrassing 26-0 scoreline that had been achieved by Preston North End in the last pre-Football League campaign. And so the Qualifying Rounds were introduced.

All of the Top 150 rankings are broken out into segments based upon the furthest round reached by clubs during each time period. The position of each club is listed alongside the club name. Many clubs have undergone name changes throughout the past 150 years and where possible all names each club used whilst participating in the FA Cup have been included even if not relevant to the period covered. To the right of each club name are details of the rounds that the club has appeared in and how many times they have done so, working down from Winning the competition and being Finalists to the point where it marks a distinction from the clubs above and below it. For example, Blackburn Rovers actually competed in four FA Cup finals during this period, but it is not necessary to record the time they were runners-up as that has no effect on the clubs 2nd position. To separate Oxford University and Royal Engineers, though, it has been necessary to record their achievements to lower rounds than the Final, but only to the differentiator of their semi-final appearances.

Best Performance - Winners

1	The Wanderers	5x Winners
2	Blackburn Rovers	3x Winners
3	Old Etonians	2x Winners
4	Oxford University	1x Winners, 4x Finalists, 6x SF
5	Royal Engineers	1x Winners, 4x Finalists, 4x SF
6	West Bromwich Albion	1x Winners, 3x Finalists
7	Clapham Rovers	1x Winners, 2x Finalists
8	Old Carthusians	1x Winners, 1x Finalists, 3x SF
9	Blackburn Olympic	1x Winners, 1x Finalists, 2x SF
10	Aston Villa	1x Winners, 1x Finalists, 1x SF

Best Performance – Runners-up

11	Queen's Park	2x Finalists
12	Preston North End	1x Finalists

Best Performance – Semi-Finalists

13	Swifts	3x SF, 5x QF
14	Nottingham Forest	3x SF, 3x QF
15	Notts County	2x SF
16	Darwen	1x SF, 3x QF
17	The (Sheffield) Wednesday	1x SF, 2x QF, 4x R4
18	Cambridge University	1x SF, 2x QF, 4x R3
19	Marlow	1x SF, 1x QF, 2x R5
20	Crewe Alexandra	1x SF, 1x QF, 2x R4
21	Old Harrovians	1x SF, 1x QF, 4x R3
22	Small Heath (Birmingham C.)	1x SF, 1x QF, 1x R3, 3x R2
23=	Crystal Palace*	1x SF, 1x QF, 1x R3, 2x R2, 5x R1
23=	Shropshire Wanderers	1x SF, 1x QF, 1x R3, 2x R2, 5x R1
25	Derby Junction	1x SF, 1x QF, 1x R3, 2x R2, 4x R1
26	Rangers (Glasgow)	1x SF, 1x QF, 1x R3, 1x R2

Best Performance – Quarter-Finalists

27	Upton Park	4x QF
28	Maidenhead (United)	3x QF, 5x R4
29	Sheffield	3x QF, 4x R4
30	Old Westminsters	3x QF, 6x R3
31	Old Foresters	1x QF, 3x R5
32	Church	1x QF, 2x R5, 3x R4, 3x R3, 5x R2
33	Middlesbrough	1x QF, 2x R5, 3x R4, 3x R3, 4x R2
34	Brentwood* / Crusaders	1x QF, 3x R4
35	Romford (Town)*	1x QF, 2x R4, 4x R3
36	Druids	1x QF, 2x R4, 3x R3
37	Hendon*	1x QF, 2x R4, 2x R3
38	Wednesbury Old Athletic* ...	1x QF, 2x R3
39	Stafford Road Works	1x QF, 1x R3, 5x R2
40=	Northwich Victoria	1x QF, 1x R3, 4x R2
40=	South Shore	1x QF, 1x R3, 4x R2
42	Redcar and Coatham	1x QF, 1x R3, 3x R2
43	Woodford Wells	1x QF, 1x R3, 2x R2
44	Hampstead Heathens	1x QF, 1x R3, 1x R2

Best Performance – 5th Round

45	Chirk (AAA)	2x R5
46	Bolton Wanderers	1x R5, 2x R4, 4x R3, 6x R2
47	Staveley	1x R5, 2x R4, 4x R3, 5x R2
48	Lockwood Brothers	1x R5, 3x R3, 4x R2, 7x R1
49	Chatham (Town)	1x R5, 3x R3, 4x R2, 6x R1
50=	Leek	1x R5, 3x R3, 3x R2
50=	Lincoln City	1x R5, 3x R3, 3x R2
52	Davenham	1x R5, 2x R3, 3x R2, 5x R1

53	Derby County	1x R5, 2x R3, 3x R2, 4x R1
54	(Burslem) Port Vale	1x R5, 2x R3, 2x R2
55	Stoke (City)	1x R5, 1x R3, 2x R2, 5x R1
56	Bootle*	1x R5, 1x R3, 2x R2, 4x R1
57	Horncastle*	1x R5, 1x R3, 1x R2, 3x R1
58	Partick Thistle	1x R5, 1x R3, 1x R2, 2x R1

Best Performance – 4th Round

59	Grimsby Town	2x R4, 3x R3, 6x R2
60	Old Wykehamists	2x R4, 3x R3, 5x R2
61	Grey Friars	2x R4, 2x R3
62	Wolverhampton Wanderers	1x R4, 3x R3
63	Reading	1x R4, 2x R3, 7x R2
64	Birmingham St George's	1x R4, 2x R3, 4x R2, 7x R1
65	Walsall Town	1x R4, 2x R3, 4x R2, 6x R1
66	Eagley	1x R4, 2x R3, 3x R2, 7x R1
67	South Reading	1x R4, 2x R3, 3x R2, 6x R1
68	Notts Rangers	1x R4, 2x R3, 3x R2, 4x R1
69	Walsall Swifts	1x R4, 2x R3, 2x R2
70	Hotspur	1x R4, 1x R3, 5x R2, 8x R1
71	Sheffield Heeley	1x R4, 1x R3, 5x R2, 7x R1
72	West End	1x R4, 1x R3, 4x R2
73	Lower Darwen........................	1x R4, 1x R3, 2x R2
74	Wednesbury Town*	1x R4, 1x R3, 1x R2, 2x R1
75=	Great Bridge Unity	1x R4, 1x R3, 1x R2, 1x R1
75=	Shankhouse	1x R4, 1x R3, 1x R2, 1x R1

Best Performance – 3rd Round

77	Pilgrims	2x R3, 8x R2
78	Barnes	2x R3, 7x R2
79	Grantham (Town)	2x R3, 5x R2
80	Rochester	2x R3, 4x R2, 13x R1
81	Windsor Home Park	2x R3, 4x R2, 7x R1
82	Oswestry Town	2x R3, 4x R2, 6x R1
83	Halliwell	2x R3, 3x R2, 6x R1
84=	Dulwich	2x R3, 3x R2, 4x R1
84=	Turton	2x R3, 3x R2, 4x R1
84=	Witton	2x R3, 3x R2, 4x R1
87	Remnants	2x R3, 2x R2, 6x R1
88	Darwen Old Wanderers	2x R3, 2x R2, 4x R1
89	Accrington*	1x R3, 4x R2
90	Hanover Utd. (Polytechnic)...	1x R3, 3x R2, 9x R1
91	Herts Rangers	1x R3, 3x R2, 7x R1
92=	Birmingham Excelsior	1x R3, 3x R2, 5x R1
92=	Derby Midland	1x R3, 3x R2, 5x R1

94	Old Brightonians	1x R3, 3x R2, 4x R1
95	Gainsborough Trinity	1x R3, 3x R2, 3x R1
96=	Reading Minster	1x R3, 2x R2, 5x R1
96=	Rossendale	1x R3, 2x R2, 5x R1
98	Dreadnought	1x R3, 2x R2, 4x R1
99	Darlington*	1x R3, 2x R2, 3x R1
100=	Padiham*	1x R3, 2x R2, 2x R1
100=	Reading Abbey	1x R3, 2x R2, 2x R1
102	Aston Unity	1x R3, 1x R2, 6x R1
103=	Higher Walton	1x R3, 1x R2, 4x R1
103=	Southport (Central)	1x R3, 1x R2, 4x R1
103=	Sunderland	1x R3, 1x R2, 4x R1
106=	Darwen Ramblers	1x R3, 1x R2, 3x R1
106=	Goldenhill	1x R3, 1x R2, 3x R1
106=	Minerva	1x R3, 1x R2, 3x R1
109=	Cliftonville	1x R3, 1x R2, 2x R1
109=	Irwell Springs (Bacup Boro)...	1x R3, 1x R2, 2x R1
109=	London Caledonians	1x R3, 1x R2, 2x R1
109=	Rangers (London)	1x R3, 1x R2, 2x R1
113=	Cowlairs	1x R3, 1x R2, 1x R1
113=	Owlerton	1x R3, 1x R2, 1x R1
113=	Phoenix Bessemer	1x R3, 1x R2, 1x R1
113=	Renton	1x R3, 1x R2, 1x R1

Best Performance – 2nd Round

117	South Norwood	5x R2
118	Astley Bridge	4x R2
119	Panthers (Sturminster N Utd)	3x R2, 6x R1
120=	Rotherham Town*	3x R2, 5x R1
120=	Wrexham / Olympic	3x R2, 5x R1
122=	1st Surrey Rifles	2x R2, 7x R1
122=	Acton*	2x R2, 7x R1
124=	Macclesfield (Town)	2x R2, 6x R1
124=	Reigate Priory	2x R2, 6x R1
124=	Southall / Park	2x R2, 6x R1
127=	High Wycombe	2x R2, 5x R1
127=	Long Eaton Rangers	2x R2, 5x R1
127=	Mosquitos	2x R2, 5x R1
130=	Forest School	2x R2, 4x R1
130=	Great Lever	2x R2, 4x R1
130=	Henley (Town)	2x R2, 4x R1
130=	Hurst (Ashton United)	2x R2, 4x R1
134=	Bolton Association	2x R2, 2x R1
134=	Fleetwood Rangers	2x R2, 2x R1

134=	Newcastle West End*	2x R2, 2x R1
134=	Newtown	2x R2, 2x R1
134=	Third Lanark Rifle Volunteers	2x R2, 2x R1
139	Blackburn Park Road	1x R2, 7x R1
140=	Civil Service	1x R2, 5x R1
140=	Hitchin (Town)*	1x R2, 5x R1
140=	Leyton*	1x R2, 5x R1
140=	Uxbridge	1x R2, 5x R1
144=	105th Regiment	1x R2, 4x R1
144=	Clapton	1x R2, 4x R1
144=	Derby St Luke's	1x R2, 4x R1
144=	Notts Olympic	1x R2, 4x R1
144=	Oswaldtwistle Rovers	1x R2, 4x R1
144=	Rawtenstall	1x R2, 4x R1
144=	Wednesbury Strollers	1x R2, 4x R1

**Different from current/later club with same/similar name*

All the Pre-World War II FA Cup Final Programmes at Wembley (*photo by Chris Wathen*).

Counting Up to 150 - Miscellaneous Facts about the FA Cup

Only **one** FA Cup match has occurred on Christmas Day, a 4th Qualifying Round 2nd Replay in the 1888/89 season between two Irish clubs, with Linfield Athletic triumphing 7-0 against Cliftonville.

Just **two** clubs have been involved in all but one FA Cup campaign: Maidenhead United only missed out in 1876/77 to save money, whilst Marlow only didn't participate in 1910/11 because the FA mislaid their entry submission.

Three clubs have lifted the FA Cup without conceding a goal en route to doing so: The Wanderers in 1873 (only played in the Final that year), Preston North End in 1889 (as part of their Invincibles season), and Bury in 1903 (culminating in a record setting 6-0 FA Cup Final victory).

Non-League clubs have contested the FA Cup Final **four** times: Tottenham Hotspur won the Cup in 1901, Southampton were runners-up in both 1900 and 1902, and Sheffield Wednesday (as The Wednesday) lost heavily in 1890.

There have only been **five** FA Cup finals where both clubs were appearing in their first Final: 1872 The Wanderers 1-0 Royal Engineers, 1898 Nottingham Forest 3-1 Derby County, 1900 Bury 4-0 Southampton, 1909 Manchester United 1-0 Bristol City, and 1914 Burnley 1-0 Liverpool.

Since The Wanderers became the first club to be known as 'the best FA Cup team of all time', only **six** other clubs have been able to make the same claim: Blackburn Rovers, Aston Villa, Newcastle United, (Aston Villa again), Manchester United, Tottenham Hotspur, (Manchester United again) and Arsenal.

Wilfred 'Billy' Minter holds the record for most goals scored in one FA Cup game by a player on a losing side when he netted **seven** times for St Albans City against Dulwich Hamlet in their 1922/23 4th Qualifying Round replay.

The most number of consecutive FA Cup ties any club has played that required a replay in every single one of them is **eight**, achieved by Lincoln City, starting with a 2-2 draw with Hereford United in the 2nd Round in the 2010/11 season, through to a 5-1 victory over Alfreton Town in a 4th Qualifying Round replay in the 2014/15 season.

The record for the same two clubs meeting each other in successive FA Cup seasons is **nine**. Kettering Town and Peterborough United faced each other in every FA Cup season from 1936/37 (won 2-0 by Peterborough) to 1950/51 (won 2-1 by Kettering in a replay). Even the intervention of World War II couldn't prevent this amazing streak.

Bury FC scored **10** goals without reply in their FA Cup Final matches, the biggest goal difference without conceding of all Cup Finalists.

Birmingham based side Headingley FC hold the record for most FA Cup campaigns without ever progressing beyond the Extra Preliminary Round. For **11** successive seasons leading up to World War II they were dispatched in the earliest round possible.

The most number of games played by a club en route to lifting the FA Cup is **12**, achieved by Barnsley FC in their 1911/12 success. Bizarrely, the Tykes scored fewer goals (11) than actual number of matches they played.

The most games played by any one club in a single FA Cup campaign is **13**, achieved by Bideford FC in the 1973/74 season. After starting with a 4-1 win over Penzance in the 1st Qualifying Round the Robins finally succumbed to Bristol Rovers in the 1st Round 'Proper'. The run included four matches against Trowbridge Town and five games against Falmouth Town.

The most number of goals scored in one FA Cup game that ended in a draw is **14**, when Dulwich Hamlet and Wealdstone played out a 7-7 draw in their 1929/30 4th Qualifying Round tie. The Hamlet won 2-1 in the replay.

The highest aggregate number of goals scored in one match with a one goal margin of victory is **15**, in that aforementioned 4th Qualifying Round replay won 8-7 by Dulwich Hamlet against St Albans City in the 1922/23 season.

The most goals scored by any club in their debut FA Cup match is **16**, achieved by New Crusaders when they defeated Woking 16-0 in their 1905/06 1st Qualifying Round tie.

The most goals scored in an FA Cup replay is **17**, achieved by Rothwell Town when winning 17-0 against Stamford in a 1927/28 Preliminary Round replay, after the sides had originally played out a 2-2 draw.

Rhyl FC conceded **18** goals in their 18-0 defeat by St Helens Recreation in the 3rd Qualifying Round in the 1902/03 season to record the heaviest defeat in the FA Cup by a non-English club.

The most goals scored by a non-league club in one FA Cup game is **19** achieved by Staveley in their 19-0 victory over Sheffield Walkley in their 1890/91 1st Qualifying Round tie, and by Oswestry Town when they defeated Badsey Rangers 19-3 in a 1933/34 Extra Preliminary Round game.

Blackburn Rovers hold the record for most consecutive FA Cup games won, when after beating Southport Central 7-1 in the 1883/84 1st Round they won a total of **20** FA Cup games before drawing 0-0 with West Bromwich Albion in the 1886 Final. (This sequence was part of a record 23 FA Cup game unbeaten run, covering 25 Rounds, over three and a bit seasons).

The Wanderers played just **21** matches across their five FA Cup winning campaigns.

Aside from the first ever FA Cup Final, **22** subsequent finals have been contested by clubs who had both at the time never won the Cup, the last such occasion being 1970 when Chelsea defeated Leeds United 2-1 in a replay at Old Trafford.

Wolverhampton Casuals hold the record for most exits in the Extra Preliminary Round, having gone out of the competition in the earliest round possible **23** times.

24 clubs that have participated in the FA Cup have a name that begins with a number rather than a letter, the latest being 1874 Northwich.

Merseyside rivals Liverpool and Everton hold the record for most FA Cup 'Proper' Round head-to-heads, meeting **25** times between 1901/02 season and 2019/20 season.

Preston North End scored **26** goals without reply against Hyde in the 1st Round in 1887/88 season to record the highest ever margin of victory in the FA Cup.

From Bedford Avenue to Worthing FC, **27** different clubs have competed in the FA Cup whilst members of the now defunct Corinthian League.

The new Wembley Stadium has hosted **28** FA Cup semi-finals (first pair of games happened in 2007/08 season).

There were **29** FA Cup Winners in the 19th Century (1871/72 to 1899/1900).

The Extra Preliminary Round of the 2020/21 season kicked off just **30** days after the 2019/20 FA Cup Final was played on August 1st 2020, the only time matches in two separate FA Cup seasons occurred in the same month.

31 - The record aggregate score on penalties occurred when Tunbridge Wells defeated Littlehampton Town 16-15 in a Preliminary round replay in 2005/06 season. Forty penalty kicks were taken in total.

Every season just **32** of usually 644 non-league teams that enter the FA Cup will qualify for the 1st Round 'Proper'. That is fewer than 5%.

35 different clubs have competed in the FA Cup whilst members of the recently closed down East Midlands Counties League.

Manchester United have scored **36** goals in FA Cup finals, the most achieved by any club.

Derby County scored **37** goals en route to lifting the FA Cup in 1945/46 season, a record for a club winning the Cup at Wembley, aided by the need to play two-legged matches in all 'Proper' Rounds before the semi-finals.

39 FA Cup finals have involved Manchester United and/or Arsenal.

Aston Villa hold the record for most goals scored en route to lifting the Trophy when they netted **40** times in their successful 1886/87 campaign.

At **41** years and 257 days old, Walter 'Billy' Hampson is the oldest verified player to feature in an FA Cup Final, doing so for Newcastle United versus Aston Villa in 1924.

Worthing FC has exited the FA Cup in the 1st Qualifying Round **43** times, the most times any club has gone out at that stage of the competition.

44 different venues have hosted FA Cup semi-finals including both the Wembley Stadiums, league grounds Old Trafford, Villa Park, Burnden Park and Elm Park to name but four, as well as one ground in Scotland and one stadium in Wales.

Marlow FC has exited the FA Cup in the Preliminary Round **45** times, the most times any club has gone out at that stage of the competition.

Manchester United and Everton jointly hold the record for most appearances in FA Cup quarter-finals, **46** times each.

A total of **47** pairs of clubs, which had both competed in the FA Cup, have merged together to form a new club that also went on to compete in the competition. Ossett Town merging with Ossett Albion to form Ossett United in 2018 is the latest such merger.

48 different clubs have been runners-up in the FA Cup Final from Manchester United and Everton who have lost the Final eight times each, through to the 13 clubs that have only ever tasted defeat in a Cup Final.

Henry 'Harry' Cursham is the FA Cup's overall top scorer netting **49** times in the competition for Notts County between 1877 and 1889, with forty-eight goals in the 'Proper' Rounds and one goal in the Qualifying Rounds.

Plymouth Argyle and Queens Park Rangers jointly hold the unwanted record of most FA Cup exits in the 3rd Round. Both clubs have been knocked out at that stage of the competition **50** times.

Rochdale hold the unwanted record of most FA Cup exits in the 1st Round. The Dale have been knocked out at that stage of the competition **52** times.

Since the current structure of the FA Cup was put in place in the 1925/26 season, **53** non-league clubs have fought their way through to the 4th Round or beyond.

54 FA Cup finals had already happened before the current record holders, Arsenal, lifted the Trophy for the first time in 1930.

The most common venue for FA Cup semi-finals is Villa Park, which has hosted a last four match **55** times.

57 different clubs have appeared in FA Cup finals from 1871/72 to 2020/21.

58 clubs had their FA Cup entry submissions accepted but then scratched without ever taking part in the competition, from Harrow Chequers and Donnington School in its first ever season through to Colne Dynamos in the 1990/91 season. *Nb. Burton Park Wanderers scratched before playing in the 2020/21 season due to Covid_19 reasons, but there is a good chance they could enter the competition again.*

Excluding replays, the FA Cup Final has occurred on **59** different dates in the calendar year from as early as 11th March in 1876 to as late as 1st August in the Covid_19 impacted 2019/20 season.

Nottingham Forest hold the record for the longest gap between their first two FA Cup Final appearances. **61** years separated their first victory over Derby County in 1898 and their second win against Luton Town in 1959.

For **62** seasons between 1920 and 1989, across two separate time periods, Aston Villa were able to claim to be the 'best FA Cup club of all time', the most amount of seasons any club has been able to make that claim.

63 different clubs have participated in the FA Cup whilst members of the Wessex League following its formation in 1986.

AFC Bournemouth hold the record for longest gap between quarter-final appearances with **64** years between the club's first appearance in 1956/57 and its second in 2020/21.

There have been **65** non-league clubs that have reached the 2nd Round or beyond having started their FA Cup campaign that season in the earliest possible qualifying round (Extra Preliminary, Preliminary or 1st Qualifying Round depending upon the season).

The FA Cup 3rd Round in the 1962/63 season took **66** days to complete owing to the prolonged severe weather conditions that winter.

Sunderland Ryhope Community Association versus Sunderland Ryhope Colliery Welfare is the longest combined named FA Cup tie of all time with a total of **67** letters in the two clubs' names.

There were **69** years between Portsmouth lifting the FA Cup in 1939 and doing so again in 2008, the longest gap for any team winning the Trophy again without being in the Final in between.

71 different players have scored more than one FA Cup Final goal. Ian Rush has scored the most with five, whilst Didier Drogba netted in four different finals.

Leicester City competed in **72** further campaigns after first appearing in an FA Cup Final before finally lifting the Trophy in 2021, the most amount of campaigns any club has had between those two feats.

75 different clubs have participated in the FA Cup whilst members of the West Midlands (Regional) League, from when it adopted its current name in 1962 formerly being known as the Birmingham and District League.

Southampton FC waited the longest between any club's first FA Cup Final appearance and finally going on to lift the Trophy. The Saints first appeared in the Final in 1900 and did so again **76** years later when they defeated Manchester United.

The original Wembley Stadium held **77** FA Cup Final matches including five replays, the most common venue to date to host these showpiece games.

79 different clubs have competed in the semi-finals of the FA Cup. Arsenal and Manchester United jointly hold the record of 30 semi-final appearances each.

Cardiff City hold the record for the longest gap between FA Cup Final appearances. **81** years elapsed between the Bluebirds lifting the FA Cup in 1927 and losing to Portsmouth in the Final in 2008.

Just **82** days passed between Manchester United finally playing their oft postponed FA Cup 3rd Round tie against Huddersfield Town in 1963 and the Red Devils lifting the Trophy at Wembley, the shortest gap between first FA Cup game played and going on to win the Cup (excluding the 1872/73 season when The Wanderers were exempted until the Final).

The most number of campaigns from first participating in FA Cup to lifting the Trophy in their debut FA Cup Final is **83** by Coventry City in 1987.

A total of **87** goals have been scored in vain in FA Cup finals by the eventual runners-up.

In 2020/21 season Chorley FC were the first club to receive a 'bye' into the FA Cup 'Proper' Rounds since Bath City received the same **89** years previously.

Players named either Bill, Billy, Will, William or Willie have won the FA Cup **90** times, a record for any name and its common variations.

The Centenary FA Cup Final between Leeds United and Arsenal in 1972 was actually the **91st** FA Cup Final.

The longest gap in seasons between successive participation in the FA Cup is **94**, achieved by Torpoint Athletic who took part in 2010/11 more than a century after appearing in the competition as Torpoint (Association).

Sutton United were involved in a record **95** FA Cup campaigns before finally reaching the 5th Round in the 2016/17 season.

It is **96** years since the current structure of the FA Cup was put in place with clubs from the top two tiers (usually) being exempt until the 3rd Round.

The original Sheppey United had **97** FA Cup campaigns, the most of any club never to appear in the 'Proper' Rounds of the competition. The club reached the 6th Qualifying Round in 1919/20 season, regarded now as the equivalent of today's 2nd Round.

Frickley Athletic had competed in the FA Cup **98** times before finally facing a club beginning with the letter 'T'. The Blues faced Tadcaster Albion in their 331st FA Cup match during the 2019/20 season.

The original Gresley Rovers (2009), King's Lynn (2010) and Windsor & Eton (2011) all folded whilst sitting on **99** FA Cup campaigns.

100 clubs entered the 1883-84 FA Cup campaign, the first time the three digit milestone had been reached.

A record **102** clubs scratched from the 1914/15 FA Cup due to the outbreak of World War I caused by many teams' players forming 'Pals Regiments'.

Macclesfield Town first reached the FA Cup 4th Round in what was then a competition record **103rd** campaign in the 2012/13 season.

Middlesbrough FC required a record **104** FA Cup campaigns before reaching the club's first ever semi-final in 1997.

In 2019/20 Notts County were the first former FA Cup winners for **105** years to have to start their FA Cup campaign in the qualifying Rounds. The previous club to have to suffer that ignominy? Nottingham Forest in the 1914/15 season.

106 clubs played their 1939/40 FA Cup Extra Preliminary Round matches before the competition was abandoned due to the outbreak of World War II.

Stourbridge hold the record for most number of campaigns before reaching the 2nd Round (**107** in 2011/12) and the Glassboys also hold the record for most campaigns before reaching the 1st Round (105 in 2009/10).

108 different clubs have participated in the FA Cup whilst members of the second oldest League in England, the Northern League.

From Addlestone and Weybridge Town to Worthing FC, **109** different clubs participated in the FA Cup whilst members of the now defunct Athenian League.

110 clubs which first entered the FA Cup in the 19th Century, are still participating in it to this day.

Chorley FC finally reached the 3rd and 4th Rounds of the FA Cup in a record setting **113th** campaign in the 2020/21 season.

Aston Villa have appeared in the 3rd Round of the FA Cup more than any other club, **115** times in total.

There was a gap of **116** years between Bury FC and Manchester City both posting their record 6-0 FA Cup Final victories.

There have been **117** different pairs of clubs that have contested the 140 FA Cup finals.

The most number of FA Cup campaigns competed in before reaching the Final for the first time is **118** by Stoke City in the 2010/11 season.

119 different clubs have participated in FA Cup quarter-final matches.

120 FA Cup matches have involved one team scoring at least a dozen goals.

The highest number of clubs making their FA Cup debut in the same season is **122**, appropriately enough in the 1921/22 season.

Lincoln City reached the FA Cup quarter-finals for the first time in their **123rd** campaign, a longevity record notable also for the Imps being the first non-league club to reach the last eight for 103 years.

Twenty-seven different clubs have competed in the FA Cup **125** times or more.

There have been **126** non-English clubs that have participated in the FA Cup representing Scotland, Wales, Ireland, Isle of Wight and Guernsey.

It is **127** years since Notts County won the FA Cup, the longest wait to repeat the feat for any former Cup winner still competing in the FA Cup to this day.

Leicester City took **130** years from first FA Cup campaign to lifting the FA Cup for the first time, the most number of years for any of the 44 FA Cup winners to do so for the first time.

Notts County participated in **133** consecutive FA Cup 'Proper' Round campaigns before being forced to withdraw due to Covid_19 positive test results ahead of their 4th Qualifying Round tie in 2020/21 season.

In 2020 Anthony Taylor became the first official in **135** years to referee the same two clubs in two separate FA Cup finals (Major Marindin the other to do so) whilst also becoming the first official in 119 years to be in the centre for a second Cup Final (Arthur Kingscott was the previous one).

137 more clubs participated in the 1946/47 FA Cup than had taken part in the 1945/46 competition. The largest jump in entrants from one season to the next caused by the staggered return of clubs following the end of World War II.

139 different clubs have participated in the FA Cup whilst members of the Western League.

140 seconds was all that was needed for Andy Locke of Nantwich Town to notch a hat-trick against Droylsden Fc in their 1995/96 1st Qualifying Round 3-0 victory.

The 2022 FA Cup Final will actually be the **141st** in the competition's history.

143 clubs that have participated in the FA Cup never exited the competition before the 'Proper' Rounds of the competition. The majority of these clubs only participated in the FA Cup in the days when there were no Qualifying Rounds. Notts County became the latest club to exit the FA Cup before the Proper Rounds for the first time when the Magpies withdrew due to Covid_19 issues in 2020/21 season.

Clubs have been disqualified from the FA Cup **144** times for a variety of different reasons, from Sheffield FC refusing to play extra time against Nottingham Forest in 1879/80 season to Peacehaven and Telscombe fielding an ineligible player in 2020/21.

From Royal Engineers Service Battalion in 1903/04 to eleven debut teams in 2020/21, there have been **145** different clubs which have so far had just one FA Cup campaign and exited in the earliest round possible, the Extra Preliminary Round.

In 2020/21 season, Harrogate Town became the **146th** different club to compete in the FA Cup whilst being a member of the Football League.

Players called John or Johnny have appeared on the pitch **147** times for FA Cup Final teams (includes a John Arne and a John Obi). Adding Jonathan and Jonny takes this up to 150, the most common name variation to play in FA Cup finals.

It is **148** years since Uxbridge FC last appeared in the FA Cup 2nd Round (played in 1873), the best performance in the club's history, and the longest wait of any club still competing in the FA Cup to replicate its best run.

The **150th** FA Cup Final won't be until the 2030/31 season.

The First 150 Clubs to have Entered FA Cup

The year refers to the first season the club entered the FA Cup (1871 = season 1871/72)

1871 Barnes .... Founder members of the FA.
Civil Service .... Known as the War Office when helping found the FA.
Clapham Rovers .... Jarvis Kenrick scored the first ever FA Cup goal.
Crystal Palace .... Founder members of the FA, unrelated to current club.
Donnington School ... Based in Lincolnshire.
Hampstead Heathens Reached quarter-finals in the club's only campaign.
Harrow Chequers ...... Entered FA Cup three times and never played a game.
Hitchin Town .... Played at same Top Field ground but unrelated to current club.
Maidenhead United Still in FA Cup and still playing at same York Road ground.
Marlow .... Still in FA Cup and only club to 'enter' every season.
Queen's Park .... First Scottish club to participate in FA Cup.
Reigate Priory .... Currently members of the Mid-Sussex League.
Royal Engineers .... Only military based club to lift the FA Cup.
Upton Park .... Reached the quarter-finals four times.
The Wanderers .... The first ever winners of the FA Cup.

1872 1st Surrey Rifles .... First club in FA Cup with a name beginning with a number.
Oxford University ..... Future FA Cup winners who also reached Final in first season.
South Norwood .... London club that never progressed further than the 2nd Round.
Windsor Home Park Club didn't play again in competition until eight years later.

1873 AAC .... Amateur Athletic Club based in West Brompton.
Brondesbury .... Played just two FA Cup games; scored nil, conceded eleven.
Cambridge University Unsupported & unofficial claim to have been formed in 1856.
Farningham .... First club to concede double figures in an FA Cup match.
Gitanos .... Based in Battersea and eventually merged with Runnymede.
High Wycombe .... Faced The Wanderers, inspiring suffix of Wycombe Wanderers.
Old Etonians .... Would go on to become the last amateur team to lift FA Cup.
Pilgrims .... Clapton based club which amalgamated into Clapton FC.
Sheffield .... Officially the 'World's Oldest Football Club' (1857).
Shropshire Wands. .... Only club to be eliminated from the FA Cup by toss of a coin.
Southall .... Became second & last club to begin in EP Rd and make 3rd Rd.
Swifts .... Jointly hold record of three semi-finals without reaching Final.
Trojans .... Scratched without playing in either of their campaigns.
Uxbridge .... 148 years later and club yet to match debut run to 2nd Round.
Woodford Wells .... Reached quarter-finals in one of their three campaigns.

1874 Leyton .... Unrelated to either same named clubs formed in 1889 & 1997.
Panthers .... Existing club, now playing as Sturminster Newton United.

1875 105th Regiment .... Formed Kings Own Yorkshire Light Infantry with 51st Regiment.
Clydesdale .... Second Scottish club to enter FA Cup but didn't play a match.
Forest School .... The Wanderers had earlier formed from Forest School players.

Herts Rangers .... A Watford based club made up of Cambridge Uni. students.
Ramblers .... Based in Woolwich and failed to win in four FA Cup campaigns.
Rochester .... Amateur side still in FA Cup after Football League was formed.

1876 Druids .... First Welsh club to participate in the FA Cup.
Gresham .... Played their home matches on what is now Hackney Downs.
Highbury Union .... Failed to win an FA Cup match in their four campaigns.
Old Harrovians .... Harrow School old boys made semi-finals in second campaign.
Old Salopians .... Scratched before playing in only time club entered the FA Cup.
Old Wykehamists ...... Still in existence competing in the Arthurian League.
Reading Hornets .... Preceded Reading FC in FA Cup, but absorbed by them in 1878.
Saffron Walden .... Still competing in the FA Cup as Saffron Walden Town.
Saxons .... One FA Cup campaign, one FA Cup game, one FA Cup defeat.
Wood Grange .... London based club that lost both its FA Cup matches.

1877 Darwen .... First northern professional side to challenge Amateur clubs.
Grantham .... Still competing in FA Cup to this day as Grantham Town.
Hawks .... London based Amateur club who won first FA Cup match 5-2.
Hendon .... Future quarter-finalists unrelated to current Hendon club.
Manchester .... A rugby focused club whose ground was used for semi-finals.
Minerva .... Kent based club which existed until 1900.
Notts County .... The World's oldest professional club & future FA Cup winners.
Old Foresters .... Still exist, now competing in the Arthurian League.
Reading .... First appearance of a current Football League club in FA Cup.
Remnants .... London based amateur club that competed in FA Cup 6 times.
St Mark's .... London based club which scratched without playing a game.
St Stephen's .... Went on to help form Shepherds Bush FC & later Acton FC.

1878 Birch .... Scratched in FA Cup & re-formed as Manchester Wanderers.
Brentwood .... Future quarter-finalist unrelated to current Brentwood Town.
Eagley .... Bolton club that held Bolton Wanderers to 5-5 draw in FA Cup.
Finchley .... Merged with Wingate to form Wingate and Finchley in 1991.
Grey Friars .... Dulwich based club also known as Greyfriars.
Nottingham Forest ... Oldest current Football League club, made SF in first campaign.
Romford .... Future quarter-finalist unrelated to other 'Romford' clubs.
Runnymede .... Surrey based club which scratched without playing a game.
Unity .... Kent based club which scratched without playing a game.
Wednesbury Strollers Inter-connected with local rivals Wednesbury Town.

1879 Acton .... Seven FA Cup campaigns going no further than 2nd Round.
Argonauts .... Unrelated to Argonauts who applied to enter League in 1930s.
Aston Villa .... First club to lift the FA Cup seven times.
Birmingham .... Unrelated to Birmingham City, also once known by this name.
Blackburn Rovers ..... One of only two clubs to win three successive FA Cup finals.
Brigg .... Unrelated to current Brigg Town, but existed at same time.
Calthorpe .... Birmingham based club that lost every FA Cup game played.

	Clarence	Based in Battersea and lost both FA Cup games played.
	Hanover United	First club called 'United' in FA Cup, now called Polytechnic.
	Henley	Continued up to 2017, named Henley Town after World War I.
	Hotspur	Unrelated to Tottenham Hotspur, also once known as Hotspur.
	Kildare	Kensal Rise club that failed to win in FA Cup in six campaigns.
	Mosquitos	Went on to merge with Lennox FC to form Dulwich FC.
	Old Carthusians	First club to win both FA Cup and FA Amateur Cup.
	Sheffield Providence	One of three clubs to merge to form Park Grange in 1882.
	St Peter's Institute ...	At some point, club amalgamated into original Staines Town.
	Stafford Road Works	Wolverhampton works team reached quarter-finals in 1881.
	Turton	Currently competing in West Lancashire League.
	Tyne Association	Lost first games in both FA Cup campaigns, seven years apart.
	West End	Uxbridge based club that entered FA Cup six times.
1880	Astley Bridge	Bolton based club that competed in FA Cup nine times.
	Blackburn Olympic ...	First northern professional club to lift the FA Cup.
	Brigg Britannia	Played two FA Cup games scoring nil and conceding thirteen.
	Caius College, Cambs.	Only University College club to enter FA Cup, but never played.
	Derbyshire	Drew 4-4 with Notts County before losing replay & that's it.
	Dreadnought	East London based club with four FA Cup campaigns in all.
	Old Philberdians	Maidenhead based club that scratched without playing.
	Rangers	London club that lost 6-0 to Royal Engineers in only game.
	Reading Abbey	Rivalled Reading FC as the major team in the town for a while.
	Reading Minster	Entered FA Cup five times all told.
	Spilsby	Now playing as Spilsby Town in the Boston League.
	St Albans (Upton)	Existed at same time as a second Hertfordshire St Albans club.
	The Wednesday	Sheffield Weds only club to win FA Cup under different names.
	Weybridge Swallows	One FA Cup campaign; won one, lost one.
1881	Accrington	Became founder members of the Football League in 1888.
	Blackburn Law	Participated in the FA Cup just the once losing 2-1 to Bootle.
	Blackburn Park Road	Club continued on in FA Cup into early years of 20th Century.
	Bolton Wanderers ...	Would go on to become first FA Cup winners at Wembley.
	Bootle	Unrelated to other 'Bootles', had 1 season in Football League.
	Derby Town	Club lost its only FA Cup match 4-1 to Small Heath Alliance.
	Esher Leopold	Surrey club that lost only FA Cup game 5-0 to Old Carthusians.
	Lockwood Brothers	Sheffield based club with seven fairly successful campaigns.
	Mitchells St George's	Reached FA Cup quarter-final as Birmingham St George's.
	Morton Rangers	London based club that lost only game 3-0 to Old Foresters.
	Olympic	London club that still took part in FA Cup in 20th Century.
	Sheffield Heeley	The first football club formed by a church in 1860.
	Small Heath Alliance	Reached FA Cup Final as Birmingham and as Birmingham City.
	St Bart's Hospital	Last club drawn to face The Wanderers in Cup, who scratched.
	Staveley	Derbyshire based club with several fairly successful campaigns.

Wednesbury Old Ath. Reached FA Cup quarter-finals in club's first campaign.
Woodford Bridge ...... Essex based club that failed to win in any of its 3 campaigns.

1882 Aston Unity .... Won first FA Cup match, but lost their following six games.
Blackpool St John's ... Blackpool FC came into being after Blackpool St John's folded.
Bolton Olympic .... Two FA Cup games; scored four, conceded sixteen.
Chatham United .... Now Chatham Town & best 'always non-league' FA Cup club.
Chesterfield Spital .... Failed to win any FA Cup game in three campaigns.
Church .... Accrington based club that reached quarter-finals in 1885.
Clitheroe .... Still competing in FA Cup as a Northern Premier League club.
Darwen Ramblers ..... Won first two FA Cup games, but lost its next three.
Etonian Ramblers ..... One FA Cup campaign, one big win, one big defeat.
Great Lever .... Bolton based club that entered the FA Cup four times.
Grimsby Town .... Twice semi-finalists in the years leading up to World War II.
Halliwell .... Bolton club that continued in FA Cup post Football League.
Haslingden .... Made only 11 FA Cup appearances spanning 116 years.
Hornchurch .... Essex club unrelated to two other Hornchurch FA Cup clubs.
Irwell Springs .... Club is still applying to play in FA Cup as Bacup Borough.
Liverpool Ramblers ... Club still in existence, still not affiliated to any League.
Lower Darwen........... Four campaigns in all, reaching the 4th Round in 1885.
Macclesfield .... Club reached 4th Round for first time 130 years after debut.
Northwich Victoria .... Reached QF in second campaign; 2 seasons in Football League.
Old Westminsters ..... Three times quarter-finalists in the club's dozen campaigns.
Oswestry .... Club had 81 FA Cup campaigns before Oswestry Town folded.
Phoenix Bessemer .... Rotherham based club that made 3rd Round in only campaign.
South Reading .... Only club to advance thanks to 2 successive disqualifications.
South Shore .... Future quarter-finalists that Blackpool FC absorbed in 1900.
Southport .... Ex-Football League club now in National League North.
United Hospital .... London club with one campaign, one win and one defeat.
Walsall Swifts .... 5 FA Cup campaigns, 4th Round reached, one half of Walsall FC.
Walsall Town .... 6 FA Cup campaigns, 4th Round reached, one half of Walsall FC.

Rank	East Midlands Counties League	Q3	Q2	Q1	PR	EP
1	Barrow Town	1			2	4
2	Radcliffe Olympic	1				1
3	Blaby and Whetstone		2	1	1	2
4	Bardon Hill		1			3
5	Ellistown and Ibstock United		1			1
6	Holbrook Sports			2	2	1
7=	Dunkirk			2		4
7=	Holwell Sports			2		4

Top Eight FA Cup Clubs whilst Members of EMCL.

Nb. Chart shows number of exits per Round

The First 150 Clubs to 'Disappear' from the FA Cup

The year refers to the last season the club entered the FA Cup (1872 = season 1871/72)

1872	Donnington School ...	Drawn to face Queen's Park in 1st & 2nd Round but withdrew.
	Hampstead Heathens	Made quarter-finals & were first club to win an FA Cup replay.
1874	AAC	Drawn to play Clapham Rovers but scratched ahead of game.
	Gitanos	A 3-0 defeat at Uxbridge was their only FA Cup game.
1875	Brondesbury	Two FA Cup games played, no goals scored, eleven conceded.
	Farningham	One game played in two seasons; lost 16-0 to The Wanderers.
1876	Clydesdale	Second Scottish club to enter FA Cup didn't even play a match.
	Crystal Palace	Lost 3-0 to The Wanderers both in 1872 SF and in last game.
	Harrow Chequers	Only club to enter FA Cup three times and never play a match.
	Woodford Wells	Reached quarter-finals in second of their 3 FA Cup campaigns.
1877	Old Salopians	Scratched before playing Oxford University only time entered.
	Saxons	Lost 4-1 at South Norwood in club's only FA Cup match.
	Trojans	Entered FA Cup twice & scratched without playing both times.
1878	High Wycombe	Played 5 FA Cup games, scored 4 (in one game); conceded 26.
	Reading Hornets	Absorbed into Reading after 2 forgettable FA Cup campaigns.
	Shropshire Wands....	Won just one game to reach SF in 1875, only win in 5 seasons.
	St Mark's	Withdrew before facing Barnes in only time entered FA Cup.
	St Stephen's	Lost 4-0 at Remnants in their only FA Cup match.
	Wood Grange	Two FA Cup campaigns, scored nil and conceded seven.
1879	105th Regiment	Four FA Cup campaigns; just one win, 3-0 vs 1st Surrey Rifles.
	Birch	Withdrew ahead of facing Darwen only time entered FA Cup.
	Forest School	Four FA Cup campaigns, won twice, scored 12, conceded 21.
	Hawks	Managed just one win in their two campaigns, 5-2 vs Minerva.
	Leyton	No wins across their five campaigns; scored 2 & conceded 27.
	Ramblers	One goal-less draw their best performance in 4 campaigns.
	Runnymede	Scratched before facing Panthers in only time entered FA Cup.
	Unity	Withdrew prior to facing Remnants in only time entered Cup.
1880	Argonauts	Lost 1-0 at home to Hotspur in replay in only FA Cup campaign.
	Birmingham	One FA Cup campaign: lost 6-0 at home to Oxford University.
	Cambridge University	Reached QF in 1876 & SF in 1877, scoring 37 across 7 seasons.
	Gresham	Managed one win, 3-0 vs Kildare, in the club's two campaigns.
	Minerva	One win, 3-0 vs Grey Friars, across their three FA Cup seasons.
	Oxford University	Won Cup & 3x runners-up; made QF at least in all 8 campaigns.
	Panthers	Two wins in six campaigns vs Wood Grange & Woodford Wells.
	South Norwood	Club recorded just three wins in their eight FA Cup campaigns.
1881	Clarence	Two campaigns, two defeats, two goals scored, 11 conceded.
	Derbyshire	Drew 4-4 with Notts County, before losing 2-4 in only season.

	Grey Friars	Club won at least one match in each of their three campaigns.
	Old Philberdians	Scratched before facing Pilgrims in only time entered FA Cup.
	St Peter's Institute ...	Two campaigns, two defeats, two goals scored, 11 conceded.
	Weybridge Swallows	Won one, 3-1 vs Henley, and lost one in only FA Cup season.
1882	Blackburn Law...........	Lost 2-1 at original Bootle in only FA Cup match played.
	Caius College, Cambs	Entered FA Cup twice, never played, even vs Nottm. Forest.
	Derby Town	Lost 4-1 at Small Heath All. (Birmingham City) in only game.
	Esher Leopold	Lost 5-0 at home to Old Carthusians in only FA Cup game.
	Herts Rangers	Won three matches across seven campaigns scoring 17 goals.
	Morton Rangers	Lost 3-0 at Old Foresters in their only FA Cup match played.
	Rangers (London)	Reached 3rd Rd in first campaign as two opponents scratched.
	Reading Abbey	Actually won more games (3) than they lost (2) in two seasons.
	Sheffield Providence	One draw, 3-3 vs Sheffield, their best result in 3 campaigns.
	St Albans (Upton)	Two campaigns, two defeats, no goals scored, four conceded.
	St Bart's Hospital	Lost 2-0 at Marlow in only game after Wanderers scratched.
	The Wanderers	Five times FA Cup winners, with most finals without defeat.
	Wednesbury Strollers	One win in four campaigns, seven goals scored, 26 conceded.
1883	Brigg Britannia	Failed to win, or even score, conceding 13 goals in 3 seasons.
	Etonian Ramblers	One campaign; one win; one loss; six scored; nine conceded.
	Highbury Union	Club lost all three games played across four FA Cup seasons.
	Phoenix Bessemer ...	Made 3rd Rd in only campaign ending with a +5 goal difference.
	Remnants	Achieved 3 wins in their 6 campaigns making 3rd Round twice.
	United Hospital	One campaign; one win; one loss; four goals; three conceded.
1884	Blackpool St John's ...	Club lost both games in two campaigns conceding 15 goals.
	Bolton Olympic	Club lost both games in two campaigns conceding 16 goals.
	Calthorpe	Club lost all for games played in 5 times they entered FA Cup.
	Dreadnought	Won one game, 2-1 vs Rochester, in club's 4 FA Cup seasons.
	Hornchurch	Lost both games at home to Marlow; scored nil, conceded 11.
	Kildare	A 1-1 draw with Acton, their best result across five campaigns.
	Manchester	One win, two goals scored & 19 conceded in two campaigns.
	Mosquitos	Managed 2 wins vs Pilgrims & St Peter's Inst. in five seasons.
	Upton Rangers	Club lost 7-0 at home to Old Wykehamists in only match.
	Woodford Bridge	A 1-1 draw with Reading Abbey, their best result in 3 seasons.
1885	Bolton Association ...	Only win, 5-1 vs Bradshaw, but made 2nd Rd in both seasons.
	Chesterfield Spital	A 1-1 draw with Rotherham Town, their best result in 3 years.
	Darwen Ramblers	Beat Haslingden & South Shore in first 2 games but lost next 3.
	Hull Town	Club lost both games played vs Grimsby Town & Lincoln City.
	Liverpool Ramblers ...	Just one win, 4-0 at Southport, in the club's three campaigns.
	Pilgrims	Twice reached FA Cup 3rd Round during a dozen campaigns.
	Preston Zingari	Scratched, as did opponents Bolton Wanderers, in only season.
	Reading Minster	Club's two wins in 5 years came when reaching 3rd Rd in 1882.
	Wednesbury Town ...	Beat West Brom en route to 4th Rd in first of two campaigns.

	West End	Three of 4 wins came when making 4th Rd in first of 6 seasons.
	Windsor Home Park	Achieved 5 wins in 7 campaigns including vs Royal Engineers.
1886	Acton	Just two wins in seven campaigns against Finchley and Kildare.
	Barnes	Won seven matches in 14 campaigns, reaching 3rd Rd twice.
	Bradshaw	Three campaigns, three defeats, three goals, 19 conceded.
	Clitheroe Low Moor	Three campaigns, three defeats, three goals, 15 conceded.
	Eagley	Reached 4th Rd in 1883, but won just 3 games in 7 seasons.
	Fishwick Ramblers	Won once, 2-1 vs Darwen Ramblers, in their two campaigns.
	Grimsby District	Lost 4-0 at Lincoln Lindum in only FA Cup game played.
	Lower Darwen	Won just 3 games in 4 campaigns, but reached 4th Rd in 1885.
	St James'	Scratched before facing Old Harrovians in only season entered.
	United London Swifts	Lost 4-2 at Upton Park in only FA Cup match played.
1887	1st Surrey Rifles	Scored in only two games in seven seasons; won both times.
	Bollington	Lost at home to Oswestry in both campaigns, aggregate 2-13.
	Caernarvon Wands.	Lost 10-1 at Stoke (City) in only FA Cup match played.
	Cannon	Scratched before facing Old Foresters in only FA Cup entered.
	Clapham Rovers	First scorers in FA Cup, winners in 1880, runners-up in 1879.
	Cowlairs	One campaign, two wins, 16 goals scored, then barred.
	Crosswell's Brewery	One campaign, one win, one defeat, one goal, 14 conceded.
	Furness Vale Rovers	One game, a 10-0 defeat at Northwich Victoria, in only season.
	Goldenhill	Won once, 3-2 vs Macclesfield, during club's three campaigns.
	Great Lever	Managed a couple of wins during their four FA Cup campaigns.
	Heart of Midlothian	One game played in two campaigns, a 7-1 defeat at Darwen.
	Luton Wanderers	One win in three campaigns, scoring four and conceding 28.
	Partick Thistle	Beat Cliftonville 11-1: English Cup, Irish hosts, Scottish winner.
	Queen's Park	Twice runners-up, 9x scratched, 69 goals scored, then barred.
	Rangers (Glasgow)	Made SF in second of two campaigns, losing 3-1 to Aston Villa.
	Renton	Ended Blackburn Rovers' record 23 game unbeaten run.
	Third Lanark RV	Won twice and lost only one game across two campaigns.
	Tyne Association	Two campaigns, seven years apart, and two defeats.
1888	Aston Unity	Won once, 3-1 vs Mitchells St George's, in six campaigns.
	Birmingham Excelsior	Achieved 3 wins in 5 campaigns including vs Birmingham City.
	Church	Made quarter-finals in 1885 & scored 51 goals in 6 seasons.
	Darwen Old Wands.	Four wins in three campaigns including 11-0 against Burnley.
	East Sheen	One FA Cup game played, a 7-2 defeat at Old St Mark's.
	Hotspur	Reached 4th Rd in 1882 and won 6 games across 8 campaigns.
	Lincoln Albion	One FA Cup game played, a 3-2 defeat at Basford Rovers.
	Lincoln Lindum	Won once, 4-0 vs Grimsby District, across three campaigns.
	Lincoln Ramblers	One FA Cup game played, a 9-0 defeat at Notts County.
	Lockwood Brothers	Reached 5th Rd in 1887, and beat Nottm. Forest among 7 wins.
	South Reading	Reached 4th Rd in 1886 but only won 3 games in 6 campaigns.
	Southfield	One FA Cup match played, a 7-0 defeat at Burton Swifts.

	Stafford Road Works	Reached QF in 1881: beat both Aston Villa & Birmingham City.
	Walsall Swifts	Reached 4th Rd in 1885, but won just 3 games in 5 campaigns.
	Walsall Town	Reached 4th Rd in 1883, and won 5 games across 6 campaigns.
1889	Astley Bridge	Won just three games during 9 campaigns & lost 11-3 to PNE.
	Aston Shakespeare ...	Won once, 1-0 vs Great Bridge Unity, during two campaigns.
	Basford Rovers	Two wins in 3 campaigns but did lose 13-0 at Notts County.
	Blackburn Olympic ...	First northern professional club to lift FA Cup in 1883.
	Davenham	Smallest village to reach last 16, beat Macclesfield 8-1 on way.
	Hartford St John's	Drew 0-0 with Newton, their best result during five campaigns.
	Hendon	Quarter-finalists in 1883 & scored 58 goals during 12 seasons.
	Lancing Old Boys	Won two, lost three in 3 seasons, but scored 15, conceded 14.
	Llangollen	Won once, 6-3 vs Oswestry, during the club's two campaigns.
	Mellors (Nottingham)	Club achieved just two wins during their four campaigns.
	Netherfield	Scratched before facing original Cleethorpes in only season.
	Old Foresters	Quarter-finalists in 1882 & scored 62 goals during 12 seasons.
	Park Grange	Two wins and two defeats during the club's two campaigns.
	Rawtenstall	Failed to win a game in the five times they entered the FA Cup.
	Royal Engineers	1875 FA Cup winners, 3x runners-up, 144 goals in 18 seasons.
	Ulster	A 7-1 home loss to Linfield Athletic in only FA Cup game.
1890	Beeston St John's	Won once, 2-0 vs Notts Olympic, in the club's two campaigns.
	Belfast North End	Scratched before facing Linfield Athletic in only campaign.
	Belfast YMCA	A 5-0 home loss to Cliftonville in only FA Cup match played.
	Distillery	One win in 2 campaigns, and lost 10-2 at Bolton Wanderers.
	Dulwich	6 campaigns, 4 wins, twice in 3rd Rd, 14 goals & 40 conceded.
	Hartford/Davenham	One campaign; beat Macclesfield 4-2, lost 4-0 to Crewe Alex.
	Long Eaton Midland	First club with just 1 game in Q1 Rd; 7-1 loss at Heanor Town.
	Lyndhurst	4 campaigns; 4 defeats; 4 goals scored; 28 conceded.
	Notts Swifts	Two campaigns & two defeats, including 2-1 at Nottm. Forest.

Rank	South West Peninsula League	Q3	Q2	Q1	PR	EP
1	Bodmin Town	1	2	4	6	
2	Saltash United		1	2	2	7
3	Tavistock		1	1	2	5
4	Plymouth Parkway			4	1	1
5	Torpoint Athletic			1	1	1
6	Witheridge			1	1	
7	St Blazey				3	3
8	AFC St Austell				2	5
9	Falmouth Town				2	3
10	Launceston				2	1

Top Ten FA Cup Clubs whilst Members of SWPL.

Nb. Chart shows number of exits per Round

The Last 150 Clubs to Reach FA Cup 1st Round 'Proper' having started in Earliest Possible Round

(Bold italics = League clubs faced)

2020/21 **Skelmersdale United** EP Rd to 1st Rd 7 ties
*Penistone Church – Congleton Town – Bootle – Lancaster City – Longridge Town – Stafford Rangers – **Harrogate Town***

2019/20 **Chichester City** EP Rd to 2nd Rd 8 ties
*Erith Town – Bridon Ropes – Chalfont St Peter – Hartley Wintney – Enfield Town – Bowers and Pitsea – bye – **Tranmere Rovers***

2016/17 **Westfields** EP Rd to 1st Rd 7 ties
Stourport Swifts – Tividale – St Ives Town – Highgate United – Walton Casuals – Leiston – Curzon Ashton

2010/11 **Hythe Town** EP Rd to 1st Rd 7 ties
*Bookham – Deal Town – Epsom and Ewell – Erith and Belvedere – Concord Rangers – Staines Town – **Hereford United***

Tipton Town
*Alvechurch – Stratford Town – Norton United – Market Drayton Town – Radcliffe Olympic – Sheffield – **Carlisle United***

2008/09 **Leiston** EP Rd to 1st Rd 7 ties
Blackstones – March Town United –Cornard United – Carshalton Athletic – Coalville Town – Lewes – Fleetwood Town

2001/02 **Brigg Town** EP Rd to 1st Rd 7 ties
*Great Harwood Town – Morpeth Town – Shildon – Gretna – Farsley Celtic – Boston United – **Tranmere Rovers***

1999/00 **Chelmsford City** Prelim Rd to 1st Rd 6 ties
*Woodbridge Town – Kingsbury Town – Aylesbury United – Moor Green – Horsham YMCA – **Oldham Athletic***

Eastwood Town
Gresley Rovers – Holbeach United – Stafford Rangers – Oadby Town – Droylsden – **Exeter City***

Oxford City
*Gosport Borough – Abingdon United – Tooting and Mitcham United – Backwell United – Salisbury City – **Wycombe Wanderers***

Whyteleafe
*Lancing – Egham Town – Thame United – Langney Sports – Bognor Regis Town – **Chester City***

'99/'00 cont. **Worthing**
Epsom and Ewell – Saltdean United – Deal Town – Chippenham Town – Burton Albion – ***Rotherham United***

1998/99 **Camberley Town** Prelim Rd to 1st Rd 6 ties
Wokingham Town – Arundel – Ringmer – Braintree Town – St Blazey – ***Brentford***

Ford United (now Redbridge)
Wellingborough Town – Barton Rovers – Woodbridge Town – Welwyn Garden City – Lowestoft Town – ***Preston North End***

1997/98 **Ilkeston Town*** Prelim Rd to 2nd Rd 7 ties
Buxton – Rossendale United – RTM Newcastle – Chorley – Hyde United – Boston United – ***Scunthorpe United***

Lincoln United Prelim Rd to 1st Rd 6 ties
Selby Town – Staveley Miners Welfare – Clitheroe – Marine – Runcorn – ***Walsall***

Tiverton Town
Weymouth – St Blazey – Wimborne Town – Dorchester Town – Sudbury Town – Cheltenham Town

1996/97 **Consett** Prelim Rd to 1st Rd 6 ties
Alnwick Town – Harrogate Town – Durham city – Bishop Auckland – Gateshead – ***Mansfield Town***

Newcastle Town
Denaby United – Willington – Winsford United – Frickley Athletic – Bamber Bridge – ***Notts County***

Whitby Town
Whickham – Garforth Town – Hyde United – Farsley Celtic – Blyth Spartans – ***Hull City***

1995/96 **Bognor Regis Town** Prelim Rd to 2nd Rd 7 ties
Whitehawk – Dover Athletic – Banstead Athletic – Dulwich Hamlet – Tiverton Town – Ashford Town (Kent) – ***Peterborough United***

Canvey Island Prelim Rd to 1st Rd 6 ties
Wroxham – Cambridge City – Braintree Town – King's Lynn (disq.) – Hednesford Town – **Brighton and Hove Albion**

Wisbech Town
Tring Town – Boston United – Eynesbury Rovers – Sudbury Town – Billericay town – Kingstonian

1994/95 **Ashford Town** (Kent) Prelim Rd to 1st Rd 6 ties

*Bracknell Town – Chatham Town – Burgess Hill Town – Gravesend and Northfleet – Salisbury – **Fulham***

Heybridge Swifts

*Holbeach United – Gorleston – Felixstowe Town – Boston United – Nuneaton Borough – **Gillingham***

Worthing

*Horsham – Horsham YMCA – Folkestone Invicta – Dulwich Hamlet – Gloucester City – **AFC Bournemouth***

1993/94 **Gretna** Prelim Rd to 1st Rd 6 ties

*Esh Winning – Seaham Red Star – Evenwood Town – Barrow – Winsford United – **Bolton Wanderers***

Metropolitan Police

Oakwood – Lewes – Leatherhead – Margate – Kingstonian – Crawley Town

Weston-super-Mare

Welton Rovers – Shortwood United – Taunton Town – Tiverton Town – Newport (IOW) – Woking

1992/93 **Dorking** Prelim Rd to 1st Rd 6 ties

*Hythe Town (w/o) – Croydon Athletic – Walton and Hersham – Dover Athletic – Farnborough Town – **Plymouth Argyle***

Nuneaton Borough*

Boldmere St Michaels – Leicester United – Matlock Town – Raunds Town – Wembley – Woking

Sutton Coldfield Town

West Bromwich Town – Stewarts and Lloyds – Eastwood Hanley – Rushall Olympic – Leyton – **Bolton Wanderers***

1991/92 **Bridlington Town*** Prelim Rd to 1st Rd 6 ties

*Evenwood Town – Blyth Spartans – Northallerton Town – North Shields – Barrow – **York City***

Lincoln United

*Dudley Town – Gainsborough Trinity – Oakham United – Frickley Athletic – Leek Town – **Huddersfield Town***

Winsford United

*Lancaster City – Nantwich Town – Mossley – Droylsden – Altrincham – **Wrexham***

1990/91 **Littlehampton Town** Prelim Rd to 1st Rd 6 ties
*Chipstead – Dulwich Hamlet – Tooting and Mitcham United – Tonbridge – Romsey Town – **Northampton Town***

Tiverton Town
*Welton Rovers – Ilfracombe Town – Saltash United – Liskeard Athletic – Peacehaven and Telscombe – **Aldershot***

1989/90 **Whitley Bay** Prelim Rd to 3rd Rd 8 ties
*Horden Colliery Welfare – Willington – Spennymoor United – Barrow – Southport – **Scarborough** – **Preston North End** – **Rochdale***

Congleton Town Prelim Rd to 1st Rd 6 ties
*Irlam Town – Denaby United – Caernarfon Town – Colwyn Bay – Witton Albion – **Crewe Alexandra***

1987/88 **Atherstone United** Prelim Rd to 1st Rd 6 ties
Northampton Spencer – Malvern Town – Lye Town – Alvechurch – Leyton-Wingate – VS Rugby

Colwyn Bay
Winsford United – Prescot Cables – Buxton – Alfreton Town – Tow Law Town – Northwich Victoria

Tamworth
Gresley Rovers – Paget Rangers – Wisbech Town – Shepshed Charterhouse – Wealdstone – **Colchester United***

1986/87 **Woking** Prelim Rd to 1st Rd 6 ties
Horndean – Lancing – Hastings Town – Crawley Town – Weymouth – Chelmsford City

1985/86 **Leyton-Wingate** Prelim Rd to 1st Rd 6 ties
Kingsbury Town – Hounslow – Harrow Borough – Crawley Town – Gresley Rovers – **Swansea City***

1984/85 **Metropolitan Police** Prelim Rd to 1st Rd 6 ties
Chatham Town – Ware – Leytonstone / Ilford – Welling United – Harlow Town – Dartford

1982/83 **Worthing** Prelim Rd to 2nd Rd 7 ties
*Fleet Town – Crawley Town – Eastleigh – Farnborough Town – Minehead – Dartford – **Oxford United***

Dartford Prelim Rd to 1st Rd 6 ties
Whitehawk – Haywards Heath – Tonbridge – Corinthian-Casuals – Boreham Wood – Worthing

'82/'83 cont. **Horwich Railway Mechanics Institute**
South Liverpool – New Mills* – Oswestry Town – Caernarfon Town – Runcorn –* ***Blackpool***

Shepshed Charterhouse
Denaby United – Alfreton Town – Goole Town – Gainsborough Trinity – King's Lynn – ***Preston North End***

Wimborne Town
Bridport – Falmouth Town – St Blazey – Bath City – Merthyr Tydfil – ***Aldershot***

Wokingham Town
Andover – Whyteleafe – Staines Town – Kingstonian – Leatherhead – ***Cardiff City***

1981/82 **Bedford Town*** Prelim Rd to 1st Rd 6 ties
Hoddesdon Town – Potton United – Barton Rovers – Ely City – Wisbech Town – ***Wimbledon***

Hastings United*
Chatham Town – Faversham Town – Canterbury City – Epsom and Ewell – Wembley – Enfield*

Hendon
Abingdon Town – Ampthill Town – Banbury United – Tring Town – Harrow Borough – Wycombe Wanderers

1980/81 **Fleetwood Town*** Prelim Rd to 1st Rd 6 ties
Emley – Worsbrough Bridge Miners Welfare – Accrington Stanley – St Helens Town – Stalybridge Celtic – Blackpool

1979/80 **Harlow Town** Prelim Rd to 4th Rd 9 ties
Lowestoft Town – Hornchurch – Bury Town – Harwich and Parkeston – Margate – Leytonstone / Ilford –* ***Southend United*** *–* ***Leicester City*** *–* ***Watford***

1978/79 **Barking*** Prelim Rd to 2nd Rd 7 ties
Clapton – Ware – Leytonstone – Billericay Town – Bedford Town – Yeovil Town –* ***Aldershot***

Boston United Prelim Rd to 1st Rd 6 ties
Heanor Town – Sutton Town – Retford Town – Gainsborough Trinity – Kettering Town – ***Tranmere Rovers***

Gravesend and Northfleet (now Ebbsfleet United)
Aveley – Welling United – Walthamstow Avenue – Dulwich Hamlet – Eastbourne United – ***Wimbledon***

'78/'79 cont. **Hillingdon Borough***
*Finchley – Molesey – Boreham Wood – Kingstonian – Tooting and Mitcham United – **Swansea City***

1977/78 **Tilbury** Prelim Rd to 3rd Rd 8 ties
Kingstonian – Bracknell Town – Witney Town – Feltham* – Tonbridge – Kettering Town (after void game) – Nuneaton Borough* – **Stoke City***

Runcorn Prelim Rd to 2nd Rd 7 ties
*Bacup Borough – Droylsden – Rossendale United – Darwen – Altrincham – **Southport** – **Hartlepool United***

Spennymoor United
*Horden Colliery Welfare – Ferryhill Athletic – Durham City – Whitley Bay – Bangor City – Goole Town – **Rotherham United***

Arnold Prelim Rd to 1st Rd 6 ties
*Spalding United – Chatteris Town – March Town United – Boston – Telford United – **Port Vale***

Bath City
*Taunton Town – Bridport – Swaythling – Dorchester Town – Merthyr Tydfil – **Plymouth Argyle***

1976/77 **Enfield*** Prelim Rd to 2nd Rd 7 ties
Hampton – Tilbury – Bracknell Town – Epsom and Ewell – Ilford – Harwich and Parkeston – **Crystal Palace***

Nuneaton Borough*
*Racing Club Warwick – Brierley Hill Alliance – Lye Town – Bromsgrove Rovers – Barton Rovers – Crook Town – **Lincoln City***

Crook Town Prelim Rd to 1st Rd 6 ties
*Eppleton Colliery Welfare – Penrith – South Bank – Bishop Auckland – Netherfield (Kendal) – Nuneaton Borough**

Dudley Town
Halesowen Town – Stratford Town – Bilston – Enderby Town – Bedford Town – **York City***

Harwich and Parkeston
*Thetford Town – Newmarket Town – Sudbury Town – Lowestoft Town – Lewes – Enfield**

1975/76 **Coventry Sporting** Prelim Rd to 2nd Rd 7 ties
*Bromsgrove Rovers – Oldbury United – Halesowen Town – Brierley Hill Alliance – Spalding United – **Tranmere Rovers** – **Peterborough United***

1974/75 **Ashford Town** (Kent) Prelim Rd to 1st Rd 6 ties
Deal Town – Sittingbourne – Dover – Canterbury City – Hillingdon Borough* – **Walsall***

Bath City
Devizes Town – Weston-super-Mare – Hungerford Town – Mangotsfield United – Yeovil Town – Wimbledon

Marine
*Ormskirk (w/o) – Witton Albion – Winsford United – Sandbach Ramblers – Telford United – **Rochdale***

1972/73 **Hayes** Prelim Rd to 2nd Rd 7 ties
Wembley – Hoddesdon Town – Erith and Belvedere – Wealdstone – Barking – **Bristol Rovers – Reading***

Walton and Hersham
*Metropolitan Police – Staines Town – Leytonstone – Wycombe Wanderers – Dartford – **Exeter City** – Margate*

Kettering Town Prelim Rd to 1st Rd 6 ties
*Spalding United – Louth United – Bourne Town – Skegness Town – Ely City – **Walsall***

Nuneaton Borough*
Kidderminster Harriers – Lockheed Leamington – Rugby Town – Alvechurch – Alfreton Town – Telford United*

Tonbridge (now Tonbridge Angels)
Maidstone United – Ramsgate Athletic – Folkestone – Sittingbourne – Romford* – **Charlton Athletic***

1971/72 **Romford*** Prelim Rd to 2nd Rd 7 ties
St *Albans City – Letchworth Town – Slough Town – Braintree and Crittall Athletic – Folkestone – Witney Town* – **Gillingham***

Ellesmere Port Town Prelim Rd to 1st Rd 6 ties
Formby – Droylsden – Ormskirk – Burscough – Macclesfield Town – Boston United

Frickley Colliery (now Frickley Athletic)
*Mexborough Town – Farsley Celtic – Yorkshire Amateur – Worksop Town – Grantham – **Rotherham United***

1969/70 **Enfield*** Prelim Rd to 1st Rd 6 ties
*Southall – Kingstonian – Grays Athletic – Edmonton – Wealdstone – **Brighton and Hove Albion***

'69/'70 cont. **Telford United**
*Lockheed Leamington – Halesowen Town – Hednesford Town – Stourbridge – Kidderminster Harriers – **Bristol Rovers***

Whitby Town
*West Auckland Town – Bedlington Colliery Welfare – Wingate (Durham) – Evenwood Town – Scarborough – **York City***

1968/69 **Brentwood Town*** Prelim Rd to 2nd Rd 7 ties
Hayes – Harlow Town – Croydon Amateurs – Metropolitan Police – Hillingdon Borough – Barnet – **Southend United***

Goole Town Prelim Rd to 1st Rd 6 ties
Barton Town – Brigg Town – Scarborough – Selby Town – Bishop Auckland – **Barrow***

Skelmersdale United
*Droylsden – Darwen – St Helens Town – Stalybridge Celtic – Northwich Victoria – **Chesterfield***

1967/68 **Spennymoor United** Prelim Rd to 2nd Rd 7 ties
Boldon Colliery Welfare – Stockton – Ferryhill Athletic – Whitby Town – Morecambe – Goole Town – Macclesfield Town*

1966/67 **Nuneaton Borough*** Q1 Rd to 3rd Rd 7 ties
*Atherstone Town – Loughborough United – Burton Albion – Macclesfield Town – Wealdstone – **Swansea Town** – **Rotherham United***

Ashford Town (Kent) Q1 Rd to 2nd Rd 6 ties
Leytonstone – Dulwich Hamlet – Margate – Guildford City – Cambridge City – **Swindon Town***

Bishop Auckland
*Willington – South Bank – Horden Colliery Welfare – Crook Town – Blyth Spartans – **Halifax Town***

Enfield*
Leyton – Hillingdon Borough* – Stevenage Town – Barnet – Chesham United – **Watford***

Bangor City Q1 Rd to 1st Rd 5 ties
Llandudno – Kirkby Town – New Brighton – Chorley – **Mansfield Town***

Blyth Spartans
Whitley Bay – Tow Law Town – Stockton – Gateshead* – Bishop Auckland*

'66/'67 cont. **Cambridge City**
Letchworth Town – Cambridge United – Bury Town –Hornchurch – Ashford Town (Kent)*

Chesham United
*Wembley – Southall – Hemel Hempstead Town – Leatherhead – Enfield**

Gainsborough Trinity
Ossett Albion – Denaby United – Farsley Celtic – Goole Town – ***Colchester United***

Horsham
Dorking – Fleet Town – Woking – Hastings United* –* ***Swindon Town***

Lowestoft Town
Gothic – Sudbury Town – Haverhill Rovers – Kettering Town – ***Orient***

Morecambe
Milnthorpe Corinthians – Nelson – Netherfield (Kendal) – South Liverpool –* ***York City***

Oxford City
Addlestone – Hounslow – Wolverton Town and BR – Finchley – ***Bristol Rovers***

Poole Town
Bridport – Portland United – Dorchester Town – Minehead – ***Queens Park Rangers***

St Neots Town
Ely City – Desborough Town – Rushden Town – Wisbech Town – ***Walsall***

Sutton United
Hatfield Town – Crittall Athletic – Kingstonian – Eastbourne United – Bath City*

Tamworth
Lockheed Leamington – Worcester City – Rugby Town – Hednesford Town –* ***Gillingham***

Welton Rovers
Devizes Town – Chippenham Town – Trowbridge Town – Fareham Town – ***Bournemouth and Boscombe Athletic***

Witton Albion
Ellesmere Port Town – Hyde United – Northwich Victoria – Rhyl – ***Bradford (Park Avenue)***

1965/66 **Altrincham** Q1 Rd to 3rd Rd 7 ties
*Prescot Town – Marine – Skelmersdale United – Bangor City – Scarborough – **Rochdale – Wolverhampton Wanderers***

Folkestone
Margate – Dover – Canterbury City – Bexley United – **Gillingham** – Wimbledon – **Crewe Alexandra***

Grantham (now Grantham T) Q1 Rd to 2nd Rd 6 ties
*Spalding United – Boston – Skegness Town – Heanor Town – Hendon – **Swindon Town***

Guildford City*
Kingstonian – Leatherhead – Woking – Bletchley Town – Wycombe Wanderers – **Queens Park Rangers***

Burton Albion Q1 Rd to 1st Rd 5 ties
Loughborough United – Hinckley Athletic – Long Eaton United – Gainsborough Trinity – Corby Town

Corinthian-Casuals
Hillingdon Borough – Windsor and Eton – Southall – Enfield* – **Watford***

Fleetwood*
Milnthorpe Corinthians – Horwich RMI – Clitheroe – Colwyn Bay – **Rochdale***

Kidderminster Harriers
*Redditch – Stafford Rangers – Worcester City – Oswestry Town – **Peterborough United***

Leytonstone
Clapton – Rainham Town – Leyton – Walthamstow Avenue – Hereford United*

Merthyr Tydfil
*Cinderford Town – Stonehouse – Gloucester City – Stourbridge – **Swindon Town***

Wealdstone
*Hertford Town – Harlow Town – Stevenage Town – Oxford City – **Millwall***

Wellingborough Town*
*Biggleswade Town – Desborough Town – Bourne Town – Harwich and Parkeston – **Aldershot***

'65/'66 cont. **Wisbech Town**
Newmarket Town – Cambridge City – Bury Town – Kettering Town – ***Brighton and Hove Albion***

1964/65 **Barnet** Q1 Rd to 3rd Rd 7 ties
Harlow Town – Hertford Town – Stevenage Town – Walthamstow Avenue – Cambridge United – Enfield – **Preston North End***

Scarborough Q1 Rd to 2nd Rd 6 ties
Farsley Celtic – Ossett Albion – Bridlington Town – Blyth Spartans –* ***Bradford City – Doncaster Rovers***

South Liverpool*
Ashton United – Skelmersdale United – Altrincham – Retford Town – ***Halifax Town – Workington AFC***

Annfield Plain Q1 Rd to 1st Rd 5 ties
Durham City – Ryhope Colliery Welfare – Tow Law Town – Horden Colliery Welfare – ***Southport***

Bideford
St Austell – Barnstaple Town – St Blazey – Cheltenham Town – ***Colchester United***

Canterbury City*
Dover – Folkestone – Deal Town – Crawley Town – ***Torquay United***

Dartford
Cray Wanderers – Chatham Town – Bexley United – Tonbridge – ***Aldershot***

Guildford City*
Woking – Walton and Hersham – Leatherhead – Maidenhead United – ***Gillingham***

Hayes
Hillingdon Borough – Windsor and Eton – Finchley – Wycombe Wanderers –* ***Exeter City***

Hendon
Leyton – Ford United – Leytonstone – Slough Town –* ***Port Vale***

Kidderminster Harriers
Redditch – Sankey of Wellington – Worcester City – Rugby Town –* ***Hull City***

Macclesfield Town
Oswestry Town – Northwich Victoria – Witton Albion – Ellesmere Port Town – ***Wrexham***

'64/'65 cont. **Salisbury***
Dorchester Town – Poole Town – Portland United – Yeovil Town – ***Peterborough United***

Spalding United
Boston United – Skegness Town – Grantham – Hinckley Athletic – ***Newport County****

Wisbech Town
March Town United – Ely City – Cambridge City – Bletchley Town – **Brentford***

1963/64 **Netherfield (Kendal)** Q1 Rd to 2nd Rd 6 ties
Clitheroe – Burscough – Lancaster City – Horden Colliery Welfare – Loughborough United - ***Chesterfield***

Altrincham Q1 Rd to 1st Rd 5 ties
Earlestown – Skelmersdale United – South Liverpool – Rhyl –* ***Wrexham***

Bangor City
Ellesmere Port Town – Runcorn – New Brighton – Wigan Athletic – ***Barrow***

Barnet
Stevenage Town – Hertford Town – Ware – Wycombe Wanderers – ***Torquay United***

Chorley
Stalybridge Celtic – Nelson – Hyde United – Morecambe – ***Rochdale***

Corby Town
St Neots Town – Bourne Town – Wellingborough Town – Lockheed Leamington –* ***Bristol City***

Frickley Colliery (now Frickley Athletic)
Ossett Albion – Farsley Celtic – Bridlington Town – Macclesfield Town –* ***Notts County***

Harwich and Parkeston
Clacton Town – Lowestoft Town – Great Yarmouth Town – King's Lynn – ***Crystal Palace***

Loughborough United
Gresley Rovers – Ilkeston Town* – Tamworth – Worcester City – Netherfield (Kendal)*

Maidenhead United
Aylesbury United – Banbury Spencer – Hemel Hempstead Town – Ilford – Bath City*

'63/'64 cont. **Tooting and Mitcham United**
Marlow – Carshalton Athletic – Walthamstow Avenue – Hayes – Gravesend and Northfleet

Trowbridge Town
*Devizes Town – Chippenham Town – Welton Rovers – Bideford – **Coventry City***

1962/63 **Gravesend and Northfleet** Q1 Rd to 4th Rd 8 ties
(now Ebbsfleet United)
*Chatham Town – Sutton United – Erith and Belvedere – Lewes – **Exeter City** – Wycombe Wanderers – **Carlisle United – Sunderland***

Bedford Town* Q1 Rd to 2nd Rd 6 ties
*Wolverton Town and BR – Hitchin Town – Cambridge City – Wisbech Town – Cambridge United – **Gillingham***

Enfield*
*Stevenage Town – Barnet – Wealdstone – Tooting and Mitcham United – Cheltenham Town – **Peterborough United***

Hinckley Athletic
*Loughborough United – Tamworth – Atherstone Town – Brierley Hill Alliance – Sittingbourne – **Queen's Park Rangers***

Wimbledon
*Leatherhead – Woking – Kingstonian – Oxford City – **Colchester United – Bristol City***

Andover Q1 Rd to 1st Rd 5 ties
*Cowes – Basingstoke Town – Alton Town – Hendon – **Gillingham***

Boston United
Spalding United – Grantham – Skegness Town – Kettering Town – King's Lynn

Buxton
*Sutton Town – Belper Town – Arnold St Mary's – Gainsborough Trinity – **Barrow***

Cheltenham Town
*Llanelli – Lovells Athletic – Gloucester City – Minehead – Enfield**

Falmouth Town
*Barnstaple Town – St Blazey – Bideford – Bath City – **Oxford United***

Maidenhead United
Windsor and Eton – Yiewsley – Finchley – Tilbury – Wycombe Wanderers

'62/'63 cont. **Poole Town**
Swanage Town – Warminster Town – Dorchester Town – Weymouth – ***Watford***

Scarborough
Bridlington Town – Harrogate Town – Ossett Albion – Hyde United –* ***Crewe Alexandra***

Sittingbourne
Whitstable – Folkestone – Dover – Guildford City – Hinckley Athletic*

Wellington Town (Telford United)
Congleton Town – Stafford Rangers – Bromsgrove Rovers – Rugby Town –* ***Bristol City***

Wigan Athletic
Milnthorpe Corinthians – Fleetwood – Netherfield (Kendal) – Ellesmere Port Town – Gateshead**

**Different from later club with same/similar name*

Rank	Northern League	R5	R4	R3	R2	R1	IR	Q6	Q5	Q4	Q3
1	Blyth Spartans	1		1	2	6				7	4
2	Bishop Auckland		1		8	11	2		10	25	5
3	Crook Town				3	7				5	3
4	Spennymoor United				3	3				3	3
5	Middlesbrough				3	1			1		3
6	Whitby Town				2	4				5	13
7	Sunderland Albion				2						
8	Stockton (1)				1	6			2	11	4
9	Shildon				1	5				5	10
10	Tow Law Town				1	3				8	6
11	Crook Town (1)				1	1		1	1	1	1
12	North Shields				1	1				4	3
13	Durham City				1	1				3	7
14	Penrith				1					2	4
15	Bedlington Terriers				1					2	2
16	Sheffield United				1						
17	Billingham Synthonia					7				7	5
18	Willington					3			1	5	6
19	West Auckland Town					3				1	5
20	Ferryhill Athletic					2				6	6

Top 20 FA Cup Clubs whilst Members of Northern League.

Nb. Chart shows number of exits per Round

Top 150 FA Cup Clubs from Start of Football League to World War I (1888/89 to 1914/15)

Almost 1,200 different clubs participated in the FA Cup in the 27 seasons from the start of the Football League to the outbreak of World War I, but fewer than 150 of them actually competed in the 'proper' rounds of the competition. Whilst the number of qualifying rounds fluctuated heavily during this period, the number of 'Proper' rounds just changed from five to six in 1905, with the 3rd Round then the 4th Round acting as the quarter-finals. As there were only two divisions within the Football League (just one in its first four seasons of existence), non-league clubs during this period, especially those from the Southern League, were regarded as being at least on a par with the predominantly northern Football League clubs.

Best Performance - Winners

1	Aston Villa	4x Winners
2	Sheffield United	3x Winners
3	Wolverhampton Wanderers	2x Winners, 4x Finalists
4	The (Sheffield) Wednesday	2x Winners, 3x Finalists
5	Blackburn Rovers	2x Winners, 2x Finalists, 7x SF
6	Bury	2x Winners, 2x Finalists, 2x SF
7	Newcastle United	1x Winners, 5x Finalists
8	Everton	1x Winners, 4x Finalists
9	West Bromwich Albion	1x Winners, 3x Finalists
10	Notts County	1x Winners, 2x Finalists, 2x SF, 5x QF
11	Barnsley	1x Winners, 2x Finalists, 2x SF, 3x QF
12	Nottingham Forest	1x Winners, 1x Finalists, 4x SF
13	Preston North End	1x Winners, 1x Finalists, 2x SF, 7x QF
14	Burnley	1x Winners, 1x Finalists, 2x SF, 5x QF
15	Newton Heath / Man. Utd.	1x Winners, 1x Finalists, 1x SF, 5x QF
16	Tottenham Hotspur	1x Winners, 1x Finalists, 1x SF, 4x QF
17	Bradford City	1x Winners, 1x Finalists, 1x SF, 3x QF, 6x R3
18	Ardwick / Manchester City	1x Winners, 1x Finalists, 1x SF, 3x QF, 5x R3

Best Performance – Runners-up

19	Derby County	3x Finalists
20	Bolton Wanderers	2x Finalists, 5x SF
21	Southampton / St Mary's ...	2x Finalists, 4x SF
22	Sunderland	1x Finalists, 4x SF, 7x QF, 11x R3
23	Liverpool	1x Finalists, 4x SF, 7x QF, 9x R3
24	Chelsea	1x Finalists, 2x SF
25	Bristol City	1x Finalists, 1x SF

Best Performance – Semi-Finalists

26	Swindon Town	2x SF, 3x QF
27	Millwall / Athletic	2x SF, 2x QF, 4x R3

28	Royal / Woolwich / Arsenal	2x SF, 2x QF, 2x R3
29	Stoke (City)	1x SF, 8x QF
30	Fulham	1x SF, 3x QF
31	Oldham Athletic	1x SF, 2x QF

Best Performance – Quarter-Finalists

32	Middlesbrough	2x QF, 5x R3
33	Small Heath (Birmingham C.)	2x QF, 4x R3
34	Queens Park Rangers	2x QF, 3x R3
35	Thames Ironworks / WHU ...	1x QF, 5x R3
36	Crystal Palace	1x QF, 3x R3, 6x R2, 10x R1
37	Bradford (Park Avenue)*	1x QF, 3x R3, 6x R2, 6x R1
38	Reading	1x QF, 3x R3, 5x R2
39	Grimsby Town	1x QF, 2x R3, 7x R2, 22x R1
40	Portsmouth	1x QF, 2x R3, 7x R2, 15x R1
41	Hull City	1x QF, 2x R3, 4x R2
42	Singers / Coventry City	1x QF, 2x R3, 3x R2
43	Leicester Fosse (City)	1x QF, 1x R3, 6x R2
44	Darwen	1x QF, 1x R3, 3x R2
45	Glossop / North End	1x QF, 1x R3, 2x R2, 14x R1
46	Middlesbrough Ironopolis ...	1x QF, 1x R3, 2x R2, 4x R1, (plus 1 pr)
47	Birmingham St George's	1x QF, 1x R3, 2x R2, 4x R1
48	Bootle*	1x QF, 1x R3, 1x R2, 3x R1
49	Chatham (Town)	1x QF, 1x R3, 1x R2, 2x R1

Best Performance – 3rd Round

50	Eastville / Bristol Rovers	3x R3
51	Norwich City	2x R3, 7x R2
52	Brentford	2x R3, 3x R2
53	Brighton & Hove Albion	1x R3, 6x R2
54	Plymouth Argyle	1x R3, 5x R2
55	Blackpool	1x R3, 4x R2, 13x R1
56	Northampton Town	1x R3, 4x R2, 11x R1
57	Darlington*	1x R3, 2x R2
58	Leyton*	1x R3, 1x R2

Best Performance – 2nd Round

59	Lincoln City	5x R2
60	Gainsborough Trinity	4x R2, 10x R1
61	New Brompton / Gillingham	4x R2, 9x R1, (plus 3x ir)
62	Leeds City*	4x R2, 9x R1, (plus 1x q3)
63	Accrington*	4x R2, 6x R1
64	Chesterfield (Town)	3x R2
65	Stockport County	2x R2, 9x R1
66	Burslem / Port Vale	2x R2, 5x R1, (plus 1x ir, 1x q6)

67	Walsall / Town Swifts	2x R2, 5x R1, (plus 1x ir, 3x q5)
68	Southend United	2x R2, 5x R1, (plus 3x q5)
69	Exeter City	2x R2, 4x R1, (plus 1x q5)
70	Huddersfield Town	2x R2, 4x R1, (plus 2x q4)
71	Sunderland Albion	2x R2, 4x R1
72	Swansea Town (City)	2x R2, 2x R1
73	Luton Town	1x R2, 12x R1
74	Crewe Alexandra	1x R2, 8x R1, (plus 1x ir)
75	(Leyton) Clapton Orient	1x R2, 8x R1, (plus 2x q3)
76	West Herts / Watford / Rov.	1x R2, 7x R1
77	Kettering (Town)	1x R2, 6x R1
78	Burton Wanderers	1x R2, 4x R1
79	Shaddongate / Carlisle Utd.	1x R2, 3x R1, (plus 2x q5)
80	Accrington Stanley*	1x R2, 3x R1, (plus 1x q5)
81	Rochdale	1x R2, 2x R1, (plus 1x q5)
82	Chester (City)*	1x R2, 2x R1, (plus 3x q4)
83	Halliwell	1x R2, 2x R1, (plus 1x q3)
84	Swifts	1x R2, 2x R1, (plus 2x q2)
85	Northwich Victoria	1x R2, 1x R1, (plus 2x q4)
86	Derby Midland	1x R2, 1x R1 (plus 1x q3)

Best Performance – 1st Round

87	Croydon Common	5x R1
88	Stockton*	4x R1, (plus 2x q5)
89	South Shore	4x R1, (plus 1x q4)
90	Heanor Town	4x R1, (plus 2x q3)
91	Old Westminsters	4x R1, (plus 1x q3)
92	Burton Swifts	3x R1, (plus 2x q5)
93	Hastings & St Leonards Utd.	3x R1, (plus 1x q5)
94	Long Eaton Rangers	3x R1, (plus 2x q4)
95	South Shields* / Gateshead*	3x R1, (plus 1x q4)
96	Casuals	3x R1, (plus 4x q2)
97	Bishop Auckland	2x R1, (plus 2x ir, 5x q5)
98	Burton United	2x R1, (plus 2x ir, 2x q5)
99	Kidderminster Rvrs / Harriers	2x R1, (plus 1x ir, 1x q5)
100	New Brighton Tower	2x R1, (plus 1x ir, 1x q3)
101	London Caledonians	2x R1, (plus 1x q6)
102	Southport / Central	2x R1, (plus 7x q5)
103	Clapton	2x R1, (plus 4x q5)
104	Oxford City	2x R1, (plus 3x q5, 8x q4)
105	Barrow	2x R1, (plus 3x q5. 3x q4)
106	Wrexham	2x R1, (plus 1x q5, 6x q4)
107	Workington*	2x R1, (plus 1x q5, 3x q4)
108	Merthyr Town*	2x R1, (plus 1x q5, 1x q4)

109	Jarrow*	2x R1, (plus 1x q4, 2x q3)
110	Crusaders	2x R1, (plus 1x q4, 1x q3)
111	Old Carthusians	2x R1, (plus 1x q3)
112	Shrewsbury Town	1x R1, (plus 1x ir)
113	Tunbridge Wells Rangers*	1x R1, (plus 3x q5, 3x q4)
114	Rotherham / Town	1x R1, (plus 3x q5, 2x q4)
115	King's Lynn	1x R1, (plus 1x q5, 1x q4, 3x q3)
116	Fairfield	1x R1, (plus 1x q5, 1x q4, 1x q3)
117	Cardiff City	1x R1, (plus 1x q5, 1x q4, 1x q2)
118	New Crusaders	1x R1, (plus 1x q5, 1x q2)
119	Halifax Town	1x R1, (plus 1x q5, 1x pr)
120	Loughborough / Town	1x R1, (plus 4x q4)
121	Marlow	1x R1, (plus 3x q4, 6x q3)
122	Chorley	1x R1, (plus 3x q4, 3x q3)
123	Worksop Town	1x R1, (plus 2x q4, 3x q3)
124	Worcester City	1x R1, (plus 2x q4, 2x q3)
125	Staple Hill	1x R1, (plus 2x q4, 1x q3)
126	Stalybridge Rovers	1x R1, (plus 1x q4, 6x q3)
127	Newcastle East End*	1x R1, (plus 1x q4, 1x q3, 1x q2)
128	Wigan County	1x R1, (plus 1x q4, 1x q3)
129	Linfield Athletic	1x R1, (plus 1x q4, 1x q1)
130	Shankhouse	1x R1, (plus 2x q3, 3x q2)
131	Hucknall St John's	1x R1, (plus 2x q3, 2x q2)
132	Old Brightonians	1x R1, (plus 2x q3, 2x q1)
133	Irthlingborough Town	1x R1, (plus 1x q3, 3x q2, 5x q1)
134	Derby Junction	1x R1, (plus 1x q3, 3x q2, 3x q1)
135	Goole Town	1x R1, (plus 1x q3, 2x q2, 4x q1)
136	Sutton Junction	1x R1, (plus 1x q3, 2x q2, 3x q1)
137	Newcastle West End*	1x R1, (plus 1x q3, 2x q2)
138	Notts Rangers	1x R1, (plus 1x q3, 1x pr)
139	Woking	1x R1, (plus 3x q2)
140=	Sheffield Heeley	1x R1, (plus 1x q2, 2x q1)
140=	Witton	1x R1, (plus 1x q2, 2x q1)
142	93rd Highland Regiment	1x R1, (plus 1x q2)
143	Distillery	1x R1
144	North Shields	(1x q6, 2x q5)
145	Rotherham County	(1x q6, 1x q5, 4x q4)
146	Southall	(1x q6, 1x q5, 2x q4)
147	Bromley	(1x q6, 3x q4)
148	Stafford Rangers	(1x q6, 2x q4)
149	Boscombe (AFC Bournem'th)	(1x q6, 2x q3)
150	Sunderland West End	(1x q6, 1x q3)

**Different from current/later club with same/similar name*

The 150 Biggest Margins of Victory in FA Cup History

26	1887/88	1st Rd	Preston North End	26 – 0	Hyde
19	1890/91	Q1 Rd	Staveley	19 – 0	Sheffield Walkley
18	1893/94	1st Rd	Preston North End	18 – 0	Reading
	1901/02	Pr Rd	Norwich CEYMS	18 – 0	Bury Town
	1902/03	Q3 Rd	St Helens Recreation	18 – 0	Rhyl
	1925/26	Pr Rd	Windsor and Eton	18 – 0	Henley Town
	1953/54	Q1 Rd	Ferryhill Athletic	18 – 0	Skinningrove Works
17	1927/28	Pr rep	Rothwell Town	17 – 0	Stamford
16	1933/34	EP Rd	Oswestry Town	19 – 3	Badsey Rangers
16	2002/03	Pr Rd	Stocksbridge PS	17 – 1	Oldham Town
16	1874/75	1st Rd	The Wanderers	16 – 0	Farningham
	1905/06	Q1 Rd	New Crusaders	16 – 0	Woking
	1909/10	Pr Rd	Kettering (Town)	16 – 0	Higham Ferrers YMCI
15	1914/15	Pr Rd	Lancaster Town (City)	17 – 2	Appleby
15	1938/39	EP Rd	Blackhall CW	16 – 1	Middleton Wanderers
15	1875/76	1st Rd	Royal Engineers	15 – 0	High Wycombe
	1880/81	1st Rd	Clapham Rovers	15 – 0	Finchley
		QF Rd	Darwen	15 – 0	Romford*
	1883/84	2nd Rd	Queen's Park	15 – 0	Manchester
	1885/86	1st Rd	Notts County	15 – 0	Rotherham Town
	1914/15	Q4 Rd	Luton Town	15 – 0	Great Yarmouth Town
	1919/20	Pr Rd	Portsmouth Ams.	15 – 0	White & Co's Sports
	1930/31	Q4 Rd	Walthamstow Ave.	15 – 0	Aldershot Traction Co.
	1931/32	EP Rd	Nuneaton Town*	15 – 0	Walsall Phoenix
	1959/60	Q2 Rd	Enfield*	15 – 0	Hoddesdon Town
14	1938/39	Q1 Rd	Burton Town	16 – 2	Sandiacre Excelsior Fndry.
14	1900/01	Q4 Rd	Bristol Rovers	15 – 1	Weymouth
	1955/56	Pr Rep	Wycombe Wands.	15 – 1	Witney Town
14	1890/91	Q1 Rd	Hurworth	0 – 14	Stockton*
		1st Rd	Clapton	0 – 14	Nottingham Forest
	1919/20	Pr Rd	Brigg Town	0 – 14	Cleethorpes Town*
	1920/21	EP Rd	Conisbrough Ath.	0 – 14	Wath Athletic
	1927/28	Pr Rd	Sandown	0 – 14	RM Portsmouth
	1964/65	Q1 Rd	Boston United	0 – 14	Spalding United
14	1886/87	2nd Rd	Wolverhampton W.	14 – 0	Crosswell's Brewery

14	1894/95	Q1 Rd	Southampton (St M)	14 – 0	Newbury*
	1899/00	Q1 Rd	Stapleford Town	14 – 0	Belper Town*
	1908/09	Q1 Rd	Exeter City	14 – 0	Weymouth
	1935/36	EP Rd	Wellington Town	14 – 0	Headingley
	1938/39	Q1 Rd	Marine	14 – 0	Sandhurst (L'pool)
	1946/47	Q2 Rd	Coalville Town*	14 – 0	Ibstock Penistone Rov.
	1954/55	Q1 Rd	Whitwick Colliery	14 – 0	Coalville Town*
13	1929/30	Pr Rd	Wimbledon	15 – 2	Polytechnic
13	1951/52	Q1 Rd	King's Lynn	14 – 1	Chatteris Town
	1955/56	Q1 Rd	Sudbury Town	14 – 1	Leiston
	1888/89	Q1 Rd	Dulwich	0 – 13	London Caledonians
	1895/96	Q1 Rd	Peterborough*	0 – 13	Lincoln City
	1930/31	Pr Rd	Cowley	0 – 13	Park Royal
	1950/51	EP Rd	Amersham Town	0 – 13	Wycombe Wanderers
13	1886/87	1st Rd	Aston Villa	13 – 0	Wednesbury Old Ath.
			Notts County	13 – 0	Basford Rovers
			Swifts	13 – 0	Luton Wanderers
	1889/90	2nd Rd	Bolton Wanderers	13 – 0	Sheffield United
	1890/91	Q1 Rd	Rotherham Town	13 – 0	Sheffield
		1st Rd	Darwen	13 – 0	Kidderminster (Harriers)
	1892/93	Q2 Rd	Gainsborough Trin.	13 – 0	Belper Town*
	1894/95	Q1 Rd	Flint	13 – 0	Warrington St Elphin's
			Leicester Fosse (City)	13 – 0	Notts Olympic
	1907/08	Q1 Rd	Denaby United	13 – 0	Wakefield City*
	1914/15	Q1 Rd	Tranmere Rovers	13 – 0	Oswestry Town
	1923/24	Pr Rd	Slough*	13 – 0	Henley Comrades
	1934/35	Pr Rd	Grantham (Town)	13 – 0	Rufford Colliery
		Q1 Rd	Vauxhall Motors	13 – 0	Bedford Queens PR
	1947/48	Pr Rd	South Shields*	13 – 0	Radcliffe Welfare Utd.
	1952/53	Q1 Rd	Great Yarmouth T.	13 – 0	Cromer
12	1927/28	Q1 Rd	Newark Town*	15 – 3	Basford United
12	1902/03	Q1 Rd	Brighton & Hove Alb.	14 – 2	Brighton Athletic
	1949/50	Q1 Rd	Hastings United*	14 – 2	Hove
12	1890/91	1st Rd	Aston Villa	13 – 1	Casuals
	1891/92	Q2 Rd	Darlington*	13 – 1	Scarborough
	1898/99	Q1 Rd	Ashton North End	13 – 1	Rhyl (United)
	1901/02	Q1 Rd	Luton Town	13 – 1	Apsley (Hemel H'stead)
	1926/27	Q1 rep	Denaby United	13 – 1	Guiseley
12	1890/91	Q1 Rd	Warmley	0 – 12	Walsall (Town Swifts)

12	1902/03	Q2 Rd	Shoreham	0 – 12	Brighton & Hove Alb.
	1911/12	Q3 Rd	Camerton	0 – 12	Merthyr Town*
	1950/51	EP Rd	Crossens	0 – 12	Skelmersdale United
	1993/94	Pr Rd	Dawlish Town	0 – 12	Taunton Town
12	1875/76	2nd Rd	Clapham Rovers	12 – 0	Leyton*
	1884/85	1st Rd	Blackburn Olympic	12 – 0	Oswaldtwistle Rovers
	1885/86	1st Rd	Clapham Rovers	12 – 0	1st Surrey Rifles
	1888/89	Q2 Rd	Chirk	12 – 0	Nantwich (Town)
	1890/91	Q1 Rd	Ardwick (Man. City)	12 – 0	Liverpool Stanley
		1st Rd	The Wednesday	12 – 0	Halliwell
	1893/94	Q1 Rd	(Woolwich) Arsenal	12 – 0	Ashford United*
	1908/09	Pr Rd	Monckton Athletic	12 – 0	Parkgate United
	1912/13	Pr Rd	Rutherford College	12 – 0	South Shields Parkside
	1913/14	Q1 Rd	Halifax Town	12 – 0	West Vale Ramblers
	1920/21	Q1 Rd	Barrow	12 – 0	Cleator Moor Celtic
	1927/28	Q1 Rd	Cowley	12 – 0	Marlow
	1929/30	EP Rd	Shrewsbury Town	12 – 0	Cannock Town
	1932/33	Q1 Rd	Brighton & Hove Alb.	12 – 0	Shoreham
	1933/34	EP Rd	Hoddesdon Town	12 – 0	Welwyn Garden City
	1935/36	Q3 Rd	Cheltenham Town	12 – 0	Chippenham Rovers
	1950/51	Pr Rd	Penrith	12 – 0	Moss Bay
	1953/54	Q3 rep	Kettering Town	12 – 0	Stamford
	2007/08	EP Rd	Dereham Town	12 – 0	Fakenham Town
	2016/17	EP Rd	Yaxley	12 – 0	Huntingdon Town
11	1929/30	EP Rd	Nuneaton Town*	13 – 2	Walsall Phoenix
	1934/35	Pr Rd	Jurgens (Purfleet)	13 – 2	Custom House
	1935/36	EP Rd	Hertford Town	13 – 2	Bushey United
	1959/60	4th rep	Tottenham Hotspur	13 – 2	Crewe Alexandra
11	1982/83	Pr Rd	Chertsey Town	1 – 12	Bromley
	2017/18	EP Rd	Stotfold	1 – 12	Berkhamsted
11	1896/97	1st Rd	Bury	12 – 1	Stockton*
	1905/06	Q4 Rd	Gainsborough Trin.	12 – 1	Weymouth
	1910/11	Q1 Rd	Tunbridge Wells Rgrs.	12 – 1	Worthing
	1919/20	Pr Rd	Maidenhead United	12 – 1	Henley Town
			Margate	12 – 1	Deal Ports (Town)
	1922/23	EP Rd	Willenhall	12 – 1	Leamington Town
	1923/24	Q1 Rd	Yeovil & Petters Utd.	12 – 1	Westbury United
	1927/28	Q1 Rd	Barry (Town)	12 – 1	Bedminster Down Sports
			Botwell Miss. (Hayes)	12 – 1	Newbury Town*
	1938/39	Pr Rd	Romford*	12 – 1	Stork (Purfleet)
		Q1 Rd	Wisbech Town	12 – 1	Chatteris Town
	1954/55	Q3 Rd	Barnstaple Town	12 – 1	Tavistock

11	1903/04	Pr rep	Hastings & St Leo. U.	0 – 11	Tunbridge Wells*
	1906/07	Q1 Rd	Birdwell	0 – 11	Rotherham Town
	1908/09	Q2 Rd	Denby Dale	0 – 11	Bradford (PA)*
			Hindpool Athletic	0 – 11	Workington*
	1909/10	Pr Rd	Basingstoke (Town)	0 – 11	Cowes
			Heckmondwike	0 – 11	Huddersfield Town
	1912/13	EP Rd	Bridlington Albion	0 – 11	Bentley Colliery
	1919/20	Pr Rd	Yiewsley (Hillingdon)	0 – 11	Slough*
	1924/25	Pr Rd	Peterboro' GN Loco	0 – 11	Peterboro & Fletton U.
	1948/49	EP Rd	David Brown Ath.	0 – 11	Ossett Town
	2007/08	EP Rd	Team Northumbria	0 – 11	Consett
11	1884/85	1st Rd	Blackburn Rovers	11 – 0	Rossendale
			Darwen	11 – 0	Bradshaw
	1885/86	1st Rd	Darwen Old Wands.	11 – 0	Burnley
	1887/88	1st Rd	Accrington	11 – 0	Rossendale
	1889/90	Q1 Rd	(Royal) Arsenal	11 – 0	Lyndhurst
	1890/91	Q1 Rd	Middlesbrough	11 – 0	Scarborough
	1896/97	Q3 Rd	Walsall	11 – 0	Dresden United
	1900/01	Q4 Rd	Reading	11 – 0	Chesham Generals
	1903/04	Q1 Rd	Hinckley Town*	11 – 0	Coalville Town*
	1905/06	Q1 Rd	Leeds City*	11 – 0	Morley
		1st Rd	Aston Vila	11 – 0	King's Lynn
	1908/09	Q1 Rd	Tunbridge Wells Rgrs.	11 – 0	Bognor Regis Town
	1911/12	EP Rd	Wrexham	11 – 0	Rhyl
	1913/14	Pr Rd	Skinningrove Steel W.	11 – 0	Saltburn
	1914/15	Pr Rd	Stoke (City)	11 – 0	Stourbridge
	1930/31	Q1 Rd	South Bank	11 – 0	Filey Town
	1932/33	EP Rd	Redditch (United)	11 – 0	Headingley
	1934/35	EP Rd	Annfield Plain	11 – 0	Dawdon Rec. Colliery
		Q1 Rd	Heanor Town	11 – 0	Gresley Rovers*
		Q2 Rd	Rushden Town	11 – 0	Desborough Town
	1935/36	EP Rd	Grays Athletic	11 – 0	Custom House
	1936/37	Pr Rd	Callendar Athletic	11 – 0	Beckenham*
		Q3 Rd	Ipswich Town	11 – 0	Cromer
	1938/39	Q3 Rd	Burton Town	11 – 0	Bolsover Colliery
	1945/46	Q1 Rd	Walton and Hersham	11 – 0	Epsom Town*
	1946/47	Pr Rd	East Grinstead (Town)	11 – 0	Shoreham
			Walton and Hersham	11 – 0	Guildford
	1947/48	Pr Rd	Hereford United	11 – 0	Thynnes Athletic
	1948/49	Q1 Rd	Milnthorpe Corinth.	11 – 0	Cockermouth
	1949/50	Pr Rd	Hinckley Athletic	11 – 0	Morris Sports
	1954/55	Pr Rd	Barnet	11 – 0	Royston Town
	1958/59	Pr Rd	Stafford Rangers	11 – 0	Dudley Town

11	1960/61	1st Rd	Bristol City	11 – 0	Chichester City*
	1965/66	Q1 Rd	Whitley Bay	11 – 0	Annfield Plain
	1970/71	Q1 Rd	Romford*	11 – 0	Rainham Town
	1971/72	1st Rd	AFC Bournemouth	11 – 0	Margate
	1975/76	Q1 Rd	Tilbury	11 – 0	Leyton-Wingate
	2014/15	EP Rd	Molesey	11 – 0	Haywards Heath Town
	2015/16	EP Rd	Coleshill Town	11 – 0	Ellesmere Rangers

**Different from current / later club with same/similar name*

Rank	Football League	W	Fin	SF	QF	R5	R4	R3	R2	R1
1	Manchester United	7	4	7	9	6	14	20	8	11
2	Tottenham Hotspur	7	1	4	12	12	11	20	4	2
3	Newcastle United	6	5	2	7	10	19	25	9	8
4	Aston Villa	6	2	8	13	8	13	30	7	9
5	Arsenal	5	6	6	12	10	9	15	9	14
6	Liverpool	5	5	9	11	14	14	15	10	5
7	Everton	4	7	11	14	13	13	15	5	10
8	Wolverhampton Wanderers	4	4	7	14	5	26	31	12	12
9	Manchester City	4	4	2	7	12	17	26	7	11
10	West Bromwich Albion	4	3	10	10	14	18	32	5	12
11	Bolton Wanderers	4	3	5	7	11	23	30	7	18
12	Sheffield United	4	2	7	10	13	28	25	9	15
13	Sheffield Wednesday	3	1	9	7	15	19	35	9	12
14	Blackburn Rovers	3	1	8	10	16	11	35	7	13
15	West Ham United	3	1	2	7	9	18	27	1	2
16	Preston North End	2	4	2	13	9	18	35	17	22
17	Sunderland	2	2	8	8	5	22	34	10	13
18	Nottingham Forest	2	1	5	14	8	22	39	11	11
19	Bury	2			3	3	16	30	27	34
20	Huddersfield Town	1	4	2	3	9	21	36	6	15
21	Leeds United	1	3	4	2	9	17	39	2	3
22	Chelsea	1	2	7	9	11	18	16	6	5
23	Burnley	1	2	5	11	11	18	34	10	20
24	Portsmouth	1	2	2	3	10	20	33	4	12
25	Cardiff City	1	2	1	2	8	20	45	3	10
26	Blackpool	1	2		3	5	17	44	13	19
27	Barnsley	1	1	1	6	10	10	41	18	17
28	Notts County	1	1	1	6	4	18	34	23	32
29	Southampton	1		5	4	11	15	31	4	1
30	Ipswich Town	1		2	3	10	18	30	3	4

Top 30 FA Cup Clubs whilst Members of the Football League.

Nb. Chart shows number of exits per Round

All the Club names that have ever entered the FA Cup

105th Regiment, 1874 Northwich, 1st Coldstream Guards, 1st Grenadier Guards, 1st Highland Light Infantry, 1st King's Royal Rifles, 1st Scots Guards, 1st Sherwood Foresters, 1st South Lancashire Regiment, 1st Surrey Rifles, 2nd Coldstream guards, 2nd Grenadier Guards, 2nd Lincolnshire Regiment, 2nd Royal Warwickshire Regiment, 2nd Scots guards, 2nd West Kent Regiment, 3rd Coldstream guards, 3rd Grenadier Guards, 4th Divisional Signals Regiment, 4th King's Royal Rifles, 4th Royal Tank Regiment, 5th Royal Tank Regiment, 8th Durham Light Infantry, 93rd Highland Regiment, Abbey Hey, Abbey Rangers, Abbey United, Aberaman, Aberaman and Aberdare, Aberaman Athletic, Aberaman United, Abercarn, Aberdare, Aberdare Amateurs, Aberdare Athletic, Aberdare Town, Abergavenny Thursdays, Abertillery, Aberystwyth, Abingdon, Abingdon Town, Abingdon United, AC London, Accrington, Accrington Stanley, Achilles, Acomb WMC, Acton, Acton Town, Addlestone, Addlestone and Weybridge Town, Addlestone United, Adlington, AEC Athletic, AFC Blackpool, AFC Bournemouth, AFC Bridgnorth, AFC Croydon Athletic, AFC Darwen, AFC Dunstable, AFC Emley, AFC Fylde, AFC Hayes, AFC Hornchurch, AFC Kempston Rovers, AFC Liverpool, AFC Lymington, AFC Mansfield, AFC Newbury, AFC Portchester, AFC Rushden and Diamonds, AFC St Austell, AFC Stoneham, AFC Sudbury, AFC Telford United, AFC Totton, AFC Uckfield, AFC Uckfield Town, AFC Varndeanians, AFC Wallingford, AFC Wimbledon, AFC Wulfrunians, Albion Sports, Alderley Edge United, Aldershot, Aldershot Albion, Aldershot Excelsior, Aldershot Institute Albion, Aldershot Town, Aldershot Traction Company, Alfold, Alford United, Alfreton Town, Allendale Park, Allerton Bywater Colliery, Allsops, Alma Swanley, Almondsbury Greenway, Almondsbury Town, Almondsbury UWE, Alnwick Town, Alresford Town, Alsager Town, Altofts, Altofts West Riding Colliery, Alton, Alton Town, Altrincham, Alvechurch, AAC, Amble, Amersham Town, Amesbury Town, Ammanford Town, Ampthill Town, Andover, Andover New Street, Andover Town, Anglo, Annfield Plain, Annfield Plain Celtic, Anstey Nomads, Anston Athletic, Anston United, AP Leamington, Apperley Bridge, Appleby, Appleby Frodingham, Appleby Frodingham Athletic, Apsley, APV Peterborough City, Aquarius, Ardley United, Ardsley, Ardsley Athletic, Ardwick, Argonauts, Arlecdon Red Rose, Arlesey Town, Arlington, Armitage, Armitage '90, Armthorpe Welfare, Arnold, Arnold St Mary's, Arnold Town, ARSENAL, Arundel, Ascot United, Ash United, Ashbourne Town, Ashby Albion, Ashby Institute, Ashby Ivanhoe, Ashby Town, Ashfield United, Ashford, Ashford Railway Works, Ashford Town (Kent), Ashford Town (Middlesex), Ashford United, Ashington, Ashton and Backwell United, Ashton Athletic, Ashton National, Ashton North End, Ashton Town, Ashton-under-Lyne, Ashton United, Ashtree Highfield, Askern Villa, Aspatria Athletic, Aspatria Spartans, Astley Bridge, Aston Shakespeare, Aston Unity, ASTON VILLA, Athersley Recreation, Atherstone Town, Atherstone Town Community Club, Atherstone United, Atherton, Atherton Collieries, Atherton Laburnum Rovers, Atlas and Norfolk Works, Atlas Hotel, Attercliffe, Auckland St Helen's United, Auckland Town, Aveley, Avro, Aylesbury, Aylesbury United, Aylesbury Vale, Aylesbury Vale Dynamos, Aylesford Paper Mills, Aylestone Park, Babbacombe, Backwell United, Bacup, Bacup Borough, Bacup of Rossendale Borough, Badsey Rangers, Badshot Lea, Baffins Milton Rovers, Baker Perkins, Baldock Town, Balham, Bamber Bridge, Banbury Spencer, Banbury United, Bangor, Bangor Athletic, Bangor City, Banstead Athletic, Banstead Mental Hospital, Bardon Hill, Bardon Hill Sports, Bargoed, Barking, Barking and East Ham United, Barking Town, Barking Woodville, Barkingside, Barnard Castle Athletic, Barnes, Barnet, Barnet Alston, Barnet and Alston, Barnoldswick and District, Barnoldswick Park Villa, Barnoldswick Town, Barnoldswick United, BARNSLEY, Barnsley St Peter's, Barnstaple Town, Barnt Green Spartak, Barnton, Barnton Rovers, Barnton Victoria, Barrow, Barrow Novocastrians, Barrow Shipbuilders, Barrow St George's, Barrow St Luke's, Barrow St Mary's, Barrow Town, Barrow YMCA, Barri, Barry AFC, Barry District, Barry Town, Bartley Green, Barton Rovers, Barton Town, Barton Town Old Boys, Barwell, Barwell Athletic, Barwell Swifts, Barwell United, Basford Rovers, Basford United, Bashley, Basildon United, Basingstoke Town, BAT Sports, Bath AFC, Bath City, Beaconsfield SYCOB, Beaconsfield Town, Bean, Bearsted, Beccles, Beccles Caxton, Beckenham, Beckenham Town, Becontree Town, Beddington Corner, Bedfont, Bedfont and Feltham, Bedfont Green, Bedfont Sports, Bedfont Town, Bedford, Bedford Avenue, Bedford Corinthians, Bedford Excelsior, Bedford North End, Bedford Queens, Bedford Queens Park Rangers, Bedford Queens Works, Bedford St Cuthbert's, Bedford Town, Bedford United, Bedford United and Valerio, Bedlington Colliery Welfare, Bedlington Mechanics, Bedlington Terriers, Bedlington United, Bedminster, Bedminster Down Sports, Bedminster St Paul's, Bedouins, Bedworth Town, Bedworth United, Beeston, Beeston Humber, Beeston St John's, Beighton Miners Welfare, Beighton Recreation, Beighton Working Men's, Belfast North End, Belfast YMCA, Belper Town, Belper United, Belvedere, Bemerton Heath Harlequins, Benfleet, Bentinck Colliery Welfare, Bentley Colliery, Benwell Adelaide, Berkhamsted, Berkhamsted Comrades, Berkhamsted Town, Berwick Rangers, Bestwood Colliery, Bethesda Athletic, Bethnal Green United, Betteshanger Welfare, Beverley Town, Bewdley Town, Bexhill, Bexhill Town, Bexhill Town Athletic, Bexhill United, Bexhill Wanderers, Bexley, Bexley United, Bexleyheath and Welling, Bexleyheath Labour, Bexleyheath Town, Bicester Town, Biddulph Victoria, Bideford, Bideford Town, Biggleswade, Biggleswade and District, Biggleswade Town, Biggleswade United, Bigrigg United, Billericay Town, Billingham, Billingham St John's, Billingham Synthonia, Billingham Town, Billingshurst, Bilsthorpe Colliery Welfare, Bilston, Bilston Borough, Bilston Town, Bilston United, Binfield, Bingley, Birch, Birch Coppice Colliery, Birdwell, Birdwell Primitive Methodists, Birkenhead, Birkenhead LNWR, Birmingham, Birmingham City, Birmingham City Transport, Birmingham Corporation Transport, Birmingham Excelsior, Birmingham St George's, Birmingham Transport, Birstall United, Birtley, Birtley New Town, Birtley Town, Bishop Auckland, Bishop Auckland Church Institute, Bishop Sutton, Bishop's Cleeve, Bishop's Stortford, Bitterne Guild, Bitterne Nomads, Bitton, Blaby and Whetstone Athletic, Black Country Rangers, Black Diamonds, Black Lane Rovers, Black Lane Temperance, Blackburn Law, BLACKBURN OLYMPIC, Blackburn Park Road, BLACKBURN ROVERS, Blackfield and Langley, Blackhall Colliery Welfare, BLACKPOOL, Blackpool Mechanics, Blackpool St John's, Blackpool (Wren) Rovers, Blackstones, Blackwell Colliery, Blackwood Town, Blaenau Ffestiniog, Blakeborough and Sons, Blakenhall, Blandford, Blandford United, Blaydon United, Bletchley and Wipac Sports, Bletchley Town, Blidworth Welfare, Bloxwich Strollers, Bloxwich Town, Bloxwich United, Blue Star, Blue Star Welfare, Blundells, Blyth, Blyth Spartans, Bodmin Town, Bognor, Bognor Regis, Bognor Regis Town, Boldmere St Michaels, Boldon Colliery, Boldon Colliery Welfare, Boldon Community Association, Bolehall Swifts, Boleyn Castle, Bollington, Bolsover Colliery, Bolton Association, Bolton Athletic, Bolton Olympic, Bolton United, BOLTON WANDERERS, Bookham, Boothtown, Bootle, Bootle Athletic, Bootle Celtic, Boots Athletic, Boreham Wood, Borough United, Borrowash Victoria, Boscombe, Bostall Heath, Boston, Boston St James', Boston St Nicholas, Boston Town, Boston United, Botley, Bottesford Town, Botwell Mission, Boulton and Paul's, Bourne Town, Bournemouth, Bournemouth and Boscombe Athletic, Bournemouth Gasworks, Bournemouth Gasworks Athletic, Bournemouth Rovers,

Bournemouth Transport, Bournemouth Tramways, Bournemouth Wanderers, Bourneville Athletic, Bowater Lloyds, Bovey Tracey, Bowers and Pitsea, Bowers United, Bowling Albion, Bowness Rovers, Bowthorn Recreation, Bowthorn United, Boxmoor, Boxmoor St John's, Brackley Town, Brackley Town Saints, Bracknell Town, Bradford, Bradford (Park Avenue), Bradford (Park Avenue) AFC, BRADFORD CITY, Bradford-on-Avon, Bradford Rovers, Bradford Town, Bradford United, Brading Town, Bradshaw, Braintree and Crittall Athletic, Braintree Town, Brandon Colliery Welfare, Brandon Rovers, Brandon Social Club, Brandon United, Brantham Athletic, Breightmet United, Brentford, Brentwood, Brentwood and Warley, Brentwood Mental Hospital, Brentwood Town, Brereton Social, Bretby Colliery, Brett Sports, Bridgend Town, Bridgnorth Town, Bridgwater, Bridgwater Town, Bridlington Albion, Bridlington Central United, Bridlington Town, Bridlington Trinity, Bridon Ropes, Bridport, Brierfield Swifts, Brierley Hill Alliance, Brierley Hill and Withymoor, Brierley Hill Town, Brigg, Brigg Britannia, Brigg Town, Brigg 2nd Lincolnshire Sugar Company, Briggs Motor Bodies, Briggs Sports, Brigham and Cowan, Brighouse Town, Brightlingsea Regent, Brightlingsea United, Brighton Amateurs, Brighton and Hove Albion, Brighton and Hove Rangers, Brighton Athletic, Brighton Corporation Tramways, Brighton Mental Hospital, Brighton Railway Athletic, Brighton United, Brighton West End, Brimington Hotspurs, Brimscombe and Thrupp, Brimsdown Rovers, Brislington, Bristol Aeroplane Company, Bristol Amateurs, Bristol City, Bristol East, Bristol Eastville Rovers, Bristol Manor Farm, Bristol Rovers, Bristol South End, Bristol St George, British Oil and Cake Mills, Broadbridge Heath, Broadfields United, Brockenhurst, Brocton, Brodsworth Main Colliery, Brodsworth Miners Welfare, Brodsworth Welfare, Bromborough, Bromley, Brompton, Bromsgrove Rovers, Bromsgrove Sporting, Bromyard Town, Brondesbury, Bronze Athletic, Brook House, Brookwood Mental Hospital, Brooms, Brotherhoods Engineering Works, Brotton, Broughton Rangers, Broxbourne Borough V&E, Brunswick Institute, Brush Sports, Brush Works, Brynn Central, Buckingham Town, Buckland Athletic, Buckley Town, Buckley United, Buckley Victoria, Bugbrooke St Michaels, Bulford United, Bullcroft Main Colliery, Bulwell United, Bungay Town, Burbage, Burberry Athletic, Burgess Hill Town, Burnham, Burnham and Hillingdon, Burnham Ramblers, Burnhope Institute, BURNLEY, Burnley Belvedere, Burnley Casuals, Burnside, Burradon Athletic, Burfield Park, Burscough, Burscough Rangers, Burslem Port Vale, Burton Albion, Burton All Saints, Burton Park Wanderers, Burton Swifts, Burton Town, Burton United, Burton Wanderers, Burton Wenerth Rangers, BURY, Bury St Edmunds, Bury Town, Bury United, Bush Hill Park, Bushey United, Bustleholme, Buxton, BWI Reading, Cadbury Athletic, Cadbury Heath, Caerau Athletic, Caerau Rovers, Caerleon Athletic, Caernarfon Town, Caernarvon Athletic, Caernarvon Wanderers, Caerphilly, Caius College Cambridge, Callendar Athletic, Callington, Calne and Harris United, Calne Corinthians, Calne Town, Calthorpe, Calverley, Camberley, Camberley and Yorktown, Camberley Town, Cambridge City, Cambridge Town, Cambridge United, Cambridge University, Camerton, Cammell Laird, Cammell Laird (Nottingham), Cammell Laird 1907, Cammell's Sports, Campion, Cannock Town, Cannon, Canterbury City, Canterbury Waverley, Canvey Island, Cardiff Albion, CARDIFF CITY, Cardiff Corinthians, Cargo Fleet, Cargo Fleet Athletic, Cargo Fleet Works, Carlin How, Carlin How Athletic, Carlisle, Carlisle City, Carlisle Red Rose, Carlisle United, Carlton Town, Carshalton Athletic, Carterton, Carterton Town, Castle Donington Town, Castle Hill, Castle Vale, Castle Vale JKS, Castleford and Allerton United, Castleford Town, Castleford United, Castleton Gabriels, Casuals, Catcliffe, Catford Southend, Causeway United, CB Hounslow United, Celtic Nation, Central Hull Rangers, Chadderton, Chalfont St Peter, Channing Rovers, Chapel-en-le-Frith, Chard Town, CHARLTON ATHLETIC, Charltons, Charnock Richard, Chasetown, Chatham, Chatham Amateurs, Chatham Town, Chatham United, Chatteris Engineers, Chatteris Town, Cheadle Town, Cheddar, Chelmsford, Chelmsford City, Chelmsford Rollers, Chelmsley Town, CHELSEA, Cheltenham Saracens, Cheltenham Town, Chepstow Town, Chertsey Town, Chesham, Chesham Generals, Chesham Town, Chesham United, Cheshunt, Chessington and Hook United, Chessington United, Chester, Chester City, Chester St Oswald's, Chesterfield, Chesterfield Corinthians, Chesterfield Municipal, Chesterfield Spital, Chesterfield Town, Chester-le-Street, Chester-le-Street Town, Chichester, Chichester City, Chichester City United, Chilton and Windlestone, Chilton Athletic, Chilton Colliery Recreation Athletic, Chingford Town, Chinnor, Chippenham Rovers, Chippenham Town, Chippenham United, Chipperfield, Chipping Norton Town, Chipping Sodbury Town, Chipstead, Chirk, Chirk AAA, Chiswick, Chiswick Town, Choppington, Chopwell Colliery, Chopwell Institute, Chorley, Christchurch, Church, Churchman Sports, Cinderford Town, Cinderhill Colliery, Cirencester Town, City of Durham, City of Liverpool, City of Norwich School Old Boys Union, City of Westminster, City Ramblers, City Wanderers, Civil Service, Clacton Town, Clandown, Clanfield '85, Clapham, CLAPHAM ROVERS, Clapton, Clapton Orient, Clarence, Clarence Iron and Steel Works, Clay Cross and Danesmoor Miners Welfare, Clay Cross Town, Clay Cross Works, Clay Cross Zingari, Clayton West, Cleator Moor Celtic, Cleethorpes Town, Clevedon, Clevedon Town, Clevedon United, Clifton, Clifton Association, Clifton Colliery, Cliftonville, Clinton, Clipstone, Clitheroe, Clitheroe Central, Clitheroe Low Moor, Close Works, Clove, Clowne Colliery, Clutton Wanderers, Clydesdale, Coalville Albion, Coalville Swifts, Coalville Town, Coalville United, Cobham, Cockermouth, Cockfield, Cockfosters, Codicote, Cogenhoe United, Coggeshall Town, Coggeshall United, Colchester Casuals, Colchester Town, Colchester United, Coleford Athletic, Coleshill Town, Collier Row, Collier Row and Romford, Colliers Wood United, Colne, Colne Carlton, Colne Dynamoes, Colne Town, Colney Heath, Columbia, Colwyn Bay, Colwyn Bay United, Concord Rangers, Congleton Hornets, Congleton Town, Conisbrough Athletic, Conisbrough St Peter's, Connah's Quay, Connah's Quay and Shotton, Connah's Quay Nomads, Consett, Consett Celtic, Consett Town Swifts, Continental Star, Coombs Wood Tube Works, Coppull Central, Corby Town, Corinthian, Corinthian-Casuals, Corinthians, Cornard United, Cornholme, Corsham Town, Cortonwood Welfare, Coundon Three Tuns, Coundon United, Courage and Co's Sports, Cove, Coventry Amateurs, COVENTRY CITY, Coventry Sphinx, Coventry Sporting, Coventry United, Cowes, Cowes Sports, Cowlairs, Cowley, Cradley Heath, Cradley Heath St Luke's, Cradley Town, Craghead Heros, Craghead United, Cramlington Welfare, Cranfield United, Cranleigh, Crawcrook Albion, Crawley Down, Crawley Down Gatwick, Crawley Green, Crawley Town, Cray Valley Paper Mills, Cray Wanderers, Crescent, Creswell Colliery, Crewe Alexandra, Cribbs, Crich Town, Crittall Athletic, Crockenhill, Croft, Crofton, Cromer, Cromptons Recreation, Crook, Crook Colliery Welfare, Crook Town, Crookhall Colliery Welfare, Crookhall Rovers, Cross Keys,

Crossens, Crosswell's Brewery, Croston, Crouch End, Crouch End Vampires, Crowborough Athletic, Crown and Manor, Croydon, Croydon Amateurs, Croydon Athletic, Croydon Common, Croydon Park, Croydon Rovers, Croydon Wanderers, Crusaders, Crystal Palace, Crystal Palace Engineers, Cudworth St Mary's, Cudworth Village, Cullompton Rangers, Curzon Ashton, Custom House, Cwmbran Town, CWS Silvertown, Dagenham, Dagenham and Redbridge, Dagenham British Legion, Dagenham Town, Daisy Hill, Dalton Casuals, Danesmoor Welfare, Darenth Heathside, Darenth Park, Darenth Training Colony, Darfield, Darfield St George, Darfield United, Darlaston, Darlington, Darlington 1883, Darlington Cleveland Bridge, Darlington Cleveland Social, Darlington Railway Athletic, Darlington St Augustine's, Darlington St Hilda's, Darlington West End, Darnall Wellington, Dartford, Dartford Amateurs, Dartmouth United, Darwen, Darwen Old Wanderers, Darwen Ramblers, Davenham, Daventry Town, Daventry United, Daventry Victoria, David Brown Athletic, Davis Athletic, Dawdon Colliery Welfare, Dawdon Recreation, Dawlish Town, De Haviland, De Haviland Vampires, Deal Cinque Ports, Deal Town, Dearne, Debenham Leisure Centre, Deeping Rangers, Deerfield Athletic, Denaby United, Denbigh Town, Denby Dale, Denton, Denton United, Depot Battalion Royal Engineers, Deptford Invicta, Deptford Town, DERBY COUNTY, Derby Hills Ivanhoe, Derby Junction, Derby Midland, Derby St Luke's, Derby Town, Derbyshire, Dereham Town, Desborough Town, Devizes Town, Dick Kerrs, Dickinsons, Didcot Town, Dilton Rovers, Dinnington Athletic, Dinnington Main Colliery, Dinnington Town, Dipton United, Diss Town, Distillery, Distington, Dobson and Barlow's, Dodworth United, Dominion, Doncaster Plant Works, Doncaster Rovers, Doncaster St George, Doncaster St James, Donnington School, Donnington Wood Institute, Dorchester Town, Dorking, Dorking Town, Dorking Wanderers, Dosthill Colts, Douglas (Kingswood), Dover, Dover Association, Dover Athletic, Downton, Dreadnought, Dresden United, Driffield Town, Dronfield Woodhouse, Droylsden, Droylsden United, Druids, Drypool Parish Church, Dudley, Dudley Phoenix, Dudley Sports, Dudley Town, Dulwich, Dulwich Hamlet, Dunkirk, Dunstable, Dunstable Thursdays, Dunstable Town, Dunston, Dunston Federation, Dunston Federation Brewery, Dunston UTS, Durham City, Eagley, Earle, Earles Welfare, Earlestown, Earlestown Bohemians, Earlestown White Star, Earlsfield Town, Earlswood Town, Easington Colliery, Easington Colliery Welfare, Easington Sports, East Bierley, East Cowes, East Cowes Victoria, East Cowes Victoria Athletic, East End Park WMC, East Grinstead, East Grinstead Town, East Ham, East Ham United, East Hull United, East Preston, East Riding Amateurs, East Sheen, East Tanfield Colliery Welfare, East Thurrock United, Eastbourne, Eastbourne Borough, Eastbourne Comrades, Eastbourne Old Comrades, Eastbourne Old Town, Eastbourne Royal Engineers Old Comrades, Eastbourne St Mary's, Eastbourne Swifts, Eastbourne Town, Eastbourne United, Eastbourne United Association, Eastern Coachworks, Eastern Counties United, Eastleigh, Eastleigh Athletic, Eastleigh LSWR, Eastville Rovers, Eastville Wanderers, Eastwood Hanley, Eastwood Rangers, Eastwood Town, Ebbsfleet United, Ebbw Vale, Eccles Borough, Eccles United, Ecclesfield, Eccleshall, Eccleshill United, Eckington Red Rose, Eckington Town, Eckington Works, Eden Colliery, Eden Colliery Welfare, Edgware, Edgware Town, Edmonton, Edmonton and Haringey, Edmonton Borough, EFC Cheltenham, Egham, Egham Town, Egremont, Ekco, Eldon Albion, Ellesmere Port Cement, Ellesmere Port Town, Ellesmere Rangers, Ellistown, Ellistown and Ibstock United, Elmore, Elsecar Athletic, Elsecar Main, Elswick Rangers, Eltham, Ely City, Emley, Emsworth, Enderby Town, Endsleigh, Enfield, Enfield (1893), Enfield Town, Epping Town, Eppleton Colliery Welfare, Epsom, Epsom and Ewell, Epsom Athletic, Epsom Town, Ericsson's Athletic, Erith, Erith and Belvedere, Erith Town, Esh Winning, Esh Winning Rangers, Esher Leopold, Eston United, Eton Manor, Etonian Ramblers, Evenwood Town, Eversley and California, EVERTON, Everwarm, Evesham Town, Evesham United, Ewell and Stoneleigh, Exeter City, Exmouth Town, Exning Town, Eynesbury Rovers, Failsworth, Fairfield, Fairford Town, Fakenham Town, Falmouth Town, Fareham, Fareham Town, Farnborough, Farnborough Town, Farncombe, Farnham, Farnham Town, Farnham United Breweries, Farningham, Farsley, Farsley Celtic, Faversham, Faversham Town, Fawley, FC Broxbourne Borough, FC Clacton, FC Halifax Town, FC Romania, FC United of Manchester, Felixstowe and Walton United, Felixstowe Port and Town, Felixstowe Town, Felixstowe United, Felling Colliery, Felling Red Star, Felstead, Feltham, Feltham and Hounslow Borough, Ferndale Athletic, Ferrybridge Amateur, Ferryhill Athletic, Filey Town, Filey United, Finchley, Finedon Revellers, Finedon United, Firbeck Main Colliery, Fisher, Fisher '93, Fisher Athletic, Fisher Athletic London, Fishwick Ramblers, Flackwell Heath, Fleet Spurs, Fleet Town, Fleetwood, Fleetwood Freeport, Fleetwood Rangers, Fleetwood Town, Fletton United, Flint, Flint Town, Flint Town United, Flixton, Florence and Ullcoats United, Fodens Motor Works, Folkestone, Folkestone and Shepway, Folkestone Invicta, Folkestone Town, Folland Sports, Foots Cray, Ford Sports (Dagenham), Ford Sports Daventry, Ford United, Forest Green Rovers, Forest School, Formby, Framingham Town, Frecheville Community Association, Freemantle, Freetown, Frenchay, Friar Lane and Epworth, Friar Lane Old Boys, Fricker Athletic, Frickley Athletic, Frickley Colliery, Frimley Green, Frizington Athletic, Frizington United, Frizington White Star, Frodingham and Appleby Athletic, Frodingham and Brumby United, Frodingham Athletic, Frome Town, Frosts Athletic, Fryston Colliery, Fulham, Fulham Amateurs, Furness Athletic, Furness Vale Rovers, Gainsborough Albion, Gainsborough Trinity, Galgate, Garforth Miners, Garforth Town, Garrards Athletic, Garston Copper Works, Garston Gasworks, Garston Woodcutters, Gateshead, Gateshead Association, Gateshead NER, Gateshead Rodsey, Gateshead Town, Gateshead United, GE Hamble, Gedling Colliery, Gedling Grove, Gedling Miners Welfare, Gedling Town, GER Loughton, GER Romford, Gilberdyke, Gilfach, Gilford Park, Gillingham, Gillingham Town, Gitanos, GKN Sankey, Glapwell, Glasgow Rangers, Glasshoughton Colliery, Glasshoughton Welfare, Glastonbury, Glastonbury Avalon Rovers, Glebe, Glossop, Glossop North End, Gloucester City, Gnome Athletic, Godalming, Godalming and Guildford, Godalming Town, Godmanchester Rovers, Golcar, Goldenhill, Golders Green, Goldthorpe Colliery, Goldthorpe United, Goodrich, Goole, Goole Chevrons, Goole Shipyards, Goole Town, Gorleston, Gornal Athletic, Gorton Villa, Gosforth and Coxlodge, Gosforth and Coxlodge British Legion, Gosport, Gosport Albion, Gosport Athletic, Gosport Borough, Gosport Borough Athletic, Gosport United, Gothic, Gradwell Sports, Graham Street Prims, Gramophone, Grangetown, Grangetown Athletic, Grangetown St Mary's, Grantham, Grantham Avenue, Grantham Rovers, Grantham Town, Grassmoor, Grassmoor Ivanhoe, Grassmoor Comrades, Gravesend, Gravesend Amateurs, Gravesend and Northfleet, Gravesend United, Gravesham Borough, Grays Athletic, Grays Sports, Grays Thurrock United, Grays United, Graysons, Great Bridge Unity, Great Harwood, Great Harwood Town, Great Lever, Great Wakering Rovers, Great Yarmouth Town, Green and Siley Weir Athletic, Green Waves, Greenhalgh's, Greenhouse London, Greenwich Borough, Greenwood Meadows, Gresford, Gresham, Gresley, Gresley Colliery, Gresley Rovers, Gresley Villa, Gretna, Grey Friars, Grimethorpe Athletic, Grimethorpe Colliery Institute, Grimethorpe Rovers, Grimethorpe United, Grimsby Albion, Grimsby All Saints, Grimsby Borough, Grimsby

District, Grimsby Haycroft Rovers, Grimsby Rangers, Grimsby Rovers, Grimsby St John's, Grimsby STC, Grimsby Town, Grimsby YMCA, Grosvenor Park, GSA Sports, Guard's Depot, Guernsey, Guildford, Guildford and Dorking United, Guildford City, Guildford United, Guinness Exports, Guisborough, Guisborough Belmont Athletic, Guisborough Red Rose, Guisborough Town, Guiseley, Guiseley Colliery, Gwynnes Athletic, Hackney Wick, Hadfield, Hadleigh United, Hadley, Haig United, Hailsham Town, Halesowen Harriers, Halesowen Town, Halifax, Halifax Town, Hall Road Rangers, Hallam, Hallen, Halliwell, Halliwell Rovers, Halliwell Unitarians, Halstead Town, Hamble ASSC, Hamble Club, Hamilton Central, Hammersmith Comrades, Hampstead, Hampstead Heathens, Hampstead Town, Hampton, Hampton and Richmond Borough, Hamworthy, Hamworthy United, Handley Page, Handsworth, Handsworth Parramore, Hanham Athletic, Hanley Town, Hanover United, Hanwell, Hanwell Athletic, Hanwell Town, Hanworth Villa, Hapton, Harborough Town, Hardwick Colliery, Harefield United, Haringey and Walthamstow Development, Haringey Borough, Harland and Wolffs, Harlandic, Harlow Town, Harpenden Town, Harrisons, Harrogate, Harrogate Hotspurs, Harrogate Railway Athletic, Harrogate Town, Harrow Borough, Harrow Chequers, Harrow Hill, Harrow Town, Harrow Weald, Harrowby, Harrowby United, Hartford and Davenham United, Hartford St John's, Hartlepool, Hartlepool United, Hartlepools United, Hartley Wintney, Harwich and Parkeston, Harworth Colliery Institute, Hashtag United, Haslingden, Haslington Villa, Hassocks, Hastings and St Leonards, Hastings and St Leonards United, Hastings Town, Hastings United, Haswell Swifts, Hatfield Main, Hatfield Town, Hatfield United, Haughmond, Havant and Waterlooville, Havant Town, Haverfordwest County, Haverhill Borough, Haverhill Rovers, Haverton Hill, Hawks, Haydock, Haydock C&B Recreation, Hayes, Hayes and Yeading United, Hayesco Sports, Hayling United, Haywards Heath, Haywards Heath Town, Haywards Sports, Hazells, Head Wrightsons, Headingly, Headington United, Heanor Athletic, Heanor Town, Heanor United, Heart of Midlothian, Heath Hayes, Heather St Johns, Heaton Stannington, Hebburn, Hebburn Argyle, Hebburn Colliery, Hebburn Leslies, Hebburn St Cuthbert's, Hebburn Town, Hebden Bridge, Heckmondwike, Hednesford, Hednesford Town, Helston Athletic, Hemel Hempstead, Hemel Hempstead Town, Hemingfield, Hemsworth, Hemsworth Colliery, Hemsworth Miners Welfare, Hemsworth West End, Hendon, Hendon Town, Hengrove Athletic, Henley Comrades, Henley, Henley Town, Hereford, Hereford City, Hereford ROAC, Hereford St Martin's, Hereford Thistle, Hereford Town, Hereford United, Herne Bay, Hersham, Hersham United, Hertford Town, Herts Rangers, Hessle, Hessle Old Boys, Hatton United, Hexham, Hexham Athletic, Hexham Excelsior, Hexham Hearts, Hexham Town, Heybridge, Heybridge Swifts, Heywood, Heywood Central, Heywood United, Hickleton Main, High Duty Alloys, High Fell, High Park, High Wycombe, Higham Ferrers Town, Higham Ferrers YMCI, Highbury Union, Higher Walton, Highgate (Rotherham), Highgate United, Highmoor-Ibis, Highthorn, Highworth Town, Hillingdon, Hillingdon Borough, Hinckley, Hinckley AFC, Hinckley Athletic, Hinckley Downes, Hinckley Town, Hinckley United, Hindley, Hindley Green Athletic, Hindpool Athletic, Histon, Histon Institute, Hitchin, Hitchin Athletic, Hitchin Blue Cross, Hitchin Blue Cross Temperance Brigade, Hitchin Town, Hitchin Union Jack, HMS Excellence, HMS Victory, Hobson Wanderers, Hoddesdon, Hoddesdon Town, Hoffmann Athletic (Chelmsford), Hoffmann Athletic (Stonehouse), Hoffmans Athletic, Holbeach United, Holbrook Miners Welfare, Holbrook Sports, Holderness Athletic, Holker Old Boys, Hollands and Blair, Hollington United, Holly Bush, Holme, Holme Head Works, Holmer Green, Holmesdale, Holt United, Holwell Sports, Holwell Works, Holyhead Town, Holyport, Hook Norton, Hook Shipyards, Hooley Hill, Horden Athletic, Horden Colliery, Horden Colliery Welfare, Horfield United, Horley Town, Horncastle, Horncastle Town, Horncastle United, Hornchurch, Hornchurch and Upminster, Horndean, Hornsea Town, Horsforth, Horsham, Horsham Trinity, Horsham YMCA, Horwich, Horwich Central, Horwich RMI, Hotspur, Houghton, Houghton Main Colliery, Houghton Rangers, Houghton Rovers, Hounslow, Hounslow Town, Hove, Hove Park, Hove United, Howden-le-Wear, Howden Rangers, Howdon British Legion, Hoxton Manor, Hoylake, Hoylake Athletic, Hoyland Common Athletic, Hoyland Common Wesleyans, Hoyland Silkstone, Hoyland St Peter's, Hoyland Town, Hucknall Byron, Hucknall Constitutional, Hucknall Portland, Hucknall St John's, Hucknall Town, Huddersfield, HUDDERSFIELD TOWN, Hudsons, Hugglescote Robin Hood, Hull Amateur, Hull Brunswick, Hull City, Hull Dairycoats, Hull Day Street Old Boys, Hull Old Boys, Hull Oriental, Hull Papermills, Hull St Peter's Old Boys, Hull Technical College Old Boys, Hull Town, Hull Wanderers, Hullbridge Sports, Humber Graving Dock, Humber United, Hungerford Town, Hunslet, Huntingdon Town, Huntingdon United, Huntley and Palmers, Hunts County, Hurst, Hurst Nook Rovers, Hurst Ramblers, Hurworth, Hyde, Hyde United, Hylton Colliery Welfare, Hythe and Dibden, Hythe Town, Hythe United, Ibstock Colliery, Ibstock Penistone Rovers, ICI Alkali, Ilford, Ilfracombe Town, Ilkeston, Ilkeston Town, Ilkeston United, Ilminster Town, Immingham, Immingham Town, Imperial Paper Mills, Industry Inn, IPSWICH TOWN, Ipswich Wanderers, Ipswich Works, Irchester United, Irlam, Irlam Town, Ironbridge, Ironbridge United, Irthlingborough Diamonds, Irthlingborough Town, Irwell Springs, Islington Town, Jardines, Jarrow, Jarrow Blackett, Jarrow Caledonians, Jarrow Croft, Jarrow Roofing Boldon Community Association, Johnson and Barnes, JS Fry and Sons, Jump Home Guard, Jump WMC, Jurgens, K Sports, Kells United, Kells Welfare Centre, Kells White Star, Kempston Rovers, Kendal Swifts, Kendal Town, Kennek Ryhope Community Association, Kennington, Kensal Rise, Kensington, Kentish Town, Keswick, Kettering, Kettering St Mary's, Kettering Town, Kettering WMC, Keynsham, Keynsham Town, Kibblesworth, Kidderminster Harriers, Kidderminster Rovers, Kidlington, Kidsgrove Athletic, Kilburn, Kildare, Kilnhurst, Kilnhurst Colliery, Kilnhurst Town, Kilnhurst United, Kimberley, Kimberley Miners Welfare, Kimberley St John's, Kimberley Town, Kimberworth Old Boys, Kinderton Victoria, Kings Langley, King's Lynn, King's Lynn DS&S, King's Lynn Town, Kings Norton Town, Kings Own Rifles, Kingsbury London Tigers, Kingsbury Town, Kingston-on-Thames, Kingston Villa, Kingstonian, Kingswood, Kingswood Rovers, Kippax Parish Church, Kirby Muxloe, Kirkby Collieries, Kirkby Town (Merseyside), Kirkham, Kirkham and Wesham, Kirkley, Kirkley and Pakefield, Kirkley and Waveney, Kiveton Park Colliery, Kiveton Park United, Knaphill, Knaresborough, Knaresborough Town, Knowsley United, Knutsford, Laceby, Knypersley Victoria, Lancaster Athletic, Lancaster City, Lancaster Town, Lanchester Rangers, Lancing, Lancing Athletic, Lancing Old Boys, Langford, Langley Green Victoria, Langley Mill Rangers, Langley Park, Langley Park Colliery Welfare, Langley Park United, Langley Park Villa, Langney Sports, Langney Wanderers, Langold WMC, Langwith Athletic, Langwith Colliery, Larkhall Athletic, Laughton Common, Launceston, Laverstock and Ford, Leadgate Exiles, Leadgate Park, Leagrave and District, Leagrave United, Leamington, Leamington Town, Leasingthorne, Leasingthorne Colliery Welfare, Leatherhead, Leavesden, Leavesden Mental Hospital, Ledbury, Ledbury Town, Leeds, Leeds Albion, Leeds Carnegie, Leeds City, Leeds Steelworks, LEEDS UNITED, Leek, Leek County School Old Boys, Leek Town, LEICESTER CITY, Leicester Fosse, Leicester Imperial, Leicester Nirvana, Leicester Nomads, Leicester Road, Leicester United, Leicester YMCA, Leigh Genesis, Leigh RMI, Leighton Cee Springs, Leighton Town, Leighton United, Leiston, Leiston Works Athletic, Lenton, Leslies, Letchworth, Letchworth Athletic, Letchworth Garden City, Letchworth Town,

Leverstock Green, Lewes, Lewisham St Mary's, Lewison, Leyland, Leyland DAF-SGL, Leyland Motors (Kingston), Leyland Motors (Lancashire), Leys Recreation, Leyton, Leyton Athletic, Leyton Orient, Leyton Pennant, Leyton-Wingate, Leytonstone, Leytonstone / Ilford, Liberty, Lichfield City, Limehouse Town, Linby Church, Linby Colliery, Lincoln Albion, Lincoln City, Lincoln Lindum, Lincoln Moorlands, Lincoln Moorlands Railway, Lincoln Ramblers, Lincoln United, Lindley Temperance, Linfield Athletic, Lingdale Mines, Lingfield, Linotype and Machinery, Lintz Institute, Liskeard Athletic, Litherland REMYCA, Little Common, Little Oakley, Littlehampton, Littlehampton Town, LIVERPOOL, Liverpool Caledonians, Liverpool Police, Liverpool Ramblers, Liverpool South End, Liverpool Stanley, Liversedge, Llandudno, Llandudno Swifts, Llanelli, Llangollen, Llanhilleth, LNWR (Wembley), Lloyds (Sittingbourne), Lock Lane Woodville, Lockheed Leamington, Lockwood Brothers, Loftus, Loftus Albion, London APSA, London Bari, London Caledonians, London Colney, London Generals, London Labour, London Lions, London Olympic, London Paper Mills, London Tigers, London Transport, London United, London Welsh, Long Buckby, Long Crendon, Long Eaton, Long Eaton Midland, Long Eaton Rangers, Long Eaton St Helen's, Long Eaton Town, Long Eaton United, Long Melford, Longfield, Longfleet St Mary's, Longlevens, Longridge Town, Longwell Green Sports, Lopham Methodists, Lordswood, Lostock Gralam, Loughborough, Loughborough Brush Sports, Loughborough Corinthians, Loughborough Dynamo, Loughborough Town, Loughborough United, Loughborough University, Louth Town, Louth United, Lovells Athletic, Lowca, Lower Breck, Lower Darwen, Lower Gornal Athletic, Lowestoft Town, Loxwood, Luddendenfoot, Luddington, Ludlow Town, Luton Amateur, Luton Amateurs and Ramblers, Luton Celtic, Luton Clarence, Luton Crusaders, Luton Reliance, Luton Town, Luton Trinity, Luton Wanderers, Lutterworth Town, Lydney Town, Lye Town, Lymington, Lymington and New Milton, Lymington Town, Lyndhurst, Lynemouth Welfare, Lynn Swifts, Lynton Works, Lyons Club, Lysaghts Excelsior, Lysaghts Sports, Lytham, Mablethorpe United, Macclesfield, Macclesfield Town, Machynlleth, Maesteg Park Athletic, Maidenhead, Maidenhead Norfolkians, Maidenhead Town, Maidenhead United, Maidstone, Maidstone Athletic, Maidstone Church Institute, Maidstone United, Maine Road, Malden Town, Malden Vale, Maldon and Heybridge, Maldon and Tiptree, Maldon Town, Malmesbury Victoria, Maltby Main, Maltby Main Colliery, Maltby Miners Welfare, Malvern Town, Manchester, Manchester Central, MANCHESTER CITY, Manchester North End, MANCHESTER UNITED, Mangotsfield PF, Mangotsfield United, Mansfield, Mansfield Colliery, Mansfield Foresters, Mansfield Mechanics, Mansfield Town, Mansfield Wesley, Mansfield Woodhouse Excelsior, Mansfield Woodhouse Rangers, Manton Colliery, Mapperley, Mapplewell and Staincross Athletic, March Great Eastern Locomotives, March Town, March Town United, Mardy, Marfleet, Margate, Margate Holy Trinity, Marine, Market Drayton Town, Market Harborough Town, Markham Main Colliery, Marlborough Old Boys, Marlow, Marlow United, Marsden, Marske United, Marston Shelton Rovers, Maryport, Mastin Moor Athletic, Matlock, Matlock Town, Mauritius Sports Association, McLaren Sports, Measham Imperial, Measham Town, Medway, Meir KA, Melksham, Melksham and Avon United, Melksham Town, Mellors, Meltham, Meltham Mills, Melton, Melton Town, Merstham, Merthyr Town, Merthyr Tydfil, Metal and Produce Recovery Depot, Methley Perseverance, Metrogas, Metropolitan Police, Metropolitan Railway, Mexborough, Mexborough Athletic, Mexborough Locomotive Works, Mexborough St John's, Mexborough Town, Mexborough Town Athletic, Mexborough West End, Mickleover, Mickleover RBL, Mickleover Sports, Mickley, Mid Kent, Mid Rhondda, Middlesbrough, Middlesbrough Ironopolis, Middlesex Wanderers, Middleton, Middleton Wanderers, Middlewich, Middlewich Athletic, Middlewich Rangers, Mildenhall Town, Mile Oak, Mile Oak Rovers and Youth, Milford Town, Millbrook, Millom Town, Millwall, Millwall Athletic, Millwall Rovers, Millwall United, Minthorpe Corinthians, Milton Keynes, Milton Keynes Borough, Milton Keynes City, Milton Keynes Dons, Milton Keynes Wolverton Town, Milton United, Minehead, Minehead Town, Minerva, Mirfield United, Mirrlees Blackstone, Mitcham Wanderers, Mitchells St George's, Moira United, Mold Town, Mole Valley Predators, Mole Valley SCR, Molesey, Monckton Athletic, Mond Nickel Works, Moneyfields, Monks Hall, Monmouth Town, Montrose Works, Moor Green, Moor Row Villa Rovers, Moore's Athletic, Morecambe, Moresby Park, Moresby Welfare Centre, Moreton Town, Morley, Morpeth Harriers, Morpeth Town, Morris Motors, Morris Sports, Morton Rangers, Mortons Athletic, Mosquitos, Moss Bay, Moss Bay Exchange, Moss Bay United, Mossley, Moulton Verdin, Mount Hill Enterprise, Mount Pleasant, Mountsorrel Town, Mulbarton Wanderers, Murton, Murton Colliery Welfare, Murton Red Star, Mytholmroyd, NAC Athletic, Nanpean Rovers, Nantwich, Nantwich Town, National Radiator Company, Needham Market, Nelson, Netherfield, Netherfield (Holbeach), Netherfield (Kendal), Netherfield Rangers, Netherseal Colliery, Neville's Athletic, New Brighton, New Brighton Tower, New Brighton Tower Amateurs, New Brompton, New Brompton Athletic, New Crusaders, New Gateshead United, New Hartley Rovers, New Hucknall Colliery, New Mills, New Milton, New Milton Town, New Peterborough Sports, New Salamis, New Tredegar, New Tupton United, New Waltham, New Whittington Exchange, Newark, Newark Athletic, Newark Castle Rovers, Newark Town, Newbiggin Athletic, Newbiggin Colliery Welfare, Newbiggin West End, Newburn, Newbury, Newbury Town, Newcastle Benfield, Newcastle Benfield Bay Plastics, Newcastle Benfield Saints, Newcastle Blue Star, Newcastle City, Newcastle East End, Newcastle Town, NEWCASTLE UNITED, Newcastle West End, Newent Town, Newhall Red Rose, Newhall St Edward's, Newhall Swifts, Newhall United, Newhall White Rose, Newhaven, Newhaven Cement Works, Newland Choir, Newmarket Town, Newport (IOW), Newport (Monmouth), Newport (Salop), Newport AFC, Newport Barbarians, Newport County, Newport Pagnell Town, Newportonians, Newquay, Newquay United, Newstead Byron, Newton Abbot, Newton Abbot Spurs, Newton Aycliffe, Newton Common Recreation, Newton Corinthians, Newton Heath, Newton Heath Athletic, Newton Heath LYR, Newton-le-Willows, Newton YMCA, Newtown, Nomads, Normanby Magnesite, Normanby Park Steel Works, North Derbyshire Ramblers, North Engineers, North Ferriby United, North Greenford United, North Hants Ironworks, North Leigh, North Lindsey Midgets, North Liverpool, North Lonsdale Amateurs, North Meols, North Shields, North Shields Athletic, North Skelton, North Skelton Athletic, North Walsham Athletic, North Wingfield, Northallerton '94, Northallerton Town, Northampton Amateurs, Northampton Nomads, Northampton ON Chenecks, Northampton Sileby Rangers, Northampton Spencer, Northampton Town, Northampton Wanderers, Northampton War Team, Northern Nomads, Northfleet, Northfleet United, Northmet, Northwich Victoria, Northwood, Norton and Stockton Ancients, Norton Sports, Norton United, Norton Woodseats, Norwich British Legion, Norwich CBS, Norwich CEYMS, Norwich City, Norwich DS&S, Norwich Priory Athletic, Norwich St Barnabas, Norwich St James', Norwich Thorpe, Norwich United, Norwich YMCA, Norwood Association, Nostell Miners Welfare, NOTTINGHAM

FOREST, NOTTS COUNTY, Notts Jardines, Notts Olympic, Notts Rangers, Notts Swifts, Notts Wanderers, Nuneaton Borough, Nuneaton Griff, Nuneaton Town, Nunhead, Oadby Town, Oak Villa, Oakdale, Oakengates Town, Oakham United, Oakmere, Oakwood, Odd Down, OJM Black Country, Old Brightonians, OLD CARTHUSIANS, Old Castle Swifts, Old Cranleighans, OLD ETONIANS, Old Foresters, Old Grammarians, Old Harrovians, Old Hill Wanderers, Old Hullensians, Old Johnians, Old Kingstonians, Old Lyonians, Old Philberdians, Old Salopians, Old St Mark's, Old St Paul's, Old St Stephen's, Old Westminsters, Old Whittington Mutuals, Old Woodstock Town, Old Wykehamists, Old Xaverians, Oldbury Town, Oldbury United, Oldfields, Oldham Athletic, Oldham Boro, Oldham County, Oldham Town, Oldland Abbotonians, Oldswinford, Ollerton Colliery, Olney Town, Olympian, Olympic, Oreston Rovers, Orient, Ormskirk, Orpington, Orrell, Orwell Works, Osberton Radiator, Osborne Athletic, Ossett Albion, Ossett Town, Ossett United, Oswaldtwistle Rovers, Oswestry, Oswestry Town, Oswestry United, Ottery St Mary, Ouston Rovers, Ouston United, Over Wanderers, Overseal Swifts, Owlerton, Owston Park Rangers, Oxford City, Oxford Cygnets, Oxford United, OXFORD UNIVERSITY, Oxhey Jets, Padiham, Page Green Old Boys, Paget Rangers, Pagham, Palmers (Jarrow), Pandon Temperance, Panthers, Park Grange, Park Royal, Park View, Parkeston Railway, Parkgate, Parkgate and Rawmarsh United, Parkgate United, Parkgate Welfare, Parkgate Works Sports, Parkhouse Colliery, Parliament Street Methodists, Parson Drove, Partick Thistle, Parton United, Paulton Rovers, Paxmans Athletic, Peacehaven and Telscombe, Pearl Assurance, Pease and Partners, Peasedown Miners Welfare, Peasedown St John, Peasley Cross Athletic, Pegasus Juniors, Pegswood United, Pelaw, Pelsall Villa, Pelton Fell, Pembroke Dock, Pendlebury, Penistone Church, Penrith, Penrith Town, Penryn Athletic, Penzance, Percy Main Amateurs, Pershore Town, Peterborough, Peterborough and Fletton United, Peterborough City, Peterborough GN Locomotives, Peterborough Northern Star, Peterborough Sports, Peterborough Town, Peterborough United, Peterborough Westwood Works, Peterlee Newtown, Petersfield Town, Petersfield United, Petter Sports, Petters United, Pewsey Vale, Pewsey YM, Phoenix Bessemer, Phoenix Sports, Phorpres Sports, Pica, Pickering St George's, Pickering Town, Pilgrims, Pilkington Recreation, Pilkington XXX, Pinchbeck United, Pinner, Pinxton, Pinxton Colliery, Pirelli General Cables, Players Athletic, Pleasley United, Plumstead St John's, Plymouth and Stonehouse Gas, Plymouth Argyle, Plymouth Civil Service, Plymouth Parkway, Plymouth United, PO Engineers (Beddington), PO Engineers (Wallington), Polytechnic, Pontefract Borough, Pontefract Collieries, Pontypridd, Poole, Poole St Mary's, Poole Town, Port Clarence, Port of London Authority, Port Sunlight, Port Sunlight Athletic, Port Talbot, Port Vale, Portfield, Porth Athletic, Porthleven, Porthmadog, Portishead Town, Portland, Portland Prison Officers and Portland United, Portland United, Portrack Shamrocks, Portsea Island Gas Company, Portslade, PORTSMOUTH, Portsmouth Albion, Portsmouth Amateurs, Portsmouth Electricity, Portsmouth Gas Company, Portsmouth Rovers, Portsmouth Royal Navy, Post Office Telecoms, Potters Bar Town, Potton United, Prescot, Prescot AFC, Prescot BICC, Prescot Cables, Prescot Town, Prescot Wire Works, Pressed Steel, Preston Colliery, PRESTON NORTH END, Preston Zingari, Prestwich Heys, Princes End United, Prospect United, Prudhoe, Prudhoe Castle, Prudhoe East End, Prudhoe Town, Punjab United (Gravesend), Purfleet, Purton, Purton West End, Pwllheli and District, Pye Radio, Pyebank, Queen's Park, Queens Park Rangers, Quorn, Racing Club Warwick, Radcliffe, Radcliffe Borough, Radcliffe Olympic, Radcliffe Welfare United, Radford, Radstock Town, RAE Farnborough, RAF Cranwell, RAF Halton, RAF Henlow, RAF Martlesham, RAF Uxbridge, Rainham Town, Rainworth Miners Welfare, Raleigh Athletic, Ramblers, RAMC Aldershot, Ramsbottom, Ramsbottom United, Ramsgate, Ramsgate Athletic, Ramsgate Grenville, Ramsgate Press Wanderers, Rangers (London), Ranks, Ransome and Marles, RAOC Cosham, RAOC Hilsea, RASC, Raunds St Peter's, Raunds Town, Ravenscourt Amateurs, Ravensthorpe, Rawmarsh Albion, Rawmarsh Athletic, Rawmarsh Town, Rawmarsh Welfare, Rawtenstall, Rayners Lane, Raynes Park Vale, Reading, Reading Abbey, Reading Amateurs, Reading City, Reading Hornets, Reading Minster, Reading Ramblers, Reading Town, Reading United, Reckitt's, Redbourne Sports, Redbridge, Redbridge Forest, Redcar, Redcar Albion, Redditch, Redditch Town, Redditch United, Redfearns, Redford Sports, Redhill, Reigate Priory, Remnants, Rendel, Renton, Retford Town, Retford United, RGA Gosport, RGA Tynemouth, RGA Weymouth, Rhiwderin, Rhosllanerchrugog, Rhyl, Rhyl Athletic, Rhyl United, Rhymney Town, Richmond Association, Richmond Town, Rickmansworth Town, Riddings, Riley Brothers, Ringmer, Ringwood Town, Ripley Athletic, Ripley Colliery, Ripley Town, Ripley Town and Athletic, Risborough Rangers, Risca Stars, RM Chatham, RM Deal, RM Portsmouth, RN Depot, RNVR Mitcham, Road Sea Southampton, Rocester, Rochdale, Rochdale Town, Rochester, Rochester United, Rock-A-Nore, Rock Ferry, Rockingham Colliery, Rogerstone, Roman Glass St George, Romford, Romford Town, Romsey Town, Romulus, Rose Green, Rosehill, Rossendale, Rossendale United, Rossington Main, Rotherham, Rotherham Amateurs, Rotherham County, Rotherham Main, Rotherham Swifts, Rotherham Town, Rotherham United, Rothwell, Rothwell Athletic, Rothwell Corinthians, Rothwell Parish Church, Rothwell Town, Rothwell Town Swifts, Rothwell White Rose, Roundell, Roundway Hospital, Rowntrees, Royal Arsenal, Royal Artillery Portsmouth, ROYAL ENGINEERS, Royal Engineers Aldershot, Royal Engineers Service Battalion, Royal Engineers Training Battalion, Royal Engineers United, Royal Ordnance Factories, Royal Scots (Chatham), Royal Scots Fusiliers, Royal Welsh Warehouse, Royal Wootton Bassett Town, Royston Midland Institute, Royston Town, Royston United, Royton, RTM Newcastle, Rufford Colliery, Rugby Town, Rugby United, Rugeley, Ruislip Manor, Ruislip Town, Runcorn, Runcorn FC Halton, Runcorn Linnets, Runcorn Town, Runnymede, Rushall Olympic, Rushden, Rushden and Diamonds, Rushden and Higham United, Rushden Fosse, Rushden Town, Rushden Windmill, Rusthall, Rutherford College, Rycroft Athletic, Ryde, Ryde Sports, Rye and Iden United, Rye United, Ryhill and Havercroft United, Ryhill Liberal, Ryhope Colliery Welfare, Ryhope Community Association, Ryhope Comrades, Ryhope Villa, Rylands, Ryton, Ryton and Crawcrook Albion, Saffron Walden, Saffron Walden Town, Sale Holmfield, Salford City, Salford United, Salisbury, Salisbury City, Salisbury Corinthians, Saltash United, Saltburn, Saltburn Swifts, Saltdean United, Salterbeck, Saltney, Sandbach Ramblers, Sandbach United, Sandhurst (Liverpool), Sandhurst Town, Sandiacre Excelsior Foundry, Sandiacre Olympic, Sandown, Sandwell Borough, Sandy Albion, Sandygate Excelsior, Sankeys of Wellington, Savoy (Southall), Savoy Hotel, Sawbridgeworth, Sawbridgeworth Town, Sawston United, Saxons, Scalegill, Scarborough, Scarborough Athletic, Scarborough Junior Imperial, Scarborough Juniors, Scarborough Penguins, Scarborough Rangers, Schorne

College, Scotswood, Scunthorpe and Lindsey United, Scunthorpe United, Seaford, Seaforth Albion, Seaham Albion, Seaham Colliery Welfare, Seaham Colliery Welfare Red Star, Seaham Harbour, Seaham Red Star, Seaham United, Seaham Villa, Seaham White Star, Seaton Delaval, Selby Mizpah, Selby Olympia, Selby Olympia Cake and Oil, Selby Town, Selsey, Selston, Seven Acre and Sidcup, Sevenoaks Town, Severalls Athletic, Shaddongate United, Shaftesbury, Shankhouse, Shanklin and Lake, Sharpness, Shaw Lane Aquaforce, Shaw Lane Association, Shawbury United, Sheepbridge Works, Sheerwater, Sheffield, Sheffield Heeley, Sheffield Providence, Sheffield Simplex Works, SHEFFIELD UNITED, Sheffield Walkley, SHEFFIELD WEDNESDAY, Shefford Town, Shell (Ellesmere Port), Shell Mex, Shelley Community, Shepherds Bush, Sheppey United, Shepshed, Shepshed Albion, Shepshed Charterhouse, Shepshed Dynamo, Shepton Mallet, Shepton Mallet Town, Sherborne Town, Sheringham, Sherwood Colliery, Shields Albion, Shifnal Town, Shilbottle Colliery Welfare, Shildon, Shildon Athletic, Shildon United, Shiphams, Shirebrook, Shirebrook Athletic, Shirebrook Miners Welfare, Shirebrook Town, Shirley Town, Shobnall Villa, Shoeburyness Garrison, Sholing, Sholing Athletic, Sholing Sports, Shoreham, Shorts Sports, Shortwood United, Shotton Colliery Welfare, Shotton Comrades, Shredded Wheat, Shrewsbury Town, Shrewton United, Shrivenham, Shropshire Wanderers, Sidlesham, Sidley United, Silksworth Colliery Welfare, Silsden, Silverwood Colliery, Singers FC, Sittingbourne, Sittingbourne Paper Mills, Skegness Town, Skelmersdale United, Skinningrove Steel Works, Skinningrove United, Skinningrove Works, Skipton Town, Slade Green, Sleaford Town, Slimbridge, Slipway, Slough, Slough Centre, Slough Town, Slough United, Slough Trading Estate, Small Heath, Small Heath Alliance, Smethwick Carriage Works, Smith's Dock, Sneinton, Snowdown Colliery Welfare, Soham Rangers, Soham Town Rangers, Solent University, Solihull Borough, Solihull Moors, Solihull Town, Somerset Rovers, Somersett Ambury V&E, Somersham Town, Somerton Amateurs, Soundwell, South Ashford Invicta, South Bank, South Bank East End, South Bank St Peter's, South Farnborough Athletic, South Hetton Colliery Welfare, South Kirkby Colliery, South Kirkby United, South Liverpool, South Lynn Youth Club, South Normanton Athletic, South Normanton Colliery, South Normanton Miners Welfare, South Normanton Rangers, South Normanton St Michael's, South Norwood, South Park, South Pontop Villa, South Reading, South Shields, South Shields Adelaide, South Shields Albion, South Shields Athletic, South Shields Corinthians, South Shields, Ex-Schoolboys, South Shields Parkside, South Shore, South Tooting, South Weald, South West Ham, South West Ham Comrades, Southall, Southall and Ealing Borough, Southall Park, Southall Town, Southam United, SOUTHAMPTON, Southampton Cambridge, Southampton Civil Service, Southampton St Mary's, Southend Amateurs, Southend Athletic, Southend Corinthians, Southend Manor, Southend United, Southern Railway, Southern United, Southfield, Southport, Southport Central, Southport Leyland Road, Southport Park Villa, Southport Vulcan, Southwick (Sussex), Southwick (Wearside), Spalding United, Spelthorne Sports, Spen Black and White, Spencer Melksham, Spencer Moulton, Spennymoor, Spennymoor Town, Spennymoor United, Spilsby, Sporting Bengal United, Sporting Club Thamesmead, Sporting Khalsa, Squires Gate, St Albans, St Albans (Upton), St Albans Abbey, St Albans City, St Andrew's, St Anne's Oldland, St Anthony's Institute, St Austell, St Bart's Hospital, St Blazey, St Cleopatra's Old Boys, St Francis Rangers, St Frideswides, St Helens Junction, St Helens Recreation, St Helens Town, St Ives Town, St James', St Leonards, St Leonards Amateurs, St Leonards Stamcroft, St Leonards United, St Luke's, St Margaretsbury, St Mark's, St Neots and District, St Neots St Mary, St Neots Town, St Peter's Albion, St Peter's Institute, St Philip's Athletic, St Philip's Marsh Adult School, St Stephen's, Stableford's Works, Stafford Rangers, Stafford Road Works, Stafford Town, Staffordshire Casuals, Staines, Staines Lagonda, Staines Lammas, Staines Town, Staithes United, Stakeford Albion, Stalybridge Celtic, Stalybridge Rovers, Stamco, Stamford, Stamford Town, Standard Telephones, Stanley (Bucks), Stanley United, Stanlow Social, Stansfeld, Stansted, Stanton Hill DS&S, Stanton Hill Victoria, Stanton ironworks, Stanway Rovers, Stapenhill, Staple Hill, Stapleford Brookhill, Stapleford Town, Staveley, Staveley Miners Welfare, Staveley Town, Staveley Welfare, Steel Peech and Tozer Social Services, Sterling Athletic, Stevenage, Stevenage Athletic, Stevenage Borough, Stevenage Town, Stewartby Works, Stewarts and Lloyds, Steyning, Steyning Town, Steyning Town Community, Stockport County, Stockport Sports, Stocksbridge Church, Stocksbridge Park Steels, Stocksbridge Works, Stockton, Stockton Heath Albion, Stockton Malleable Institute, Stockton Shamrocks, Stockton St John's, Stockton Town, Stoke, Stoke City, Stoke United, Stokenchurch, Stokesley, Stokesley Sports Club, Stone Dominoes, Stone Old Alleynians, Stonehouse, Stoneycroft, Stork, Stork (Purfleet), Stotfold, Stourbridge, Stourport Swifts, Stourton United, Stowmarket, Stowmarket Corinthians, Stowmarket Town, Stratford Town, Stratford Town Amateurs, Streatham Town, Street, Stroud, Studley, Sudbury Town, Sudbury Wanderers, Summerstown, Sun Sports, Sunbeam Motors, SUNDERLAND, Sunderland Albion, Sunderland East End Black Watch, Sunderland Nissan, Sunderland Olympic, Sunderland Rovers, Sunderland Royal Rovers, Sunderland Ryhope Colliery Welfare, Sunderland Ryhope Community Association, Sunderland West End, Sunniside Rangers, Surbiton Hill, Surbiton Town, Surrey Wanderers, Sutton (Hull), Sutton Athletic, Sutton Coldfield Town, Sutton Common Rovers, Sutton Court, Sutton Junction, Sutton Town, Sutton Town (2002), Sutton Town (Ashfield), Sutton United, Suttons, Swadlincote, Swadlincote Town, Swaffham Town, Swaine Hill United, Swalwell Axwell Rovers, Swanage Town, Swanage Town and Herston, Swanley Athletic, Swanscombe, Swansea City, Swansea Town, Swaythling, Swifts, Swindon Amateurs, Swindon BR Corinthians, Swindon Corinthians, Swindon GWR Corinthians, Swindon Supermarine, Swindon Town, Swindon Victoria, Swinton Town, Symingtons Recreation, Tadcaster Albion, Tadley Calleva, Takeley, Talbot Stead, Tamworth, Tamworth Castle, Tanfield Lea Rovers, Tankersley, Tankersley United, Tate Institute, Taunton, Taunton and Newtons United, Taunton Castle, Taunton Town, Taunton United, Tavistock, Team Bath, Team Bury, Team Northumbria, Team Solent, Telford United, Terrington, Teversal, Teversal and Silverhill Colliery Welfare, Thackley, Thame, Thame Rangers, Thame United, Thames, Thames Association, Thames Ironworks, Thamesmead Town, Thanet United, Thatcham, Thatcham Town, Thetford Recreation, Thetford Town, Third Lanark Rifle Volunteers, Thoresby Colliery Welfare, Thornaby, Thornaby Amateurs, Thornaby-on-Tees, Thornaby St Patrick, Thornaby Utopians, Thornbury Town, Thorndale, Thorne Colliery, Thornhill Lees Albion, Thornhill United, Thornley Albion, Thornley Colliery Welfare, Thornton United, Thornycroft Athletic, Thornycrofts (Basingstoke), Thornycrofts (Woolston), Thorpe Hesley, Thrapston Town, Three Bridges, Threlkeld, Throckley Welfare, Thurnby Nirvana, Thurnscoe Park Avenue, Thurnscoe Victoria, Thurrock, Thynnes Athletic, Tibshelf Colliery, Tilbury, Timperley, Timsbury, Timsbury Athletic, Tinsley Park, Tipton Town, Tiptree United, Tiverton Town, Tividale, Tokyngton Manor, Ton Pentre, Tonbridge, Tonbridge Angels, Tonge, Tonge Temperance, Tooting and Mitcham United,

Tooting Bec, Tooting Graveney, Tooting Town, Torpoint Association, Torpoint Athletic, Torquay Town, Torquay United, Torrington, TOTTENHAM HOTSPUR, Tottington, Totton, Totton and Eling, Tow Law, Tow Law Town, Tower Hamlets, Trafalgar, Trafalgar Sports, Trafford, Tranmere Rovers, Trawden Forest, Treeton, Treeton Reading Room, Treherbert, Trent Rovers, Trimdon Grange, Trimdon Grange Colliery, Tring Athletic, Tring Town, Troedyrhiw, Troedyrhiw Stars, Trojans, Trowbridge Town, Truro City, Tuffley Rovers, Tufnell Park, Tufnell Park Edmonton, Tufnell Spartans, Tunbridge Wells, Tunbridge Wells Rangers, Tunbridge Wells United, Turton, Tushingham Brick Works, Tutbury Town, Twerton St Michael's, Twickenham, Twizell United, Tyldesley Albion, Tyne Association, UGB St Helens, UGBM Sports, Ulster, Ulverston Town, Union Jack, United Hospital, United London Swifts, United Services Portsmouth, Unity, Upminster, Upper Armley, Upton Colliery, Upton Park, Upton Rangers, Urmston, Urmston Old Boys, Ushaw Moor, Usworth Colliery, Usworth Social Club, Uxbridge, Uxbridge Town, Vampires, Vauxhall GM, Vauxhall Motors, Vauxhall Motors (Ellesmere Port), Vauxhall Motors (Luton), VCD Athletic, Venner Sports, Vernon Athletic, Verwood Town, Vickers Armstrong, Vickerstown, Viking Greenford, Viking Sports, Virginia Water, VS Rugby, VT FC, Vulcans, Wadebridge Town, Wadham Lodge, Wakefield, Wakefield and Emley, Wakefield City, Wakefield-Emley, Walgrave Amber, Walkden Central, Walker Celtic, Walker Church Institute, Walker Parish Church, Walker Park, Wallasey Borough, Wallasey Rovers, Wallasey Transport, Wallasey United, Wallingford Town, Wallington, Wallsend, Wallsend Elm Villa, Wallsend Park Villa, Wallsend Town, Walsall, Walsall Borough, Walsall Jolly Club, Walsall LMS, Walsall Phoenix, Walsall Swifts, Walsall Town, Walsall Town Swifts, Walsall Wood, Walsden United, Walsham-le-Willows, Walshaw, Waltham Abbey, Waltham Comrades, Waltham Forest, Waltham Glendale, Walthamstow, Walthamstow Avenue, Walthamstow Grange, Walthamstow Pennant, Walthamstow Town, Walton and Hersham, Walton Casuals, Walton-on-Thames, THE WANDERERS, Wandsworth, Wandsworth and Norwood, Wandsworth United, Wanstead, Wantage Town, War Office, Warboys Town, Wardle and Barbridge United, Wardley Welfare, Ware, Wareham Town, Warley, Warley County Borough, Warlingham, Warminster Town, Warmley, Warmley Amateurs, Warrington Rylands, Warrington St Elphin's, Warrington Town, Warwick County, Washington, Washington Chemical Works, Washington Colliery, Washington Nissan, Washington United, Waterlooville, Waterlows, Waterlows Athletic, Watford, Watford British Legion, Watford Old Boys, Watford Orient, Watford Rovers, Watford Spartans, Watford St Mary's, Watford Victoria Works, Wath Athletic, Wath Brow United, Wath-upon-Dearne, Watton United, Wealden, Wealdstone, Wednesbury Old Athletic, Wednesbury Strollers, Wednesbury Town, THE WEDNESDAY, Wednesfield, Wednesfield Social, Welbeck Colliery, Welling Town, Welling United, Wellingborough, Wellingborough Redwell Stars, Wellingborough Town, Wellingborough Whitworth, Wellington (Herefordshire), Wellington (Somerset), Wellington St George's, Wellington Town, Wellington Works, Wells Amateurs, Wells City, Wells St Cuthbert's, Welshpool, Welton Rovers, Welwyn, Welwyn Garden City, Wembley, Wesley Rangers, West Allotment Celtic, West Auckland, West Auckland Town, West Birmingham, West Bridgford, WEST BROMWICH ALBION, West Bromwich Town, West Croydon, West Didsbury and Chorlton, West End, West End Rovers, West Essex, West Ham Garfield, WEST HAM UNITED, West Hampstead, West Hartlepool, West Hartlepool Expansion, West Hartlepool NER, West Hartlepool Perseverance, West Hartlepool Rovers, West Hartlepool St Joseph's, West Herts, West Hull Albion, West Kirby, West London Old Boys, West Manchester, West Midlands Police, West Norwood, West Sleekburn Welfare, West Stanley, West Thurrock Athletic, West Vale Ramblers, West Wylam Colliery Welfare, Westbury United, Westfield, Westfields, Westham, Westhoughton, Westland Works, Weston-super-Mare, Weston-super-Mare St John's, Westside, Weybridge, Weybridge Swallows, Weymouth, Weymouth SAA, Wheatley Hill Colliery, Wheelock Albion, Whickham, Whiston, Whitburn, Whitburn Colliery Welfare, Whitby, Whitby Albion Rangers, Whitby Town, Whitby United, Whitchurch, Whitchurch Alport, Whitchurch United, White Ensign, White Star Wanderers, White's Sports Club, Whitehaven, Whitehaven Athletic, Whitehaven Colliery Recreation, Whitehaven Wellington Villa, Whitehaven White Rose, Whitehawk, Whiteheads, White-le-Head Rangers, Whitley and Monkseaton, Whitley Bay, Whitley Bay Athletic, Whitstable Town, Whitton United, Whitwell Colliery, Whitwick Colliery, Whitwick Imperial, Whitwick White Cross, Whyteleafe, Whyteleafe Albion, Wick, Wick and Barnham United, Widnes, Widnes County, Widnes DS&S, WIGAN ATHLETIC, Wigan Borough, Wigan County, Wigan Robin Park, Wigan Rovers, Wigan Town, Wigan United, Wigmore Athletic, Wigston Fields, Wigton Athletic, Wigton Harriers, Willand Rovers, Willaston White Star, Willenhall, Willenhall Pickwick, Willenhall Swifts, Willenhall Town, Willesden, Willesden Town, William Colliery, Willington, Willington Athletic, Willington Temperance, Wills Sports, Wilmslow Albion, Wiltshire County Mental Hospital, WIMBLEDON, Wimblington Old Boys, Wimborne, Wimborne Town, Wincanton Town, Winchester, Winchester City, Windermere, Windsor, Windsor and Eton, Windsor and Eton Temperance, Windsor Home Park, Windsor Phoenix Athletic, Windy Nook, Wingate (Barnet), Wingate (Durham), Wingate Albion, Wingate Albion Comrades, Wingate and Finchley, Wingate Athletic, Wingate Colliery Welfare, Winsford United, Winslow United, Winterbourne United, Winterton Rangers, Wirral Railway, Wisbech Town, Witham Town, Withdean 2000, Witheridge, Withernsea, Witney Town, Witney United, Witton, Witton Albion, Witton Park Institute, Wivenhoe Town, Wodson Park, Woking, Wokingham and Emmbrook, Wokingham Town, Wolesley Athletic, Wolsingham, Wolsingham Town, Wolsingham Welfare, Wolverhampton Amateur, Wolverhampton Casuals, Wolverhampton Sporting Community, WOLVERHAMPTON WANDERERS, Wolverton, Wolverton L&NWR, Wolverton Town, Wolverton Town (Milton Keynes), Wolverton Town and BR, Wombwell, Wombwell Athletic, Wombwell Main Welfare, Wombwell Rising Star, Wombwell Sporting Association, Wombwell Town, Wood Grange, Wood Green Town, Wood Skinners, Woodbridge Town, Woodford, Woodford Albion, Woodford Bridge, Woodford Crusaders, Woodford Town, Woodford United, Woodford Wells, Woodhouse, Woodhouse Britannia, Woodley Sports, Woodley United, Woodstock Sports, Woolston, Woolwich, Woolwich Arsenal, Woolwich Borough Council Athletic, Woolwich Ordnance, Woolwich Polytechnic, Woolwich Royal Artillery, Wootton Bassett Town, Wootton Blue Cross, Worcester City, Workington, Workington AFC, Workington DS&S, Worksop Parramore, Worksop Town, Worsbrough Bridge Miners Welfare, Worthing, Worthing United, Wren Rovers, Wrexham, Wrexham Olympic, Wrockwardine Wood, Wroxham, Wycliffe, Wycombe Wanderers, Wymondham Town, Wythenshawe Amateurs, Yate Town, Yaxley, Yeading, Yeadon Celtic, Yeovil & Petters United, Yeovil Casuals, Yeovil Town, Yiewsley, York City, Yorkshire Amateur, Youlgrave

The Best 150 Debut Performances in FA Cup

16 – 0	Home	**New Crusaders**	vs	*Woking*	1905/06	Q1 Rd
14 – 0	Home	**Exeter City**	vs	*Weymouth*	1908/09	Q1 Rd
12 – 0	Home	**Ardwick** (Man City)	vs	*Liverpool Stanley*	1890/91	Q1 Rd
11 – 0	Away	**Huddersfield Town**	vs	*Heckmondwike*	1909/10	Pr Rd
		Bentley Colliery	vs	*Bridlington Albion*	1912/13	EP Rd
11 – 0	Home	**(Royal) Arsenal**	vs	*Lyndhurst*	1889/90	Q1 Rd
		Walton & Hersham	vs	*Epsom Town*	1945/46	Q1 Rd
10 – 0	Home	**Portsmouth**	vs	*Ryde*	1899/00	Q1 Rd
		West Hampstead	vs	*Hampstead**	1899/00	Q1 Rd
		Gilfach	vs	*Cross Keys*	1921/22	EP Rd
9 – 0	Away	**Old St Paul's**	vs	*Dulwich*	1889/90	Q1 Rd
9 – 0	Home	**Wednesbury Old Ath.**	vs	*Mitchells St George's*	1881/82	1st Rd
		Eastleigh LSWR (Ath.)	vs	*Clifton*	1895/96	Q1 Rd
		Eastern Counties Utd.	vs	*Orwell Works*	1936/37	EP Rd
		Long Eaton United	vs	*Players Athletic*	1956/57	Q1 Rd
12 – 4	Home	**Thurnscoe Victoria**	vs	*Sheffield*	1930/31	Pr Rd
9 – 1	Away	**Achilles**	vs	*Old Grammarians*	1948/49	Pr Rd
9 – 1	Home	**Peterboro/Fletton U.**	vs	*Leighton Utd (Town)*	1923/24	Pr Rd
		Bexley	vs	*Woolwich Boro Coun.*	1932/33	EP Rd
		North Skelton Ath.	vs	*Bridlington Trinity*	1954/55	Q1 Rd
		Alfold	vs	*Shoreham*	2020/21	EP Rd
8 – 0	Home	**Scunthorpe & Lynd U.**	vs	*Withernsea*	1909/10	Pr Rd
		Retford Town	vs	*British Oil & Cake M.*	1921/22	EP Rd
		Humber United	vs	*Pickering St George's*	1929/30	EP Rd
		Harrow Town (Boro.)	vs	*Berkhamsted Town*	1945/46	Pr Rd
		Stowmarket Cor. (T.)	vs	*Norwich SOBU*	1948/49	Pr Rd
9 – 2	Home	**Leyton***	vs	*Upton Park*	1896/97	Q1 Rd
8 – 1	Away	**Fryston Colliery**	vs	*Brigg**	1913/14	EP Rd
		BWI Reading	vs	*Henley Town*	1924/25	EP Rd
		Garrards Athletic	vs	*Chippenham Town*	1929/30	EP Rd
		Wingate (Barnet)*	vs	*Acton Town*	1948/49	EP Rd
8 – 1	Home	**Bradford (Park Ave.)***	vs	*South Kirkby Colliery*	1908/09	Q1 Rd
		Grimsby Rangers	vs	*Selby Mizpah*	1908/09	Q1 Rd
		Pontypridd	vs	*Lysaghts Excelsior*	1912/13	Pr Rd
		Harworth Coll. Ath.	vs	*Upton Colliery*	1946/47	Pr Rd

7 – 0	Away	**Broughton Rangers**	vs	*Reckitt's (Hull)*	1926/27	EP Rd
7 – 0	Home	**Turton**	vs	*Brigg**	1879/80	1st Rd
		93rd Highland Reg.	vs	*Luton Town*	1890/91	Q1 Rd
		1st Highland Light Inf.	vs	*Maidstone**	1891/92	Q1 Rd
		Oldham County	vs	*Oswaldtwistle Rovers*	1896/97	Q1 Rd
		Plymouth Argyle	vs	*Whiteheads*	1903/04	Q3 Rd
		Crystal Palace	vs	*Clapham*	1905/06	Q1 Rd
		Spalding United	vs	*Bourne Town*	1921/22	EP Rd
		Park Royal	vs	*Abingdon Town*	1930/31	EP Rd
		Eynesbury Rovers	vs	*Luton Amateur*	1935/36	PR Rd
		Newquay	vs	*Weston-s-Mare St J.*	1950/51	EP Rd
		Bishop's Cleeve	vs	*Minehead (Town)*	2004/05	EP Rd
9 – 3	Home	**Sheringham**	vs	*March Great East. U.*	1927/28	EP Rd
8 – 2	Away	**Crook CW** (Town)	vs	*Eden Colliery*	1946/47	Pr Rd
8 – 2	Home	**Sunderland Albion**	vs	*Shankhouse*	1888/89	Q1 Rd
		Brighton United	vs	*Romford (Town)**	1898/99	Pr Rd
8 – 2	Home	**Dudley** (Town)	vs	*Brierley Hill Alliance*	1899/00	Q1 Rd
		Black Lane Rovers	vs	*Croston*	1924/25	EP Rd
		Garston Woodcutters	vs	*Oakmere (Liverpool)*	1938/39	Pr Rd
7 – 1	Away	**Lancing Old Boys**	vs	*Barnes*	1885/86	1st Rd
		Nantwich (Town)	vs	*Hartford St John's*	1888/89	Q1 Rd
		Linfield Athletic	vs	*Ulster*	1888/89	Q2 Rd
		Royal Artillery	vs	*Eastleigh LSWR (Ath.)*	1896/97	Q1 Rd
		Aberaman	vs	*Caerphilly*	1902/03	Q2 Rd
		Dover*	vs	*Betteshanger CW*	1937/38	EP Rd
7 – 1	Home	**L'pool Caledonians**	vs	*Wrexham*	1892/93	Q1 Rd
		Ardsley Athletic	vs	*Goldthorpe Colliery*	1920/21	EP Rd
		Fleetwood*	vs	*Great Harwood*	1947/48	Pr Rd
6 – 0	Away	**New Brighton Tower**	vs	*Middlewich Rangers*	1897/98	Q1 Rd
		South Liverpool*	vs	*Warrington St Elphin*	1898/99	Q1 Rd
		Mitcham Wanderers	vs	*Gwynnes Athletic*	1923/24	EP Rd
		New Mills*	vs	*North Liverpool*	1923/24	EP Rd
		Corsham Town	vs	*Odd Down*	1950/51	EP Rd
		Bethesda Athletic	vs	*Pwllheli & District*	1969/70	Q1 Rd
6 – 0	Home	**Southwick** (Wearside)	vs	*Bishop Auckland CI*	1890/91	Q1 Rd
		Heywood	vs	*North Meols*	1891/92	Q1 Rd
		Buxton	vs	*Gedling Grove*	1891/92	Q2 Rd
		Garston Copper Wrks.	vs	*Birkenhead LNWR*	1897/98	Q1 Rd
		Newport County*	vs	*Mond Nickel Works*	1913/14	Pr Rd

6 – 0	Home	**Chesham United**	vs	*Tufnell Spartan*	1919/20	Pr Rd
		Chepstow Town	vs	*Oakdale*	1920/21	EP Rd
		Parkhouse Colliery	vs	*Jump Home Guard*	1949/50	EP Rd
		East Preston	vs	*Peacehaven & Telsc.*	1998/99	Q1 Rd
		Biggleswade United	vs	*Haverhill Rovers*	2005/06	EP Rd
8 – 3	Home	**Hyde United**	vs	*Timperley*	1935/36	EP Rd
7 – 2	Home	**Old St Mark's**	vs	*East Sheen*	1887/88	1st Rd
		Tavistock	vs	*Taunton (Town)*	1948/49	EP Rd
6 – 1	Away	**Sheffield United**	vs	*Scarborough*	1889/90	Q1 Rd
		1st Scots Guards	vs	*Slough**	1896/97	Pr Rd
		Guildford United*	vs	*East Grinstead (T.)*	1921/22	EP Rd
		Alfreton Town	vs	*Shirebrook MW*	1960/61	Q1 Rd
		AFC Sudbury	vs	*Diss Town*	1999/00	Pr Rd
6 – 1	Home	**Windsor Phoenix Ath.**	vs	*Schorne College*	1890/91	Q1 Rd
		Sheepbridge Works	vs	*Clay Cross Town*	1892/94	Q2 Rd
		Brentford	vs	*1st Coldstream Grds.*	1897/98	Q1 Rd
		Hindley	vs	*Blackburn Park Road*	1898/99	Q1 Rd
		Bradford City	vs	*Rockingham Colliery*	1903/04	Q1 Rd
		Chelsea	vs	*1st Grenadier Guards*	1905/06	Q1 Rd
		Newark Castle Rovers	vs	*Sneinton (Carlton T.)*	1930/31	Pr Rd
		Aberaman/Aberdare	vs	*Llanelli*	1945/46	Q1 Rd
		Chippenham United	vs	*Radstock Town*	1948/49	EP Rd
		Fleet Town	vs	*Alton Town*	1966/67	Q1 Rd
		King's Lynn Town	vs	*Whitton United*	2011/12	EP Rd
		Longridge Town	vs	*Barnoldswick Town*	2019/20	EP Rd
5 – 0	Away	**Wigan United**	vs	*Haydock*	1901/02	Q1 Rd
		Maidstone Cl (Ath.)	vs	*Royal Eng. Serv. Batt.*	1903/04	EP Rd
		1st King's Royal Rifles	vs	*Sth. Farnborough Ath.*	1911/12	Pr Rd
		Lenton	vs	*Basford United*	1920/21	EP Rd
		Wombwell Athletic	vs	*Thurnscoe Victoria*	1946/47	Pr Rd
		Walthamstow Penn.	vs	*Beckenham Town*	1989/90	Pr Rd
		Almondsbury (UWE)	vs	*Amesbury Town*	2010/11	EP Rd
5 – 0	Home	**Church**	vs	*Clitheroe (Central)*	1882/83	1st Rd
		Darlington St August.	vs	*Darlington**	1889/90	Q1 Rd
		Langley Green Vic.	vs	*Kettering (Town)*	1890/91	Q1 Rd
		Kensal Rise	vs	*Middlesex Wanderers*	1904/05	Pr Rd
		Linby Church	vs	*Kimberley St John's*	1904/05	Q1 Rd
		Newport (Wales)	vs	*Frome Town*	1906/07	Q1 Rd
		Walthamstow Grange	vs	*Woodford*	1908/09	Pr Rd
		Wood Green Town*	vs	*Chesham Town*	1909/10	Q1 Rd
		Gateshead (Town)*	vs	*Pelaw*	1912/13	EP Rd

5 – 0	Home	**Bideford Town**	vs	*Glastonbury*	1925/26	EP Rd
		5th Royal Tank Rgmt.	vs	*Coleford Athletic*	1927/28	EP Rd
		Lysaghts Sports	vs	*Selby Olympia C&O*	1933/34	Pr Rd
		New Gateshead Utd.	vs	*St Peter's Albion*	1935/36	EP Rd
		Vickers Armstrong	vs	*PO Engineers*	1946/47	PR Rd
		Tonbridge (Angels)	vs	*Bexley*	1948/49	EP Rd
		Hatfield Main	vs	*Yorkshire Amateur*	1968/69	Q1 Rd
		Shifnal Town	vs	*New Mills**	1981/82	Pr Rd
		Oakwood	vs	*Camberley Town*	1990/91	Pr Rd
		Somersett Ambury VE	vs	*Clapton*	2001/02	Pr Rd
		Holbrook MW	vs	*Heanor Town*	2009/10	EP Rd
		Dorking Wanderers	vs	*Canterbury City*	2013/14	EP Rd
		Salisbury	vs	*Bitton*	2016/17	Pr Rd
9 – 5	Home	**Hoylake Athletic**	vs	*Southport Leyland Rd*	1949/40	EP Rd
7 – 3	Away	**Head Wrightsons**	vs	*Filey Town*	1950/51	Pr Rd
7 – 3	Home	**Newark***	vs	*Spilsby*	1884/85	1st Rd
		Llangollen	vs	*Oswestry (Town)*	1887/88	1st Rd
		Pease & Partners	vs	*Whitby Albion Rgrs.*	1931/32	Pr Rd
		Stewarts & Lloyds*	vs	*Wellingborough T.**	1936/37	Pr Rd
		Wolsingham Welfare	vs	*Chilton Athletic*	1954/55	Q1 Rd
6 – 2	Away	**Higham Ferrers Town**	vs	*Spilsby*	1921/22	EP Rd
		Gosport Borough (A.)	vs	*Salisbury Corinthians*	1945/46	Q1 Rd
		Tividale	vs	*Heanor Town*	1975/76	Q1 Rd
6 – 2	Home	**Etonian Ramblers**	vs	*Romford (Town)**	1882/83	1st Rd
		Rossendale	vs	*Irwell Springs (Bacup)*	1883/84	1st Rd
		Crouch End	vs	*Ashford United**	1891/92	Q1 Rd
		Crook (Town)*	vs	*Seaham Albion*	1897/98	Pr Rd
		Brighton & Hove Alb.	vs	*Brighton Athletic*	1901/02	Pr Rd
		Sutton (Hull)	vs	*Grimsby Rovers*	1912/13	EP Rd
		Christchurch	vs	*Wareham Town*	1913/14	EP Rd
		Lancaster Town (City)	vs	*Appleby*	1913/14	Pr Rd
		Bigrigg United	vs	*Barrow Novocasts.*	1914/15	Pr Rd
		Bridlington Town*	vs	*Redcar*	1920/21	EP Rd
		Goldthorpe United	vs	*Maltby Main Coll.**	1927/28	EP Rd
		Stoneycroft	vs	*Thorndale*	1938/29	Pr Rd
		Ruislip Manor	vs	*Tufnell Park**	1948/49	EP Rd

**Different from current / later club with same/similar name*

The Worst 150 Debut Performances in FA Cup

0 – 26	Away	**Hyde***	vs	*Preston North End*	1887/88	1st Rd
3 – 19	Away	**Badsey Rangers**	vs	*Oswestry Town*	1933/34	EP Rd
1 – 16	Away	**Middleton Wanderers**	vs	*Blackhall Coll. Welf.*	1938/39	EP Rd
0 – 15	Away	**White's Sports Club**	vs	*Portsmouth Ams.*	1919/20	Pr Rd
0 – 14	Home	**Hurworth**	vs	*Stockton**	1890/91	Q1 Rd
		Brigg Town	vs	*Cleethorpes Town**	1919/20	Pr Rd
0 – 13	Home	**Amersham Town**	vs	*Wycombe Wanderers*	1950/51	EP Rd
0 – 13	Away	**Basford Rovers**	vs	*Notts County*	1886/87	1st Rd
		Warrington St Elphin	vs	*Flint (Town Utd.)*	1894/95	Q1 Rd
		Wakefield City*	vs	*Denaby United*	1907/08	Q1 Rd
		Radcliffe Welfare Utd.	vs	*South Shields**	1947/48	Pr Rd
1 – 13	Away	**Rhyl** (United)	vs	*Ashton North End*	1898/99	Q1 Rd
		Apsley (Hemel Hemp.)	vs	*Luton Town*	1901/02	Q1 Rd
0 – 12	Home	**Oswaldtwistle Rovers**	vs	*Blackburn Olympic*	1884/85	1st Rd
		Warmley	vs	*Walsall (Town Swifts)*	1890/91	Q1 Rd
1 – 12	Away	**Deal Ports** (Town)	vs	*Margate*	1919/20	Pr Rd
0 – 11	Home	**Bridlington Albion**	vs	*Bentley Colliery*	1912/13	EP Rd
		David Brown Athletic	vs	*Ossett Town*	1948/49	EP Rd
		Team Northumbria	vs	*Consett*	2007/08	EP Rd
0 – 11	Away	**Burnley**	vs	*Darwen Old Wands.*	1885/86	1st Rd
		Bognor (Regis Town)	vs	*Tunbridge Wells Rgrs.*	1908/09	Q1 Rd
		Epsom Town	vs	*Walton & Hersham*	1945/46	Q1 Rd
1 – 11	Away	**Blackpool St John's**	vs	*Blackburn Rovers*	1882/83	1st Rd
		Raleigh Athletic	vs	*Ransome & Marles*	1930/31	Pr Rd
		East Riding Amateurs	vs	*Boston**	1931/32	Pr Rd
0 – 10	Home	**Crewe Alexandra**	vs	*Queen's Park*	1883/84	1st Rd
		Croydon Park	vs	*2nd Scots Guards*	1893/94	Q1 Rd
0 – 10	Away	**Furness Vale Rovers**	vs	*Northwich Victoria*	1886/87	1st Rd
		Cross Keys	vs	*Gilfach*	1921/22	EP Rd
1 – 10	Home	**Reading Ramblers**	vs	*Bristol St George*	1898/99	Q1 Rd
1 – 10	Away	**Caernarvon Wands.**	vs	*Stoke (City)*	1886/87	1st Rd
		Jardines (Nottm.)	vs	*Notts Rangers*	1887/88	1st Rd
		Selby Olympia (C&O)	vs	*Apperley Bridge*	1920/21	EP Rd
		Dawdon Recreation	vs	*Spennymoor United*	1932/33	EP Rd

1 – 10	Away	**Tate Institute**	vs	*Grays Athletic*	1932/33	Pr Rd
0 – 9	Away	**Mitchells St George's**	vs	*Wednesbury Old Ath.*	1881/82	1st Rd
		Lincoln Ramblers	vs	*Notts County*	1887/88	1st Rd
		Hurst Nook Rovers	vs	*Heywood Central*	1893/94	Q1 Rd
		Carlisle City*	vs	*Oswaldtwistle Rovers*	1895/96	Pr Rd
		Newport (Salop)	vs	*Stourbridge*	1897/98	Q1 Rd
		Barrow Novocasts.	vs	*Workington**	1908/09	Q1 Rd
		Ringwood Town	vs	*Newport (IOW)*	1934/35	EP Rd
		London Transport	vs	*Barking**	1946/47	EP Rd
		Crowborough Ath.	vs	*Corinthian*	1994/95	Pr Rd
4 – 12	Away	**Thame** (United)	vs	*Wealdstone*	1931/32	EP Rd
1 – 9	Home	**Doncaster Rovers**	vs	*Rotherham Town*	1888/89	Q1 Rd
1 – 9	Away	**Blackburn Park Road**	vs	*Blackburn Rovers*	1881/82	1st Rd
		(L'boro) **Brush Works**	vs	*L'borough Corinth.*	1919/20	Q1 Rd
		Wolesley Athletic	vs	*Stafford Rangers*	1922/23	EP Rd
		Beccles	vs	*Wisbech Town*	1925/26	Pr Rd
0 – 8	Home	**Barrow St Luke's**	vs	*Workington**	1909/10	Q1 Rd
		Acomb WMC	vs	*Mexborough Town**	1914/15	Pr Rd
0 – 8	Away	**Hoddesdon** (Town)	vs	*Old Foresters*	1884/85	1st Rd
		Darlington*	vs	*Grimsby Town*	1885/86	2nd Rd
		Hednesford (Town)	vs	*Small Heath (B'ham)*	1890/91	Q1 Rd
		Leeds	vs	*Barnsley (St Peter's)*	1894/95	Q2 Rd
		Newhall St Edmunds	vs	*Ripley Athletic*	1908/09	Pr Rd
		Withernsea	vs	*Scunthorpe & Lind. U.*	1909/10	Pr Rd
		Rhiwderin	vs	*Newport County**	1914/15	Pr Rd
		British Oil & Cake M.	vs	*Retford Town*	1921/22	EP Rd
		Pickering St George's	vs	*Humber United*	1929/30	EP Rd
		Monmouth Town	vs	*Barry (Town)*	1937/38	Pr Rd
		Norwich SOBU	vs	*Stowmarket Cor. (T.)*	1948/49	Pr Rd
		Ottery St Mary	vs	*Newquay*	1980/81	Pr Rd
3 – 10	Away	**West End Rovers**	vs	*Spencer Moulton*	1948/49	EP Rd
2 – 9	Away	**Burton Wanderers**	vs	*Small Heath Alliance*	1885/86	1st Rd
		Grimsby YMCA	vs	*Frodingham Athletic*	1926/27	EP Rd
		Ware	vs	*Aylesbury United*	1926/27	EP Rd
1 – 8	Home	**Moresby Park**	vs	*Barrow*	1906/07	Q1 Rd
		Bedford Queens Wrk.	vs	*Letchworth (Town)*	1947/48	Pr Rd
1 – 8	Away	**Heywood Central**	vs	*Higher Walton*	1887/88	1st Rd
		Selby Mizpah	vs	*Grimsby Rangers*	1908/09	Q1 Rd
		Lysaghts Excelsior	vs	*Pontypridd*	1912/13	Pr Rd

1 – 8	Away	**St Cleo's Old Boys**	vs	*Lostock Gralam*	1920/21	Pr Rd
		Darenth Training Col.	vs	*Callendar Athletic*	1935/36	EP Rd
		Dagenham Brit. Leg.	vs	*Harwich & Parkeston*	1946/47	EP Rd
		Wheelock Albion	vs	*Northwich Victoria*	1947/48	Pr Rd
0 – 7	Home	**Upton Rangers**	vs	*Old Wykehamists*	1883/84	1st Rd
		Derby County	vs	*Walsall Town*	1884/85	1st Rd
		Boston St James'	vs	*Stamford (Town)*	1920/21	Pr Rd
		Yorkshire Amateur	vs	*Castleford Town*	1925/26	EP Rd
		Cinderhill Colliery	vs	*Heanor Ath. (Town)*	1949/50	EP Rd
		East Ham United	vs	*Sudbury Wanderers*	1995/96	Pr Rd
0 – 7	Neut.	**Spilsby**	vs	*Stafford Road Works*	1880/81	1st Rd
0 – 7	Away	**Wednesbury Strollers**	vs	*Oxford University*	1878/79	1st Rd
		Brigg*	vs	*Turton*	1879/80	1st Rd
		Matlock (Town)	vs	*Stafford Road Works*	1885/86	1st Rd
		Attercliffe	vs	*Staveley*	1886/87	1st Rd
		Boston*	vs	*Gainsborough Trinity*	1887/88	1st Rd
		Southfield	vs	*Burton Swifts*	1887/88	1st Rd
		Maidstone*	vs	*1st Highland Light Inf.*	1891/92	Q1 Rd
		Rushden (Town)	vs	*Leicester Fosse (City)*	1892/93	Q1 Rd
		Mickley	vs	*Bishop Auckland*	1892/93	Q2 Rd
		Leytonstone	vs	*Gravesend United*	1896/97	Pr Rd
		Lewisham St Mary's	vs	*Sheppey United**	1896/97	Q1 Rd
		Wombwell Town*	vs	*Sheffield*	1896/97	Q1 Rd
		Chippenham Town	vs	*Staple Hill*	1898/99	Q1 Rd
		Bury St Edmunds (T.)	vs	*Colchester Town*	1900/01	Pr Rd
		Basford United	vs	*Mansfield Mechanics*	1908/09	Pr Rd
		Apperley Bridge	vs	*Halifax Town*	1919/20	EP Rd
		Pearl Assurance	vs	*Wimbledon*	1919/20	Pr Rd
		Dronfield W'dhouse	vs	*Staveley Town*	1919/20	Q1 Rd
		Machynlleth	vs	*Chester (City)**	1921/22	EP Rd
		Dorchester Town	vs	*Poole (Town)*	1926/27	Pr Rd
		Lynton Works	vs	*Leighton United (T.)*	1927/28	EP Rd
		RNVR Mitcham	vs	*Carshalton Athletic*	1931/32	PR Rd
		Urmston Old Boys	vs	*Stalybridge Celtic*	1933/34	Pr Rd
		Stanlow Social	vs	*Prescot Cables*	1937/38	Pr Rd
		Pirelli General Cables	vs	*Andover*	1947/48	EP Rd
		Colne	vs	*Ashington*	2002/03	PR Rd
		Woodford United	vs	*Cogenhoe United*	2004/05	Pr Rd
		Wick & Barnham Utd.	vs	*Horley Town*	2015/16	EP Rd
3 – 9	Home	**Appleby Works**	vs	*Milnthorpe Corinths.*	1947/48	Pr Rd
3 – 9	Away	**Oldland Abbotonians**	vs	*Bristol Manor Farm*	2013/14	EP Rd

2 – 8	Home	**Eden Colliery**	vs	*Crook CW (Town)*	1946/47	Pr Rd
		Sawston United	vs	*Parson Drove United*	1948/49	Pr Rd
2 – 8	Away	**Halesowen Town**	vs	*Wellington T (Telford)*	1898/99	Q1 Rd
		Hersham	vs	*Tooting Town*	1920/21	PR Rd
		Croston	vs	*Black Lane Rovers*	1924/25	EP Rd
		Fakenham Town	vs	*Eastern Coachworks*	1950/51	EP Rd
1 – 7	Home	**Chesterfield Spital**	vs	*Wednesbury Old Ath.*	1882/83	1st Rd
		Derby Junction	vs	*West Bromwich Alb.*	1884/85	1st Rd
		Clifton (Association)	vs	*Wednesbury Old Ath.*	1890/91	Q1 Rd
		Prescot (Cables)	vs	*Crewe Alexandra*	1891/92	Q1 Rd
		Wirral Railway	vs	*New Brighton Tower*	1899/00	Q1 Rd
		Caerphilly	vs	*Aberaman*	1902/03	Q2 Rd
		Grangetown (S'land.)	vs	*Craghead United*	1911/12	EP Rd
		Pontefract Borough	vs	*Altofts West Rid. Coll.*	1927/28	EP Rd
1 – 7	Away	**Long Eaton Midland**	vs	*Heanor Town*	1889/90	Q1 Rd
		Ashton North End	vs	*Blackpool*	1895/96	Q1 Rd
		Berkhamsted*	vs	*Apsley (Hemel Hemp.)*	1902/03	Pr Rd
		Barrow St George's	vs	*Barrow*	1904/05	Q2 Rd
		Margate Holy Trinity	vs	*Sittingbourne*	1906/07	Q1 Rd
		Brierfield Swifts	vs	*Rossendale United*	1907/08	Pr Rd
		Darlaston	vs	*Coventry City*	1907/08	Q1 Rd
		Louth Town*	vs	*Boston**	1920/21	Pr Rd
		Frodingham/Appleby	vs	*Selby Olympia C&O*	1929/30	Pr Rd
		Felling Red Star	vs	*Newburn*	1936/37	EP Rd
		Willesden	vs	*Leavesden*	1947/48	EP Rd
0 – 6	Home	**Sittingbourne**	vs	*1st Highland Light Inf.*	1893/94	Q1 Rd
		Moore's Athletic	vs	*Burton United*	1908/09	Pr Rd
		Kempston Rovers	vs	*Biggleswade/Dist. (T.)*	1910/11	Pr Rd
		Rawmarsh Town	vs	*Darfield United*	1912/13	EP Rd
0 – 6	Away	**Forest School**	vs	*Oxford University*	1875/76	1st Rd
		Clitheroe Low Moor	vs	*Blackburn Park Road*	1883/84	1st Rd
		Bournemouth (Rvrs.)	vs	*Old Westminsters*	1884/85	1st Rd
		Workington*	vs	*Bootle**	1887/88	1st Rd
		North Meols	vs	*Heywood*	1891/92	Q1 Rd
		Gedling Grove	vs	*Buxton*	1891/92	Q2 Rd
		Thornaby Utopians	vs	*Birtley*	1898/99	Q1 Rd
		Pyebank	vs	*Mexborough**	1899/00	Pr Rd
		Royal Engineers Utd.	vs	*Thames Iron. (WHU)*	1899/00	Pr Rd
		Raunds Town*	vs	*Desborough Town*	1902/03	Q1 Rd
		Kensington	vs	*Crouch End Vampires*	1903/04	Pr Rd
		Kettering WMC	vs	*Peterborough City**	1908/09	Pr Rd

0 – 6	Away	**Ramsgate** (Town)*	vs	*Sittingbourne*	1911/12	EP Rd
		Sutton United	vs	*Redhill*	1911/12	Pr Rd
		Mond Nickel Works	vs	*Newport County**	1913/14	Pr Rd
		Parkgate Works Sp.	vs	*Grimethorpe CI*	1919/20	Pr Rd
		Heaton Stannington	vs	*Preston Coll. (N Shields)*	1920/21	EP Rd
		Oakdale	vs	*Chepstow*	1920/21	EP Rd
		Distington	vs	*Penrith*	1920/21	Pr Rd
		Staithes United	vs	*Bridlington Town**	1921/22	EP Rd
		Truro City	vs	*Green Waves*	1924/25	EP Rd
		Twerton St Michael's	vs	*Radstock Town*	1936/37	EP Rd
		(Royal) **Wootton BT**	vs	*Wilts County Hosp.*	1938/39	PR Rd
		Jump Home Guard	vs	*Parkhouse Colliery*	1949/50	EP Rd
		Dunstable Town*	vs	*Biggleswade Town*	1950/51	EP Rd
		Kidlington	vs	*(Oxford) Headington U.*	1950/51	EP Rd
		Mablethorpe United	vs	*Ransome & Marles*	1950/51	EP Rd
		Bracknell Town	vs	*Wokingham Town*	1965/66	Q1 Rd
		Darenth Heathside	vs	*Welling United*	1986/87	Q1 Rd
		Eccleshill United	vs	*Great Harwood Town*	1991/92	Pr Rd
		Wodson Park	vs	*Oxhey Jets*	2011/12	EP Rd

**Different from current / later club with same/similar name*

Rank	Alliance / Conference / National League	QF	R5	R4	R3	R2	R1
1	Lincoln City	1				2	3
2	Telford United		1	2	1	4	7
3	Kidderminster Harriers		1	1	1	2	12
4	Sutton United		1	1	1	1	5
5	Luton Town		1		1	2	1
6	Crawley Town		1				
7	Kettering Town			2	1	3	14
8	Altrincham			1	4	8	9
9	Barnet			1	2	3	10
10	Macclesfield Town			1	2	3	4
11	Dagenham and Redbridge			1	2	1	4
12	Stevenage			1	1	5	5
13	Farnborough Town			1	1		6
14	Hednesford Town			1		2	4
15	Havant and Waterlooville			1		1	4
16	Torquay United			1		1	3

Top 16 FA Cup Clubs whilst Members of the National League.

Nb. Chart shows number of exits per Round

The 150 Clubs with the Most FA Cup Campaigns**

(** Includes seasons when clubs withdrew or were disqualified without playing)

139	Maidenhead United	1871/72	2020/21	3x Quarter-Finalists
	Marlow	1871/72	2020/21	Semi-Finalists in 1882
134	Notts County	1877/78	2020/21	FA Cup Winners 1894
	Reading	1877/78	2020/21	2x Semi-Finalists
133	Nottingham Forest	1878/79	2020/21	2x FA Cup Winners
132	Aston Villa	1879/80	2020/21	7x FA Cup Winners
132	Blackburn Rovers	1879/80	2020/21	6x FA Cup Winners
130	Sheffield Wednesday	1880/81	2020/21	3x FA Cup Winners
	Bolton Wanderers	1881/82	2020/21	4x FA Cup Winners
129	Birmingham City	1881/82	2020/21	2x FA Cup Finalists
	Grimsby Town	1882/83	2020/21	2x Semi-Finalists
128	Crewe Alexandra	1883/84	2020/21	Semi-Finalists in 1888
	Middlesbrough	1883/84	2020/21	FA Cup Finalists 1997
	Stoke City	1883/84	2020/21	FA Cup Finalists 2011
	West Bromwich Albion	1883/84	2020/21	5x FA Cup Winners
	Wolverhampton Wanderers	1883/84	2020/21	4x FA Cup Winners
	Wrexham	1883/84	2020/21	3x Quarter-Finalists
127	Preston North End	1883/84	2020/21	2x FA Cup Winners
	Derby County	1884/85	2020/21	FA Cup Winners 1946
	Lincoln City	1884/85	2020/21	Quarter-Finalists 2017
	Sunderland	1884/85	2020/21	2x FA Cup Winners
126	Burnley	1885/86	2020/21	FA Cup Winners 1914
	Gainsborough Trinity	1885/86	2020/21	Reached 3rd Round 1887
	Luton Town	1885/86	2020/21	FA Cup Finalists 1959
125	Clapton	1884/85	2020/21	Reached 3rd Round 1926
	Everton	1886/87	2020/21	5x FA Cup Winners
	Swindon Town	1886/87	2020/21	2x Semi-Finalists
124	Southport	1882/83	2020/21	Quarter-Finalists 1931
	Watford	1886/87	2020/21	2x FA Cup Finalists
	Millwall	1887/88	2020/21	FA Cup Finalists 2004
123	Chatham Town	1882/83	2020/21	Quarter-Finalists 1889
	Kettering Town	1888/89	2020/21	2x reached 4th Round
	Walsall	1888/89	2020/21	6x reached 5th Round
122	Manchester United	1886/87	2020/21	12x FA Cup Winners
	Doncaster Rovers	1888/89	2020/21	5x reached 5th Round

122	Arsenal	1889/90	2020/21	14x FA Cup Winners
	Bishop Auckland	1889/90	2020/21	Reached 4th Round 1955
	Sheffield United	1889/90	2020/21	4x FA Cup Winners
121	Port Vale	1885/86	2020/21	Semi-Finalists 1954
	Leicester City	1890/91	2020/21	FA Cup Winners 2021
120	Bury	1887/88	2019/20	2x FA Cup Winners
	Manchester City	1890/91	2020/21	6x FA Cup Winners
	Blackpool	1891/92	2020/21	FA Cup Winners 1953
	Southampton	1891/92	2020/21	FA Cup Winners 1976
119	Uxbridge	1873/74	2020/21	Reached 2nd Round 1874
	Chesterfield	1892/93	2020/21	Semi-Finalists 1997
	Liverpool	1892/93	2020/21	7x FA Cup Winners
	Newcastle United	1892/93	2020/21	6x FA Cup Winners
	Stockport County	1892/93	2020/21	3x reached 5th Round
118	Barnsley	1893/94	2020/21	FA Cup Winners 1912
	Gillingham	1893/94	2020/21	Quarter-Finalists 2000
117	Darlington*	1885/86	2011/12	Reached 5th Round 1958
	Coventry City	1892/93	2020/21	FA Cup Winners 1987
	Tottenham Hotspur	1894/95	2020/21	8x FA Cup Winners
116	Stourbridge	1891/92	2020/21	Reached 3rd Round 2017
	Bristol City	1895/96	2020/21	FA Cup Finalists 1909
	Bristol Rovers	1895/96	2020/21	3x Quarter-Finalists
	West Ham United	1895/96	2020/21	3x FA Cup Winners
	Wycombe Wanderers	1895/96	2020/21	Semi-Finalists 2001
115	Weymouth	1893/94	2020/21	Reached 4th Round 1962
	Queens Park Rangers	1895/96	2020/21	FA Cup Finalists 1982
114	Darwen	1877/78	2008/09	Semi-Finalists 1881
	Tranmere Rovers	1891/92	2020/21	3x Quarter-Finalists
	Brentford	1897/98	2020/21	4x Quarter-Finalists
113	Shrewsbury Town	1887/88	2020/21	2x Quarter-Finalists
	Sittingbourne	1893/94	2020/21	2x reached 2nd Round
	Worksop Town	1893/94	2020/21	Reached 3rd Round 1956
	Chorley	1894/95	2020/21	2x reached 2nd Round
	Fulham	1896/97	2020/21	FA Cup Finalists 1975
	Northampton Town	1898/99	2020/21	3x reached 5th Round
112	Northwich Victoria	1882/83	2020/21	Quarter-Finalists 1884
	Oxford City	1895/96	2020/21	2x reached 2nd Round
	Lowestoft Town	1898/99	2020/21	6x reached 1st Round
	Portsmouth	1899/00	2020/21	2x FA Cup Winners

111	Grantham Town	1877/78	2020/21	3x reached 3rd Round
	Macclesfield Town	1882/83	2020/21	Reached 4th Round 2013
	Kidderminster Harriers	1890/91	2020/21	Reached 5th Round 1994
110	Buxton	1891/92	2020/21	Reached 3rd Round 1952
	Bromley	1898/99	2020/21	3x reached 2nd Round
	Worthing	1899/00	2020/21	Reached 2nd Round 1983
	Barrow	1901/02	2020/21	12x reached 3rd Round
	Brighton and Hove Albion	1901/02	2020/21	FA Cup Finalists 1983
	Carlisle United	1901/02	2020/21	Quarter-Finalists 1975
109	Stafford Rangers	1884/85	2020/21	Reached 4th Round 1975
	Redhill	1897/98	2020/21	Reached 1st Round 1958
	Norwich City	1902/03	2020/21	3x Semi-Finalists
108	Bradford City	1903/04	2020/21	FA Cup Winners 2011
	Plymouth Argyle	1903/04	2020/21	Semi-Finalists 1984
107	Dartford	1895/96	2020/21	2x reached 3rd Round
	Shildon	1898/99	2020/21	Reached 2nd Round 1937
	Woking	1903/04	2020/21	Reached 4th Round 1991
	Leyton Orient	1904/05	2020/21	Semi-Finalists 1978
106	Sheffield	1873/74	2020/21	3x Quarter-Finalists
	Chester City*	1886/87	2009/10	2x reached 5th Round
	Chippenham Town	1898/99	2020/21	3x reached 1st Round
	Hull City	1904/05	2020/21	FA Cup Finalists 2014
	Chelsea	1905/06	2020/21	8x FA Cup Winners
	Crystal Palace	1905/06	2020/21	2x FA Cup Finalists
	Oldham Athletic	1905/06	2020/21	3x Semi-Finalists
105	Hednesford Town	1890/91	2020/21	Reached 4th Round 1997
104	Ashington	1888/89	2020/21	Reached 3rd Round 1927
	Tow Law Town	1891/92	2013/14	Reached 2nd Round 1968
	Great Yarmouth Town	1900/01	2020/21	2x reached 2nd Round
	Worcester City	1905/06	2020/21	Reached 4th Round 1959
	Southend United	1907/08	2020/21	4x reached 5th Round
103	Bath City	1890/91	2020/21	6x reached 3rd Round
	Aylesbury United	1897/98	2020/21	Reached 3rd Round 1995
	Exeter City	1908/09	2020/21	2x Quarter-Finalists
	Hartlepool United	1908/09	2020/21	6x reached 4th Round
	Rochdale	1908/09	2020/21	3x reached 5th Round
	St Albans City	1908/09	2020/21	3x reached 2nd Round
102	Basingstoke Town	1902/03	2020/21	3x reached 2nd Round
	Witton Albion	1907/08	2020/21	3x reached 2nd Round

102	Huddersfield Town	1909/10	2020/21	FA Cup Winners 1922
	Mansfield Town	1909/10	2020/21	Quarter-Finalists 1969
	Scunthorpe United	1909/10	2020/21	2x reached 5th Round
101	Matlock Town	1885/86	2020/21	Reached 3rd Round 1977
	Scarborough	1887/88	2007/08	Reached 4th Round 2004
	Frome Town	1906/07	2020/21	Reached 1st Round 1955
	AFC Bournemouth	1909/10	2020/21	2x Quarter-Finalists
	Cardiff City	1910/11	2020/21	FA Cup Winners 1927
100	Desborough Town	1899/00	2020/21	Reached 1st Round 1927
	Hemel Hempstead Town	1901/02	2020/21	2x reached 1st Round
	Penrith	1906/07	2020/21	Reached 2nd Round 1982
	Frickley Athletic	1910/11	2020/21	Reached 3rd Round 1986
99	Winsford United	1887/88	2020/21	Reached 2nd Round 1888
	Windsor and Eton	1892/93	2010/11	Reached 2nd Round 1984
	Gresley Rovers*	1895/96	2008/09	3x reached 1st Round
	King's Lynn	1900/01	2009/10	Reached 3rd Round 1962
	Altrincham	1906/07	2020/21	Reached 4th Round 1986
	Blyth Spartans	1909/10	2020/21	Reached 5th Round 1978
	Sutton United	1911/12	2020/21	Reached 5th Round 2017
	Barnet	1912/13	2020/21	3x reached 4th Round
	Stalybridge Celtic	1912/13	2020/21	3x reached 2nd Round
98	Swansea City	1913/14	2020/21	2x Semi-Finalists
97	Southall	1873/74	2020/21	Reached 3rd Round 1936
	Nantwich Town	1888/89	2020/21	3x reached 1st Round
	Sheppey United*	1892/93	2000/01	Reached Q6 Round 1920
	Glossop North End	1894/95	2020/21	Quarter-Finalists 1909
	West Auckland Town	1905/06	2020/21	3x reached 1st Round
	Stamford	1911/12	2020/21	Reached 1st Round 2017
	Hendon	1912/13	2020/21	Reached 3rd Round 1974
	Lancaster City	1913/14	2020/21	2x reached 2nd Round
	Charlton Athletic	1914/15	2020/21	FA Cup Winners 1947
96	Poole Town	1891/92	2020/21	Reached 3rd Round 1927
	Harwich and Parkeston	1898/99	2020/21	6x reached 1st Round
	Melksham Town	1909/10	2020/21	2x reached Q3 Round
	Kingstonian	1919/20	2020/21	Reached 4th Round 2001
	Yeovil Town	1919/20	2020/21	Reached 5th Round 1949
95	Horsham	1903/04	2020/21	Reached 2nd Round 2008
	Skelmersdale United	1905/06	2020/21	3x reached 1st Round
	Grays Athletic	1911/12	2020/21	Reached 2nd Round 2006
	Wealdstone	1913/14	2020/21	Reached 3rd Round 1978

95	Dulwich Hamlet	1919/20	2020/21	15x reached 1st Round
	Leeds United	1920/21	2020/21	FA Cup Winners 1972
	Marine	1920/21	2020/21	Reached 3rd Round 1993

**Different from current / later club with same/similar name*

Rank	Southern League	W	Fin	SF	QF	R5	R4	R3	R2	R1
1	Tottenham Hotspur	1			3			2	1	3
2	Southampton		2	2	3			1	4	10
3	Swindon Town			2	1			2	2	3
4	Millwall			2				2	3	12
5	Queens Park Rangers				2			1	3	6
6	West Ham United				1			4	3	2
7	Crystal Palace				1			2	3	5
8	Reading				1			2	2	11
9	Portsmouth				1			1	5	9
10	Coventry City				1			1	1	3
11	Fulham				1				2	1
12	Yeovil Town					1		7	7	16
13	Colchester United					1				3
14	Bedford Town (1)						2	2	2	6
15	Hereford United						1	2	10	10
16	Chelmsford City						1	1	8	18
17	Weymouth						1	1	6	17
18	Wimbledon						1	1	3	4
19	Ebbsfleet United						1	1	1	6
20	Oxford United						1	1	1	3
21	Worcester City						1		1	6
22	Bath City							3	9	11
23	Bristol Rovers							3	2	9
24	Kettering Town							2	7	14
25	Dartford							2	6	16
26	Gillingham							2	5	6
27	Norwich City							2	5	3
28	Plymouth Argyle							2	4	7
29	Folkestone							2	3	11
30	Margate							2	3	8
31	Barnet							2	2	5
32	Hastings United (1)							2	1	5
33	Brentford							2	1	4
34	King's Lynn							1	7	4
35	Brighton and Hove Albion							1	5	4

Top 35 FA Cup Clubs whilst Members of Southern League.

Nb. Chart shows number of exits per Round

Where are they now?

Existing Clubs which last played in the FA Cup prior to the 21st Century.

Clubs that still exist but which have not participated in the FA Cup during the 21st Century typically fall into three main camps. First are those amateur clubs that participated in the formative years of the competition, and which broke away from the FA to form the Amateur Football Association in the early 20th Century. The majority of these clubs can be found today playing in one of the Arthurian League, the Amateur Football Combination or the Southern Amateur League.

Second are the non-English clubs, split into the Scottish and Irish teams that played in the competition during its first 20 years, and the Welsh non-league clubs that participated in it any time up to the 1991/92 season. All three country FAs have at some point in history had their member clubs banned from taking part in non-country FA affiliated competitions. Those clubs still in existence are now members of Leagues in their own country.

Third are the lower level non-league clubs that have either not progressed into the formal English football pyramid or which are currently plying their trade in Step Six leagues, or their feeder leagues. In theory all these clubs could one day participate in the FA Cup again, but for most of them the level of investment required to climb the pyramid to put themselves in a position to do so is prohibitive.

Researching club histories is always fraught with challenges as indicated in the introductory passages, and it is likely that several of the clubs listed below could be argued to not be continuations of the sides that participated in the FA Cup. I'm very happy to add or remove clubs from the list for future books upon receipt of physical or visual evidence of their individual circumstances.

(Nb. All League statuses refer to 2020/21 season).

Aberystwyth Town (Welsh Premier League)
Six campaigns as Aberystwyth between 1896/97 and 1909/10 reaching the 4th Qualifying Round in 1897/98 by defeating Glossop North End.

Achilles (Suffolk and Ipswich League Senior Division)
Two campaigns in 1948/49 and 1949/50 reaching 2nd Qualifying Round and recording a 9-1 victory over Old Grammarians.

Altofts (West Yorkshire League Division Two)
Twelve campaigns from 1898/99 to 1937/38, the last seven as Altofts West Riding Colliery, reaching 1st Qualifying Round twice scoring five goals including once against Guiseley.

Amersham Town (Spartan South Midlands League Division One)
Six campaigns between 1950/51 and 1969/70 appearing in 1st Qualifying Round five times but without winning an FA Cup match, a 2-2 draw with Wolverton Town and British Rail the best result achieved.

Annfield Plain (Wearside League Division One)
Seventy-three campaigns from 1906/07 to 1992/93, the first four as Annfield Plain Celtic, reaching the 1st Round 'Proper' on three occasions, the latter two being drawn against and losing heavily to Southport FC in 1928/29 and 1964/65.

Appleby (Westmorland League Division One)
Eight campaigns between 1913/14 and 1948/49, exiting in the Preliminary Round every time (an unwanted FA Cup record) with a 2-2 draw against Penrith being the best result achieved.

Bangor City (Cymru North Division)
Sixty-four campaign from 1896/97 to 1991/92, initially as Bangor FC then Bangor Athletic, reaching the 2nd Round 'Proper' on four occasions with victories over Football League sides Wrexham (1960/61) and Rochdale (1972/73).

Barry Town United (Cymru Premier Division)
Seventy-one campaigns from 1911/12 to 1992/93 competing under the names Barry and District, Barry AFC, Barry Town and Barri, reaching the 2nd Round 'Proper' in 1929/30, and continuing on for one season longer than the majority of other Welsh non-league clubs when new rules for participating in outside national FA cup competitions came into effect.

Beccles Caxton (Anglian Combination Division Two)
Just one campaign in 1905/06 losing 5-1 to Lowestoft Town in the club's only FA Cup match.

Beccles Town (Anglian Combination Premier Division)
Ten campaigns between 1925/26 and 1957/58 when known as Beccles, reaching the 3rd Qualifying Round three times with their biggest win being a 7-1 victory over Sheringham.

Bexley (Kent County League Division One)
Ten campaigns from 1932/33 to 1949/50 reaching the 1st Qualifying Round in the club's debut campaign, opening with a 9-1 victory over Woolwich Borough Council Athletic (now Greenwich Borough).

Blackpool (Wren) Rovers (West Lancashire League Premier Division)
Sixteen campaigns between 1983/84 and 1998/99, twice reaching 2nd Qualifying Round when known simply as Wren Rovers, and with a 4-1 victory over Liversedge being the club's biggest FA Cup win.

Blaenau Ffestiniog Amateurs (Welsh Ardal League North West Division)
Three consecutive campaigns across 1972–75 as Blaenau Ffestiniog, exiting in the 1st Qualifying Round each time, with goal-less draws against Marine (twice) and Oswestry Town the best result the club achieved.

Blandford United (Dorset Premier League)
Seventeen campaigns from 1920/21 to 1952/53, the first ten of which simply known as Blandford, and posting the club's best FA Cup run to the 3rd Qualifying Round in its debut season, with 6-2 wins over Bournemouth (Amateurs) and Dorchester Town being the club's largest victories.

Blidworth Welfare (Central Midlands League Southern Division)
Also known as Blidworth Miners Welfare, with five consecutive campaigns straddling the mid-1990s, just one of which went beyond the Preliminary Round thanks to the club's only victory, 2-1 in a replay against Harworth Colliery Institute.

Boldon Community Association (Wearside League Division One)
Thirty-three campaigns from 1949/50 to 1981/82, playing as Boldon Colliery Welfare up until 1976, reaching the 3rd Qualifying Round four times and with a 4-0 victory over West Auckland Town being the club's best FA Cup result.

Breightmet United (Manchester League Division Two)
Twenty-five campaigns leading up to World War II with sixteen Preliminary Round exits and nine 1st Qualifying Round knock-outs, the club's last FA Cup match being a 3-0 defeat to future winners Wigan Athletic.

Brereton Social (Midland Combination Division One)
Seven campaigns from 1973/74 to 1981/82 reaching the 3rd Qualifying Round in 1978/79 courtesy of successive 3-2 victories over Bedworth United and Sutton Coldfield Town.

Bungay Town (Anglian Combination Division One)
Eighteen campaigns from 1935/36 to 1963/64 reaching the 3rd Qualifying Round on three occasions with a 4-0 victory over the original Walton United being the club's best result.

Burnley Belvedere (East Lancashire League Division One)
Five successive campaigns from 1904/05 exiting in 1st Qualifying Round three times and Preliminary Round twice, but actually losing all five matches scoring just twice and conceding twenty-seven.

Caerleon (Gwent County League Premier Division)
Two campaigns as Caerleon Athletic just prior to the outbreak of WWI reaching 1st Qualifying Round in 1913/14 season culminating in an 8-1 defeat to Swansea Town (now Swansea City).

Caernarfon Town (Cymru Premier Division)
Seventeen successive campaigns from 1979/80 until returning to compete in Welsh football and reached the 3rd Round 'Proper' in 1986/87 following victories over Football League sides Stockport County and York City, before losing just 1-0 in a replay at second tier Barnsley.

Cambridge University (British Universities and Colleges Sports (BUCS) League)
Seven consecutive campaigns from 1873/74 reaching the semi-finals in 1876/77 losing 1-0 to The Wanderers thereby just missing out on a varsity FA Cup Final with Oxford University.

Cardiff Corinthians (South Wales Alliance League Division One)
Twenty-four campaigns from 1911/12 to 1949/50 reaching the 3rd Qualifying Round in 1922/23 losing 2-0 to Bath City.

Carlisle City (Northern League Division Two)
Five successive campaigns from 1976/77 appearing in the 1st Qualifying Round in each of the first four, but a 4-2 victory over Annfield Plain being the club's only success.

Cefn Druids (Cymru Premier)
Twenty-two campaigns from 1876/77 to 1910/11 under their original name of Druids, the first Welsh club to enter the FA Cup, reaching the quarter-finals in 1882/83 season, achieved by a 1-0 victory over Bolton Wanderers in a second replay.

Chatteris Town (Cambridgeshire League Division One B)
Fifty-six campaigns between 1930/31 and 1994/95 reaching the 3rd Qualifying Round three times with a 5-1 win over Sheringham being the club's best result.

Chepstow Town (Welsh Ardal League South East)
Just two campaigns in 1920/21 and 1921/22 playing as Chepstow, but managing to post two 6-0 victories in that short time against Oakdale and Rhiwderin.

Chipping Norton Town (Witney and District League Division Three)
Just two campaigns across 1982–84 losing both games played, first to Highgate United then to Bourne Town.

Chirk AAA (Welsh Ardal League North East)
Twenty campaigns covering 1884/85 to 1924/25, twice reaching the 5th Round of the FA Cup when known as Chirk in the days before the Football League was founded, with the club's 10-2 victory over Shrewsbury Town still their opponent's heaviest FA Cup defeat.

Civil Service (Southern Amateur League Senior Division Two)
Thirty campaigns spread across 100 years starting with the very first FA Cup season 1871/72 through to a special invitation to the centenary season in 1971/72. The club did not register an FA Cup win until the 1899/00 season.

Cleator Moor Celtic (North West Counties League Division One North)
Twenty-nine campaigns starting in 1919/20 and ending in 1991/92 reaching the 1st Round 'Proper' in 1950/51 season losing 5-0 to Tranmere Rovers.

Cliftonville (Northern Ireland Football League Premiership)
Five successive campaigns spanning across the formation of the Football League reaching the 3rd Round in the club's debut season in 1886/87 only to lose 11-1 to Partick Thistle in the only FA Cup game between two non-English sides from two different countries.

Coleford Athletic (Mid-Somerset League Premier Division)
Sixteen campaigns from 1922/23 to 1950/51 reaching the 3rd Qualifying Round in the club's debut season and a 5-1 victory over Spencer Melksham being the club's biggest FA Cup win.

Connah's Quay Nomads (Cymru Premier)
Three successive campaigns across 1971–74, reaching 2nd Qualifying Round in first and last campaigns, and with a 5-1 win over Prescot Town (now Prescot Cables) being the club's biggest victory.

Cranleigh (Surrey Intermediate League West)
Seven campaigns from 1912/13 to 1938/39 with just two Preliminary Round appearances and just one FA Cup victory, a 2-0 win in their first match against Surrey Wanderers.

Crockenhill (Kent County League Premier Division)
Five successive campaigns across 1984–89 with just one 1st Qualifying Round appearance and just one FA Cup victory, 3-0 versus Flackwell Heath in 1987/88 season.

Crouch End Vampires (Southern Amateur League Senior Division Two)
Eleven successive campaigns from 1897/98 to 1907/08, reaching the 4th Qualifying Round in the first season after the two clubs Crouch End FC and Vampires FC merged, and involved in one of the rare 6-6 draws in the FA Cup against Page Green Old Boys in 1906/07 season.

Cwmbran Town (Gwent County League Premier Division)
Four successive campaigns from 1988/89 until the time Welsh FA clubs could no longer participate in English FA Cup, reaching the 2nd Qualifying Round in the club's second campaign, and three 1-0 results their only FA Cup victories.

Denbigh Town (Welsh Ardal League North West)
Just one campaign in 1910/11 whilst members of The Combination with just one 3-2 defeat to Middlewich to their name.

Filey Town (Scarborough and District League Division One)
Twenty-one campaigns from 1920/21 to 1950/51, reaching the 2nd Qualifying Round four times, with a 4-0 win over Normanby Magnesite being the club's biggest victory.

Flint Town United (Cymru Premier)
Sixteen campaigns from 1892/93 through to 1961/62 under the names Flint, Flint Town and Flint Town United, reaching the 3rd Qualifying Round three times and with a record FA Cup win for a Welsh side of 13-0 against Warrington St Elphin's in 1894/95 season.

Frecheville Davys (Sheffield County Senior League Premier Division)
Just one FA Cup campaign in 1976/77 season as Frecheville Community Association and just one FA Cup game, a 1-0 defeat at the hands of Winterton Rangers.

Glasgow Rangers (Scottish Premier League)
Just two campaigns before the Scottish FA banned the club from participating in the FA Cup, scratching in the first in 1885/86, but only a 3-1 defeat against Aston Villa prevented the club from becoming the second Scottish team in an FA cup final in the 1886/87 season.

Glastonbury Town (Somerset County League Division Two)
Seventy-three campaigns covering the 20th century from 1901/02 to 1998/99, first as Glastonbury Avalon Rovers then as Glastonbury, reaching the 1st Round 'Proper' in 1950/51 losing 2-1 to Exeter City.

Gonville and Caius AFC (Cambridge University Association Football League Premier Division)
Entered the FA Cup twice as Caius College, Cambridge, in 1880/81 and 1881/82 but scratched both times before facing Nottingham Forest and Dreadnought respectively.

Hanham Athletic (Gloucestershire County League)
Thirty-two campaigns from 1912/13 to 1954/55, reaching the 3rd Qualifying Round in 1921/22 season, with a 6-0 victory over Paulton Rovers being the club's biggest FA Cup win.

Haverfordwest County (Cymru Premier)
Four successive campaigns from 1981/82 season when the club posted its best run to the 3rd Qualifying Round, winning just four games in total all by a one goal margin.

Heart of Midlothian (Scottish Championship)
Two campaigns in 1885/86 and 1886/87, but just one FA Cup match, a 7-1 defeat to Darwen in the club's second campaign, the last season Scottish FA clubs could compete in the English FA Cup.

Hollington United (Mid Sussex League Premier Division)
Just one campaign in 1927/28 season involving a victory against East Grinstead (Town), a walkover versus Bognor Regis Town and a heavy 5-0 defeat at the hands of Worthing.

Holt United (Anglian Combination Division Two)
Five campaigns between 1936/37 and 1950/51 with one 2nd Qualifying Round appearance in the last season before WWII, a campaign that included a 6-0 victory over Bungay Town.

Holyhead Town (North Wales Coast West Football League Division One)
Five campaigns between 1964/65 and 1970/71 with one 2nd Qualifying Round appearance in 1967/68 season, with a 4-0 victory over Porthmadog the club's only FA Cup win.

Horncastle Town (Lincolnshire Football League)
If the current club is the same as the one formed in 1873, it has had twelve campaigns under three different names, Horncastle, Horncastle United and Horncastle Town, reaching the 5th Round in 1886/87 season where it lost 5-0 to Aston Villa.

Hornsea Town (Humber Premier League Premier Division)
Two campaigns in 1921/22 and 1923/24, losing both games played and exiting in the Extra Preliminary Round both times.

Horsham Trinity (West Sussex League Championship North Division)
Two consecutive campaigns across 1925–27, exiting in the Extra Preliminary Round both times, and a 1-1 draw with East Grinstead (Town) the club's best result.

Ilminster Town (Somerset County League Premier Division)
Seventeen campaigns from 1948/49 to 1981/82, reaching the 2nd Qualifying Round seven times, and with a 4-1 victory over Street FC being the club's biggest FA Cup win.

Keswick (Westmorland League Division One)
Eighteen campaigns from 1900/01 to 1932/33, twice reaching the 3rd Qualifying Round, and with a 5-1 victory over Bowthorn Recreation being the club's biggest FA Cup win.

Knutsford (Cheshire League Premier Division)
Just one FA Cup campaign in 1949/50 season, exiting in the Extra Preliminary Round after a 2-1 defeat to Barnton following a 1-1 draw.

Lancing Old Boys (Arthurian League Division One)
Three campaigns straddling the formation of the Football League, reaching 2nd Round in 1885/86 season following a 7-1 victory over Barnes.

Linby Colliery Welfare (Central Midlands League Southern Division)
Nine consecutive campaigns from 1948/49 season playing as Linby Colliery, reaching the 1st Round 'Proper' in 1950/51 as a Central Alliance side, one of the lowest level clubs to reach the 1st Round, losing 4-1 to Gillingham.

Linfield (Northern Ireland Football League Premiership)
Three successive campaigns during the first three seasons of the Football League playing as Linfield Athletic, reaching the 1st Round 'Proper' in the club's debut season only to withdraw before facing Nottingham Forest in a replay following a 2-2 draw.

Lisburn Distillery (Northern Ireland Football League Premier Intermediate League)
Two campaigns as Distillery in 1887/88 and 1889/90 with just one win against Linfield Athletic and a 10-2 defeat versus Bolton Wanderers amongst their games.

Liverpool Ramblers (Not affiliated to any League)
Three successive campaigns starting from 1882/83 season when the club reached the 2nd Round following their only FA Cup win, 4-0 versus Southport FC in a 1st Round replay.

Llandudno (Cymru North Division)
Thirty-six campaigns from 1914/15 to 1966/67, reaching the 3rd Qualifying Round twice, posting the club's best FA Cup win, 7-0 versus Merseyside club Stork FC, during the second of the club's two best runs in 1958/59 season.

London Welsh (Amateur Football Combination Intermediate South Division)
Five campaigns from 1898/99 to 1904/05, appearing the 1st Qualifying Round just once in 1900/01, although lost all five FA Cup matches played, including a 4-2 defeat by Queens Park Rangers.

Lostock Gralam (Cheshire League Premier Division)
Forty-two campaigns from 1909/10 through to 1970/71, reaching the 2nd Qualifying Round eight times, and with an 8-1 victory over St Cleopatra's Old Boys being the club's biggest FA Cup win.

Machynlleth (Welsh Ardal League North East)
Just one FA Cup campaign in 1921/22 season and just one FA Cup match, a 7-0 defeat at original Chester (City).

Marsden (Huddersfield and District League Division Four)
Just one FA Cup campaign in 1950/51 season, reaching the Preliminary Round after a 3-2 victory over Meltham FC.

Marston Shelton Rovers (Bedfordshire League Premier Division)
Just one FA Cup campaign in 1950/51 season, reaching the Preliminary Round after a 3-0 victory over Bedford Corinthians.

Meltham Athletic (Huddersfield and District League Division Three)
Ten campaigns from 1934/35 to 1950/51, first as Meltham Mills and then as Meltham, appearing in the 1st Qualifying Round in 1945/46 season, even though the club's only victory was a 3-2 win over Hessle Old Boys three years later.

Metrogas (Kent County League Division One West)
Two campaigns in 1921/22 and 1922/23, reaching the 5th Qualifying Round in the club's debut season courtesy of a 5-0 victory over Aylesbury United in a replay.

Middlesex Wanderers (Not affiliated to any League)
Just one FA Cup campaign in 1904/05 season and just one FA Cup match, a 5-0 defeat at Kensal Rise.

Milnthorpe Corinthians (West Lancashire League Division One)
Twenty-four campaigns from 1937/38 to 1969/70, reaching the 2nd Qualifying Round nine times, including both their first and last campaigns, and with an 11-0 thrashing of Cockermouth FC being the club's biggest FA Cup win.

Monmouth Town (Welsh Ardal League South East)
Three FA Cup campaigns either side of WWII, with three defeats (scoring one and conceding nineteen goals) despite appearing in 2nd Qualifying Round in 1945/46 season.

Newtown (Cymru Premier)
Twelve campaigns, notable for a 90 year gap between the first ten campaigns which started in 1884/85 and the final two campaigns than began in 1990/91, and with two 2nd Round appearances in the club's first two campaigns.

Norwich CEYMS (Anglian Combination Premier Division)
Forty-two campaigns from 1889/90 through to 1948/49, reaching the 4th Qualifying Round in 1906/07 season, and including an 18-0 thrashing of Bury St Edmunds (now Bury Town) which was the joint biggest margin of victory in the FA Cup in the 20th Century.

Old Carthusians (Arthurian League Premier Division)
Thirteen consecutive campaigns from 1879/80 to 1891/92, incorporating five quarter-finals, three semi-finals and lifting the Trophy in 1880/81 season at the Kennington Oval thirteen years before becoming the inaugural FA Amateur Cup winners.

Old Etonians (Arthurian League Premier Division)
Nineteen campaigns from 1873/74 to 1892/93 that encompassed two FA Cup winning seasons (1878/79 and 1881/82) and four other times when finishing as runners-up, including the first time the Trophy was won by a northern professional club in 1882/83 season.

Old Foresters (Arthurian League Premier Division)
Twelve consecutive campaigns from 1877/78 to 1888/89, reaching the 5th Round three times, the first one of which was also the quarter-finals in 1881/82 season, losing 1-0 to Marlow in a replay.

Old Harrovians (Arthurian League Premier Division)
Thirteen campaigns from 1876/77 to 1892/93 that included a semi-final appearance in the club's second campaign, losing 2-1 to Royal Engineers at Kennington Oval.

Old Lyonians (Southern Amateur League Senior Division Three)
Fifteen campaigns in the years leading up to the outbreak of WWII, reaching 4th Qualifying Round in 1933/34 season, and with a 5-0 win over Bushey United being the club's biggest FA Cup win.

Old Salopians (Arthurian League Division One)
Entered the FA Cup just once in 1876/77 season, but withdrew ahead of facing Oxford University.

Old Westminsters (Arthurian League Division One)
Twelve consecutive campaigns from 1882/83 to 1893/94, reaching the quarter-finals on three separate occasions, and with an 11-3 victory over Norwich Thorpe being the club's biggest FA Cup win.

Old Wykehamists (Arthurian League Premier Division)
Twelve campaigns from 1876/77 to 1892/93, reaching the 4th Round twice, and with a 10-0 victory over Luton Wanderers being the club's biggest FA Cup win.

Old Xaverians (Liverpool County Premier League Premier Division)
Eight consecutive campaigns from 1920/21 season, reaching 1st Qualifying Round in 1926/27, courtesy of the club's only FA Cup victory, 2-1 against Earle FC in the Preliminary Round.

Ottery St Mary (Devon Football League South West Division)
Six FA Cup campaigns starting in 1980/81 season and culminating in the club's only 2nd Qualifying Round appearance in 1987/88, and with a 4-1 win over Sharpness being the club's biggest FA Cup victory.

Oxford University (British Universities and Colleges Sports (BUCS) League)
Eight consecutive FA Cup campaigns from 1872/73 to 1879/80, reaching at least the quarter-finals in every single campaign, being runners-up three times including in both the club's first and last campaigns, and winning the FA Cup in 1873/74 season.

Partick Thistle (Scottish League One)
Just two campaigns in 1885/86 and 1886/87 ahead of Scottish FA banning their member clubs from competing in non-Scottish FA affiliated competitions, reaching the 5th Round in the latter season, losing 1-0 to Old Westminsters.

Peasedown Miners Welfare (Somerset County League Division Two)
Twenty-two campaigns from 1912/13 to 1956/57, under the name Peasedown St John's for the first nine of them, reaching the 4th Qualifying Round in 1945/46 season, and with a 7-0 win over Radstock Town being the club's biggest FA Cup victory.

Percy Main Amateurs (Northern Alliance Premier Division)
Just two FA Cup campaigns, a record 54 years apart for a club only participating in the competition twice, exiting in the Preliminary Round in both 1927/28 and 1981/82, and losing both games played.

Polytechnic (Southern Amateur League Senior Division One)
Twenty-six campaigns from 1879/80 to 1950/51, the first nine pre-Football League campaigns under the club's original name Hanover United, reaching the 3rd Round in 1884/85 season, and with a 6-2 win over Hertford Town being the club's biggest FA Cup victory.

Port Talbot Town (Cymru South Division)
Three consecutive campaigns playing as Port Talbot in the years leading up to WWI, exiting in the Preliminary Round on each occasion, disqualified in the club's final campaign after achieving their best result, a goal-less draw against Caerleon Athletic who were also disqualified.

Porthmadog (Welsh Ardal League North West)
Fourteen consecutive campaigns from 1967/68 season, reaching 3rd Qualifying Round in 1973/74, and with a 6-0 victory against Holyhead Town being the club's biggest FA Cup win.

Purton (Wiltshire League)
Fourteen campaigns from 1929/30 to 1950/51, the first six as Purton West End, reaching 1st Qualifying Round in 1935/36 season, and with just two FA Cup wins to their name.

Pwllheli (North Wales Coast West Premier Division)
Seventeen campaigns from 1953/54 to 1975/76, all played under the club's original name Pwllheli and District, reaching the 4th Qualifying Round in their second campaign, and with a 7-0 victory over Prescot Cables being the club's biggest FA Cup win.

Queen's Park (Scottish League Two)
A dozen campaigns in total starting from the inaugural FA Cup season in 1871/72 up to 1886/87 after which Scottish clubs were banned from participating in English FA Cup, scratching from the competition nine times, twice at the semi-finals stage, and twice being runners-up to Blackburn Rovers in consecutive Final in 1884 and 1885.

Rayners Lane (Spartan South Midlands League Division One)
Seven consecutive campaigns from 1986/87 season culminating in reaching the 2nd Qualifying Round in 1992/93, and with five one-goal margin of victories the best the club could muster in that time.

Reigate Priory (Mid Sussex League Championship Division)
One of the 15 clubs which participated in the inaugural FA Cup in 1871/72, with nine campaigns in total through to 1929/30 season, reaching 2nd Round twice in the early days despite just one FA Cup victory to their name, a 1-0 win over Barnes.

Rogerstone (Gwent County League Division Two)
Three consecutive campaigns in the years immediately following the end of WWI, exiting in the Preliminary Round in each season, but managing one victory, 4-1 against Risce Stars.

Royal Engineers (Army Football Association Division One)
Eighteen consecutive campaigns from the inaugural FA Cup in 1871/82 through to the first season of the Football League in 1888/89, appearing in four FA Cup finals (including the first one), and lifting the famous Trophy in 1874/75 season.

Sandown (Isle of Wight League Division One)
Nine campaigns from 1926/27 to 1949/50, appearing in the 1st Qualifying Round in 1945/46 season, but with just one FA Cup victory under their belt, a 7-4 win over Gosport Albion in the 1926/27 season.

Sawston United (Cambridgeshire League Division 3A)
Just one FA Cup campaign in 1948/49 season and just one FA Cup match, an 8-2 defeat at home to Parson Drove United.

Seaford Town (Southern Combination Football League Division One)
Three consecutive FA Cup campaigns across 1909–12 under the club's initial name Seaford, losing all three matches played despite two 1st Qualifying Round appearances.

Shankhouse (Northern Alliance Premier Division)
Forty campaigns spanning 1887/88 to 1954/55, reaching the 4th Round in the club's debut season losing 9-0 at home to Aston Villa after defeating both Scarborough and Darlington.

Sharpness (Gloucestershire County League)
Six consecutive FA Cup campaigns from 1985/86, reaching 2nd Qualifying Round in both first two seasons, and with a 5-1 victory over Shortwood United being the club's biggest FA Cup win.

Sheringham (Eastern Counties League Division One North)
Twenty-seven campaigns from 1927/28 to 1961/62, reaching the 2nd Qualifying Round five times including in the club's debut campaign, and setting their biggest win in their last campaign, a 9-3 victory versus March Great Eastern United.

Skegness Town (Northern Counties East League Division One)
Thirty-six campaigns from 1949/50 to 1985/86, reaching the 1st Round 'Proper' in 1955/56 season, losing 4-0 at home to Worksop Town.

Somersham Town (Cambridgeshire League Senior Division A)
Three campaigns between 1954/55 and 1958/59, appearing in 1st Qualifying Round in both the first and last campaigns, with a 3-0 win over Newmarket Town being the club's only FA Cup victory to date.

South Kirkby Colliery (Sheffield County Senior League Division One)
Forty consecutive campaigns from 1905/06 to 1954/55 spanning two World Wars, reaching the 4th Qualifying Round three times including in the club's debut season, and with a 6-1 win over Darfield United being the club's biggest FA Cup victory.

Spilsby Town (Boston League Premier Division)
Seven campaigns from 1880/81 through to 1921/22 under the name Spilsby, with five appearances in the 1st Round, but just suffered seven defeats in seven matches (seven goals scored, 43 conceded).

Stokenchurch (Hellenic League Division Two East)
Five successive campaigns from 1930/31 with five Extra Preliminary Round exits, and with a 1-1 draw against Old Lyonians preventing just five FA Cup defeats.

Stonehouse Town (Hellenic League Division One West)
Twenty-nine successive campaigns covering 1947/48 to 1975/76, with seven appearances in 2nd qualifying Round, and with a 4-0 defeat of Cinderford Town being the club's biggest FA Cup win.

Stoneycroft (Liverpool County Premier League Division One)
Five campaigns from 1938/39 through to 1950/51, reaching the 3rd Qualifying Round in the club's debut campaigns, and with defeating Thorndale 6-2 being the club's biggest FA Cup win.

Sturminster Newton United (Dorset Premier League)
Six consecutive campaigns from 1874/75 to 1879/80 all played under the club's first name, Panthers, reaching the 2nd Round three times with a 3-0 victory over Wood Grange being the club's biggest FA Cup win.

Swanage Town and Herston (Dorset Premier League)
Nine consecutive FA Cup campaigns starting from 1987/88, the first four of which all saw the club reach the 2nd Qualifying Round, and with 5-1 win against Melksham Town being the club's biggest FA Cup victory.

Terrington Tigers (North West Norfolk League Division One)
Just one FA Cup campaign in 1920/21 season under the club's original name Terrington, and just one FA Cup match, a 5-1 defeat at home to Morton's Athletic.

Thorne Colliery (Central Midlands League North Division)
Thirteen consecutive FA Cup campaigns crossing World War II from 1934/35 to 1950/51, reaching 2nd Qualifying Round five times, and with 4-1 victories against Monckton Athletic and Denaby United being the club's biggest FA Cup wins.

Ton Pentre (Welsh Ardal League South West)
Twenty-four consecutive campaigns right up until 1991/92 season when non-league Welsh clubs were prevented from participating in the English FA Cup, reaching the 1st Round 'Proper' in 1986/87 losing 4-1 at home to Cardiff City.

Turton (West Lancashire League Premier Division)
Five campaigns from 1879/80 to 1900/01, reaching the 3rd Round twice in the pre-Football league days, and with a 7-0 win against Brigg FC in their debut FA Cup match being the club's biggest victory.

Walsall Phoenix (Staffordshire County Senior League Premier Division)
Eleven campaigns from 1921/22 to 1935/36, with just once reaching Preliminary Round in 1932/33 season, courtesy of the club's one FA Cup win, 2-1 at home to Wolverhampton Amateur (now Wolverhampton Casuals).

Watton United (Anglian Combination Division One)
Ten campaigns from 1987/88 to 1999/00, reaching 1st Qualifying Round four times, and with just two FA Cup victories against the original Barking FC and Burnham Ramblers.

Welshpool (Welsh Ardal League North East)
Eight FA Cup campaigns from 1898/99 to 1908/09, reaching the 1st Qualifying Round in 1900/01 season, and with a 2-1 win at Chirk the club's only victory in the FA Cup.

West Kirby (West Cheshire League Division Two)
Three consecutive FA Cup campaigns across 1922–25, reaching 1st Qualifying Round in final campaign, with a 2-0 victory over Lostock Gralam that season the club's only FA Cup win.

Wigan Rovers (Wigan and District League Premier Division)
Four FA Cup campaigns between 1967/68 and 1972/73, exiting in the 1st Qualifying Round in all four seasons, and with a 1-1 draw against Horwich Railway Mechanics Institute the best FA Cup result achieved by the club to date.

Wilmslow Albion (Manchester Football League Division One)
Four campaigns from 1935/36 to 1949/50, reaching Preliminary Round only in 1948/49 season, but actually lost all four FA Cup matches played.

Wombwell Main (Sheffield County Senior League Premier Division)
Ten campaigns from 1906/07 to 1946/47 playing as Wombwell Main Welfare, reaching 2nd Qualifying Round in 1908/09 season, and with a 3-1 win against Worksop Town the club's only FA Cup victory.

Wymondham Town (Anglian Combination Division One)
Six consecutive FA Cup campaigns culminating in reaching 2nd Qualifying Round in 1955/56 season, with a 2-1 victory over Cromer FA the club's only FA Cup win.

Youlgrave United (Hope Valley Amateur League Premier Division)
Seven campaigns from 1921/22 to 1947/48 playing under the name Youlgrave, achieving five Preliminary Round exits but no actual FA Cup wins, although was involved in one of the rare 6-6 draws with Droylsden FC in 1947/48 season.

Rank	Spartan South Midlands League	Q4	Q3	Q2	Q1	PR	EP
1	Aylesbury	1		1		1	2
2	St Margaretsbury		2	2	5	5	4
3	Welwyn Garden City		2		4	3	5
4	Royston Town		1	2	2	5	5
5	Dunstable Town		1	1	3	2	1

Top Five FA Cup Clubs whilst Members of SSML.
Nb. Chart shows number of exits per Round

150 Clubs with Most Seasons between Consecutive FA Cup Campaigns

94	Torpoint (Association)	1906/07 Q2 Rd	Lost 0-2 at Radstock Town
	Torpoint Athletic	2010/11 EP Rd	Drew 1-1 at St Blazey
92	Knaresborough	1912/13 Q2 Rd	Lost 0-6 at Halifax Town
	Knaresborough Town	2014/15 EP Rd	Won 2-1 at Glasshoughton Welf.
87	Brotherhoods Works	1922/23 Pr Rd rep	Lost 1-2 at Desborough Town
	Peterborough Sports	2015/16 EP Rd	Won 1-0 at Eynesbury Rovers
85	Holwell Works	1914/15 EP Rd	Lost 1-4 at Grantham
	Holwell Sports	2009/10 EP Rd	Drew 2-2 vs. Ellistown
81	Newtown	1899/00 Q2 Rd rep	Lost 1-3 vs. Oswestry United
		1990/91 Pr Rd	Drew 1-1 vs. Eastwood Town
75	Harpenden Town	1913/14 EP Rd	Lost 0-2 at Luton Trinity
		1998/99 Pr Rd	Won 3-2 vs. Burnham
75	Christchurch	1914/15 Pr Rd	Scratched along with Poole
		1999/00 Pr Rd	Drew 1-1 vs. Bridport
73	Haslingden	1914/15 Q3 Rd rep 2	Lost 0-1 vs. Southport
		1997/98 Pr Rd	Lost 2-4 at Gretna
73	Ledbury	1928/29 EP Rd	Lost 1-4 at Oakengates Town
	Ledbury Town	2007/08 EP Rd	Lost 2-6 vs. Boldmere St Mich.
71	Cadbury Heath YMCA	1934/35 PR Rd	Lost 0-6 at Lovell's Athletic
	Cadbury Heath	2011/12 EP Rd	Won 6-1 at Corsham Town
69	Irchester United	1936/37 Pr Rd	Scratched before Desborough T.
		2011/12 EP Rd	Lost 2-3 at Thrapston Town
67	Sneinton	1930/31 Pr Rd	Lost 1-6 at Newark Castle Rovers
	Carlton Town	2003/04 EP Rd	Lost 0-3 to Shirebrook Town
67	Ringwood Town	1935/36 Q1 Rd	Lost 1-7 to Newport (IOW)
		2008/09 EP Rd	Won 1-0 vs. Hallen
67	Barnton	1949/50 EP Rd rep	Lost 1-2 at Knutsford
		2016/17 EP Rd	Lost 1-2 at 1874 Northwich
66	Steyning	1904/05 Q1 Rd	Lost 3-6 at Worthing
	Steyning Town	1980/81 Q1 Rd	Lost 1-3 at Sutton United
66	Brantham Athletic	1938/39 EP Rd	Lost 0-4 at Crittall Athletic
		2010/11 EP Rd	Won 4-2 vs. Woodbridge Town
66	Kings Langley	1945/46 Q1 Rd	Lost 1-7 at Harrow Town
		2011/12 EP Rd	Won 5-2 vs. Stotfold, Disqualified

65	Bristol St George	1953/54 Q2 Rd	Lost 1-4 at Chippenham United
	Roman Glass St George	2018/19 EP Rd	Lost 2-5 at Bradford Town
63	Sherborne	1937/38 EP Rd	Lost 1-2 vs. Weymouth
	Sherborne Town	2006/07 EP Rd	Lost 1-4 at Liskeard Athletic
62	Staffordshire Casuals	1949/50 Pr Rd	Lost 0-4 at Sutton Town
	Wolverhampton Casuals	2011/12 EP Rd	Lost 1-3 at Rocester
61	Pewsey Vale	1950/51 EP Rd	Lost 3-5 at Purton
		2011/12 EP Rd	Lost 0-2 vs. Bishop Sutton
59	Basford United	1954/55 Q1 Rd	Lost 1-7 vs. Gresley Rovers*
		2013/14 EP Rd	Won 1-0 vs. Holwell Sports
57	Kidlington	1950/51 EP Rd	Lost 0-6 at Headington United
		2007/08 EP Rd	Drew 1-1 vs. Shrivenham
57	Rufford Colliery	1950/51 Pr Rd	Lost 0-2 vs. Shirebrook
	Rainworth Miners Colliery	2007/08 EP Rd	Drew 0-0 at Teversal
56	Hanwell Town	1926/27 Pr Rd	Lost 3-4 vs. Hounslow
		1988/89 Pr Rd	Won 4-0 vs. Corinthian-Casuals
56	Newton Abbot Spurs	1964/65 Q1 Rd rep	Lost 2-3 at Falmouth Town
		2020/21 EP Rd	Won 3-0 vs. AFC St Austell
55	St Ives Town	1950/51 Pr Rd	Lost 2-5 at St Neots & District
		2005/06 EP Rd	Lost 1-2 at St Margaretsbury
54	Saffron Walden	1880/81 1st Rd	Lost 0-7 at Old Carthusians
	Saffron Walden Town	1938/39 Pr Rd	Lost 0-3 vs. Hoddesdon Town
54	Walsall Wood*	1920/21 EP Rd	Lost 0-1 at Talbot Stead
		1980/81 Pr Rd	Lost 0-3 vs. Winsford United
54	Henley Town	1949/50 Pr Rd	Lost 0-3 vs. Yiewsley
		2003/04 EP Rd	Drew 0-0 at St Margaretsbury
54	Wootton Bassett Town	1950/51 Pr Rd	Lost 0-4 at Devizes Town
		2004/05 Pr Rd	Lost 2-3 at Exmouth Town
54	Shaftesbury	1953/54 Q1 Rd	Lost 1-1 at Portland United
		2007/08 EP Rd	Drew 2-2 at Liskeard Athletic
54	Gedling Colliery	1954/55 Q2 Rd	Lost 2-3 at Gresley Rovers*
	Gedling Miners Welfare	2008/09 EP Rd	Lost 1-7 at Westfields
53	Sholing Athletic	1924/25 Pr Rd	Lost 1-2 vs. B'mouth Tramways
	Sholing Sports	1983/84 Q1 Rd	Won 2-1 vs. Salisbury

53	Wells City	1958/59 Q1 Rd	Lost 1-2 at Weston-super-Mare
		2011/12 EP Rd	Won 3-0 at Hengrove Athletic
52	Wimborne	1924/25 EP Rd	Lost 0-2 at Salisbury Corinthians
	Wimborne Town	1982/83 Pr Rd	Won 3-2 at Bridport
51	Woolwich Boro Council Ath.	1936/37 Pr Rd	Lost 1-2 at Swanley Athletic
	Greenwich Borough	1993/94 Q1 Rd	Won 2-0 at Eastbourne United
51	Sawbridgeworth	1949/50 EP Rd	Lost 0-6 vs. Tilbury
	Sawbridgeworth Town	2000/01 Pr Rd	Lost 1-3 at Chelmsford City
50	Corsham Town	1952/53 Pr Rd	Lost 1-4 vs. Chippenham Town
		2002/03 Pr Rd	Won 3-1 vs. Portland United
49	Rossington Main	1938/39 EP Rd	Lost 0-3 at Rawmarsh Welfare
		1993/94 Pr Rd	Lost 0-3 at Rossendale United
49	Cobham	1950/51 Pr Rd	Lost 0-3 at Camberley
		1999/00 Pr Rd	Drew 1-1 vs. Farnham Town
49	East Cowes Victoria	1950/51 Pr Rd	Lost 2-3 at Romsey Town
	East Cowes Victoria Athletic	1999/00 Pr Rd	Lost 0-1 vs. Sittingbourne
49	Whitton United	1959/60 Q1 Rd	Lost 1-2 vs. Harwich & Parkeston
		2008/09 EP Rd	Drew 1-1 vs. Cornard United
48	Percy Main Amateurs	1927/28 Pr Rd	Lost 1-2 at Walker Celtic
		1981/82 Pr Rd	Lost 1-3 at Lancaster City
47	Reigate Priory	1876/77 1st Rd	Lost 0-5 at Clapham Rovers
		1927/28 Pr Rd	Lost 4-7 at West Norwood
47	Keynsham	1937/38 Pr Rd	Scratched before St Philips MAS
	Keynsham Town	1990/91 Pr Rd	Lost 1-2 at Melksham Town
47	Stansted	1949/50 EP Rd	Lost 0-5 vs. Grays Athletic
		1996/97 Pr Rd	Won 2-1 vs. Aveley
47	Tavistock	1959/60 Pr Rd	Lost 3-4 at Bideford
		2006/07 Pr Rd	Won 4-2 vs. Bridport
46	Langford	1937/38 Pr Rd	Lost 1-3 vs. Kempston Rovers
		1989/90 Pr Rd	Lost 0-3 vs. Canvey Island
46	Leiston	1958/59 Q1 Rd	Lost 2-6 vs. Whitton United
		2004/05 EP Rd	Drew 1-1 vs. Felixstowe/Walton
46	Long Melford	1958/59 Q1 Rd rep	Lost 2-4 at Haverhill Rovers
		2004/05 EP Rd	Drew 1-1 at Great Yarmouth T.

44	Stewarts & Lloyds (Corby)	1948/49 Q1 Rd	Lost 0-1 at Wellingborough Town
		1992/93 Pr Rd	Won 4-2 vs. Evesham United
44	Atherton Collieries	1950/51 Pr Rd	Lost 0-5 at Hyde United
		1994/95 Pr Rd	Drew 1-1 vs. Blidworth MW
43	Hoddesdon	1884/85 1st Rd	Lost 0-8 at Old Foresters
	Hoddesdon Town	1931/32 Pr Rd	Won 6-2 at Waltham Comrades
43	Thatcham	1938/39 EP Rd	Lost 0-3 vs. Morris Motors
	Thatcham Town	1987/88 Pr Rd	Lost 0-3 vs. Worthing
43	Liversedge	1948/49 EP Rd	Lost 0-6 at Farsley Celtic
		1991/92 Pr Rd	Won 3-1 vs. Maine Road
43	Brightlingsea United	1949/50 EP Rd	Lost 0-4 at Clapton
		1992/93 Pr Rd	Lost 1-2 vs. Fisher Athletic
43	Fakenham Town	1950/51 EP Rd	Lost 2-8 at Eastern Coachworks
		1993/94 Pr Rd	Drew 2-2 vs. Great Yarmouth T.
43	Odd Down	1950/51 EP Rd	Lost 0-6 vs. Corsham Town
		1993/94 Pr Rd	Drew 1-1 vs. Ilfracombe Town
43	South Normanton MW	1962/63 Q1 Rd	Scratched before Belper Town
	South Normanton Athletic	2005/06 Pr Rd	Won 1-0 vs. Arnold Town
42	Normanby Park Steel Works	1931/32 Pr Rd	Lost 0-1 at Brigg Town
		1979/80 Pr Rd	Lost 1-3 vs. Whitby Town
42	Brodsworth Main Colliery ...	1955/56 Q1 Rd	Lost 1-2 vs. Langold WMC
	Brodsworth Miners Welfare	1997/98 Pr Rd	Lost 0-3 at Billingham Town
39	Peterboro Westwood Wrks	1948/49 Q1 Rd	Scratched before Desborough T.
	Baker Perkins	1987/88 Pr Rd	Drew 2-2 vs. Rushall Olympic
39	Harworth Colliery Athletic	1949/50 Pr Rd rep	Lost 4-8 at Stocksbridge Works
	Harworth Colliery Institute	1988/89 Pr Rd	Drew 0-0 vs. Belper Town
39	Ruislip Town	1949/50 EP Rd	Lost 2-6 at Hatfield Town
		1988/89 Pr Rd	Won 2-0 vs. Crockenhill
39	Bournemouth (Amateurs) ...	1950/51 Q1 Rd	Lost 2-6 at Blandford United
		1989/90 Pr Rd	Won 2-0 vs. Bracknell Town
39	Bicester Town	1955/56 Pr Rd	Lost 0-4 at Slough Town
		1994/95 Q1 Rd	Lost 0-5 at Wokingham Town
39	Warboys Town	1958/59 Pr Rd	Lost 2-4 at Soham Town Rangers
		1997/98 Pr Rd	Drew 0-0 at N'hampton Spencer

39	Heaton Stannington	1976/77 Q1 Rd	Lost 0-3 vs. Shildon
		2015/16 EP Rd	Won 3-1 vs. Norton & Stockton
38	Andover	1898/99 Q1 Rd	Lost 0-2 at Freemantle
		1946/47 Pr Rd	Lost 0-2 at Thornycroft Athletic
38	Guiseley	1945/46 Q1 Rd rep	Lost 0-7 at Frickley Colliery
		1983/84 Q1 Rd	Lost 0-1 at Morecambe
38	Cleator Moor Celtic	1950/51 1st Rd	Lost 0-5 vs. Tranmere Rovers
		1988/89 Pr Rd	Drew 0-0 vs. Bridlington Town
37	Barnard Castle Athletic	1890/91 Q1 Rd	Lost 2-3 at Darlington St August.
		1931/32 EP Rd	Drew 2-2 at Durham City
37	Lymington	1953/54 Q1 Rd	Lost 0-9 at Dorchester Town
	AFC Lymington	1990/91 Pr Rd	Won 5-1 at Chichester City
37	Morpeth Town	1958/59 Q1 Rd rep	Lost 0-2 vs. Ferryhill Athletic
		1995/96 Pr Rd	Drew 2-2 at Ryhope Comm. Ass.
36	Hallam	1958/59 Q2 Rd	Lost 1-4 at Norton Woodseats
		1994/95 Pr Rd	Drew 1-1 at Denaby United
35	Wrockwardine Wood	1897/98 Q3 Rd	Lost 3-5 vs. Burton Wanderers
		1936/37 EP Rd	Lost 2-3 at Hednesford Town
35	Metropolitan Railway	1898/99 Q3 Rd	Lost 2-8 at Gravesend United
		1937/38 EP Rd	Lost 1-5 vs. Slough
35	Armthorpe Welfare	1950/51 EP Rd	Lost 1-8 at Ashby Institute
		1985/86 Q1 Rd	Drew 1-1 at Burscough
35	Exmouth Town*	1950/51 EP Rd rep	Lost 1-4 vs. St Blazey
		1985/86 Pr Rd	Won 5-0 at Glastonbury
35	Langley Park Colliery Welf.	1950/51 EP Rd	Lost 2-5 at Evenwood Town
		1985/86 Pr Rd	Lost 2-6 vs. Horden CW
35	Farnham Town	1951/52 Pr Rd	Lost 3-5 vs. Hounslow Town
		1986/87 Pr Rd	Drew 1-1 at Devizes Town
35	Diss Town	1959/60 Q1 Rd rep 2	Lost 1-2 vs. Gorleston
		1994/95 Pr Rd	Drew 2-2 at Lowestoft Town
35	Prestwich Heys	1983/84 Q2 Rd	Lost 0-1 vs. Southport
		2018/19 EP Rd	Won 2-1 vs. Abbey Hey
34	Ipswich Town	1892/93 Q2 Rd	Lost 1-4 at Old Westminsters
		1930/31 EP Rd	Won 5-0 vs. Harwich & Parkeston

34	Hastings and St Leonards	1947/48 Pr Rd	Lost 1-2 vs Horsham
	Hastings Town	1981/82 Q1 Rd	Lost 0-1 at Ashford Town (Kent)
34	Arlesey Town	1950/51 EP Rd	Lost 2-3 at Letchworth Town
		1984/85 Pr Rd	Drew 2-2 vs. Cheshunt
34	Harrogate Railway Athletic	1956/57 Q2 Rd	Lost 0-4 at Goole Town
		1990/91 Q4 Rd	Lost 1-3 at Chorley
34	Nelson	1968/69 Pr Rd	Lost 0-4 vs. Netherfield (Kendal)
		2002/03 EP Rd	Drew 0-0 vs. Norton & Stockton
33	Ecclesfield	1890/91 Q3 Rd	Lost 0-3 at Lincoln City
		1927/28 EP Rd	Won 5-3 vs. Grimethorpe CI
33	Arnold St Mary's	1922/23 Pr Rd	Lost 0-3 vs. Sutton Junction
		1961/62 Q1 Rd	Lost 1-5 vs. Matlock Town
33	Romsey Town	1950/51 Q1 Rd rep	Lost 0-2 at Dorchester Town
		1983/84 Pr Rd	Drew 1-1 vs. Chippenham Town
33	Welwyn Garden City	1955/56 Pr Rd	Lost 0-3 vs. Clapton
		1988/89 Pr Rd	Lost 0-2 at Potton United
33	Ossett Town	1957/58 Q2 Rd rep	Lost 3-4 vs. Stocksbridge Works
		1990/91 Pr Rd	Drew 1-1 at Knowsley United
32	Brigg*	1881/82 1st Rd	Lost 0-6 at Grantham
		1913/14 EP Rd	Lost 1-8 vs. Fryston Colliery
32	Spilsby	1884/85 1st Rd	Lost 3-7 at Newark
		1920/21 EP Rd	Lost 2-3 at Horncastle Town
32	Casuals	1894/95 Q2 Rd rep	Lost 1-3 vs. Ilford
		1930/31 Pr Rd	Won 3-1 vs. Redhill
32	South West Ham	1896/97 Pr Rd	Lost 1-4 at Windsor and Eton
		1932/33 Pr Rd	Lost 2-5 at Clapton
32	Faversham	1907/08 Q1 Rd	Lost 0-3 vs. Bromley
	Faversham Town	1949/50 EP Rd	Won 3-1 at Margate
32	Thame	1938/39 EP Rd	Lost 1-6 vs. Aylesbury United
	Thame United	1976/77 Q1 Rd	Won 1-0 vs. Witney Town
32	Shepshed Albion	1949/50 Pr Rd rep	Lost 2-8 at Atherstone Town
	Shepshed Charterhouse	1981/82 Q1 Rd	Won 2-1 at Kidderminster H.
32	Newhaven	1962/63 Q1 Rd rep	Lost 0-2 vs. Bexhill Town
		1994/95 Pr Rd	Lost 0-6 at Canterbury City

32	Portland United	1970/71 Q1 Rd 2002/03 EP Rd	Lost 0-3 at Salisbury Won 6-2 vs. Welton Rovers
32	Bodmin Town	1972/73 Q1 Rd 2004/05 Pr Rd	Lost 1-3 at Barnstaple Town Won 4-0 vs. Clevedon United
31	Thornaby*	1901/02 Q3 Rd 1936/37 Pr Rd	Lost 1-2 vs. Sunderland Royal R. Lost 2-5 vs. South Bank
31	Eldon Albion	1907/08 Pr Rd 1948/49 EP Rd	Lost 0-1 at Spennymoor United Lost 0-5 vs. South Hetton CW
31	New Mills*	1932/33 Pr Rd 1969/70 Q1 Rd	Lost 1-3 at Earle Lost 0-1 vs. Mossley
31	Shoreham	1955/56 Pr Rd 1986/87 Pr Rd	Lost 1-6 vs. Bognor Regis Town Lost 0-4 at Camberley Town
31	Radstock Town	1955/56 Q1 Rd 1986/87 Pr Rd	Lost 2-3 vs. Weston-super-Mare Drew 1-1 at Havant Town
31	Eton Manor	1958/59 Q1 Rd 1989/90 Pr Rd	Lost 2-9 vs. Romford Drew 2-2 at Hailsham Town
31	Winchester City	1972/73 Q1 Rd rep 3 2003/04 Pr Rd	Lost 0-3 vs. Basingstoke Town Won 2-0 at Banstead Athletic
30	Flint .... Flint Town	1894/95 Q3 Rd 1928/29 Pr Rd	Lost 1-2 vs. Fairfield Won 1-0 vs. Altrincham
30	Lewes	1926/27 Pr Rd 1962/63 Q1 Rd	Lost 4-5 at Southwick Won 5-1 vs. Horsham
30	Wootton Blue Cross	1950/51 Q2 Rd 1980/81 Pr Rd	Lost 3-4 vs. Hitchin Town Lost 0-3 at Tiptree United
30	Ilfracombe Town	1959/60 Q1 Rd 1989/90 Pr Rd	Scratched before Truro City Won 1-0 at Clevedon Town
30	Sheffield	1959/60 Q1 Rd 1989/90 Pr Rd	Lost 2-3 vs. Worksop Town Won 1-0 vs. Armthorpe Welfare
30	Larkhall Athletic	1978/79 Q1 Rd rep 2008/09 EP Rd	Lost 1-2 at Paulton Rovers Won 5-0 at Liskeard Athletic
29	Addlestone	1930/31 Pr Rd 1965/66 Q1 Rd	Lost 1-7 vs. RAMC Aldershot Lost 0-9 at Woking
29	Epping Town*	1937/38 EP Rd 1972/73 Q1 Rd	Lost 0-3 at Tufnell Park Lost 0-1 at Bishop's Stortford

29	Buckingham Town	1950/51 EP Rd	Lost 1-5 vs. Yiewsley
		1979/80 Q1 Rd	Lost 0-7 vs. Hendon
28	Bridport	1906/07 Q1 Rd	Lost 0-3 vs. Whiteheads
		1938/39 EP Rd	Lost 0-5 at Bournemouth (Ams.)
28	Shepton Mallet Town*	1950/51 EP Rd	Lost 1-5 vs. Devizes Town
		1978/79 Q1 Rd	Won 3-1 at Llanelli
28	Royston Town	1954/55 Pr Rd	Lost 0-11 at Barnet
		1982/83 Q1 Rd	Lost 0-5 vs. Leytonstone/Ilford
28	Street	1971/72 Q1 Rd	Lost 2-4 at Trowbridge Town
		1999/00 Pr Rd	Lost 0-1 vs. Eastleigh
27	Alford United	1912/13 EP Rd	Lost 1-4 vs. Hull Day Street OB
		1949/50 EP Rd	Won 6-4 vs. Skegness Town
27	Felixstowe United	1950/51 EP Rd	Lost 1-3 at Sheringham
	Felixstowe Town	1977/78 Q1 Rd	Lost 2-4 vs Gorleston
27	Kempston Rovers	1950/51 EP Rd	Lost 1-2 at St Ives Town
		1977/78 Pr Rd	Won 2-1 vs. Potton United
27	Alnwick Town	1958/59 Q1 Rd rep	Lost 2-3 at Cockfield
		1985/86 Q1 Rd	Lost 0-1 at Bridlington Trinity
27	Sidley United	1978/78 Q1 Rd	Lost 1-4 at Medway
		2005/06 EP Rd	Won 3-1 vs. Pagham
27	Gornal Athletic	1980/81 Q1 Rd	Lost 0-2 at Bedworth United
		2007/08 EP Rd	Lost 0-3 vs. Meir KA
26	Camberley	1950/51 Q1 Rd	Lost 2-3 at Tooting & Mitcham U.
	Camberley Town	1976/77 Q1 Rd	Drew 1-1 vs. Epsom and Ewell
25	Rockingham Colliery	1906/07 Q1 Rd	Lost 1-4 at Castleford Town
		1935/36 EP Rd	Drew 1-1 vs. Mexborough Ath.
25	Players Athletic	1920/21 Pr Rd	Lost 0-4 at Welbeck Colliery
		1951/52 Q1 Rd	Lost 1-4 at Ransome and Marles
25	Willesden	1950/51 Pr Rd	Lost 1-5 at Enfield
		1975/76 Q1 Rd	Lost 1-4 at Molesey
25	Paulton Rovers	1953/54 Pr Rd	Lost 1-4 at Hanham Athletic
		1978/79 Q1 Rd	Drew 3-3 at Larkhall Athletic
25	Boldmere St Michaels	1958/59 Q1 Rd	Lost 2-4 vs. Evesham United
		1983/84 Pr Rd	Lost 0-2 vs. Dudley Town

25	Wellington (Somerset)	1984/85 Q1 Rd	Lost 2-3 vs. Glastonbury
		2009/10 EP Rd	Lost 1-3 vs. Bideford
24	Redcar*	1889/90 Q2 Rd	Lost 1-8 vs. Rotherham Town
		1913/14 Pr Rd	Lost 2-8 at Spennymoor United
24	Prescot	1892/93 Q2 Rd	Lost 1-2 at Chester
		1920/21 Pr Rd	Won 4-2 vs. Northern Nomads
24	Whitley and Monkseaton	1908/09 Pr Rd	Lost 0-3 at Seaham White Star
		1936/37 EP Rd	Won 3-2 at Consett
24	Sandbach Ramblers*	1938/39 EP Rd	Lost 1-2 vs. Nantwich
		1968/69 Pr Rd	Lost 4-5 at Nantwich
24	Parson Drove	1950/51 Q1 Rd	Lost 0-1 at Histon Institute
		1974/75 Q1 Rd	Lost 0-9 at King's Lynn
24	Eppleton Colliery Welfare	1951/52 Q1 Rd	Lost 2-4 at Chilton Athletic
		1975/76 Q1 Rd	Won 1-0 vs. Ferryhill Athletic
24	Stockton Heath Albion	1959/60 Pr Rd	Lost 0-3 vs. Congleton Town
	Warrington Town	1983/84 Pr Rd	Lost 0-3 vs. Stalybridge Celtic
24	Newquay	1981/82 Q1 Rd	Lost 0-2 at Falmouth Town
		2005/06 EP Rd	Lost 1-2 at Westbury United
23	Finchley	1881/82 1st Rd rep	Lost 0-4 at Acton
		1904/05 Q1 Rd	Lost 1-2 at West Hampstead
23	Hurst	1888/89 Q1 Rd	Drew 0-0 vs. Bolton Wanderers
		1911/12 Pr Rd	Won 6-1 vs. Macclesfield Town
23	Cleethorpes Town*	1888/89 Q3 Rd	Lost 0-5 at Grimsby Town
		1911/12 EP Rd	Won 5-0 at Allerton Bywater Col.
23	Douglas (Kingswood)	1921/22 EP Rd	Scratched before Clutton Wands.
		1950/51 Pr Rd	Lost 0-5 at Clevedon
23	St Austell	1967/68 Q2 Rd	Lost 0-2 at Bideford
		1990/91 Pr Rd	Lost 0-4 vs. Falmouth Town
23	Almondsbury Greenway ...	1981/82 Pr Rd	Drew 1-1 vs. Wellington (Somer.)
	Almondsbury Town	2004/05 Pr Rd	Lost 0-4 at Fairford Town
23	Penzance	1982/83 Q1 Rd	Lost 1-2 at Chard Town
		2005/06 Pr Rd	Drew 2-2 vs. Street
23	Coleshill Town	1984/85 Pr Rd	Lost 1-6 at St Helens Town
		2007/08 EP Rd	Drew 1-1 vs. Wellington (Mids.)

**Different from current / later club with same/similar name*

Top 150 FA Cup Clubs Between the Wars (1919/20 to 1938/39)

During the 20 years between the Wars, the FA Cup underwent its last two major changes. After three seasons at Stamford Bridge, the first FA Cup Final at the original Wembley Stadium took place in 1923. Bolton Wanderers won the first of three finals in the 1920s, to become the most successful inter-war club of the FA Cup. The second major change saw the current structure of the FA Cup put in place for the 1925/26 season, driven by the Football League doubling in size to four divisions soon after the Great War. Lower down the rankings some clubs that made the later qualifying rounds in the early 1920s may be disadvantaged by one or two positions during this period, but it doesn't affect clubs at the top of the rankings.

Best Performance - Winners

1	Bolton Wanderers	3x Winners
2	Arsenal	2x Winners, 4x Finalists
3	Newcastle United	2x Winners, 2x Finalists
4	Huddersfield Town	1x Winners, 5x Finalists
5	Manchester City	1x Winners, 3x Finalists, 5x SF
6	Preston North End	1x Winners, 3x Finalists, 4x SF
7	Portsmouth	1x Winners, 3x Finalists, 3x SF
8	Aston Villa	1x Winners, 2x Finalists, 5x SF
9	Sheffield United	1x Winners, 2x Finalists, 4x SF
10	West Bromwich Albion	1x Winners, 2x Finalists, 3x SF, 6x QF
11	Cardiff City	1x Winners, 2x Finalists, 3x SF, 5x QF
12	Sunderland	1x Winners, 1x Finalists, 3x SF
13	Tottenham Hotspur	1x Winners, 1x Finalists, 2x SF, 8x QF
14	Everton	1x Winners, 1x Finalists, 2x SF, 5x QF
15	Blackburn Rovers	1x Winners, 1x Finalists, 2x SF, 4x QF
16	The / Sheffield Wednesday	1x Winners, 1x Finalists, 2x SF, 2x QF

Best Performance – Finalists

17	Wolverhampton Wanderers	2x Finalists
18	West Ham United	1x Finalists, 2x SF
19	Birmingham (City)	1x Finalists, 1x SF

Best Performance – Semi-Finalists

20	Chelsea	2x SF, 6x QF
21	Derby County	2x SF, 3x QF, 7x R5
22	Burnley	2x SF, 3x QF, 5x R5
23	Southampton	2x SF, 3x QF, 3x R5
24	Grimsby Town	2x SF, 2x QF
25	Millwall	1x SF, 3x QF
26	Leicester City	1x SF, 2x QF, 6x R5
27	Swansea Town (City)	1x SF, 2x QF, 4x R5
28	Manchester United	1x SF, 2x QF, 3x R5, 8x R4

29 Hull City .... 1x SF, 2x QF, 3x R5, 4x R4
30 Fulham .... 1x SF, 2x QF, 2x R5
31 Reading .... 1x SF, 1x QF, 3x R5
32 Notts County .... 1x SF, 1x QF, 2x R5, 5x R4
33 Bristol City .... 1x SF, 1x QF, 2x R5, 3x R4

Best Performance – Quarter-Finalists

34 Liverpool .... 4x QF
35 Nottingham Forest .... 3x QF
36 Stoke / City .... 2x QF
37 Bradford (Park Avenue)* ..... 1x QF, 7x R5
38 Middlesbrough .... 1x QF, 6x R5
39 Bradford City .... 1x QF, 3x R5
40 Bury .... 1x QF, 2x R5, 10x R4
41 Blackpool .... 1x QF, 2x R5, 7x R4, 15x R3
42 Swindon Town .... 1x QF, 2x R5, 7x R4, 9x R3
43 Luton Town .... 1x QF, 2x R5, 5x R4, 12x R3
44 Brentford .... 1x QF, 2x R5, 5x R4, 10x R3
45 Barnsley .... 1x QF, 2x R5, 4x R4, 13x R3, 16x R2
46 Charlton Athletic .... 1x QF, 2x R5, 4x R4, 13x R3, 15x R2
47 Watford .... 1x QF, 2x R5, 4x R4, 8x R3
48 Exeter City .... 1x QF, 2x R5, 3x R4
49 (Leyton) Clapton Orient .... 1x QF, 1x R5, 4x R4, 7x R3
50 Southport .... 1x QF, 1x R5, 4x R4, 6x R3
51 Queens Park Rangers .... 1x QF, 1x R5, 2x R4, 8x R3
52 York City .... 1x QF, 1x R5, 2x R4, 6x R3

Best Performance – 5th Round

53 Leeds United 3x R5
54 Brighton & Hove Albion 2x R5, 4x R4, 10x R3
55 Crystal Palace 2x R5, 4x R4, 7x R3
56 Chesterfield 2x R5, 3x R4
57 South Shields* / Gateshead* 2x R5, 2x R4
58 Port Vale 1x R5, 5x R4
59 Walsall 1x R5, 4x R4
60 (AFC) Bournemouth & Bosc. 1x R5, 3x R4, 9x R3
61 Southend United 1x R5, 3x R4, 8x R3
62 Stockport County 1x R5, 2x R4, 7x R3, 12x R2
63 Norwich City 1x R5, 2x R4, 7x R3, 11x R2
64 Northampton Town 1x R5, 2x R4, 7x R3, 10x R2
65 Coventry City 1x R5, 1x R4, 5x R3, 9x R2
66 Aldershot / Town* 1x R5, 1x R4, 5x R3, 8x R2
67 Halifax Town 1x R5, 1x R4, 4x R3

Best Performance – 4th Round

68	Plymouth Argyle	5x R4
69	Oldham Athletic	3x R4, 11x R3
70	Darlington*	3x R4, 7x R3, 11x R2
71	Tranmere Rovers	3x R4, 7x R3, 9x R2
72	Chester (City)*	3x R4, 5x R3
73	New Brighton	3x R4, 3x R3
74	Corinthians	2x R4, 8x R3
75	Doncaster Rovers	2x R4, 6x R3
76	Accrington Stanley*	2x R4, 5x R3
77	Wrexham	2x R4, 4x R3
78	Bristol Rovers	1x R4, 7x R3
79	Crewe Alexandra	1x R4, 4x R3
80	Mansfield Town	1x R4, 3x R3
81	Workington AFC	1x R4, 2x R3
82	Chelmsford City	1x R4, 1x R3

Best Performance – 3rd Round

83	Lincoln City	6x R3
84	Carlisle United	4x R3, 9x R2
85	Rotherham United	4x R3, 7x R2
86	Yeovil & Petter's U. (Town)	3x R3
87	Newport County*	2x R3, 9x R2
88	Scarborough	2x R3, 5x R2
89	Wigan Borough	2x R3, 4x R2, 8x R1, (plus 1x q6)
90	Bath City	2x R3, 4x R2, 8x R1, (plus 1x q5)
91	Dartford	2x R3, 4x R2, 7x R1
92	Gillingham	1x R3, 8x R2
93	(Hartlepool) Hartlepools U.	1x R3, 7x R2, 15x R1
94	Torquay United	1x R3, 7x R2, 13x R1
95	Folkestone	1x R3, 4x R2
96	Burton Town	1x R3, 3x R2, 5x R1
97	Margate	1x R3, 3x R2, 4x R1
98	Spennymoor United	1x R3, 2x R2, 6x R1
99	Crook Town*	1x R3, 2x R2, 4x R1, (plus 1x q6)
100	Rhyl	1x R3, 2x R2, 4x R1, (plus 2x q3)
101	Ipswich Town	1x R3, 2x R2, 3x R1
102	Chilton Colliery Rec. Ath.	1x R3, 2x R2, 2x R1
103	Ashington	1x R3, 1x R2, 7x R1
104	Peterborough & Fletton Utd.	1x R3, 1x R2, 5x R1, (plus 1x q5)
105	Darwen	1x R3, 1x R2, 5x R1, (plus 4x q4)
106	Southall	1x R3, 1x R2, 5x R1, (plus 2x q4, 3x q3)
107	Aberdare Athletic	1x R3, 1x R2, 5x R1, (plus 2x q4, 1x pr)
108	Cheltenham Town	1x R3, 1x R2, 4x R1, (plus 2x q4)

109	Wigan Athletic	1x R3, 1x R2, 4x R1, (plus 1x q4)
110	London Caledonians	1x R3, 1x R2, 3x R1, (plus 1x q6, 4x q5)
111	Clapton	1x R3, 1x R2, 3x R1, (plus 1x q6, 3x q5)
112	Boston*	1x R3, 1x R2, 3x R1, (plus 1x q5)
113	Poole / St Mary's / Town	1x R3, 1x R2, 3x R1, (plus 1x q4)
114	Runcorn (FC Halton)	1x R3, 1x R2, 1x R3

Best Performance – 2nd Round

115	Gainsborough Trinity	8x R2
116	Barrow	5x R2
117	Scunthorpe & Lindsey Utd.	4x R2
118	Northfleet United	3x R2, 8x R1
119	Walthamstow Avenue	3x R2, 6x R1
120	Rochdale	2x R2, 16x R1
121	Ilford*	2x R2, 8x R1
122	Kettering Town	2x R2, 7x R1, (plus 1x q6, 2x q5)
123	Blyth Spartans	2x R2, 7x R1, (plus 1x q6, 6x q4)
124	Guildford City*	2x R2, 7x R1, (plus 8x q4)
125	Nelson	2x R2, 6x R1, (plus 2x q6)
126	Tunbridge Wells Rangers* ...	2x R2, 6x R1, (plus 2x q4)
127	Leyton*	2x R2, 5x R1
128	Sittingbourne	2x R2, 4x R1
129	Bromley	2x R2, 2x R1, (plus 1x q6)
130	South Liverpool*	2x R2, 2x R1, (plus 1x q4)
131	Merthyr Town*	1x R2, 8x R1, (plus 1x q6)
132	Wellington Town (Telford U)	1x R2, 8x R1, (plus 1x q4)
133	Stalybridge Celtic	1x R2, 6x R1
134	Worksop Town	1x R2, 4x R1, (plus 1x q6, 1x q5, 4x q4)
135	Shildon / Athletic	1x R2, 4x R1, (plus 1x q6, 1x q5, 2x q4)
136	Nunhead	1x R2, 4x R1, (plus 2x q5)
137	Wimbledon	1x R2, 4x R1, (plus 6x q4)
138	Chatham (Town)	1x R2, 4x R1, (plus 4x q4, 2x q3)
139	Newark Town*	1x R2, 4x R1, (plus 4x q4, 1x q3)
140	West Stanley	1x R2, 3x R1, (plus 7x q4)
141	Stockton*	1x R2, 3x R1, (plus 5x q4)
142	Kidderminster Harriers	1x R2, 3x R1, (plus 1x q4, 1x q3, 3x q1)
143	Boston United	1x R2, 3x R1, (plus 1x q4, 1x q3)
144	Durham City	1x R2, 2x R1, (plus 4x q5)
145	Grantham (Town)	1x R2, 2x R1, (plus 3x q4, 5x q3)
146	Preston Coll. / North Shields	1x R2, 2x R1, (plus 3x q4, 4x q2)
147	Barry (Town)	1x R2, 2x R1, (plus 2x q4)
148	Manchester Central	1x R2, 2x R1, (plus 1x q4)
149	Castleford Town	1x R2, 1x R1, (plus 1x q5)
150	Sutton Town (Ashfield Utd.)	1x R2, 1x R1, (plus 2x q4)

**Different from current/later club with same/similar name*

150 FA Cup Giant-Killings

(Which is the greatest Giant-Killing of them all? Is your favourite listed here?)

Classic Giant-killing Folklore (15)

These 'David overcoming Goliath' matches are well known to all fans of English football.

1932/33 R3 **Walsall** (3N) 2-0 Arsenal (1)
The first real 'shock' of the FA Cup – Arsenal were Champions and would retain their title.

1948/49 R4 **Yeovil Town** (NL) 2-1 Sunderland (1)
Seismic shock as Sunderland at the time were known as the 'Bank of England' club.

1955/56 R2 Derby County (3N) 1-6 **Boston United** (NL)
The biggest away win by a non-league side over a Football League club.

1958/59 R3 **Worcester City** (NL) 2-1 Liverpool (2)
Liverpool may have been a second tier club at the time, but this result still resonates.

1970/71 R5 **Colchester United** (4) 3-2 Leeds United (1)
A shock considered on a par with Walsall beating Arsenal. Colchester had been 3-0 up.

1971/72 R3r **Hereford United** (NL) 2-1 Newcastle United (1)
The most cited FA Cup giant-killing of all time; has become synonymous with the feat.

1974/75 R3 Burnley (1) 0-1 **Wimbledon** (NL)
First time a top-flight club lost at home to a non-league side in current FA Cup structure.

1977/78 R4 Stoke City (2) 2-3 **Blyth Spartans** (NL)
This was Blyth Spartans' eighth victory of their FA Cup campaign that season.

1979/80 R3 **Halifax Town** (4) 1-0 Manchester City (1)
Halifax Town only reached the 3rd Round 13 times so opportunity to giant-kill was limited.

1979/80 R3r **Harlow Town** (6) 1-0 Leicester City (2)
The Leicester City side included a very young Gary Lineker.

1985/86 R3 Birmingham City (1) 1-2 **Altrincham** (5)
Unsurprisingly, Birmingham City were relegated from the top flight at the end of the season.

1988/89 R3 **Sutton United** (5) 2-1 Coventry City (1)
Coventry City had lifted the FA Cup just 20 months earlier.

1990/91 R3 West Bromwich Albion (2) 2-4 **Woking** (5)
Noted for the stunning hat-trick by Woking's Tim Buzaglo.

1991/92 R3 **Wrexham** (4) 2-1 Arsenal (1)
Arsenal were current League Champions, Wrexham had finished bottom of Division Four.

1993/94 R3 Birmingham City (2) 1-2 **Kidderminster Harriers** (5)
Unsurprisingly, Birmingham City were relegated from the second tier at the end of season.

Early Acts of Giant-Killing (10 / 25)

In the very early days of the Football League, clubs outside of the League were often considered as good as, if not better than, League sides, and there would be many instances of League clubs being knocked out by non-league sides up until World War I. Listed here are the more notable ones.

1888/89 Q1 Stoke (City) (1) 1-2 **Warwick County** (NL)
The first time a top-flight club was knocked out of the FA Cup by a non-league side.

1888/89 Q3 **Linfield Athletic** (NL) 4-0 Bolton Wanderers (1)
The first instance of a top-flight club knocked out by a non-English non-league team.

1888/89 R2 **The Wednesday** (NL) 3-2 Notts County (1)
The first time a top-flight club lost to a non-league side in the 'Proper' rounds.

1889/90 SF **The Wednesday** (NL) 2-1 Bolton Wanderers (1)
The first non-league side to beat a top-flight club in the FA Cup semi-finals.

1890/91 R1 **Stoke** (City) (NL) 3-0 Preston North End (1)
The first time a non-league club defeated the current League Champions in the FA Cup.

1900/01 R1 **Tottenham Hotspur** (NL) 2-1 Bury (1)
The first time a non-league club knocked out the FA Cup holders.

1900/01 Fin r **Tottenham Hotspur** (NL) 3-1 Sheffield United (1)
The only time a non-league side has won the FA Cup.

1905/06 Q3 **Crystal Palace** (NL) 7-1 Chelsea (2)
The biggest margin of victory by a non-league club over a Football League side.

1905/06 R3 **Southampton** (NL) 6-1 Middlesbrough (1)
The biggest margin of victory by a non-league club over a top-flight team.

1910/11 R1 Bristol City (1) 0-3 **Crewe Alexandra** (NL)
First top-flight club to lose to a non-Southern League / Football Alliance non-league side.

Rank	North West Counties League	R1	Q4	Q3	Q2	Q1	PR	EP
1	Penrith	2	1	1	1	2	3	
2	Colwyn Bay	1	1	1		3	1	
3	Skelmersdale United	1		2	2	9	9	
4	Newcastle Town	1		1	3	9	4	1
5	Stalybridge Celtic	1		1	1		2	
6	Leigh Genesis	1						

Top Six FA Cup Clubs whilst Members of NWCL.

Nb. Chart shows number of exits per Round

Early Giant-Killings within current FA Cup structure in place from 1925/26 Season (10 / 35)

The FA Cup was restructured for the 1925/26 season into a format almost the same as would be recognised today whereby clubs from the top two Football League divisions were exempted until the 3rd Round 'Proper'. All non-league clubs, bar some early exemptions, would have to try to qualify for the 'Proper' Rounds.

1933/34 R2 Carlisle United (3N) 1-2 **Cheltenham Town** (NL)
The first non-league club to start its FA Cup campaign in the Extra Preliminary Round to go on to beat a Football League team in same run.

1935/36 R1 **Southall** (NL) 3-1 Swindon Town (3S)
Arguably the lowest level non-league club to beat a Football League side.

1947/48 R3 **Colchester United** (NL) 1-0 Huddersfield Town (1)
The first instance of a non-league club defeating a top-flight club in the current structure.

1947/48 R4 **Colchester United** (NL) 3-2 Bradford (Park Avenue) (2)
The first instance of a non-league club defeating a second tier side in the current structure.

1948/49 R3 **Yeovil Town** (NL) 3-1 Bury (2)
Yeovil Town would go on become noted for their Giant-Killing exploits.

1954/55 R3 r **Bishop Auckland** (NL) 3-0 Ipswich Town (2)
Bishop Auckland would win the first of three consecutive FA Amateur Cup finals this season.

1956/57 R3 Notts County (2) 1-3 **Rhyl** (Athletic) (NL)
First away win by a non-league side over a club from the top two tiers of Football League.

1956/57 R3 r Lincoln City (2) 4-5 **Peterborough United** (NL)

1959/60 R3 Ipswich Town (2) 2-3 **Peterborough United** (NL)
First non-league club to knock out two clubs from second tier both away from home.

1963/64 R3 Newcastle United (2) 1-2 **Bedford Town** (NL)
Newcastle United had lifted the FA Cup less than nine years earlier than this giant-killing.

Rank	Sussex County League / Southern Combination League	R1	Q4	Q3	Q2	Q1	PR	EP
1	Southwick	1	3	5	13	18	15	4
2	Worthing	1	2	2	5	9	3	
3	Littlehampton Town	1	2	1	11	33	26	8
4	Chichester City (1)	1	1	3	9	20	22	
5	Horsham	1	1	1	3	6	2	
6	Ringmer	1		1	3	14	24	3

Top Six FA Cup Clubs whilst Members of SCFL.
Nb. Chart shows number of exits per Round

Non-League Clubs Giant-Killing after Formalisation of the Football Pyramid (40 / 75)

The 1979/80 season saw the introduction of the Alliance Premier League, a division made up of the top non-league clubs at the time, and the start of what is now known as the Football Pyramid (although its structure has evolved several times). From this time onward comparative levels between clubs can be identified to 'scale' the magnitude of Giant-killing achieved.

1993/94 R1 **Halifax Town** (5) 2-1 West Bromwich Albion (2)
Nb: Top two tiers had 46 clubs this season so recently promoted clubs appeared in 1st Rd.

1997/98 R3 Swindon Town (2) 1-2 **Stevenage** (Borough) (5)

2003/04 R3 Crewe Alexandra (2) 0-1 **Telford United** (5)

2004/05 R1 **Histon** (7) 2-0 Shrewsbury Town (4)

2004/05 R1 **Slough Town** (7) 2-1 Walsall (3)
The first instance of a four tier gap giant-killing.

2004/05 R1 **Hinckley United** (6) 2-0 Torquay United (3)

2005/06 R1 **Burscough** (7) 3-2 Gillingham (3)

2006/07 R1 Chesterfield (3) 0-1 **Basingstoke Town** (6)

2007/08 R1r **Staines Town** (7) 1-1 Stockport County (4)
(won 6-5 on pens)

2007/08 R2r **Chasetown** (8) 1-0 Port Vale (3)
The largest giant-killing gap (5 tiers) between levels of David and Goliath.

2007/08 R3r **Havant & Waterlooville** (6) 4-2 Swansea City (3)

2008/09 R1 **Curzon Ashton** (8) 3-2 Exeter City (4)

2008/09 R2 **Eastwood Town** (7) 2-0 Wycombe Wanderers (4)

2008/09 R2 **Histon** (5) 1-0 Leeds United (3)

2008/09 R3 **Torquay United** (5) 1-0 Blackpool (2)

2009/10 R1 **Northwich Victoria** (6) 1-0 Charlton Athletic (3)

2010/11 R1 Rochdale (3) 2-3 **FC United of Manchester** (7)
The largest gap between levels for a non-league club away victory over a third tier club.

2010/11 R3 **Crawley Town** (5) 2-1 Derby County (2)

2011/12 R1r **Stourbridge** (7) 2-0 Plymouth Argyle (4)

2012/13 R1 **Chelmsford City** (6) 3-1 Colchester United (3)

2012/13 R3 **Macclesfield Town** (5) 2-1 Cardiff City (2)

2012/13	R3	**Luton Town** (5)	1-0	Wolverhampton Wanderers (2)
2012/13	R4	Norwich City (1)	0-1	**Luton Town** (5)

The first instance of a non-league side beating a Premier League club.

2013/14	R1	**Macclesfield Town** (5)	4-0	Swindon Town (3)
2013/14	R1r	**Brackley Town** (6)	1-0	Gillingham (3)
2014/15	R1	**Warrington Town** (8)	1-0	Exeter City (4)
2014/15	R1	Coventry City (3)	1-2	**Worcester City** (6)
2014/15	R1r	**Maidstone United** (7)	2-1	Stevenage (4)
2014/15	R2	Hartlepool United (4)	1-2	**Blyth Spartans** (7)
2015/16	R1	Bristol Rovers (4)	0-1	**Chesham United** (7)
2015/16	R1	**Salford City** (7)	2-0	Notts County (4)
2016/17	R1r	**Brackley Town** (6)	4-3	Gillingham (3)
2016/17	R2	**Stourbridge** (7)	1-0	Northampton Town (3)
2016/17	R3r	**Lincoln City** (5)	1-0	Ipswich Town (2)
2016/17	R4	**Lincoln City** (5)	3-1	Brighton & Hove Albion (2)
2016/17	R4	**Sutton United** (5)	1-0	Leeds United (2)
2016/17	R5	Burnley (1)	0-1	**Lincoln City** (5)

Burnley are the only top-flight club to lose twice at home to a non-league side.

2018/19	R3	Sheffield United (2)	0-1	**Barnet** (5)
2019/20	R1	Leyton Orient (4)	1-2	**Maldon & Tiptree** (8)

Joint largest gap between levels for a non-league club away victory over a fourth tier club.

2019/20	R1	Macclesfield Town (4)	0-4	**Kingstonian** (7)
2020/21	R1	Wigan Athletic (3)	2-3	**Chorley** (6)
2020/21	R1	Swindon Town (3)	1-2	**Darlington** (6)
2020/21	R1	Colchester United (4)	1-1 (Penalties 3-4)	**Marine** (8)

Joint largest gap between levels for a non-league club away victory over a fourth tier club.

2020/21	R1	**Oxford City** (6)	2-1	Northampton Town (3)
2020/21	R2	Peterborough United (3)	1-2	**Chorley** (6)
2020/21	R3	**Chorley** (6)	2-0	Derby County (2)

Largest gap between levels for a non-league club victory over a second tier club.

Modern Day Giant-Killing by League Clubs over Higher Level League Clubs (39 / 114)

As the financial gap between the 'haves' and the 'have-nots' widens with every passing season, defeats of top level teams by other League clubs two or more divisions below them raise eyebrows, tempered only by the fact that maybe the higher level club did not play its full strength team.

2003/04	R3r	Bolton Wanderers (1)	1-2	**Tranmere Rovers** (3)
2003/04	R3r	Rotherham United (2)	1-2	**Northampton Town** (4)
2004/05	R3	**Oldham Athletic** (3)	1-0	Manchester City (1)
2005/06	R3	Fulham (1)	1-2	**Leyton Orient** (4)
2005/06	R4	**Brentford** (3)	2-1	Sunderland (1)
2006/07	R3	**Nottingham Forest** (3)	2-0	Charlton Athletic (1)
2007/08	R3	**Huddersfield Town** (3)	2-1	Birmingham City (1)
2007/08	R3	Everton (1)	0-1	**Oldham Athletic** (3)
2008/09	R3	**Hartlepool United** (3)	2-0	Stoke City (1)
2009/10	R3	Manchester United (1)	0-1	**Leeds United** (3)
2009/10	R4r	Wigan Athletic (1)	0-2	**Notts County** (4)
2010/11	R3	**Stevenage** (4)	3-1	Newcastle United (1)
2010/11	R3	**Southampton** (3)	2-0	Blackpool (1)
2010/11	R3	Sunderland (1)	1-2	**Notts County** (3)
2011/12	R3	**Swindon Town** (4)	2-1	Wigan Athletic (1)
2011/12	R4	Hull City (2)	0-1	**Crawley Town** (4)
2012/13	R4	Queens Park Rangers (1)	2-4	**Milton Keynes Dons** (3)
2012/13	R4	**Oldham Athletic** (3)	3-2	Liverpool (1)
2013/14	R3	Aston Vila (1)	1-2	**Sheffield United** (3)
2013/14	R4r	Fulham (1)	0-1	**Sheffield United** (3)
2014/15	R3	Queens Park Rangers (1)	0-3	**Sheffield United** (3)
2014/15	R4	Chelsea (1)	2-4	**Bradford City** (3)

Arguably the greatest FA Cup shock of all time because of the two-goal down comeback and the financial disparity between the clubs.

2014/15	R5	**Bradford City** (3)	2-0	Sunderland (1)
2015/16	R3	**Oxford United** (4)	3-2	Swansea City (1)

2016/17	R3	**Millwall** (3)	3-0	AFC Bournemouth (1)
2016/17	R3r	Barnsley (2)	1-2	**Blackpool** (4)
2016/17	R4	**Millwall** (3)	1-0	Watford (1)
2016/17	R5	**Millwall** (3)	1-0	Leicester City (1)
2017/18	R3	Brentford (2)	0-1	**Notts County** (4)
2017/18	R3	**Coventry City** (4)	2-1	Stoke City (1)
2017/18	R3r	**Wigan Athletic** (3)	3-0	AFC Bournemouth (1)
2017/18	R4	**Wigan Athletic** (3)	2-0	West Ham United (1)
2017/18	R5	**Wigan Athletic** (3)	1-0	Manchester City (1)

A record-breaking third victory over top-flight clubs in the same FA Cup campaign.

2018/19	R3	**Gillingham** (3)	2-1	Cardiff City (1)
2018/19	R3	Fulham (1)	1-2	**Oldham Athletic** (4)
2018/19	R3	**Newport County** (4)	2-1	Leicester City (1)
2018/19	R4	**AFC Wimbledon** (3)	4-2	West Ham United (1)
2019/20	R3r	**Tranmere Rovers** (3)	2-1	Watford (1)
2020/21	R3	**Crawley Town** (4)	3-0	Leeds United (1)

Lower Level Non-League clubs beating Higher Level Non-League Opponents (26 / 140)

1979/80	Q1	**Parson Drove United** (9)	2-0	Chelmsford City (6)
1986/87	Q2	**Yeading** (9)	4-1	Sutton United (5)
1994/95	Q1	**Romford** (10)	4-3	Grays Athletic (6)
1994/95	Q2	Hayes (6)	1-2	**Romford** (10)
2010/11	Q4	**Hythe Town** (9)	2-0	Staines Town (6)
2011/12	Q1	**Hartley Wintney** (10)	1-0	Bashley (7)
2011/12	Q2	Mickleover Sport (7)	1-4	**Barrow Town** (10)
2011/12	Q2r	Vauxhall Motors (6)	0-1	**Ashington** (9)
2011/12	Q3	**Ashington** (9)	1-0	Guiseley (6)
2011/12	Q4	**Redbridge** (8)	2-0	Ebbsfleet United (5)
2013/14	Q1	Redditch United (7)	1-2	**Atherstone Town** (10)
2013/14	Q3	Weston-super-Mare (6)	2-3	**Brislington** (9)

2013/14	Q4	Aldershot Town (5)	1-2	**Shortwood United** (8)
2014/15	Q1	**Ellistown & Ibstock Utd** (10)	3-2	Hereford United (7)
2014/15	Q2	**Shildon** (9)	1-0	Stalybridge Celtic (6)
2014/15	Q2	Barrow (6)	0-1	**Runcorn Town** (9)
2015/16	Q2	**Hinckley AFC** (10)	2-1	Redditch United (7)
2015/16	R1r	Boreham Wood (5)	1-2	**Northwich Victoria** (8)
2016/17	Q2	**Felixstowe & Walton Utd** (9)	2-1	Bishop's Stortford (6)
2016/17	Q4	Wrexham (5)	2-3	**Stamford** (8)
2017/18	Q2	**1874 Northwich** (9)	1-0	North Ferriby United (6)
2018/19	PR	Bedworth United (7)	1-2	**Racing Club Warwick** (10)
2018/19	Q3	**Dunston UTS** (9)	4-3	Chester (6)
2020/21	Q2	**Sheppey United** (9)	2-0	Welling United (6)
2020/21	Q2	**Christchurch** (9)	1-1 (6-5 on pens)	Gloucester City (6)
2020/21	Q4	Maidenhead United (5)	2-3	**Cray Valley Paper Mills** (8)

FA Cup Final Shocks (10 / 150)

1894	**Notts County** 4-1 Bolton Wanderers	First time 2nd tier club won FA Cup.
1901	**Tottenham Hotspur** 3-1 Sheffield United	Only non-league FA Cup winners.
1908	**Wolves** 3-1 Newcastle United	Wolves finished 9th in Division Two.
1912	**Barnsley** 1-0 West Bromwich Albion	Barnsley scored fewer goals than games.
1931	**West Bromwich Albion** 2-1 Birmingham	Only club to win Cup and be promoted.
1939	**Portsmouth** 4-1 Wolverhampton Wands.	Wolves were hot favourites to win.
1973	**Sunderland** 1-0 Leeds United	Arguably the biggest FA Cup Final upset.
1976	**Southampton** 1-0 Manchester United	Separated by 25 league places.
1980	**West Ham United** 1-0 Arsenal	Last 2nd tier club to lift FA Cup.
2013	**Wigan Athletic** 1-0 Manchester City	Only club to win Cup and be relegated.

150 Longest and Shortest Named Clubs to have Played in FA Cup

The most common number of characters in the names of clubs that have participated in the FA Cup is thirteen, with the names of 315 different clubs containing that amount of letters covering AFC Bridgnorth, Farsley Celtic, Old Harrovians and Wymondham Town to name but four. However, the longest names used are as many as 39 characters long and the shortest contain just four.

When determining the length of a club's name certain rules have been followed. Initials remain as initials and so for example 'AFC' is recorded as three characters rather than the 22 characters required for 'Associated Football Club'. This applies to many military clubs using initials such as 'RAF', 'RN' and 'RAE' in their names, and for all 'YMCA' teams. Some clubs competed in the FA Cup using just initials and some of these appear in the list of shortest named clubs.

Abbreviations have been extended to their full word spelling such as 'Lancs.' to 'Lancashire' and 'Co.' to 'Company' except where the abbreviation is recognised as a way of spelling the word such as 'St' which counts as two characters rather than the five needed for 'Saint'. (Turn to page 181 for an explanation of initials and abbreviations used by clubs in the FA Cup).

All spaces, commas, brackets and apostrophes have been discounted in determining length of names, but all numbers have been spelt out, especially for example '2nd' which becomes 'second and '3rd' which becomes 'third'. This is true, too, for club names that contain a year within it unless the year is just used as a differentiator from a previous club. So 1874 Northwich is 'Eighteen Seventy Four Northwich' whereas Enfield (1893) is just recorded as plain 'Enfield'.

The 150+ Longest Names

39 Jarrow Roofing Boldon Community Association ◆ Portland Prison Officers and Portland United

36 Sunderland Ryhope Community Association ◆ Teversal and Silverhill Colliery Welfare

35 Brigg 2nd Lincolnshire Sugar Company

33 Chilton Colliery Recreation Athletic

32 Steel, Peech and Tozer Social Services

31 4th Divisional Signals Regiment ◆ Frecheville Community Association ◆ Mapplewell and Staincross Athletic ◆ Royal Engineers Training Battalion ◆ Sunderland Ryhope Colliery Welfare

30 Royal Engineers Service Battalion ◆ Wolverhampton Sporting Community ◆ Worsborough Bridge Miners Welfare

29 Bishop Auckland Church Institute ◆ Swindon British Rail Corinthians

28 Clay Cross and Danesmoor Welfare ◆ Depot Battalion Royal Engineers ◆ 1874 Northwich ◆ 1st South Lancashire Regiment ◆ Frodingham and Appleby Athletic ◆ Gateshead North Eastern Railway ◆ Grimethorpe Colliery Institute ◆ March Great Eastern Locomotives ◆ Metal and Produce Recovery Depot ◆ Peterborough and Fletton United ◆ Whitehaven Colliery Recreation

27 Atherstone Town Community Club ◆ Birdwell Primitive Methodists ◆ Bournemouth Gasworks Athletic ◆ Brighton Corporation Tramways ◆ Castleford and Allerton United ◆ Eastbourne United Association ◆ East Tanfield Colliery Welfare ◆ Hastings and St Leonards United ◆ Hull Technical College Old Boys ◆ Mansfield Woodhouse Excelsior ◆ 93rd Highland Regiment ◆ Port of London Authority Police ◆ Sunderland East End Black Watch ◆ Wombwell Sporting Association

26 Addlestone and Weybridge Town ◆ Boldon Community Association ◆ East End Park Working Men's Club ◆ 1st Highland Light Infantry ◆ Green and Silley Weir Athletic ◆ Guisborough Belmont Athletic ◆ 105th Regiment ◆ Parliament Street Methodists ◆ Ryhope Community Association ◆ 2nd Lincolnshire Regiment ◆ South Hetton Colliery Welfare ◆ Stockton Malleable Institute ◆ Third Lanark Rifle Volunteers ◆ West Hartlepool Perseverance

25 Appleby Frodingham Athletic ◆ Bilsthorpe Colliery Welfare ◆ Blaby and Whetstone Athletic ◆ Clarence Iron and Steel Works ◆ Darlington Cleveland

Social ◆ Darlington Railway Athletic ◆ East Cowes Victoria Athletic ◆ 8th Durham Light Infantry ◆ Ellistown and Ibstock United ◆ Felixstowe and Walton United ◆ Florence and Ullcoats United ◆ Frodingham and Brumby United ◆ Guildford and Dorking United ◆ Hampton and Richmond Borough ◆ Hartford and Davenham United ◆ Harworth Colliery Institute ◆ Mansfield Woodhouse Rangers ◆ Mexborough Locomotive Works ◆ Norton and Stockton Ancients ◆ Norwich School Old Boys Union ◆ Parkgate and Rawmarsh United ◆ Peterborough GN Locomotives ◆ Ryhill and Havercroft United ◆ Sandiacre Excelsior Foundry ◆ Scarborough Junior Imperial ◆ Shilbottle Colliery Welfare ◆ Silksworth Colliery Welfare ◆ St Philips Marsh Adult School ◆ Whitehaven Wellington Villa

24 Aldershot Traction Company ◆ Bedford Queens Park Rangers ◆ Blackhall Colliery Welfare ◆ Brierley Hill and Withymoor ◆ Chessington and Hook United ◆ Crookhall Colliery Welfare ◆ Harrogate Railway Athletic ◆ Kettering Working Men's Club ◆ Newbiggin Colliery Welfare ◆ New Brighton Tower Amateurs ◆ Northampton Sileby Rangers ◆ Peterborough Northern Star ◆ Plymouth and Stonehouse Gas ◆ Royal Artillery Portsmouth ◆ South Farnborough Athletic ◆ South Normanton St Michael's ◆ South Shields Ex-Schoolboys ◆ United Services Portsmouth ◆ Wardle and Barbridge United ◆ West Wylam Colliery Welfare

23 Allerton Bywater Colliery ◆ Ashton and Backwell United ◆ Barnoldswick and District ◆ Bemerton Heath Harlequins ◆ Bentinck Colliery Welfare ◆ Birmingham City Transport ◆ Brentwood Mental Hospital ◆ Brighton Railway Athletic ◆ Bristol Aeroplane Company ◆ Brodsworth Miners Welfare ◆ Brookwood Mental Hospital ◆ Chesterfield Corinthians ◆ Donnington Wood Institute ◆ Eppleton Colliery Welfare ◆ 4th Royal Tank Regiment ◆ Irthlingborough Diamonds ◆ Leek County School Old Boys ◆ Lincoln Moorlands Railway ◆ Loughborough Corinthians ◆ Middlesbrough Ironopolis ◆ National Radiator Company ◆ North Derbyshire Ramblers ◆ Royal Engineers Aldershot ◆ Royal Wootton Bassett Town ◆ Royston Midland Institute ◆ Ryton and Crawcrook Albion ◆ Shirebrook Miners Welfare ◆ Sittingbourne Paper Mills ◆ Snowdown Colliery Welfare ◆ Southampton Civil Service ◆ South Shields Corinthians ◆ Taunton and Newtons United ◆ Thoresby Colliery Welfare ◆ Thornley Colliery Welfare ◆ Tooting and Mitcham United ◆ Washington Chemical Works ◆ Wellingborough Whitworth ◆ West Didsbury and Chorlton ◆ West Hartlepool Expansion ◆ West Hartlepool St Joseph's ◆ Whitburn Colliery Welfare

22 Atherton Laburnum Rovers ◆ Banstead Mental Hospital ◆ Brandon Colliery Welfare ◆ Brighton and Hove Rangers ◆ Brighton Mental Hospital ◆ British Oil and Cake Mills ◆ Crystal Palace Engineers ◆ Darlington St Augustine's ◆ Farnham United Breweries ◆ 5th Royal Tank Regiment ◆ 1st Sherwood Foresters ◆ 4th Kings Royal Rifles ◆ Havant and Waterlooville ◆ Haydock C&B Recreation ◆ Hemsworth Miners Welfare ◆ Hoyland Common Wesleyans ◆ Hucknall Constitutional ◆ Ibstock Penistone Rovers ◆ Kimberley Miners Welfare ◆ Langold Working Men's Club ◆ Loughborough University ◆ Mexborough Town Athletic ◆ Newton Common Recreation ◆ New Whittington Exchange ◆ Normanby Park Steel Works ◆ Peacehaven and Telscombe ◆ Peasedown Miner's Welfare ◆ Radcliffe Welfare United ◆ Rainworth Miners Welfare ◆ Ramsgate Press Wanderers ◆ Royal Ordnance Factories ◆ Rushden and Higham United ◆ 2nd Coldstream Guards ◆ 2nd West Kent Regiment ◆ Selby Olympia Cake and Oil ◆ Shotton Colliery Welfare ◆ Skinningrove Steel Works ◆ Smethwick Carriage Works ◆ South Normanton Athletic ◆ South Normanton Colliery ◆ Sporting Club Thamesmead ◆ Stewarts and Lloyds (Corby) ◆ Stocksbridge Park Steels ◆ Weston-super-Mare St Johns ◆ Windsor Phoenix Athletic ◆ Wolverhampton Wanderers ◆ Woolwich Royal Artillery

The longest named club to win the FA Cup is **Wolverhampton Wanderers** (with 22 characters).

The club with the longest single word name to have played in the FA Cup is **Rhosllanerchrugog** (with 17 characters).

The multiple named clubs which have competed in the FA Cup with the most letters per word in their names are **Chesterfield Corinthians**, **Irthlingborough Diamonds**, **Loughborough Corinthians**, **Middlesbrough Ironopolis** and **Wellingborough Whitworth** (all with 11.5 characters per word).

The shortest named club to win the FA Cup is **Bury** (with four characters).

Excluding abbreviations, the clubs with the shortest two word names to have played in the FA Cup are **East Ham**, **Ely City**, **K Sports**, **Mid Kent**, **Mile Oak**, **Odd Down** and **West End** (all with seven characters).

The 150+ Shortest Names

4 Avro ◆ Bean ◆ Bury ◆ Cove ◆ Ekco ◆ Hyde ◆ Leek ◆ Pica ◆ RASC ◆ Rhyl ◆ Ware ◆ Wick

5 Acton ◆ Alton ◆ Amble ◆ Anglo ◆ Birch ◆ Blyth ◆ Brigg ◆ Clove ◆ Colne ◆ Cowes ◆ Croft ◆ Dover ◆ Earle ◆ Egham ◆ Erith ◆ Glebe ◆ Goole ◆ Hawks ◆ Hayes ◆ Holme ◆ Irlam ◆ Leeds ◆ Lewes ◆ Lowca ◆ Mardy ◆ Pelaw ◆ Quorn ◆ Ranks ◆ Savoy ◆ Shell ◆ Stork ◆ Tonge ◆ Unity

6 Alfold ◆ Arnold ◆ Aveley ◆ Balham ◆ Barnes ◆ Barnet ◆ Barrow ◆ Bexley ◆ Bitton ◆ Bootle ◆ Boston ◆ Botley ◆ Brooms ◆ Buxton ◆ Cannon ◆ Church ◆ Cobham ◆ Cowley ◆ Cribbs ◆ Cromer ◆ Darwen ◆ Dearne ◆ Denton ◆ Druids ◆ Eagley ◆ Elmore ◆ Eltham ◆ Fawley ◆ Fisher ◆ Formby ◆ Fulham ◆ Golcar ◆ Gothic ◆ Gretna ◆ Hadley ◆ Hallam ◆ Hallen ◆ Hapton ◆ Hendon ◆ Hessle ◆ Hexham ◆ Histon ◆ Ilford ◆ Jarrow ◆ Laceby ◆ Lenton ◆ Leyton ◆ Loftus ◆ Lytham ◆ Marine ◆ Marlow ◆ Meir KA ◆ Melton ◆ Morley ◆ Murton ◆ Nelson ◆ Newark ◆ Nomads ◆ Orrell ◆ Pagham ◆ Pinner ◆ Purton ◆ Rawden ◆ Rendel ◆ Renton ◆ RM Deal ◆ Royton ◆ Saxons ◆ Selsey ◆ Slough ◆ Street ◆ Sutton ◆ Swifts ◆ Thames ◆ Totton ◆ Turton ◆ Ulster ◆ Warley ◆ Welwyn ◆ Whitby ◆ Widnes ◆ Witton ◆ Woking ◆ Yaxley

7 Allsops ◆ Altofts ◆ Andover ◆ Appleby ◆ Ardsley ◆ Arsenal ◆ Arundel ◆ Bargoed ◆ Barking ◆ Barnton ◆ Barwell ◆ Bashley ◆ Beccles ◆ Bedfont ◆ Bedford ◆ Beeston ◆ Bingley ◆ Birtley ◆ Bookham ◆ Boxmoor ◆ Brocton ◆ Bromley ◆ Brotton ◆ Burbage ◆ Burnham ◆ Burnley ◆ Campion ◆ Casuals ◆ Cheddar ◆ Chelsea ◆ Chester ◆ Chinnor ◆ Chorley ◆ Clapham ◆ Clapton ◆ Clifton ◆ Clinton ◆ Consett ◆ Crofton ◆ Croston ◆ Croydon ◆ Dorking ◆ Douglas ◆ Downton ◆ Dulwich ◆ Dunkirk ◆ Dunston ◆ East Ham ◆ Ely City ◆ Enfield ◆ Everton ◆ Fareham ◆ Feltham ◆ Flixton ◆ Galgate ◆ Gilfach ◆ Gitanos ◆ Gresham ◆ Halifax ◆ Hanwell ◆ Haydock ◆ Hazells ◆ Hersham ◆ Heywood ◆ Hindley ◆ Horsham ◆ Horwich ◆ Hotspur ◆ Hoylake ◆ Hudsons ◆ Hunslet ◆ Jurgens ◆ K Sports ◆ Keswick ◆ Kilburn ◆ Kildare ◆ Kirkley ◆ Lancing ◆ Leiston ◆ Lewison ◆ Leyland ◆ Liberty ◆ Loxwood ◆ Lye Town ◆ Margate ◆ Marsden ◆ Mellors ◆ Meltham ◆ Mickley ◆ Mid Kent ◆ Mile Oak ◆ Minerva ◆ Molesey ◆ Moss Bay ◆ Mossley ◆ Newburn ◆ Newbury ◆ Newport ◆ Newquay ◆ Newtown ◆ Nunhead ◆ Oakdale ◆ Oakmere ◆ Oakwood ◆ Odd Down ◆ Olympic ◆ Padiham ◆ Penrith ◆ Pinxton ◆ Prudhoe ◆ Pyebank ◆ Radford ◆ Rangers ◆ Reading ◆ Redhill ◆ Ringmer ◆ RN Depot ◆ Romford ◆ Romulus ◆ Rugeley ◆ Saltney ◆ Sandown ◆ Seaford ◆ Selston ◆ Shildon ◆ Sholing ◆ Silsden ◆ Slipway ◆ Spilsby ◆ St James ◆ St Luke's ◆

St Mark's ◆ Stanley ◆ Studley ◆ Suttons ◆ Takeley ◆ Tilbury ◆ Treeton ◆ Trojans ◆ Urmston ◆ Vulcans ◆ Walsall ◆ Walshaw ◆ Warmley ◆ Watford ◆ Wembley ◆ West End ◆ Westham ◆ Whiston ◆ Windsor ◆ Wingate ◆ Wrexham ◆ Wroxham ◆ Yeading

---

Rank	Northern Premier League	R4	R3	R2	R1	Q4	Q3	Q2
1	Stafford Rangers	1		1	4	4	2	5
2	Northwich Victoria	1		1		3	2	3
3	Scarborough		3	2	3	2		1
4	Wigan Athletic		2	3	4	1		
5	Boston United		2	2	5	4	2	2
6	Altrincham		2	2	5	4	1	4
7	Marine		2		3	12	10	5
8	Gateshead United		1	3	6			
9	Blyth Spartans		1	1	1	5	1	5
10	Whitley Bay		1	1		2	1	
11	Stourbridge		1	1		1	1	
12	Matlock Town		1		3	3	9	12
13	Burton Albion		1		3	3		2
14	Wakefield		1		2	2	4	7
15	Eastwood Town		1		1		2	6
16	Caernarfon Town		1			2		2
17	Bangor City			2	4	5	2	3
18	Barrow			2	4	4	3	3
19	Chorley			2	2	2	7	8
20	Morecambe			1	7	5	3	2
21	Runcorn FC Halton			1	6	5	4	4
22	Mossley			1	5	4	4	6
23	Lancaster City			1	3	6	8	11
24	Goole Town			1	3	6	2	8
25	Southport			1	3	2	2	4
26	Gateshead			1	2	3	3	6
27	Bishop Auckland			1	2	2	3	6
28	Colwyn Bay			1	2	1	3	7
29	Leek Town			1	1	6	5	5
30	Accrington Stanley			1	1	2	3	6

Top 30 FA Cup Clubs whilst Members of Northern Premier League.

Nb. Chart shows number of exits per Round

Only 150 Years of FA Cup Facts & Stats

Only **Abingdon Town** have competed in the FA Cup whilst members of the still active North Berks Football League (in 1938/39 season).

Only **Alan Taylor** scored for West Ham United in their quarter-final, semi-final and Cup Final matches en route to lifting the FA Cup in 1975, netting three braces in the four games played.

Only **Alex Jackson** of Huddersfield Town in 1928 scored for a losing Cup Finalist between Harry Tufnell for Barnsley in 1910 and Joe Bradford for Birmingham in 1931.

Only **Alvechurch** have made it as far as the FA Cup 3rd Round whilst members of the West Midlands (Regional) League (in 1973/74 season).

Only **Arsene Wenger** has managed seven FA Cup winning sides (all managing Arsenal from 1998 to 2017).

Only **Arsenal** have appeared in more than 20 FA Cup finals (winning a record 14 times and runners-up seven times).

Only **Arthur Turner** has played in an FA Cup Final for a club for which he never played any League games (since League began in 1888/89, for Charlton Athletic in 1946 Cup Final).

Only **Ashley Cole** has won the FA Cup as a player as many as seven times (three times for Arsenal and four times for Chelsea between 2002 and 2012).

Only **Barnsley** have scored fewer goals (11) than games played (12) in the season they lifted the FA Cup (1912).

Only **Barrow** have appeared in the FA Cup 3rd Round as many as a dozen times and failed to as yet go any further.

Only **Bideford** have played as many as 13 matches in one FA Cup campaign, making 1st Round 'Proper' in 1973/74 season after having started in 1st Qualifying Round.

Only **Bishop Auckland** have participated in the FA Cup more than 100 times as a member of the Northern League.

Only **Blyth Spartans** have made it as far as the 5th Round of the FA Cup whilst members of the Northern League (in 1977/78 season).

Only **Bolton Wanderers** have benefited from opposition being disqualified on as many as three separate occasions (1885/86 vs Rawtenstall and Preston North End, 1887/88 vs Everton, although Bolton were also subsequently disqualified).

Only **Boothtown** have competed in the FA Cup whilst members of the still active Halifax and District League (in 1914/15 and 1919/20 seasons).

Only **Boxmoor St John's** have competed in the FA Cup whilst members of the still active West Herts League (in 1933/34 season).

Only **Burnley** have twice lost at home to non-league opposition when playing as a top-flight club (0-1 versus Wimbledon in 1975 and 0-1 versus Lincoln City in 2017).

Only **Bury** have appeared in more than one FA Cup Final but not conceded a goal in Cup Final games (1900 & 1903).

Only **Cardiff City** have taken the FA Cup outside of England when defeating Arsenal 1-0 in the 1927 Cup Final.

Only **Charlton Athletic** have reached an FA Cup Final after legitimately losing a game in an earlier round (lost 2-1 at Fulham FC in 3rd Round second leg in 1945/46 season).

Only **Chatham Town** has made it as far as the quarter-finals having started its FA Cup campaign in the earliest qualifying round, doing so in the 1888/89 season.

Only **Cheltenham Town** have competed in the FA Cup whilst members of the still active North Gloucestershire League (from 1919/20 to 1912/22).

Only **Chesterfield Corinthians** have played as many as five FA Cup games without scoring a goal in the competition. The club conceded 34 goals in those games played during the mid-1920s.

Only **Chorley** have defeated two Step Three clubs (Wigan Athletic and Peterborough United) in the same season whilst competing as a Step Six side (National League North).

Only **Civil Service** accepted an invitation from the FA to participate in the centenary competition in 1971/72 despite being outside of the acceptable leagues. They promptly lost 10-0 at Bromley and would probably refuse a similar invitation for the 2021/22 season.

Only the original **Coalville Town** have both won and lost an FA Cup game by more than 13 goals (14-0 versus Ibstock Penistone Rovers in 1946 and 0-14 versus Whitwick Colliery in 1954).

Only **Columbia FC** have competed in the FA Cup whilst members of the still active Surrey Intermediate League (in 1931/32 season).

Only **Coventry City** have beaten Tottenham Hotspur in an FA Cup Final despite Spurs having competed in nine finals (in 1987).

Only **Crystal Palace** have scored as many as seven goals as a non-league club in an FA Cup match against Football League opposition (beating Division Two Chelsea FC 7-1 in 1905/06 season).

Only **Curzon Ashton** have played in the 'Proper' Rounds of the FA Cup with the letter 'Z' contained within their name (Preston Zingari scratched before playing in 1884/85).

Only **Darlington** have advanced to the next round of the FA Cup on the basis of a 'lucky losers draw' (in 1999/2000 season).

Only **Darwen** have scored as many as fifteen goals in a quarter-final tie, winning 15-0 against original Romford in 1880/81 season.

Only **Didier Drogba** has scored a goal in four different FA Cup finals (2007, 2009, 2010 and 2012).

Only **Dulwich Hamlet** have twice conceded as many as seven goals in one FA Cup match and not lost either of them (8-7 versus St Albans City in 1922/23 and 7-7 versus Wealdstone in 1929/30).

Only **Eric Cantona** has scored two penalties in one FA Cup Final match (in Manchester United's 4-0 win over Chelsea in 1994).

Only **Falmouth Town** have competed in the FA Cup whilst members of the still active Cornwall Combination (in 1983/84 season).

Only **Frank Stapleton** has scored an FA Cup Final goal both for and against the same club (excluding own goals), scoring for Arsenal against Manchester United in 1979, and for Manchester United against Brighton and Hove Albion in 1983.

Only **Fulham** have lost a semi-final by as much as a six goal margin, doing so against Newcastle United in 1908.

Only **Gorleston** have competed in the FA Cup whilst members of the still active Anglian Combination League (from 1964/65 to 1968/69).

Only **Gosforth and Coxlodge** have appeared in the FA Cup 1st Qualifying Round as many as fifteen times and failed to go any further.

Only **Greenwich Borough** have been disqualified from the FA Cup more than once in the 21st Century (in 2000/01 and 2004/05).

Only **Harrogate Railway Athletic** have made it as far as the FA Cup 2nd Round whilst members of the Northern Counties East League (in 2002/03 season).

Only **Harrow Chequers** have entered the FA Cup as many as three times, but never actually played a match (1871/72, 1874/75 and 1875/76).

Only **Headingley** have entered the FA Cup more than ten times and been knocked out in the Extra Preliminary Round every time (1928/29 to 1938/39).

Only **John Anderson** has been the same moniker of two different FA Cup Final scorers, for Portsmouth in 1939 and for Manchester United in 1948. Both clubs lifted the FA Cup in their respective seasons.

Only **Leyton Orient** have scored six goals in extra time in an FA Cup match, winning 8-2 against Droylsden FC in a 2nd Round replay in 2010/11 season.

Only **Lincoln City** have reached the quarter-finals of the FA Cup as a National League club (in 2016/17).

Only **Lincoln United** have appeared in the 'Proper' Rounds of the FA Cup whilst members of the Central Midlands League (in 1990/91 season).

Only **Linfield Athletic** have won an FA Cup match on Christmas Day (winning 7-0 against Cliftonville in 1888/89 season).

Only **Linotype and Machinery** have competed in the FA Cup whilst members of the still active Lancashire and Cheshire League (in 1935/36 and 1936/37 seasons).

Only **Lord Arthur Kinnaird** has played in as many as nine FA Cup Finals (appearing for The Wanderers and Old Etonians from 1873 to 1883).

Only **Manchester United** have never defended their FA Cup crown (in 1999/2000 after being required to compete in the Club World Championship).

Only **Marine** have faced a top-flight side whilst competing at Level Eight of the football pyramid – Marine versus Tottenham Hotspur, January 2021.

Only **Merchiston Castle School** in Edinburgh has hosted an FA Cup semi-final in Scotland (1884/85 season).

Only **The Millennium Stadium** in Cardiff has hosted both FA Cup finals and semi-finals outside of England (2005).

Only **Millwall and Southampton** contested an FA Cup semi-final match whilst both clubs were classed as non-league teams (1899/1900 season).

Only **Milnthorpe Corinthians** have appeared in the FA Cup 2nd Qualifying Round as many as nine times and failed to go any further.

Only **Newcastle United** have twice lost consecutive FA Cup finals (1905 & 1906 and 1998 & 1999).

Only **Newport (IOW)** have 'lost' as many as four FA Cup matches in one season, in 1945/46, losing 1-0 to Cowes in 3rd Qualifying Round (who were disqualified), losing 2-1 to Clapton Orient in 1st Round 1st leg, and losing both legs to Aldershot in the 2nd Round.

Only **Nottingham Forest** have been scheduled to play FA Cup games in all four countries of the United Kingdom (although Linfield Athletic scratched before their replay happened).

Only **Nunhead** have scored nine goals against fellow non-league opposition in the 'Proper' Rounds of the FA Cup and conceded nine goals against fellow non-league opposition in the 'Proper' Rounds of the FA Cup (1926 beat Kingstonian 9-0, 1931 lost 9-0 to Bath City).

Only **Old Carthusians and Wimbledon** have won both the FA Cup and the FA Amateur Cup, with Middlesbrough FC and Wycombe Wanderers the only marginally realistic other clubs likely to achieve the feat.

Only **Old Etonians** have won the FA Cup and subsequently had to start future competitions in the Qualifying Rounds as many as five times (1888/89 to 1892/93).

Only **One Goal** was scored in each of the three FA Cup finals played at Stamford Bridge in the early 1920s.

Only **One Top-Flight Club** was part of the quartet of sides in two season's FA Cup semi-finals, separated by exactly 100 years, Newcastle United in 1908 and Portsmouth in 2008.

Only **Osborne Athletic** have appeared in the FA Cup Preliminary Round as many as a dozen times and failed to go any further.

Only **Oxford University** have reached at least the quarter-finals of the FA Cup in all their multiple campaigns (from 1872/73 to 1879/80). They are also the only club whose last campaign in the FA Cup culminated in a Cup Final appearance (1880).

Only **Partick Thistle and Cliftonville** have contested an FA Cup tie between two non-English sides not from the same other country. Partick Thistle romped to an 11-1 victory in 1886/87.

Only **Paul Bracewell** has appeared in as many as four FA Cup finals and failed to be called an FA Cup winner, three times a losing Finalist with Everton in the 1980s, and once again with Sunderland in 1992 (with Liverpool the victors on three of the four occasions).

Only **Paul Jones** has come on as a goalkeeping substitute in an FA Cup Final (in 2003 for Southampton against Arsenal).

Only **Pierre-Emerick Aubameyang** has scored FA Cup Final goals with a hyphenated first name (for Arsenal in 2020).

Only **Pontefract Borough** have competed in the FA Cup with a name that contains all the letters of the words 'The FA Cup' within it (1927/28 and 1928/29).

Only one **Preliminary Round** tie was required the first time that round was introduced in 1890/91 season (Crusaders beat Rochester 5-0 in 1890/91).

Only **Preston North End** have scored more than 20 goals in one FA Cup match (26-0 versus Hyde in 1887/88).

Only **Raich Carter** won FA Cup Winners medals either side of World War II, for Sunderland in 1937 and for Derby County in 1946.

Only **Rhyl** has competed in Proper Rounds of the FA Cup with a name that contains no vowels in it (from 1931/32 to 1991/92).

Only **Rotherham United** have failed to reach at least the FA Cup quarter-finals of the 44 clubs in the top two divisions of English football in 2020/21 season.

Only **Royal Engineers** scored an FA Cup Final goal where the identity of the goal-scorer is still unknown (1878).

Only **Sheffield FC** have faced as many as 17 different clubs playing in their first ever FA Cup match.

Only **Sheffield Wednesday** have appeared in as many as nine consecutive FA Cup quarter-finals (for the first five seasons as a non-league club), achieving the feat from 1887/88 to 1895/96 when the club lifted the Trophy for the first time.

Only the original **Shepherd's Bush** appeared in the FA Cup 5th Qualifying Round as many as four times and failed to go any further.

Only **Shropshire Wanderers** have exited the FA Cup due to the toss of a coin (in 1873/74 season against Sheffield FC after two nil-nil draws).

Only **Slough Town** have appeared in the FA Cup 2nd Round as many as eight times and failed to as yet go any further.

Only **Southampton** have appeared in more than one FA Cup Final as a non-league club (1900 and 1902).

Only **Southport Leyland Road** have competed in the FA Cup whilst members of the still active Lancashire Amateur League (in 1949/50 season).

Only **St Albans City** have scored seven goals in an FA Cup match and still ended up on the losing side (losing 7-8 against Dulwich Hamlet in 1922/23 season).

Only **Stamford** have played as many as 14 consecutive FA Cup ties against clubs all with same suffix in their name. The Daniels faced fourteen different 'Towns' across 18 consecutive FA games from 1953/54 to 1963/64.

Only **Stan Crowther** played for more than one club in the FA Cup in the same season (for Aston Villa and then for Manchester United following the Munich air crash in 1958).

Only **Stan Mortensen** has scored a hat-trick in an FA Cup Final played at Wembley (for Blackpool in 1953).

Only **Sunderland Ryhope Colliery Welfare** have competed in the FA Cup in the 21st Century with all the letters of the words 'FA Cup' in their name (2015/16 to 2020/21).

Only **Ted MacDougall** has scored as many as nine goals in one FA Cup 'Proper' Round match, doing so for AFC Bournemouth in their 11-0 win over Margate in 1971/72.

Only **Tottenham Hotspur** have been defeated in eight consecutive FA Cup semi-final appearances (from 1992/93 to 2017/18).

Only **Union Jack** have competed in the FA Cup whilst members of the still active Bristol Downs League (in 1925/26 season).

Only **Villa Park** has hosted more than 50 FA Cup semi-finals, 55 in total, but the last one was back in 2007 (Manchester United 4-1 Watford).

Only **The Wanderers** have appeared in an FA Cup Final without actually playing any games to get there (1873).

Only **Watford** have appeared in more than one FA Cup Final and failed to score a goal in Cup Final games (1984 and 2019).

Only **West Bromwich Albion** have appeared in three successive FA Cup finals and not lifted the Trophy until the third time (1885/86 to 1887/88).

Only **Westfields** have so far appeared in the 'Proper' Rounds of the FA Cup whilst members of the Midland Football League (in 2016/17 season).

Only **Weymouth** have lost more than one FA Cup game by a 14 goal margin or greater (1-15 versus Bristol Rovers in 1900 and 0-14 versus Exeter City in 1908).

Only **Wigan Athletic** have won the FA Cup and been relegated in the same season (defeated Manchester City 1-0 in 2013).

Only **Wilfred 'Billy' Minter** has scored seven goals in one FA Cup match and been on the losing side (for St Albans City in their 7-8 defeat to Dulwich Hamlet in 1922/23 season).

Only **Wimbledon** have lost FA Cup matches in EP Round, Preliminary Round, Q1 Round, Q2 Round, Q3 Round, Q4 Round, Round 1, Round 2, Round 3, Round 4, Round 5, Round 6 and semi-finals. In fact the only round Wimbledon did not lose a game in is the Final itself.

Only the original **Witney Town** have played in the 'Proper' Rounds of the FA Cup whilst members of the Hellenic League (in 1971/72 season).

Only **Yeovil Town** have knocked out as many as 20 Football League clubs whilst competing in the FA Cup as a non-league team (1934/35 Crystal Palace to 2000/01 Blackpool).

Rank	Western League	W	Fin	SF	QF	R5	R4	R3	R2	R1	IR	Q6	Q5	Q4
1	Tottenham Hotspur	1			2			2	1	2				
2	Southampton		1	1	3				2	3				
3	Millwall			1				1	2	3	1			
4	Portsmouth				1			2	2	3	1			
5	Reading				1				2	6				
6	Fulham				1				2					
7	Bath City							2	2	4				6
8	Bristol Rovers							2	1	4	2		1	1
9	Brentford							2	1	1	3			
10	Yeovil Town							1	3	2			1	3
11	Plymouth Argyle							1	2	3				
12	West Ham United							1	2	1	2	1		1
13	Crystal Palace							1	1					
14	Poole Town							1		1				2
15	Dorchester Town								2	3				7
16	Bridgwater Town (1)								2	2				2
17	Queens Park Rangers								1	3		1	2	
18	Salisbury City								1	3				3
19	Weymouth								1	2		1		2
20	Brighton and Hove Albion								1	1				
21	Bristol City								1		1			
22	Barnstaple Town									4				2
23	Tiverton Town									4				3
24	Bideford									3				14
25	Trowbridge Town									3				5

Top 25 FA Cup Clubs whilst Members of Western League.

Nb. Several clubs competed in both Southern League and Western League concurrently

150 Unique Suffixes of Clubs which have Participated in the FA Cup

More than 480 clubs have competed in the FA Cup with 'Town' in their name, the most common suffix of clubs which have taken part in the competition. The first to do so was a short-lived club called Derby Town which lost 4-1 at Small Heath Alliance (Birmingham City) in the 1st Round of the 1881/82 season.

Almost 280 other clubs have participated in the FA Cup with 'United' as the last part of their name, the first with that suffix being Hanover United in the 1879/80 season. The club were beaten 2-1 by Grey Friars in the first of its nine campaigns, before changing its name to Polytechnic, a club still in existence and competing in the Southern Amateur League and which played in the FA Cup on-and-off, up until the 1950/51 season.

The third most common suffix used by clubs that have played in the FA Cup is 'Athletic'. A club known by the moniker AAC, which stood for Amateur Athletic Club, entered the competition in 1873/74 season but withdrew before facing Clapham Rovers, so the first such club to actually play a game in the competition with the 'Athletic' suffix was the original Wednesbury Old Athletic club. They first participated in the FA Cup in the 1881/82 season going as far as the quarter-finals in their debut campaign.

Other common suffixes used by clubs in the FA Cup include 'Rovers', 'City', 'Rangers', 'Albion', 'Swifts' and 'Wanderers', whilst there have been many other clubs with 'Colliery' and 'Welfare' as the last part of their names.

But there have also been hundreds of clubs who can lay claim to be the only one with a particular suffix, and 150 of those are listed below.

Oldland ABBOTONIANS – This Western League club has had two FA Cup campaigns so far winning just one of three games played to date, 1-0 versus Newport (IOW) in 2016/17. The suffix reflects one of two clubs that merged together in 1998, Longwell Green Abbotonians, which had originally been formed in 1947 by pupils of Hanham Abbots school.

Crewe ALEXANDRA – There have been a few clubs named after Queen Victoria in the FA Cup, but Crewe is the only one to be named after Princess Alexandra. The club has participated in the FA Cup every season since 1883/84 and reached the semi-finals in their fifth campaign.

Whitchurch ALPORT – This Shropshire side has competed in the last four FA Cup campaigns, reaching the 1st Qualifying Round in 2019/20. The suffix remembers the home of a local fallen war hero and footballer, Coley Maddox, who had lived on Alport Farm.

Walgrave AMBER – Two FA Cup campaigns in the late 1920s whilst members of the Northants League (now the United Counties League), reaching the Preliminary round in their second campaign in 1927/28.

Norton and Stockton ANCIENTS – Twenty-one FA Cup campaigns straddling the turn of the 21st Century as members of the Northern League, reaching the 3rd Qualifying Round in 2010/11.

Newport BARBARIANS – Entered the FA Cup three times either side of WWI but only actually participated in 1919/20 season whilst members of Monmouthshire Senior League, losing 2-0 to Cardiff Corinthians in their only match played.

London BARI – Two FA Cup campaigns as members of the Essex Senior League in 2014/15 and 2015/16, losing both matches played before being absorbed into Hackney Wick.

Tooting BEC – Just one FA Cup campaign so far in 2019/20 with just one FA Cup match, a 3-2 defeat at Guildford City. The suffix reflects the name of the owners of Upper Tooting as detailed in the Domesday Book, the Abbey of Hellouin Bec in Normandy.

Phoenix BESSEMER – Just one FA Cup campaign for this Rotherham based club in 1882/83, reaching the 3rd Round and inflicting a 9-1 defeat on Grimsby Town in the Mariners first ever FA Cup match played. The suffix is in reference to Henry Bessemer, the founder of a South Yorkshire steel-making company that bore his name, and who invented the Bessemer Process, the first inexpensive industrial way of mass-producing steel from molten pig iron.

Spen BLACK AND WHITE – Seventeen FA Cup campaigns from 1912/13 to 1933/34, this Tyne & Wear based club reached the 3rd Qualifying Round in 1922/23 season.

Jarrow BLACKETT – Two FA Cup campaigns in the final seasons before WWI as members of the Tyneside League, winning one of their three matches 1-0 versus Shields Albion.

Earlestown BOHEMIANS – This Merseyside based club had two FA Cup campaigns just before the outbreak of WWII whilst members of the Liverpool County Combination and reached the 2nd Qualifying Round in the second run.

Oldham BORO – The club's first 16 FA Cup campaigns were under the name Oldham Town, but they changed to this name for their final season in 2009/10. Suffix was adopted to disassociate the club from the one founded by disgraced chairman, Ken Hughes, and to give in a distinct, fresh identity.

Stapleford BROOKHILL – Just one FA Cup campaign and one FA Cup game for this Notts Spartan League side in 1934/35, a 3-1 defeat at Boots Athletic. The suffix references Brookhill Street in Stapleford.

Hull BRUNSWICK – Originally competed in FA Cup as Brunswick Institute when in the East Riding Amateur League, but used this name in the last six of their 18 campaigns whilst members of the higher level Yorkshire League.

Tadley CALLEVA – Competed in seven of the last eight FA Cup campaigns, posting their best run to 1st Qualifying Round in the latest 2020/21 season. The suffix reflects the Roman name for nearby village of Silchester, Calleva Atrebatum.

Southampton CAMBRIDGE – Four FA Cup campaigns in the years leading up to WWI, the club reached the 3rd Qualifying Round in their debut season in 1910/11. The suffix is likely to be a reference to Cambridge Road in Southampton.

Colne CARLTON – Just two FA Cup campaigns for this North East Lancashire Combination club in 1924/25 and 1925/26, exiting in Extra Preliminary Round both times.

Leeds CARNEGIE – Following a whole host of name changes this educational college competed in the FA Cup three times from 2008/09 to 2010/22 whilst members of the Northern Counties East League, exiting in the Extra Preliminary Round each time.

Beccles CAXTON – Just one FA Cup campaign in 1905/06 season whilst members of the Norfolk and Suffolk League losing 5-1 at Lowestoft Town in the club's only FA Cup match. Probably named for Caxton Road in Beccles.

Ellesmere Port CEMENT – Ten FA Cup campaigns spanning the 1920s and '30s for this Cheshire based club reaching the 2nd Qualifying Round twice in that time. Note, Newhaven Cement Works also have competed in FA Cup.

Norwich CEYMS – Both the abbreviated version and the full Norwich Church of England Young Men's Society name provide a unique suffix for this Norfolk club that participated in the FA Cup 42 times, reaching the 4th Qualifying Round in 1906/07 season.

Harrow CHEQUERS – Entered the FA Cup three times in the competition's first five years, but never actually played a match, choosing to scratch every time.

Goole CHEVRONS – Just one FA Cup campaign in 1919/20 whilst members of the Goole and District League, exiting in the Preliminary Round following a 2-1 defeat to Beverley Town in their only match. The suffix is likely to represent the fact that this was a temporary team made up of soldiers who'd been active during World War I, the name reflecting the overseas Service Chevron awarded for each year of overseas service.

Newland CHOIR – Just one FA Cup campaign in 1920/21 as members of the East Riding Amateur League, losing 2-1 to Hull Old Boys in an Extra Preliminary Round replay.

Dosthill COLTS – Just one FA Cup campaign in 2010/11 season whilst members of the Midland Combination, reaching the 1st Qualifying Round.

Hucknall CONSTITUTIONAL – Just one FA Cup campaign in 1905/06 as members of the Notts and District League, reaching the 3rd Qualifying Round after three straight victories. The suffix suggests affiliation with the Hucknall Constitutional Club.

Beddington CORNER – The Cornerites competed in the FA Cup for eight seasons in the years leading up to WWII whilst members of the Surrey Senior League, with a best run to the 3rd Qualifying Round in the 1933/34 season.

Oxford CYGNETS – Participated in the FA Cup in each of the final four years of the 19th Century, reaching the 2nd Qualifying Round in both their first and last campaigns.

Stone DOMINOES – Ten consecutive FA Cup campaigns starting from 2003/04, with a best run to the 2nd Qualifying Round in their second campaign. The suffix is a derivative of St Dominic's, the scouts group for which the club was originally formed as a youth side.

Milton Keynes DONS – Competed in the last 17 FA Cup campaigns reaching the 5th Round 'Proper' in 2012/13 season. The suffix reflects the connection of the club to Wimbledon FC.

Mount Hill ENTERPRISE – A dozen FA Cup campaigns, with ten before WWII and two after, reaching the 1st Qualifying Round in half of them. Thirty years after their last campaign the club was absorbed into Hanham Athletic.

South Shields EX-SCHOOLBOYS – Just one FA Cup campaign as a Sunderland Amateur League club in 1950/51, losing 3-1 to Annfield Plain in a replay.

Leadgate EXILES – Five FA Cup campaigns in the final years of the 19th Century, reaching the 2nd Qualifying Round when members of the Northern League in 1897/98 season.

Bristol MANOR FARM – The Farm reached the 3rd Qualifying Round for the third successive season in 2020/21 season, the best the club has achieved in 35 campaigns. Named for the small area in north Bristol.

Sandiacre EXCELSIOR FOUNDRY – Participated in the last seven FA Cup campaigns prior to WWII as a Notts Alliance club, reaching the 1st Qualifying Round in five of them. The club was the works team of the Excelsior Foundry Co.

West Ham GARFIELD – Five FA Cup campaigns at the start of the 20th Century, reaching 1st Qualifying Round in their first two campaigns.

Shoeburyness GARRISON – Thirteen FA Cup campaigns either side of the Great War for this Essex based military club, reaching the 2nd Qualifying Round in three of their first five campaigns.

Leigh GENESIS – The final name of the club that had been previously known as Horwich RMI and Leigh RMI, they played just the last three of their 86 FA Cup campaigns under this name. The suffix was adopted to signify a new beginning for the club, being distinct from Railway Mechanics Institute names.

Ramsgate GRENVILLE – Four FA Cup campaigns in the run up to the outbreak of WWII, this original Kent League club appeared in the Preliminary Round in both their first two seasons.

Nuneaton GRIFF – Nine FA Cup campaigns so far from 2007/08 to 2016/17, reaching the 2nd Qualifying Round in 2012/13. The suffix reflects the Griff and Coton Coal Miners Welfare ground where the club moved to be based a year after forming as Nuneaton Amateurs.

Gedling GROVE – Six FA Cup campaigns in the 1890s for this Nottinghamshire based club, with three 1st Qualifying Round and three 2nd Qualifying Rounds exits.

Monks HALL – This Cheshire based club had three FA Cup campaigns immediately after the end of WWI, reaching the 4th Qualifying Round in their debut campaign in 1919/20.

Dulwich HAMLET – The Hamlet appeared in the FA Cup for the 95th time in the 2020/21 season. They have reached the 1st Round 'Proper' 15 times over those years, which is a record number for a club yet to progress further in the competition.

Seaham HARBOUR – Twenty-six FA Cup campaigns in total from 1892/93 to 1928/29, although four were under the name Seaham White Star, the club reached the 4th Qualifying Round in 1909/10 season.

Bemerton Heath HARLEQUINS – The Quins had their 29th consecutive FA Cup campaign in the 2020/21 season, but the club has never bettered its debut campaign performance of reaching the 3rd Qualifying Round. The club's kit reflects the suffix name, or the suffix name reflects the kit colours of black and white.

Hexham HEARTS – Eight consecutive FA Cup campaigns spanning the late 1940s and '50s whilst members of the Northern Alliance, and making it as far as the 4th Qualifying Round in 1953/54.

Hampstead HEATHENS – Only participated in the FA Cup in the competition's debut campaign, reaching the quarter-finals courtesy of the first ever replay victory in the competition.

Darenth HEATHSIDE – This Kent League club participated in the FA Cup six times in the 1980s and '90s reaching the 2nd Qualifying Round in their second campaign.

Craghead HEROS – This County Durham based club had one FA Cup campaign whilst members of the Northern Combination in 1919/20 season, losing 1-0 at Boldon Colliery in their only match. The suffix is likely to reflect the fact that this was a temporary team made up of military personnel with no formal team to sign on to for at least a year after the War.

Prestwich HEYS – Fifteen campaigns in total, returning to the FA Cup in 2018/19 twenty-five years after the third of their three visits to the 2nd Qualifying Round. The suffix represents the Heys Road School whose former students formed an old boys club that adopted the current name in 1964.

Sale HOLMEFIELD – Three FA Cup campaigns for this Manchester League club from 1906/07 to 1909/10, reaching the 1st Qualifying Round in their middle campaign. Holmefield is a small suburb of Sale.

Jump HOME GUARD – This South Yorkshire club participated in FA Cup twice in 1949/50 and 1950/51 whilst members of the Barnsley Association League, achieving one draw and two heavy defeats. Note, several clubs with the suffix 'Guards' have also competed in FA Cup but this is the only one in the singular.

Beeston HUMBER – A Nottinghamshire based club which participated in the FA Cup twice in the late 19th Century whilst members of the Nottinghamshire and District League. The club exited in the 1st Qualifying Round both times.

Industry INN – This Rotherham based club competed in FA Cup just once whilst members of the Sheffield Licenced Victuallers League in 1912/13, losing 2-1 to Kilnhurst Town in a second replay.

Middlesbrough IRONOPOLIS – Five FA Cup campaigns at the start of the 1890s, reaching the quarter-finals in 1892/93 just ahead of their one season as a Football League club. The suffix was created to reflect the industrial nature of the town and to distinguish the club from Middlesbrough FC.

Oxhey JETS – This Hertfordshire club has competed in all the last 16 FA Cup campaigns reaching the 2nd Qualifying Round on two occasions.

Castle Vale JKS – Formed from the reserves of Castle Vale Kings Heath, the Junior Kick Stars had one FA Cup campaign of their own whilst members of the Midland Combination Premier Division in 2010/11, only reaching the Preliminary Round courtesy of a walkover against Ledbury Town.

Sporting KHALSA – Participated in eight of the last nine FA Cup seasons, reaching the 4th Qualifying Round in 2015/16.

Staines LAMMAS – Four FA Cup campaigns so far from 2011/12 to 2014/15, with a best run to the 1st Qualifying Round in their debut campaign. The suffix represents the Lammas Recreational Ground in Staines.

Esher LEOPOLD – Just one FA Cup campaign and just one FA Cup match for this Surrey based club, losing 5-0 at home to Old Carthusians in their only match in 1881/82. The suffix is in honour of Leopold I, husband of Princess Charlotte, who both lived at Claremont Mansion.

Hebburn LESLIES – The football club of Hawthorn Leslies shipyard competed in the FA Cup four times in 1920s and '30s whilst members of the Tyneside League, but were defeated in all four games they played.

Ryhill LIBERAL – Just one FA Cup campaign and one FA Cup game, a 2-1 defeat at Horsforth in 1920/21 season. Associated with the Ryhill Liberal Club in Wakefield.

Lincoln LINDUM – Competed in FA Cup in the last three years before the Football League was founded, winning their debut match but losing the other three. The suffix reflects the Roman name for Lincoln, Lindum Colonia.

Runcorn LINNETS – The Linnets have participated in the FA Cup in each of the last 13 seasons, reaching the 3rd Qualifying Round in 2013/14. The suffix is a nod to Runcorn FC's nickname, originally chosen due to the high numbers of the birds around their ground.

London LIONS – Four FA Cup campaigns across nine seasons from 2012/13 to 2020/21 reaching the 1st Qualifying Round in their debut campaign.

Normanby MAGNESITE – Fourteen FA Cup campaigns leading up to the outbreak of WWII, this Teesside League club reached the 3rd Qualifying Round twice. Works team of local magnesium producing brick works factory.

Greenwood MEADOWS – Three FA Cup campaigns for the Magpies in the early 2010s exiting in the Extra Preliminary Round each time.

North Lindsey MIDGETS – Just one FA Cup campaign for this North Lindsey League club, and just one FA Cup match in 1911/12 losing 2-1 to Hull Day Street Old Boys. The suffix appears to reflect the fact that the club was formed from a boys' club set up by R.A.C. Symes.

Lingdale MINES – Participated in the FA Cup in both of the last two seasons prior to WWI while members of the Cleveland League, losing both matches they actually played.

Reading MINSTER – Five FA Cup campaigns before the formation of the Football League reaching the 3rd Round in 1881/82 season.

Selby MIZPAH – Two FA Cup campaigns in 1908/09 and 1909/10 as members of the West Yorkshire League, exiting in the 1st Qualifying Round both times. Mizpah is the Hebrew word for Watchtower original coined in the biblical story of Jacob and Laban.

Lincoln MOORLANDS – Four FA Cup campaigns whilst members of the North East Counties League prior to merging with Lincoln Railway to form Lincoln Moorlands Railway. That new club also participated in the FA Cup in each of the next eight seasons.

Solihull MOORS – Participated in each of the last 14 FA Cup campaigns since Solihull Borough and Moor Green merged in 2007, reaching the 2nd Round 'Proper' in four of their last five campaigns.

Old Whittington MUTUALS – This Derbyshire based club had one FA Cup campaign and one FA Cup match, losing 3-0 at the original Belper Town in 1909/10.

Ashton NATIONAL – A Tameside club that were also known as Ashton National Gas which participated in the FA Cup three times in the mid-1930s, reaching the 1st Qualifying Round in their middle campaign.

Peterlee NEWTOWN – Twenty-seven consecutive FA Cup campaigns starting in 1979/80, reaching the 4th Qualifying Round in 1985/86 season.

Leicester NIRVANA – Initially participated in FA Cup as Thurnby Nirvana but included here as is a continuation of the same club, they have been involved in the last ten FA Cup seasons, and reached the 1st Qualifying Round in their first two campaigns. The suffix was chosen to reflect the inclusive nature of the club, an open and idyllic place for all.

Sunderland NISSAN – Initially participated in FA Cup as Washington Nissan but included here as was a continuation of the same club, competing in the FA Cup six times, and reaching the 1st Qualifying Round in 2006/07.

Maidenhead NORFOLKIANS – Competed in the FA Cup in the each of the final 16 seasons prior to the Great War, reaching the 3rd Qualifying round three times, and subsequently being absorbed into Maidenhead United after the War.

Barrow NOVOCASTRIANS – A Cumbrian club who were members of the North West Association League when reaching the FA Cup 1st Qualifying Round four times during their six campaigns prior to WWI. A Novocastrian is an inhabitant of Newcastle-upon-Tyne.

Stone OLD ALLEYNIANS – Participated in both the last two FA Cup campaigns, exiting in the Extra Preliminary Round both times. The suffix reflects a connection to Alleyne's grammar School in Stone.

Northampton ON CHENECKS – Five successive FA Cup campaigns up to 2020/21 season with a 1-0 victory over Histon the club's only win so far. The 'ON' part of their name stands for 'Old Northamptonian'. According to Wikipedia, Chenecks is derived from the four School Houses at Northampton Grammar School; CHipseys, SpENcer, BECKett and St CrispinS.

Hull ORIENTAL – Just one campaign in FA Cup whilst members of the East Riding Counties League in 1910/11, losing 5-1 to Mexborough town in their only match.

South Shields PARKSIDE – Competed in the FA Cup in the final six seasons prior to the outbreak of WWI, reaching the 2nd Qualifying Round in 1909/10 whilst members of the Tyneside League. Parkside is a small suburb of South Shields.

Plymouth PARKWAY – The Parkway have competed in the FA Cup in each of the last nine seasons, reaching the 2nd Qualifying Round in 2018/19. Named for the Parkway Sports Club where home games are played.

Scarborough PENGUINS – Five FA Cup campaigns in the late 1920s before being absorbed into Scarborough FC, reaching the 1st Qualifying Round three times.

Willenhall PICKWICK – Seven FA Cup campaigns in the years leading up to WWI as members of the Birmingham Combination, reaching the 4th Qualifying Round in the 1913/14 season. The suffix is likely to reflect the popularity at the time of the Charles Dickens novel *"The Posthumous Papers of the Pickwick Club"*.

Annfield PLAIN – First entered the FA Cup in 1909/10 season as Annfield Plain Celtic, but have had 69 subsequent campaigns under the current name, and appeared in the 1st Round 'Proper' for the third time in 1964/65 season. 'Plain' in the town's name is derived from the inclined plane used to move wagons on the Stanhope and Tyne Railway.

Hucknall PORTLAND – Six FA Cup campaigns spanning the turn of the 20th Century, reaching the 5th Qualifying Round in 1899/1900 season. Likely to have been associated with the Portland pub.

Mole Valley PREDATORS – Formerly known as Chessington United the club played the last of its five FA Cup campaign under this name in 2015/16, reaching the third of their three Preliminary Round appearances. Named for Predators Youth FC, one of the teams that were amalgamated with Chessington United in 2005 to form the club.

Graham Street PRIMS – Two FA Cup campaigns so far for this Derbyshire club in the mid-2010s, exiting in Extra Preliminary Round both times as members of the East Midlands Counties League. Suffix is an abbreviation of 'Primitives' associated with Primitive Methodist Church.

Reigate PRIORY – Entered the first FA Cup but scratched before facing Royal Engineers. The club twice reached the 2nd Round over the next five years, before returning for three campaigns in the late 1920s whilst members of the Surrey Senior League, exiting in the Preliminary Round each time.

Sheffield PROVIDENCE – Three FA Cup campaigns in the early 1880s, but a 3-3 draw against Sheffield FC was the only game they didn't lose.

Bedford QUEENS – Two FA Cup campaigns at the start of the 20th Century whilst members of the Bedfordshire and District League, exiting in the 2nd Qualifying Round on both occasions. Bedford Queens Park Rangers and Bedford Queens Works also participated in the competition later in the century, both of which may be connected, and the 'Queens' name is also now adopted by Queens Park Rangers who dropped the apostrophe some time during the 1960s.

Brightlingsea REGENT – Formed as a result of a merger between Brightlingsea United and Regent Park Rangers in 2005, the Rs competed in the FA Cup for the eighth successive season in the 2020/21 season, having had one run to the 3rd Qualifying Round in the previous seven.

Luton RELIANCE – Participated in the FA Cup in each of the last three seasons before the outbreak of WWI whilst members of the Luton and District League, reaching the 2nd Qualifying Round in their middle campaign.

Finedon REVELLERS – Six FA Cup campaigns straddling the turn of the 20th Century whilst members of the Northants League (now the United Counties League), reaching the 3rd Qualifying Round in the 1900/01 season.

Third Lanark RIFLE VOLUNTEERS – This Scottish club participated in the FA Cup twice, reaching the 2nd Round in both their 1885/86 and 1886/87 campaigns.

Hugglescote ROBIN HOOD – This Leicestershire Senior League club had one FA Cup campaign in 1898/99, losing 4-1 to Burton Swifts in their only match.

Gateshead RODSLEY – Two FA Cup campaign just prior to outbreak of WWI exiting in Preliminary Round in first campaign when members of the Tyneside League, and in the Extra Preliminary Round in their second campaign whilst a Northern Alliance club. Possibly connected to Rodsley Avenue in Gateshead.

Bridon ROPES – The Charlton based club has twice competed in FA Cup in last five years with a 3-1 win over Broadfields United the club's only victory to date, earning a Preliminary Round appearance in 2019/20 season. Connected to the British Ropes Factory in Charlton.

Cheltenham SARACENS – The Saracens participated in the FA Cup for the fifth time in 2020/21, having posted just one run as far as the 1st Qualifying Round to date.

Aston SHAKESPEARE – Most likely to be football club of the Shakespeare Inn in Birmingham in the 19th Century. The club entered the FA Cup twice either side of the formation of the Football League before amalgamating into Aston Victoria.

Barrow SHIPBUILDERS – Just one FA Cup campaign and one FA Cup match for this Cumbrian based North West Association League club, losing 2-1 at home to Kells White Star in the Preliminary Round of the 1919/20 competition.

Hoyland SILKSTONE – Six FA Cup campaigns whilst members of the Barnsley Association League with three Preliminary Round and three 1st qualifying Round exits. Connected to the Hoyland Silkstone Colliery named after the Silkstone coal seam it was sunk to exploit.

Steel, Peech and Tozer SOCIAL SERVICES – Three FA Cup campaigns, from 1948/49 to 1950/51 whilst members of the Sheffield Association League, reaching the 1st Qualifying Round in the club's first and last campaigns.

Catford SOUTHEND – A couple of other clubs competed in FA Cup with 'South End' as their suffix, but only the Kittens used the name without the space when adopting it in 1900 following two years as Catford Rovers. The club twice made the 5th Qualifying Round in a dozen campaigns either side of the Great War.

Coventry SPHINX – The Sphinx competed in the FA Cup for the 14th consecutive season in 2020/21, and have a best Cup run to the 3rd Qualifying Round. Connected to the Armstrong Siddeley Motor Company which used a sphinx as a badge.

Chesterfield SPITAL – Three campaigns in the early 1880s, but only made the 2nd Round once courtesy of a bye in 1884/85 season. Spital is a small suburb of Chesterfield.

Darlington ST AUGUSTINE'S – Twenty-five FA Cup campaigns in the 19th century and leading up to WWI whilst members of the Northern League, reaching the 5th Qualifying Round in the 1901/02 season.

Norwich ST BARNABAS – Six FA Cup campaigns in the years leading up to WWII, the club posted their best run in the first of them, to the 3rd Qualifying Round in 1933/34.

Newhall ST EDWARD'S – This Derbyshire based club had just one FA Cup campaign in 1908/09 whilst members of the Burton and District League, losing 8-0 at Ripley Athletic in their only match.

Warrington ST ELPHIN'S – Competed in the FA Cup in the last six seasons of the 19th Century, reaching the 2nd Qualifying Round in their final campaign in 1899/1900.

Darlington ST HILDA'S – Just three FA Cup campaigns either side of the turn of the 20th Century, twice appearing in the 1st Qualifying Round, latterly as members of the Teesside League.

West Hartlepool ST JOSEPH'S – Entered the FA Cup in both the last two seasons before WWI, but played just one game in 1913/14, a 4-0 defeat at Dipton United.

Hereford ST MARTINS – Three FA Cup campaigns for one of the clubs that helped create Hereford United, all in the early 1920s, and all ending in a heavy defeat and an Extra Preliminary Round exit.

Boston ST NICHOLAS – Just one FA Cup campaign as members of the South Lincolnshire League in 1921/22 season, losing 2-0 to Peterborough GN Locomotives in the Extra Preliminary Round.

Chester ST OSWALD'S – Five FA Cup campaigns in the years straddling the formation of the Football League, the club achieved just two wins in the competition against Druids and Shrewsbury Town.

Thornaby ST PATRICK – Three FA Cup campaigns in the late 1930s, the first two as Thornaby Amateurs, exiting in the Preliminary Round in all three campaigns.

Chalfont ST PETER – Several clubs have used the suffix 'St Peter's', but this Buckinghamshire based club is the only one to exclude the apostrophe and the 's' in their name. The Saints competed in the FA Cup for the 44th consecutive time in 2020/21 and have reached the 3rd Qualifying Round four times.

Heaton STANNINGTON – The 2020/21 FA Cup campaign for the Stan was just the 13th in its history despite coming 100 years after their first appearance in the competition. Connected to Stannington Avenue in Heaton.

Stocksbridge Park STEELS – This Sheffield club has participated in each of the last 29 FA Cup campaigns, reaching the 4th Qualifying Round in 2003/04.

Leeds STEELWORKS – competed in the first three FA Cup campaigns following the end of WWI, reaching the 2nd Qualifying Round in their debut campaign, and losing 7-0 to Leeds United the following season.

Swindon SUPERMARINE – Have participated in the last 20 FA Cup campaigns and reached the 2nd Round 'Proper' in 2010/11. Named for the Supermarine aircraft company.

Weybridge SWALLOWS – Just one FA Cup campaign in 1880/81 reaching the 2nd Round after a 3-1 victory over Henley.

Alma SWANLEY – A Kent League club that participated in the FA Cup five times in the 1980s and '90s, reaching the 2nd Qualifying Round in their final campaign in 1992/93 season. Named for the Alma pub in Swanley.

Billingham SYNTHONIA – With a suffix derived from 'Synthetic Ammonia', a chemical fertiliser produced by major local employer ICI, the club has competed in the FA Cup 77 times since 1934/35 season, reaching the 1st Round 'Proper' on seven occasions, most latterly in 1989/90.

Hitchin Blue Cross TEMPERANCE BRIGADE – Eventually became simply Hitchin Blue Cross but had one FA Cup campaign using this moniker in 1909/10 losing 4-2 to Leighton Town.

Bedlington TERRIERS – Formed in 1949, the club adopted the 'Terriers' suffix in 1981 after previous incarnations as 'Mechanics', 'United' (twice) and 'Colliery Welfare', and last appeared in the FA Cup in 2016/17 season with 35 campaigns and one 2nd Round 'Proper' appearance under their belt.

Norwich THORPE – Competed in the FA Cup in four campaigns at the start of the 1890s reaching the 2nd Qualifying Round in the first two of them.

Coundon THREE TUNS – This Wearside League club only participated in the FA Cup once, losing 2-0 to Billingham Town in their only match in 1984/85 season. Named for the Three Tuns pub.

London TIGERS – The first three of the club's eight FA Cup campaigns were played under the name Kingsbury London Tigers, and the club reached the 2nd Qualifying Round in 2014/15.

New Brighton TOWER – Five FA Cup campaigns straddling the turn of the 20th Century, the middle three of which were as a Football League side, and reaching the 1st Round 'Proper' twice. Named for the observation tower in New Brighton built at the end of the 19th Century. A separate club, New Brighton Tower Amateurs, competed in FA Cup soon after.

Merthyr TYDFIL – Sixty-four FA Cup campaigns after WWII until folding in 2010, reaching the 2nd Round 'Proper' six times, most recently in 1990/91 season. The town is named after the fifth Century Saint Tydfil.

Halliwell UNITARIANS – Two FA Cup campaigns for this Lancashire based club whilst members of local Bolton and District Leagues in 1906/07 and 1908/09, playing just two matches losing both of them by a 4-0 scoreline.

Farnham UNITED BREWERIES – Seven FA Cup campaigns in the 1920s whilst members of the Surrey Senior league, making the 1st Round 'Proper' in 1925/26 only to lose 10-1 at home to Swindon Town. Note, two clubs have appeared in FA Cup with 'Brewery' as their suffix, Crosswell's Brewery and Dunston Federation Brewery.

Thornaby UTOPIANS – Three FA Cup campaigns straddling the turn of the 20th Century as members of the Northern League, reaching the 3rd Qualifying Round in their final campaign.

Moulton VERDIN – This Cheshire based club participated in the FA Cup in each of the final six seasons before the outbreak of WWII whilst members of the Crewe and District League, reaching the 2nd Qualifying round in 1934/35 season.

Cudworth VILLAGE – Many village clubs have participated in the FA Cup, but this Barnsley-based club is the only one to include the word in their name. They competed in the FA Cup 17 times between the two Wars, twice making the 2nd Qualifying Round.

Canterbury WAVERLEY – Eight FA Cup campaigns for the Waves leading up to the outbreak of WWII, setting their best run to the 4th Qualifying Round in that final season before the War.

Sheffield WEDNESDAY – Originally name The Wednesday, the Owls have won the FA Cup three times in their 130 campaigns, which all started in the 1880/81 season. They were the first non-league club to reach an FA Cup Final (in 1890).

Hoyland Common WESLEYANS – Two FA Cup campaigns immediately after end of WWI whilst members of local Sheffield leagues, losing both matches played.

Rushden WINDMILL – Seven FA Cup campaigns in the seasons leading up to WWI as members of the Northants League, reaching the 1st Qualifying Round in each even numbered campaign.

Garston WOODCUTTERS – As members of the Liverpool League this club played in the FA Cup in the last season before WWII and achieved two wins on their way to the 2nd Qualifying Round, including an 8-2 victory over Oakmere.

Dronfield WOODHOUSE – Three campaigns immediately after WWI for this Derbyshire side competing in the Sheffield Amateur League and reaching the 1st Qualifying Round in their debut season. Note that two Mansfield Woodhouse clubs competed in FA Cup but both had a further third word in their respective names, Excelsior and Rangers.

Norton WOODSEATS – This South Yorkshire club participated in the FA Cup 37 times from 1926/27 to 1973/74, twice falling one round short of appearing in the 'Proper' Rounds. For a short while some time after their FA Cup exploits the Hammers were known as Dronfield United before reverting to their original name.

Pilkington XXX – Five FA Cup campaigns whilst members of the Midlands Combination from 2007/08 to 2012/13, reaching the 1st Qualifying Round just once. Their suffix reflected the Triple X glass product manufactured by its parent company.

Mile Oak Rovers and YOUTH – This Staffordshire club competed in the FA Cup for nine consecutive seasons up until 1990/91, reaching the 2nd Qualifying Round three times.

Clay Cross ZINGARI – Two FA Cup campaigns in the early 1920s whilst members of the Derbyshire Senior League, but lost both games played. Note, Preston Zingari entered the FA Cup in 1884/85 season but scratched alongside their opponents before playing their match.

Rank	Combined Counties League	Q4	Q3	Q2	Q1	PR	EP
1	Hartley Wintney	1	2		1	5	2
2	South Park	1			2	1	
3	Hanworth Villa	1				8	1
4	Badshot Lea		1	2		7	2
5	Chipstead		1	1	3	12	1
6	Abbey Rangers		1			1	3
7	AFC Wallingford			3		1	1
8	Bedfont			2	10	5	1

Top Eight FA Cup Clubs whilst Members of CCL.

Nb. Chart shows number of exits per Round

Top 150 FA Cup Clubs from End of World War II to End of 20th Century (1945/46 to 1999/2000)

The second half of the 20th Century is regarded by many to be the FA Cup's halcyon days. A post-war boom in attendances was followed by the advent of televised football that brought football as a whole to a much larger audience. The FA Cup Final was the showpiece event of the season, the only domestic club match shown live on television until the second last decade of the century. The FA made some rule changes to entry criteria that limited the number of entrants in the last 30 years or so of the 20th Century, meaning just over 1,200 clubs participated in the FA Cup from the end of World War II, despite covering a 55 year period.

Best Performance - Winners

1	Manchester United.............	9x Winners
2	Tottenham Hotspur	6x Winners
3	Liverpool	5x Winners, 10x Finalists
4	Arsenal	5x Winners, 9x Finalists
5	Everton	3x Winners, 7x Finalists
6	Newcastle United	3x Winners, 6x Finalists
7	Chelsea	3x Winners, 5x Finalists
8	West Ham United	3x Winners, 3x Finalists
9	Manchester City	2x Winners, 4x Finalists
10	Wolverhampton Wanderers	2x Winners, 2x Finalists, 7x SF
11	West Bromwich Albion	2x Winners, 2x Finalists, 6x SF
12	Leeds United	1x Winners, 4x Finalists
13	Blackpool	1x Winners, 3x Finalists
14	Aston Villa	1x Winners, 2x Finalists, 5x SF, 13x QF
15	Nottingham Forest	1x Winners, 2x Finalists, 5x SF, 12x QF
16	Sunderland	1x Winners, 2x Finalists, 4x SF, 8x QF
17	Bolton Wanderers	1x Winners, 2x Finalists, 4x SF, 7x QF
18	Charlton Athletic	1x Winners, 2x Finalists, 2x SF
19	Southampton	1x Winners, 1x Finalists, 4x SF
20	Derby County	1x Winners, 1x Finalists, 3x SF, 11x QF
21	Ipswich Town	1x Winners, 1x Finalists, 3x SF, 7x QF
22	Wimbledon	1x Winners, 1x Finalists, 2x SF
23	Coventry City	1x Winners, 1x Finalists, 1x SF

Best Performance – Runners-up

24	Leicester City	4x Finalists
25	Sheffield Wednesday	2x Finalists, 6x SF
26	Burnley	2x Finalists, 4x SF
27	Preston North End	2x Finalists, 2x SF
28	Birmingham City	1x Finalists, 7x SF
29	Luton Town	1x Finalists, 4x SF

30	Blackburn Rovers	1x Finalists, 3x SF, 6x QF, 19x R5
31	Watford	1x Finalists, 3x SF, 6x QF, 12x R5
32	Crystal Palace	1x Finalists, 3x SF, 5x QF, 9x R5
33	Fulham	1x Finalists, 3x SF, 5x QF, 7x R5
34	Middlesbrough	1x Finalists, 1x SF, 7x QF
35	Queens Park Rangers	1x Finalists, 1x SF, 6x QF
36	Brighton & Hove Albion	1x Finalists, 1x SF, 2x QF

Best Performance – Semi-Finalists

37	Sheffield United	3x SF, 10x QF
38	Norwich City	3x SF, 6x QF
39	Portsmouth	2x SF, 5x QF
40	Stoke City	2x SF, 3x QF
41	Oldham Athletic	2x SF, 2x QF
42	Leyton / Orient	1x SF, 3x QF
43	Swansea Town / City	1x SF, 1x QF, 6x R5, 18x R4
44	Port Vale	1x SF, 1x QF, 6x R5, 15x R4
45	Plymouth Argyle	1x SF, 1x QF, 3x R5, 13x R4
46	York City	1x SF, 1x QF, 3x R5, 10x R4
47	Chesterfield	1x SF, 1x QF, 2x R5

Best Performance – Quarter-Finalists

48	Barnsley	4x QF
49	Hull City	3x QF, 9x R5
50	Notts County	3x QF, 5x R5, 17x R4
51	Wrexham	3x QF, 5x R5, 14x R4
52	Brentford	3x QF, 4x R5
53	Huddersfield Town	2x QF, 8x R5
54	Bristol Rovers	2x QF, 6x R5, 17x R4
55	Millwall	2x QF, 6x R5, 16x R4
56	Shrewsbury Town	2x QF, 6x R5, 12x R4
57	Abbey / Cambridge United ...	2x QF, 4x R5
58	Bristol City	1x QF, 10x R5
59	Swindon Town	1x QF, 7x R5
60	Headington / Oxford United	1x QF, 5x R5
61	Carlisle United	1x QF, 4x R5, 15x R4
62	Peterborough United	1x QF, 4x R5, 14x R4
63	Bradford City	1x QF, 4x R5, 11x R4
64	Mansfield Town	1x QF, 4x R5, 7x R4
65	Tranmere Rovers	1x QF, 3x R5, 8x R4
66	Colchester United	1x QF, 3x R5, 6x R4
67	AFC Bournemouth / & Bosc.	1x QF, 2x R5, 8x R4
68	Gillingham	1x QF, 2x R5, 5x R4
69	Bradford (Park Avenue)*	1x QF, 1x R5, 4x R4
70	Wigan Athletic	1x QF, 1x R5, 3x R4, 15x R3

71 Exeter City .... 1x QF, 1x R5, 3x R4, 13x R3
72 Gateshead* .... 1x QF, 1x R5, 3x R4, 7x R3

Best Performance – 5th Round

73 Cardiff City 6x R5
74 Grimsby Town 4x R5, 15x R4
75 Doncaster Rovers 4x R5, 7x R4
76 Walsall 3x R5, 10x R4
77 Southend United 3x R5, 6x R4
78 Rotherham United 2x R5, 17x R4
79 Bury 2x R5, 9x R4
80 Scunthorpe / & Lindsey Utd. 2x R5, 8x R4
81 Chester / City* 2x R5, 6x R4
82 Northampton Town 2x R5, 5x R4
83 Reading 1x R5, 10x R4, 33x R3
84 Stockport County 1x R5, 10x R4, 22x R3
85 Crewe Alexandra 1x R5, 7x R4
86 Newport County* 1x R5, 6x R4, 19x R3
87 Aldershot 1x R5, 6x R4, 16x R3
88 Darlington* 1x R5, 3x R4, 12x R3
89 Halifax Town 1x R5, 3x R4, 9x R3
90 Rochdale 1x R5, 2x R4, 12x R3
91 Wellington T. / Telford Utd. 1x R5, 2x R4, 3x R3
92 Yeovil & Petters Utd. / Town 1x R5, 1x R4, 9x R3
93 Southport 1x R5, 1x R4, 8x R3
94 Blyth Spartans 1x R5, 1x R4, 2x R3
95 Kidderminster Harriers 1x R5, 1x R4, 2x R2

Best Performance – 4th Round

96 Hereford United 6x R4
97 Torquay United 5x R4
98 Hartlepool / Hartlepools / U. 4x R4
99 Lincoln City 3x R4
100 Sutton United 2x R4, 4x R3, 6x R2, 16x R1
101 Bedford Town* 2x R4, 4x R3, 6x R2, 12x R1
102 Altrincham 1x R4, 8x R3
103 Accrington Stanley* 1x R4, 6x R3
104 Enfield* 1x R4, 4x R3, 18x R2
105 Kettering Town 1x R4, 4x R3, 9x R2, 31x R1
106 Woking 1x R4, 4x R3, 9x R2, 16x R1
107 Weymouth 1x R4, 3x R3
108 Rhyl 1x R4, 2x R3, 4x R2, 17x R1
109 Worcester City .... 1x R4, 2x R3, 4x R2, 9x R1, (plus 16x q4)
110 Tooting and Mitcham United 1x R4, 2x R3, 4x R2, 9x R1, (plus 10x q4)
111 G'send & N'fleet (Ebbsfleet) 1x R4, 2x R3, 3x R2, 11x R1

112 New Brighton 1x R4, 2x R3, 3x R3, 6x R1
113 (Stevenage) Borough 1x R4, 2x R3, 3x R3, 4x R1
114 Bishop Auckland 1x R4, 1x R3, 10x R2
115 Northwich Victoria 1x R4, 1x R3, 6x R2, 15x R1
116 Walthamstow Avenue 1x R4, 1x R3, 6x R2, 13x R1
117 Stafford Rangers 1x R4, 1x R3, 4x R2, 14x R1
118 Leatherhead 1x R4, 1x R3, 4x R2, 6x R1
119 Hednesford Town 1x R4, 1x R3, 3x R2
120 Harlow Town 1x R4, 1x R3, 1x R2

Best Performance – 3rd Round
121 Barrow 9x R3
122 Workington AFC 7x R3, 18x R2
123 Barnet 7x R3, 12x R2
124 Wycombe Wanderers 5x R3, 15x R2
125 Maidstone United* 5x R3, 11x R2
126 Bath City 4x R3
127 Scarborough 3x R3, 11x R2
128 Boston United 3x R3, 8x R2
129 Macclesfield / Town 3x R3, 6x R2
130 Nuneaton Borough* 2x R3, 6x R2
131 Hastings United* 2x R3, 3x R2
132 Burton Albion 2x R3, 2x R2, 12x R1
133 Marlow .... 2x R3, 2x R2, 4x R1, (plus 3x q4)
134 Rushden and Diamonds ...... 2x R3, 2x R2, 4x R1, (plus 2x q4)
135 Chelmsford City 1x R3, 9x R2
136 South Shields*/ Gateshead U 1x R3, 8x R2
137 King's Lynn 1x R3, 7x R2
138 Hendon 1x R3, 6x R2, 18x R1
139 Grantham / Town 1x R3, 6x R2, 13x R1
140 Margate / Thanet United ..... 1x R3, 5x R2, 15x R1, (plus 8x q4)
141 Dagenham .... 1x R3, 5x R2, 15x R1, (plus 6x q4)
142 Aylesbury United 1x R3, 4x R2
143 Cheltenham Town 1x R3, 3x R2, 18x R1
144 Marine .... 1x R3, 3x R2, 9x R1, (plus 9x q4)
145 Bishop's Stortford .... 1x R3, 3x R2, 9x R1, (plus 6x q4)
146 Welling United .... 1x R3, 3x R2, 9x R1, (plus 2x q4)
147 Morecambe 1x R3, 2x R2, 16x R1
148 Wealdstone 1x R3, 2x R2, 13x R1
149 Goole Town 1x R3, 2x R2, 10x R1
150 Frickley Colliery / Athletic 1x R3, 2x R2, 9x R1

**Different from current/later club with same/similar name*

Achieved Most Times

Most FA Cup Wins – **Arsenal** (14)

Most FA Cup Finals – **Arsenal** (21)

Most FA Cup Finals without losing – **The Wanderers** (5)

Most Consecutive FA Cup Final Wins – **The Wanderers** and **Blackburn Rovers** (3)

Most FA Cup Finals before losing in Final for first time – **Tottenham Hotspur** (lost in 8th Final)

Most FA Cup Final Wins in Successive Final Appearances – **Arsenal** and **Tottenham Hotspur** (7)

Most FA Cup Finals before Lifting Trophy – **Leicester City** (won in 5th Final)

Most FA Cup Final Defeats – **Everton** and **Manchester United** (8)

Most FA Cup Final Defeats in Successive Final Appearances – **Leicester City** (4)

Most FA Cup Finals without lifting Trophy – **Queen's Park**, **Birmingham City**, **Crystal Palace** and **Watford** (2)

Most FA Cup Finals without conceding – **Bury** (2)

Most FA Cup Finals without scoring – **Watford** (2)

Most FA Cup Finals across five consecutive Seasons – **Old Etonians**, **Blackburn Rovers**, **Arsenal** and **Chelsea** (4)

Most times appearing in three Consecutive Finals – **Arsenal** (twice)

Most times losing consecutive FA Cup Finals – **Newcastle United** (twice)

Most times knocked out FA Cup holder – **Manchester United** (10)

Most times knocked out by eventual FA Cup Winner – **Aston Villa**, **Liverpool** and **West Bromwich Albion** (25)

Most FA Cup Semi-Finals appearances – **Arsenal** and **Manchester United** (30)

Most FA Cup Semi-Finals without defeat – **Old Etonians** (6, includes one 'bye')

Most FA Cup Semi-Finals defeats – **Everton** (13)

Most Consecutive FA Cup Semi-Finals appearances – **Arsenal** and **Manchester United** (5)

Most Consecutive FA Cup Semi-Finals defeats – **Manchester United** (3)

Most Successive FA Cup Semi-Finals appearances ending in defeat – **Tottenham Hotspur** (8)

Most FA Cup Semi-Finals without reaching a Cup Final – **Norwich City**, **Oldham Athletic** and **Swifts** (3)

Most FA Cup Semi-Finals and never yet won FA Cup – **Birmingham City** (9)

Most FA Cup Quarter-Finals appearances – **Everton** and **Manchester United** (46)

Most Consecutive FA Cup Quarter-Finals appearances – **Sheffield (The) Wednesday** (9)

Most FA Cup campaigns reaching at least Quarter-Finals every time – **Oxford University** (8)

Most FA Cup Quarter-Finals defeats – **Everton** (20)

Most FA Cup Quarter-Finals without ever reaching Semi-Finals – **Brentford** and **Upton Park** (4)

Most FA Cup Quarter-Finals without appearing in an FA Cup Final – **Norwich City** (7)

Most FA Cup Quarter-Finals without yet lifting FA Cup Trophy – **Birmingham City** (21)

Most times reached at least the FA Cup 5th Round – **Everton** (61)

Most times exited FA Cup in 5th Round – **Blackburn Rovers** (20)

Most times exited FA Cup in 5th Round and never yet gone further – **Walsall** (6)

Most times reached FA Cup 5th Round but not appeared in FA Cup Final – **Norwich City** (21)

Most times reached FA Cup 5th Round but not won FA Cup – **Birmingham City** (34)

Most times reached at least the FA Cup 4th Round – **Everton** (81)

Most times reached at least the FA Cup 4th Round in Consecutive Seasons – **Chelsea** (23)

Most times exited FA Cup in 4th Round – **Wolverhampton Wanderers** (30)

Most times reached FA Cup 4th Round but never went further – **Hereford United** (8)

Most times an existing club has reached FA Cup 4th Round and never yet gone further – **Torquay United** (7)

Most times reached FA Cup 4th Round but not appeared in FA Cup Final – **Swansea City** and **Swindon Town** (34)

Most times reached FA Cup 4th Round but not won FA Cup – **Middlesbrough** (58)

Most times reached at least the FA Cup 3rd Round – **Aston Villa** (115)

Most times exited FA Cup in the 3rd Round – **Plymouth Argyle** and **Queens Park Rangers** (50)

Most times reached FA Cup 3rd Round and never yet gone further – **Barrow** (12)

Most times appeared in FA Cup 3rd Round as a non-league club (since 1925/26) – **Yeovil Town** (13)

Most times exited in FA Cup 2nd Round – **Northampton Town** (31)

Most times reached FA Cup 2nd Round and never yet gone further – **Slough Town** (8)

Most times appeared in 'Proper' Rounds of FA Cup but never went further than 2nd Round – **Hayes** (22)

Most times an existing club has appeared in 'Proper' Rounds of FA Cup but never gone further than 2nd Round – **Slough Town** (21)

Most times exited in FA Cup 1st Round – **Rochdale** (52)

Most times reached FA Cup 1st Round and never yet gone further – **Dulwich Hamlet** (15)

Most appearances in 1st Round 'Proper' as a non-league club – **Kettering Town** and **Yeovil Town** (51)

Most Consecutive appearances in 1st Round 'Proper' as a non-league club – **Hereford United** (17)

Most FA Cup campaigns without ever appearing in 1st Round 'Proper' – original **Sheppey United** (97)

Most FA Cup campaigns by an existing club without yet appearing in 1st Round 'Proper' – **Melksham Town** (96)

Most times exited FA Cup in the short-lived Intermediate Round – **Brentford, Darwen, Gillingham** and **West Ham United** (3)

Most times exited FA Cup in the short-lived 6th qualifying round – **Chesterfield** and **Rotherham County** (6)

Most times exited FA Cup in 6th qualifying round and never reached 'Proper' Rounds – original **Alfreton Town, Green Waves, Loughborough Corinthians**, original **Sheppey United, Sunderland West End**, original **Tufnell Park** and **Walthamstow Town** (1)

Most times exited FA Cup in the short-lived 5th qualifying round – **Bishop Auckland** (10)

Most times exited FA Cup in 5th qualifying round and never going further – original **Shepherds Bush** (4)

Most times exited FA Cup in the 4th qualifying round – **Bath City** (30)

Most times exited FA Cup in the 4th qualifying round and never yet gone further – **Bedworth United, Cowes, Hucknall Town** and **Portland United** (6)

Most times exited FA Cup in the 3rd qualifying round – **Worksop Town** (24)

Most times exited FA Cup in the 3rd qualifying round and never yet gone further – **Chertsey Town** and **Gateshead North Eastern Railway** (5)

Most times exited FA Cup in the 2nd qualifying round – **Lowestoft Town** (32)

Most times exited FA Cup in the 2nd qualifying round and never went further – **Milnthorpe Corinthians** (9)

Most times an existing club has exited FA Cup in the 2nd qualifying round and has never yet gone further – **Lostock Gralam** (8)

Most times exited FA Cup in 1st qualifying round – **Worthing** (43)

Most times exited FA Cup in the 1st qualifying round and never went further – **Gosforth and Coxlodge** (15)

Most times an existing club has exited FA Cup in the 1st qualifying round and has never yet gone further – **Horndean** (11)

Most times exited FA Cup in the preliminary round – **Marlow** (45)

Most times exited FA Cup in the preliminary round and never went further – **Osborne Athletic** (12)

Most times an existing club has exited FA Cup in the preliminary round and has never yet gone further – **Appleby** (8)

Most times exited FA Cup in the extra preliminary round – **Wolverhampton Casuals** (23)

Most times exited FA Cup in the extra preliminary round and never went further – **Headingly** (11)

Most times an existing club has exited FA Cup in the extra preliminary round and has never yet gone further – **Holyport** (7)

Most FA Cup games scoring double figures – **Tunbridge Wells Rangers** and **Yeovil Town** (5)

Most 'Proper' Round FA Cup games scoring double figures – **Clapham Rovers** (4)

Most FA Cup games played without ever scoring a goal – **Chesterfield Corinthians** (5)

Most FA Cup campaigns – **Maidenhead United** and **Marlow** (139)

Most FA Cup goals scored – **Tottenham Hotspur** (900)

Most FA Cup goals conceded – **Maidenhead United** (619)

Most FA Cup games played – **Arsenal** (480)

Most FA Cup goals scored per game played – **Somerset Rovers** (5.5 across two games)

Most FA Cup goals scored per game played (minimum of 10 games) – **Park Royal** (4.25)

Most FA Cup goals scored per game played (minimum of 20 games) – **Old Carthusians** (3.45)

Most FA Cup goals scored per game played (minimum of 50 games) – **Burton Town** (3.32)

Most FA Cup goals scored per game played (minimum of 100 games) – original **Tunbridge Wells Rangers** (2.87)

Most FA Cup goals scored per game played (minimum of 200 games) – original **Bedford Town** (2.36)

Most FA Cup goals scored per game played (minimum of 300 games) – **King's Lynn** (2.33)

Most FA Cup goals scored per game played (minimum of 400 games) – **Kettering Town** (2.12)

Most different clubs played against in FA Cup matches – **Kettering Town** (181)

Most common FA Cup games – **Chippenham Town vs Trowbridge Town** and **Barry Town vs Llanelli** (26 games each)

Most common FA Cup games in 'Proper' Rounds – **Everton vs Liverpool** (25 games)

Most common FA Cup tie drawn out of the hat – **Great Yarmouth Town vs Lowestoft Town** (21 times)

Most common FA Cup tie played in consecutive seasons – **Kettering Town vs Peterborough United** (9)

Most consecutive different FA Cup winners – **1931 to 1949** and **1966 to 1978** (13)

Most consecutive different Runners-up – **1909–1927** (15)

Most FA Cup Final appearances by a player – **Lord Arthur Kinnaird** (9)

Most FA Cup Final wins by a player – **Ashley Cole** (7)

Most FA Cup Final goals scored by a team – **Manchester United** (36)

Most FA Cup Final goals scored by a player – **Ian Rush** (5)

Most FA Cup Final goals conceded by a team – **Chelsea** and **Manchester United** (21)

Most common scoreline in FA Cup Finals – **1-0** (45 times)

Most goals scored in one FA Cup Final match – **Blackburn Rovers 6-1 The Wednesday** and **Blackpool 4-3 Bolton Wanderers** (7)

Most goals scored in an FA Cup Final in one season – **Manchester United 4-0 Brighton & Hove Albion (after a 2-2 draw)** (8)

Most goals scored in one FA Cup Semi-Final match – **West Bromwich Albion 6-2 Nottingham Forest, Manchester United 5-3 Fulham, Hull City 5-3 Sheffield United** and **Liverpool 4-4 Sheffield United** (8)

Most goals scored in an FA Cup Semi-Final in one season – **Sheffield United 1-0 Liverpool (after 2-2 and 4-4 draws)** (13)

Most goals scored in one FA Cup Quarter-Final match – **Darwen 15-0** original **Romford** (15)

Most FA Cup entries in one season – **2011/12** (763 clubs)

Most non-league clubs in 2nd Round of FA Cup (since 1925/26) – **1975/76, 2007/08** and **2020/21** (18)

Most non-league clubs in 3rd Round of FA Cup (since 1925/26) – **2008/09** (8)

Most non-league clubs in 4th Round of FA Cup (since 1925/26) – **1956/57** and **1974/75** (3)

Most top-flight clubs in FA Cup Quarter-Finals – **1894/95, 1895/96, 1995/96, 2005/06** and **2019/20** (8)

Most common date for FA Cup Final matches – **24th April** and **26th April** (6 times)

Most common result in FA Cup matches – **2-1 / 1-2** (9,894 times)

The League with most member clubs to have participated in FA Cup over its 140 seasons – **Southern League** (381 clubs)

Rank	Isthmian League	R4	R3	R2	R1	Q6	Q5	Q4	Q3	Q2
1	Enfield	1	2	9	8			6	3	2
2	Sutton United	1	1	2	7			14	2	9
3	Woking	1	1	2	7			1	5	14
4	Tooting and Mitcham United	1	1	2	4			10	8	15
5	Walthamstow Avenue	1		5	7			12	4	9
6	Leatherhead	1		4	3			7	6	6
7	Harlow Town	1			4			7	5	6
8	Marlow		2		2			3		8
9	Wycombe Wanderers		1	6	15			10	4	6
10	Hendon		1	4	12			12	10	10
11	Bishop's Stortford		1	2	7			7	4	4
12	Aylesbury United		1	2	3			3	1	5
13	Canvey Island		1	2	2			5	3	4
14	London Caledonians		1		4	1	4	7	1	2
15	Clapton		1		3	1	5	5	2	13
16	Chesham United		1		3			4	6	9
17	Yeading		1		2			2	2	4
18	Yeovil Town		1		1			3		
19	Hastings United		1						4	3
20	Tilbury		1						2	9
21	Slough Town			5	6			6	3	5
22	Hitchin Town			4	2			9	5	9
23	Bognor Regis Town			4	2			6	2	14
24	Barking (1)			4				5	3	11
25	Ilford (1)			3	7	1	2	14	6	11
26	Hayes			3	6			3	3	6
27	St Albans City			3	5	1	1	7	9	19
28	Wimbledon			3	5			7	3	6
29	Kingstonian			3	4			17	14	18
30	Leytonstone			2	8	1		8	7	16

Top 30 FA Cup Clubs whilst Members of Isthmian League.

Nb. Chart shows number of exits per Round

FA Cup Team Name Initials & Abbreviations Explained

AAA

Amateur Athletic Association – As used by **Chirk AAA** after the end of World War I, having previously been known simply as Chirk.

AAC

Amateur Athletic Club – A 19th Century club formed in 1868 in Middlesex which converted to rugby in 1874 causing it to withdraw from the FA Cup before facing Clapham Rovers in the only season it entered the competition.

AC

Academic Club – Used by **AC London**, a club from Tadworth which entered the FA Cup just once in 2017/18 season whilst members of the Combined Counties League reaching the Preliminary Round.

AEC

Associated Equipment Company – Used by the football club of that company based in Southall, **AEC Athletic**, entering the FA Cup five times in the mid-1930s whilst members of the Southwest Middlesex League, twice reaching the Preliminary Round.

AFC

Association Football Club – The most common meaning for this abbreviation used as a prefix by several phoenix clubs to keep the original club name alive, such as **AFC Darwen**, **AFC Telford United** and **AFC Wimbledon**, or by clubs' fans running an alternate club such as **AFC Mansfield**, or used as a suffix by clubs wanting to distinguish themselves from other sports in their location such as **Workington AFC**.

AFC

Affordable Football Club – Used by **AFC Liverpool**, a club set up in 2008 by fans of Liverpool FC priced out of attending games at Anfield.

AFC

Amalgamated Football Club – Used by **AFC Sudbury** to reflect that the club is a 1999 merger between Sudbury Town and Sudbury Wanderers.

AP

Automotive Products – As used by Leamington FC from the mid-1970s to mid-1980s when known as **AP Leamington**, prior to the club's current name and after being known as Lockheed Leamington

APSA

Asian People's Sports Association / All People's Sports Association – As used by East London outfit **London APSA** during their nine FA Cup campaigns ahead of renaming as Newham in 2014, but reverting back to original name two years later.

APV

Aluminium Plant and Vessel Company – As used by the now defunct Peterborough City, which originally competed in FA Cup as Peterborough Westwood Works, then as Baker Perkins from the mid-1980s, and for one season as **APV Peterborough City** in 1991/92.

ASSC

Aerostructures Sports and Social Club – As used by the current club Folland Sports when first appearing in the FA Cup as **Hamble ASSC**, a reflection of one of the club's previous names of many, Aerostructures Sports and Social Club.

BAT — **British American Tobacco** – A former name of current club Totton and Eling was **BAT Sports** reflecting the fact they were the sports team of that company having previously been known as Bramtoco FC.

BICC — **British Insulated Callendar Cable** – As used by **Prescot BICC**, a member of the Liverpool County Combination also known as Prescot BI which competed in the FA Cup three times in total, either side of World War II, appearing in the Preliminary Round in its pre-war campaign.

BR — **British Rail** – Adopted by **Swindon BR Corinthians** when the railways were nationalised and used by Wolverton Town when known as **Wolverton Town and BR** from the early 1950s to the mid-1970s.

BWI — **British Workmen's Institute** – As used by **BWI Reading** which entered the FA Cup three times in the mid-1920s reaching the 1st Qualifying Round twice.

C&B — **Community and Bowling** – As used by **Haydock C&B Recreation**, a sports and social club which participated in the FA Cup five times in the late 1940s and early '50s, reaching the 4th Qualifying Round in their debut season whilst members of the Liverpool County Combination.

CA — **Community Association** – Used by several clubs, particularly in the north-east, such as **Jarrow Roofing Boldon CA** and **Sunderland Ryhope CA**.

CB — **Cater Bank** – As used by **CB Hounslow United** reflecting the organisation of their main sponsor and employer of their club chairman.

CBS — **County Building Services** – The current name of the club formed as Norwich Union FC in 1888 is **Norwich CBS**, the name used for the club's one and only FA Cup campaign to date in 2019/20 season.

CEYMS — **Church of England Young Men's Society** – The name of a current Norfolk club, **Norwich CEYMS**, which has 42 FA Cup campaigns under its belt, but last appeared in the competition in 1948/49.

CNSOBU — **City of Norwich School Old Boys Union** – A Norfolk and Suffolk League club that competed in the FA Cup three times spanning 1950, reaching the 1st Qualifying Round in 1949/50.

CSOB — **County School Old Boys** – A current Staffordshire club, **Leek CSOB**, which has competed in the FA Cup 13 times, last doing so in 2011/12, and one which reached the 2nd Qualifying Round in its debut campaign.

CW — **Colliery Welfare** – An abbreviation used by many clubs which were formed in mining communities, such as **Eppleton CW**, and many of which have been renamed following their pit's closure such as **Langley Park** and **Murton**.

CWS — **Co-operative Wholesale Society** – As used by CWS Silvertown, an Essex based club that competed in the FA Cup twice in the late 1930s as members of the London League.

DAF-SGL **Van Doorne's Automobiel Fabriek-Saum Gottschalk Limited** – Lancashire based club Leyland Motors entered the last two of its 48 FA Cup campaigns as Leyland DAF-SGL in recognition of its affiliated company's new ownership.

DS&S **Demobilised Soldiers and Sailors** – A suffix used in names of temporary clubs formed by groups of players immediately after the end of WWI whilst awaiting for historical clubs to restart after the War or new permanent clubs to be formed. Examples include **King's Lynn DS&S**, **Norwich DS&S**, and **Widnes DS&S** which all participated in the FA Cup just once.

EFC **Endsleigh Football Club** – As used by **EFC Cheltenham** for the club's final FA Cup campaign in 1998/99, having previously participated in the competition named simply as Endsleigh.

FC **Football Club** – Used as a prefix by clubs to either differentiated themselves from an associated bigger club e.g. **FC United of Manchester**, or as a way to affiliated themselves with a folded club e.g. **FC Clacton** and **FC Halifax Town**, or as just an alternative to the usual use of the initials as a suffix.

GE **General Electric** – As used by the current club Folland Sports when the company the club was affiliated with was acquired by GE Aviation, renaming the club as **GE Hamble** for its 2011/12 and 2012/13 FA Cup campaigns.

GER **Great Eastern Railway** – Used by **GER Romford / GER Loughton**, a club that participated in the FA Cup for a dozen seasons post World War I as members of the Spartan League, reaching the 4th Qualifying Round in 1920/21.

GKN **Guest, Keen and Nettlefolds** – Used by Sankeys of Wellington FC for the last three of their FA Cup campaigns as members of the West Midlands (Regional) League, playing as **GKN Sankey** to reflect the company name to which the club was affiliated.

GM **General Motors** – The name used by Vauxhall Motors when first entering the FA Cup in 1989/90 was **Vauxhall GM**, a name used for just three campaigns.

GN **Great Northern** – As used by **Peterborough GN Locomotives**, a Cambridgeshire based club that competed in the FA Cup either side of the Great War, with reaching the 2nd Qualifying Round in 1912/13 the best of their 15 campaigns.

GWR **Great Western Railway** – As used by Swindon BR Corinthians for FA Cup and Wiltshire League campaigns either side of World War II when known as **Swindon GWR Corinthians** following a name change from the club's original name of Swindon Corinthians.

Hayesco **Hayes Cocoa Company** – Two FA Cup campaigns for **Hayesco Sports** just prior to the outbreak of World War II, being eliminated in the Extra Preliminary Round both times.

HMS — **His / Her Majesty's Ship** – Used by two clubs, **HMS Excellence** and **HMS Victory** in the years leading up to the outbreak of World War II, both members of the United Services League.

ICI — **Industrial Chemicals Incorporated** – As used by **ICI Alkali** when participating in the FA Cup in the mid-1930s as members of the Manchester League, reaching the 2nd Qualifying Round in the club's debut campaign.

IOW — **Isle of Wight** – As used by **Newport (IOW)** to help differentiate that club from others that use or have used the same name. There have been four 'Newport' clubs that have competed in the FA Cup from different parts of the country.

JKS — **Junior Kick Starts** – As used by **Castle Vale JKS**, a name adopted by the reserve side of Castle Vale FC when establishing themselves as a separate club in 2006, which competed in the FA Cup just once in 2010/11 season.

JS — **Joseph Storrs** – As used by the works team of **JS Fry and Sons** in the early 1930s whilst members of the Bristol and District League.

KA — **King's Arms –** As used by current club **Meir KA** which last competed for the third time in the FA Cup in 2009/10, named for the pub where the club was founded.

LC — **Leisure Centre** – As used by current club **Debenham LC** which last appeared in the FA Cup in the 2015/16 season.

LMS — **London Midland Scottish** – As used by **Walsall LMS**, a Birmingham Combination club which appeared in the FA Cup four times spanning 1930, reaching the Preliminary Round in three of those campaigns.

LNWR — **London North West Railway** – As used by **LNWR (Wembley)**, a club that entered the FA Cup just once as members of the Middlesex and District League in 1922/23, exiting in the Preliminary Round.

LSWR — **London South West Railway** – As used by **Eastleigh LSWR**, a former name of Eastleigh Athletic when first competing in the FA Cup in the late 19th Century.

LYR — **Lancashire and Yorkshire Railway** – As used by **Newton Heath LYR**, the original name of Manchester United when first competing in the FA Cup in the late 1880s and early 1890s.

MK — **Milton Keynes** – Used as an abbreviations by clubs such as **MK Dons** and **MK City**

MW — **Miners Welfare** – An abbreviation used by many clubs formed in mining communities such as **Staveley MW**, and many of which have since been renamed such as **Holbrook Sports** and **Maltby Main**.

NAC **Northern Aluminium Company** – Used by Banbury based **NAC Athletic** for the club's three FA Cup campaigns spanning 1950 whilst members of the Oxford Senior League, reaching the Preliminary Round in 1950.

NER **North Eastern Railway** – As used by **Gateshead NER**, a club that participated in the FA Cup for 13 seasons crossing the end of the 19th Century, reaching the 3rd Qualifying Round five times in total, and **West Hartlepool NER**, a Teesside League club at the same time with four FA Cup campaigns, three of which ended in the 1st Qualifying Round.

OCO **Olympia Cake and Oil** – The more common name used by **Selby OCO** which competed in the FA Cup a dozen times after World War I, twice reaching the 2nd Qualifying Round.

OJM **Oliver James Mee** – The current name of the club formed as Black Country Rangers is **OJM Black Country**, the name being adopted when amalgamating a Sunday League side called OJM named in the memory of Oliver James Mee.

ON **Old Northamptonian** – As used by current club **Northampton ON Chenecks** which has competed in the FA Cup in each of the last five seasons, reaching the Preliminary Round just once.

PF **Park Furnishers** – A brief rename for Mangotsfield United for the 1978/79 season saw the club play as **Mangotsfield PF** in the FA Cup, a name that reflected the club's sponsors.

PM **Paper Mills** – An abbreviation used by current club **Cray Valley PM**, the fifth 'Paper Mills' club to compete in the FA Cup.

PO **Post Office** – Used by a couple of clubs connected to the Post Office, **PO Engineers (Beddington)**, competing in FA Cup for seven seasons prior to World War II, and **PO Engineers (Wallington)** which participated twice after the War.

RA **Railway Athletic** – As used by two separate clubs called **Darlington RA**, two of four 'Railway Athletics' to have competed in the FA Cup.

RAE **Royal Aircraft Establishment** – Used by **RAE Farnborough** during their four FA Cup campaigns in the early 1920s, reaching the Preliminary Round just once.

RAF **Royal Air Force** – There have been five RAF clubs that have participated in the FA Cup representing **Cranwell**, **Halton**, **Henlow**, **Martlesham** and **Uxbridge**, and all doing so between the Wars.

RAMC **Royal Army Medical Corps** – Sixteen FA Cup campaigns for **RAMC Aldershot** between the Wars, twice reaching the 3rd Qualifying Round.

RAOC **Royal Army Ordnance Corps** – As used by **Hereford RAOC**, a military club that participated in the FA Cup just once in 1924/25, losing their only game in the

Extra Preliminary Round, as well as **RAOC Corsham / RAOC Hilsea** with 13 FA Cup campaigns in all, including two 3rd Qualifying round appearances.

RASC — **Royal Army Service Corps** – A Feltham based military club that competed under the name **RASC** and which entered the FA Cup twice in mid-1920s whilst members of the South West Middlesex League.

RBL — **Royal British Legion** – As used by **Mickleover RBL**, a Central Midlands League South Division club which participated in the FA Cup just once in 1992/93, exiting in the Preliminary Round.

REC — **Recreation** – As used by **Thetford REC**, a Norfolk and Suffolk league club which participated in the FA Cup just once in 1921/22, reaching the Preliminary Round.

REMYCA — **Rem Young Christians Association** – As used by current club **Litherland REMYCA**, with the suffix created from amalgamating elements of two associated clubs' names, Rem Social club and Bootle YMCA.

RGA — **Royal Garrison Artillery** – Three RGA clubs have competed in the FA Cup from **Gosport**, **Tynemouth** and **Weymouth** spanning the Great War with none progressing further than the Preliminary round.

RM — **Royal Marines** – The Royal Marines have had three representations in the FA Cup from **Chatham**, **Deal** and **Portsmouth**, all occurring between the Wars, and with three 3rd Qualifying Round appearances between them.

RMI — **Railway Mechanics Institute** – The original name of the club that became to be called Leigh Genesis was **Horwich RMI**, renamed as **Leigh RMI** when the club was relocated in 1995, and one which competed in the FA Cup 86 times.

RN — **Royal Naval** – As used by **RN Depot (Chatham)** during that club's two FA Cup campaigns whilst members of the original Kent League just after the end of World War I.

RNVR — **Royal Naval Volunteer Reserves** – As used by **RNVR Mitcham** during that club's one FA Cup campaign in 1931/32 season where it reached the Preliminary Round.

RS — **Road Sea** – The more common name used by **RS Southampton**, a Southern League club which had four FA Cup campaigns in the mid-1980s, twice reaching the 3rd Qualifying Round.

SAA — **Sub Aqua Association** – As used by **Weymouth SAA** which entered the FA Cup in 1946/47 but withdrew before facing Bournemouth Gasworks Athletic.

SCR — **Sutton Common Road** – Used in a former name of current club Sutton Common Rovers in their first five FA Cup campaigns as **Mole Valley SCR**, reflecting the location of the club that had gone through various name changes since its conception as Inrad FC in 1978.

Stamco — **Sussex Turney and Moulding Company** – The name originally adopted by the club formed in 1971 which eventually became known as St Leonards FC was **Stamco**, reflecting the company name with which it was affiliated. The club folded in 2004 and had nine FA Cup campaigns.

STC — **Steam Trawling Company –** The affiliated company name of **Grimsby STC** which participated in the FA Cup just once in 1920/21, playing one game and exiting in the Extra Preliminary Round.

SYCOB — **Slough Youth Centre Old Boys** – As used by Beaconsfield Town when forming in 1994 as **Beaconsfield SYCOB** reflecting that the club was a merger of Beaconsfield United and Slough Youth Centre Old Boys FC.

UGB — **United Glass Bottlers** – As used by **UGB St Helens**, a Liverpool County Combination club which competed in the FA Cup three times spanning across 1950 and which exited in the Extra Preliminary Round each time.

UGBM — **United Glass Bottles Manufacturers** – As used by **UGBM Sports**, a Charlton based club which competed in the FA Cup five times prior to the outbreak of World War II whilst members of the London League, and which had a best run to the 2nd Qualifying Round in the 1938/39 season.

US — **United Services** – The more common used name of current club **US Portsmouth** formerly known as Portsmouth Royal Navy, which has twice reached the 2nd Qualifying Round.

UTS — **Utility Technology Services** – As used by Dunston FC when known as **Dunston UTS** prior to promotion to level eight in the football pyramid, the lowest level where company names are not allowed to be used in football club names. The club had previously also competed in the FA Cup under Dunston Federation Brewery and Dunston Federation.

UWE — **University of West England** – Used by **Almondsbury UWE** (from 2017 plain Almondsbury) whilst participating in FA Cup for the first half of the 2010s, twice reaching the 1st Qualifying Round.

V&E — **Victoria and Elm** – Used by FC Broxbourne Borough when first forming as **Somersett Ambury V&E** in 1991 to reflect the two clubs involved in the merger, with Ambury V&E named after the Victoria and Elm social club on Goff's Lane in Cheshunt, and subsequently when the name changed to **Broxbourne Borough V&E** in 2002.

VCD — **Vickers Crayford / Dartford** – Formed in 1916, Vickers FC adopted the name **VCD Athletic** just prior to World War II and has appeared in the last 21 FA Cup campaigns under that name.

VS — **Valley Sports** – The name used by the current Rugby Town when it first competed in the FA Cup was **VS Rugby**, adopted in 1973 after having previously been called Valley Sports.

VT — **Vosper Thornycroft** – The name used by the current Sholing FC when it first competed in the FA Cup was **VT FC**, adopted in 2003 after having previously been called Vosper Thornycroft.

WIPAC — **Wico-Pacy** – The name of the automotive electrical company in Bletchley which was reflected by the now defunct Milton Keynes City when first competing in the FA Cup in 1954/55 as **Bletchley and WIPAC Sports**.

WMC — **Working Men's Club** – Used by several clubs which have participated in the FA Cup including **Acomb WMC**

XXX — **Triple X** – As used by **Pilkington XXX**, which entered the FA Cup five times spanning 2010 whilst members of the Midland Combination, their name reflecting the Triple X glass product manufactured by its parent company.

YM — **Young Men** – The original name of Pewsey Vale was **Pewsey YM**, reflecting the club's connections to a pre-World War II club, Pewsey Boys, and competing in the FA Cup under that name in the first season after the War was over.

YMCA — **Young Men's Christian Association** – Used by several clubs such as **Barrow YMCA** and **Horsham YMCA** either because they were representing the YMCA at the time of competing in FA Cup or as a recognition of that association being responsible for their formation.

YMCI — **Young Men's Christian Institute** – As used by **Higham Ferrers YMCI**, a Northamptonshire club which competed in the FA Cup three times spanning 1910, exiting in the Preliminary Round in all three campaigns.

Rank	Northern Counties East League	R2	R1	Q4	Q3	Q2	Q1	PR	EP
1	Harrogate Railway Athletic	1		2		1	9	5	2
2	Brigg Town		1	1	4	1	7	9	1
3	Spennymoor United		1		1		1		
4	Shepshed Charterhouse		1						
5	North Ferriby United			1	4	2	5	6	
6	Eastwood Town			1	3	1		1	
7	Arnold Town			1	2	3	3	3	7
8	North Shields			1	2				
9	Buxton			1	1			5	
10	Liversedge			1		5	6	8	10

Top Ten FA Cup Clubs whilst Members of NCEL.

Nb. Chart shows number of exits per Round

Top 150 'Always Non-League' FA Cup Clubs (1888/89 to 2020/21)

Non-League clubs are often at the heart of what is known as the 'Magic of the FA Cup' and their exploits in David versus Goliath encounters against top-flight opponents are legendary. From Warwick County being the first non-league club to defeat a top-flight opponent, Stoke (City), during the inaugural season of the Football League in 1888/89 through to the historic Cup runs of Chorley FC and Marine FC in the most recent 2020/21 campaign, non-league clubs have captured the imagination of fans across the ages and across the world.

But only a handful of non-league clubs enjoy such limelight, whilst the vast majority of them participate year-in, year-out in the FA Cup without appearing on the radar of mainstream reporters and higher level clubs' fans. But the FA Cup would not be the FA Cup without them, so this list celebrates those 'always non-league' clubs that have had the biggest impact on the competition over its 150 years of existence.

Best Performance – Quarter-Finalists

1 Chatham Town .... 1x QF, 2x R2, 6x R1
Quarter-finalists in 1888/89 as Chatham United – no league status at time

2 Birmingham St George's ..... 1x QF, 2x R2, 4x R1
Quarter-finalists in 1888/89 – no league status at time

Best Performance – Round Five

3 Sutton United 1x R5, 3x R4, 5x R3
Reached Round 5 in 2016/17 (National League)
Nb: Sutton United will be removed from this list after being promoted to EFL

4 Telford United...................... 1x R5, 3x R4, 4x R3
Reached Round 5 in 1984/85 (Alliance Premier)

5 Blyth Spartans 1x R5, 4x R3
Reached Round 5 in 1977/78 (Northern League)

Best Performance – Round Four

6 Corinthians 2x R4, 8x R3
Last reached Round 4 in 1928/29 – no league status at time

7 Kettering Town 2x R4, 5x R3
Last reached Round 4 in 2008/09 (Conference Premier)

8 Bedford Town * 2x R4, 4x R3
Last reached Round 4 in 1965/66 (Southern League Premier)

9 Altrincham 1x R4, 8x R3
Reached Round 4 in 1985/86 (Alliance Premier)

10 Woking 1x R4, 5x R3
Reached Round 4 in 1990/91 (Isthmian League Premier)

11 Enfield * 1x R4, 4x R3
Reached Round 4 in 1980/81 (Isthmian League Premier)

12 Weymouth 1x R4, 3x R3, 11x R2
Reached Round 4 in 1961/62 (Southern League Premier)
13 Rhyl 1x R4, 3x R3, 6x R2
Reached Round 4 in 1956/57 (Cheshire County League)
14 Chelmsford City 1x R4, 2x R3, 13x R2
Reached Round 4 in 1938/39 (Southern League)
15 Worcester City 1x R4, 2x R3, 6x R2
Reached Round 4 in 1958/59 (Southern League North)
16 Ebbsfleet United 1x R4, 2x R3, 4x R2, 20x R1
Reached Round 4 as Gravesend & Northfleet in 1962/63 (Southern League)
17 Tooting & Mitcham United ... 1x R4, 2x R3, 4x R2, 10x R1
Reached Round 4 in 1975/76 (Isthmian League 1)
18 Farnborough Town 1x R4, 2x R3, 16x R1
Reached Round 4 in 2002/03 (Conference)
19 Bishop Auckland 1x R4, 10x R2
Reached Round 4 in 1954/55 (Northern League)
20 Walthamstow Avenue 1x R4, 9x R2
Reached Round 4 in 1952/53 (Isthmian League)
21 Stafford Rangers 1x R4, 5x R2, 17x R1
Reached Round 4 in 1974/75 (Northern Premier League)
22 Kingstonian 1x R4, 5x R2, 11x R1
Reached Round 4 in 2000/01 (Conference)
23 Leatherhead 1x R4, 5x R2, 8x R1
Reached Round 4 in 1974/75 (Isthmian League 1)
24 Chorley 1x R4, 3x R2, 13x R1
Reached Round 4 in 2020/21 (National League North)
25 Hednesford Town 1x R4, 3x R2, 8x R1
Reached Round 4 in 1996/97 (Conference)
26 Havant & Waterlooville 1x R4, 2x R2
Reached Round 4 in 2007/08 (Conference South)
27 Harlow Town 1x R4, 5x R1
Reached Round 4 in 1979/80 (Isthmian League Premier)

Best Performance – Round Three

28 Bath City 6x R3
Last reached Round 3 in 1993/94 (Conference)
29 Nuneaton Borough * 3x R3, 8x R2
Last reached Round 3 in 2005/06 (Conference North)
30 Tamworth 3x R3, 6x R2
Last reached Round 3 in 2011/12 (Conference Premier)
31 Dartford 2x R3, 10x R2
Last reached Round 3 in 1936/37 (Southern League)
32 Margate 2x R3, 9x R2
Last reached Round 3 in 1972/73 (Southern League Premier)

33 Folkestone 2x R3, 6x R2
Last reached Round 3 in 1965/66 (Southern League Premier)

34 Marine 2x R3, 4x R2, 11x R1
Last reached Round 3 in 2020/21 (Northern Premier League 1 North West)

35 Dover Athletic 2x R3, 4x R2, 8x R1
Last reached Round 3 in 2014/15 (Conference National)

36 Eastleigh 2x R3, 4x R2, 6x R1
Last reached Round 3 in 2016/17 (National League)

37 Hastings United * 2x R3, 3x R2
Last reached Round 3 in 1954/55 (Southern League)

38 Marlow 2x R3, 5x R1
Last reached Round 3 in 1994/95 (Isthmian League Premier)

39 Runcorn * 1x R3, 8x R2, 22x R1
Reached Round 3 in 1938/39 (Cheshire County League)

40 Gateshead United 1x R3, 8x R2, 19x R1
Reached Round 3 as South Shields in 1969/70 (Northern Premier League)*

41 King's Lynn 1x R3, 8x R2, 16x R1
Reached Round 3 in 1961/62 (Southern League)

42 Grantham Town 1x R3, 7x R2
Reached Round 3 in 1973/74 (Southern League Premier)

43 Hendon 1x R3, 6x R2
Reached Round 3 in 1973/74 (Isthmian League 1)

44 Spennymoor United 1x R3, 5x R2, 17x R1
Reached Round 3 in 1936/37 (North Eastern League)

45 Dagenham 1x R3, 5x R2, 15x R1
Reached Round 3 in 1984/85 (Alliance Premier)

46 Welling United 1x R3, 5x R2, 13x R1
Reached Round 3 in 1988/89 (Conference)

47 Boreham Wood 1x R3, 4x R2, 14x R1
Reached Round 3 in 2020/21 (National League)

48 Salisbury City .... 1x R3, 4x R2, 12x R1 (plus 15x q4)
Reached Round 3 in 2011/12 (Conference South)

49 Gateshead .... 1x R3, 4x R2, 12x R1 (plus 8x q4)
Reached Round 3 in 2014/15 (Conference National)

50 Leyton * .... 1x R3, 4x R2, 11x R1 (plus 1x q5)
Reached Round 3 in 1909/10 (Southern League 1)
Nb: Round 3 in 1909/10 is equivalent to Round 5 nowadays (last 16), so Leyton could arguably be the 3rd best 'Always Non-League' club

51 Aylesbury United .... 1x R3, 4x R2, 11x R1 (plus 8x q4)
Reached Round 3 in 1994/95 (Isthmian League Premier)

52 Stourbridge 1x R3, 4x R2, 6x R1
Reached Round 3 in 2016/17 (Northern Premier League Premier)

53 Bishop's Stortford 1x R3, 3x R2, 14x R1
Reached Round 3 in 1982/83 (Isthmian League Premier)

54 Stockton * 1x R3, 3x R2, 12x R1
Reached Round 3 in 1951/52 (North Eastern League)
55 Canvey Island 1x R3, 3x R2, 3x R1
Reached Round 3 in 2001/02 (Isthmian League Premier)
56 Burton Town .... 1x R3, 3x R2, 5x R1 (plus 7x q4)
Reached Round 3 in 1931/32 (Birmingham and District League)
57 Histon .... 1x R3, 3x R2, 5x R1 (plus 2x q4)
Reached Round 3 in 2008/09 (Conference Premier)
58 Wealdstone 1x R3, 2x R2, 15x R1
Reached Round 3 in 1977/78 (Southern League Premier)
59 Frickley Athletic .... 1x R3, 2x R2, 11x R1 (plus 11x q4)
Reached Round 3 in 1985/86 (Alliance Premier)
60 Goole Town .... 1x R3, 2x R2, 11x R1 (plus 9x q4)
Reached Round 3 in 1956/57 (Midland League)
61 Worksop Town 1x R3, 2x R2, 9x R1
Reached Round 3 in 1955/56 (Midland League)
62 Chesham United 1x R3, 2x R2, 8x R1
Reached Round 3 in 1979/80 (Isthmian League 1)
63 Hillingdon Borough * 1x R3, 2x R2, 7x R1
Reached Round 3 in 1969/70 (Southern League Premier)
64 AFC Fylde 1x R3, 2x R2, 6x R1
Reached Round 3 in 2019/20 (National League)
65 Crook Town * 1x R3, 2x R2, 4x R1
Reached Round 3 in 1931/32 (North Eastern League 1)
66 Buxton 1x R3, 2x R2, 3x R1
Reached Round 3 in 1951/52 (Cheshire County League)
67 Chilton Colliery Rec. Ath. ..... 1x R3, 2x R2 (plus 1x q5)
Reached Round 3 in 1925/26 (Northern Alliance)
68 Whitley Bay .... 1x R3, 2x R2 (plus 6x q4)
Reached Round 3 in 1989/90 (Northern Premier League 1)
69 Brentwood Town * .... 1x R3, 2x R2 (plus 2x q4)
Reached Round 3 in 1969/70 (Southern League Premier)
70 Bromsgrove Rovers 1x R3, 11x R1
Reached Round 3 in 1993/94 (Conference)
71 Corby Town 1x R3, 8x R1
Reached Round 3 in 1965/66 (Southern League Premier)
72 Poole Town 1x R3, 7x R1
Reached Round 3 in 1926/27 (Southern League Eastern / Western League 1)
73 Clapton .... 1x R3, 6x R1 (plus 1x q6, 7x q5)
Reached Round 3 in 1925/26 (Isthmian League)
74 Southall .... 1x R3, 6x R1 (plus 1x q6, 1x q5)
Reached Round 3 in 1935/36 (Athenian League)
75 London Caledonians .... 1x R3, 5x R1 (plus 2x q6)
Reached Round 3 in 1927/28 (Isthmian League)

76 Peterborough & Fletton Utd. 1x R3, 5x R1 (plus 1x q5)
Reached Round 3 in 1927/28 (Southern League Eastern)
77 Matlock Town .... 1x R3, 5x R1 (plus 5x q4)
Reached Round 3 in 1976/77 (Northern Premier League)
78 Yeading 1x R3, 4x R1
Reached Round 3 in 2004/05 (Isthmian league Premier)
79 Boston * .... 1x R3, 3x R1 (plus 1x q5)
Reached Round 3 in 1925/26 (Midland League)
80 Emley * .... 1x R3, 3x R1 (plus 2x q4, 9x q3)
Reached Round 3 in 1997/98 (Northern Premier League Premier)
81 Finchley .... 1x R3, 3x R1 (plus 2x q4, 7x q3)
Reached Round 3 in 1952/53 (Athenian League)
82 Eastwood Town .... 1x R3, 3x R1 (plus 1x q4)
Reached Round 3 in 2008/09 (Northern Premier League Premier)
83 Hastings United .... 1x R3, 2x R1 (plus 6x q4)
Reached Round 3 in 2012/13 (Isthmian League Premier)
84 Tilbury .... 1x R3, 2x R1 (plus 3x q4)
Reached Round 3 in 1977/78 (Isthmian League Premier)
85 Alvechurch .... 1x R3, 2x R1 (plus 2x q4, 5x q3)
Reached Round 3 in 1973/74 (West Midlands (Regional) League Premier)
86 Lovells Athletic .... 1x R3, 2x R1 (plus 2x q4, 4x q3)
Reached Round 3 in 1945/46 (Welsh League (South) 1)
87 Chasetown .... 1x R3, 2x R1 (plus 3x q3)
Reached Round 3 in 2007/08 (Southern League 1 Midland)
88 Caernarfon Town .... 1x R3 (plus 3x q4)
Reached Round 3 in 1986/87 (Northern Premier League)

Best Performance – Round Two
89 Slough Town 8x R2
Last reached Round 2 in 2018/19 (National League South)
90 Guildford City * 6x R2, 21x R1
Last reached Round 2 in 1971/72 (Southern League Premier)
91 Merthyr Tydfil .... 6x R2, 17 x R1
Last reached Round 2 in 1990/91 (Conference)
92 Hayes 4x R2, 22x R1
Last reached Round 2 in 1999/00 (Conference)
93 Bangor City 4x R2, 13x R1
Last reached Round 2 in 1983/84 (Alliance Premier)
94 Dorchester Town 4x R2, 11x R1
Last reached Round 2 in 2012/13 (Conference South)
95 Hitchin Town 4x R2, 10x R1
Last reached Round 2 in 1995/96 (Isthmian League Premier)
96 South Liverpool * 4x R2, 8x R1
Last reached Round 2 in 1964/65 (Lancashire Combination 1)

97 Bognor Regis Town 4x R2, 7x R1
Last reached Round 2 in 1995/96 (Isthmian League 1)

98 Barking * .... 4x R2, 6x R1 (plus 9x q4)
Last reached Round 2 in 1983/84 (Isthmian League Premier)

99 Maidstone United .... 4x R2, 6x R1 (plus 1x q4)
Last reached Round 2 in 2019/20 (National League South)

100 Solihull Moors 4x R2, 5x R1
Last reached Round 2 in 2020/21 (National League)

101 Bromley 3x R2, 18x R1
Last reached Round 2 in 1945/46 (Athenian League)

102 Oxford City 3x R2, 15x R1
Last reached Round 2 in 2020/21 (National League South)

103 Witton Albion .... 3x R2, 13x R1 (plus 11x q4)
Last reached Round 2 in 1991/92 (Conference)

104 Romford * .... 3x R2, 13x R1 (plus 6x q4)
Last reached Round 2 in 1971/72 (Southern League Premier)

105 St Albans City 3x R2, 11x R1
Last reached Round 2 in 1996/97 (Isthmian League Premier)

106 Ilford * .... 3x R2, 10x R1 (plus 1x q6)
Last reached Round 2 in 1974/75 (Isthmian League 1)

107 Ashford Town *(Kent)* .... 3x R2, 10x R1 (plus 8x q4)
Last reached Round 2 in 1996/97 (Southern League Premier)

108 Crook Town .... 3x R2, 10x R1 (plus 5x q4)
Last reached Round 2 in 1964/65 (Northern League)

109 Northfleet united .... 3x R2, 8x R1 (plus 1x q5)
Last reached Round 2 in 1929/30 (Southern League East)

110 Basingstoke Town .... 3x R2, 8x R1 (plus 8x q4)
Last reached Round 2 in 2006/07 (Conference South)

111 Droylsden .... 3x R2, 5x R1 (plus 7x q4)
Last reached Round 2 in 2010/11 (Conference North)

112 Brackley Town .... 3x R2, 5x R1 (plus 3x q4)
Last reached Round 2 in 2020/21 (National League North)

113 Lancaster City 2x R2, 14x R1
Last reached Round 2 in 1972/73 (Northern Premier League)

114 North Shields .... 2x R2, 10x R1 (plus 1x q6, 2x q5)
Last reached Round 2 in 1982/83 (Northern League 1)

115 Leytonstone .... 2x R2, 10x R1 (plus 1x q6, 1x q5)
Last reached Round 2 in 1951/52 (Isthmian League)

116 Newport *(IOW)* .... 2x R2, 10x R1 (plus 7x q4)
Last reached Round 2 in 1945/46 (Hampshire League 1)

117 Wisbech Town .... 2x R2, 9x R1 (plus 8x q4)
Last reached Round 2 in 1997/98 (Southern League Midland)

118 Alfreton Town .... 2x R2, 9x R1 (plus 4x q4)
Last reached Round 2 in 2012/13 (Conference National)

119 Kendal Town .... 2x R2, 8x R1 (plus 12x q4)
Last reached Round 2 as Netherfield in 1963/64 (Lancashire Combination 1)

120 Whitby Town .... 2x R2, 8x R1 (plus 6x q4, 19x q3)
Last reached Round 2 in 1985/86 (Northern League 1)

121 Mossley .... 2x R2, 8x R1 (plus 6x q4, 9x q3)
Last reached Round 2 in 1980/81 (Northern Premier League)

122 Guiseley .... 2x R2, 8x R1 (plus 6x q4, 7x q3)
Last reached Round 2 in 2018/19 (National League North)

123 Tunbridge Wells Rangers * ... 2x R2, 7x R1 (plus 3x q5)
Last reached Round 2 in 1936/37 (Southern League)

124 Walton & Hersham .... 2x R2, 7x R1 (plus 6x q4, 7x q3)
Last reached Round 2 in 1973/74 (Isthmian League 1)

125 Leamington .... 2x R2, 7x R1 (plus 6x q4, 4x q3)
Last reached Round 2 as AP Leamington in 1978/79 (Southern League Prem.)

126 Minehead .... 2x R2, 6x R1 (plus 9x q4)
Last reached Round 2 in 1977/78 (Southern League Premier)

127 FC Halifax Town .... 2x R2, 6x R1 (plus 6x q4)
Last reached Round 2 in 2018/19 (National League)

128 Ilkeston Town * .... 2x R2, 6x R1 (plus 5x q4)
Last reached Round 2 in 1999/00 (Southern League Premier)

129 Rugby Town .... 2x R2, 6x R1 (plus 4x q4)
Last reached Round 2 as VS Rugby in 1992/93 (Southern League Premier)

130 Sittingbourne .... 2x R2, 5x R1 (plus 1x q6)
Last reached Round 2 in 1928/29 (Southern League East)

131 Staines Town .... 2x R2, 5x R1 (plus 5x q4)
Last reached Round 2 in 2009/10 (Conference South)

132 Hinckley United .... 2x R2, 4x R1 (plus 4x q4)
Last reached Round 2 in 2004/05 (Conference North)

133 Bridgwater Town * .... 2x R2, 4x R1 (plus 2x q4)
Last reached Round 2 in 1961/62 (Western League)

134 Sunderland Albion 2x R2, 4x R1
Last reached Round 2 in 1891/92 (Northern League)
Nb: Round 2 in 1891/92 is equivalent to Round 5 nowadays (last 16), so Sunderland Albion could arguably be the 3rd best 'Always Non-League' club

135 Great Yarmouth Town 2x R2, 3x R1
Last reached Round 2 in 1953/54 (Eastern Counties League)

136 Hinckley Athletic .... 2x R2 (plus 1x q5)
Last reached Round 2 in 1954/55 (Birmingham and District League North)

137 Harrogate Railway Athletic ... 2x R2 (plus 2x q4)
Last reached Round 2 in 2007/08 (Northern Premier League 1 North)

138 Curzon Ashton .... 2x R2 (plus 7x q3)
Last reached Round 2 in 2016/17 (National League North)

139 Cambridge City 1x R2, 9x R1
Reached Round 2 in 2004/05 (Conference South)

140 Shildon 1x R2, 8x R1
Reached Round 2 in 1936/37 (Northern League)

141 Grays Athletic .... 1x R2, 7x R1 (plus 11x q4)
Reached Round 2 in 2005/06 (Conference National)

142 Windsor & Eton .... 1x R2, 7x R1 (plus 1x q4)
Reached Round 2 in 1983/84 (Isthmian League 1)

143 Horden Colliery Welfare .... 1x R2, 6x R1 (plus 14x q4)
Reached Round 2 in 1938/39 (North Eastern League)

144 Gloucester City .... 1x R2, 6x R1 (plus 11x q4)
Reached Round 2 in 1989/90 (Southern League Premier)

145 Braintree Town .... 1x R2, 6x R1 (plus 7x q4)
Reached Round 2 in 2016/17 (National League)

146 Carshalton Athletic .... 1x R2, 6x R1 (plus 3x q4)
Reached Round 2 in 1982/83 (Isthmian League Premier)

147 Burscough .... 1x R2, 5x R1 (plus 6x q4)
Reached Round 2 in 2005/06 (Northern Premier League Premier)

148 Barry Town .... 1x R2, 5x R1 (plus 5x q4)
Reached Round 2 in 1929/30 (Southern League West)

149 Weston-super-Mare .... 1x R2, 5x R1 (plus 3x q4)
Reached Round 2 in 2003/04 (Southern League Premier)

150 AFC Telford United .... 1x R2, 5x R1 (plus 1x q4)
Reached Round 2 in 2014/15 (Conference National)

**Different from current / later club with same/similar name*

Rank	Essex Senior League	Q4	Q3	Q2	Q1	PR	EP
1	Southend Manor	1		1	4	7	11
2	Canvey Island	1		1	1	4	
3	Romford (1)		2				
4	Stansted		1	2	3	8	9
5	Basildon United		1		6	11	2
6	Hadley		1			1	
7	Walthamstow			3	1		3
8	Burnham Ramblers			2	7	14	4
9	Redbridge			2	2	5	4
10	Heybridge Swifts			2	1		

Top Ten FA Cup Clubs whilst Members of ESL.

Nb. Chart shows number of exits per Round

150 Years of FA Cup Firsts

1871/72 First ever FA Cup matches on 11 November 1871 including Maidenhead versus Marlow, the oldest fixture still viably possible today, plus the first ever FA Cup goal scored by Jarvis Kenrick for Clapham Rovers in their 3-0 win against Upton Park.

Jarvis Kenrick was also the first player to score a brace in one FA Cup game, and Clapham Rovers were the first club to score three goals in one game.

First goal-less draw in the FA Cup between the original Hitchin FC and the original Crystal Palace in the 1st Round. In a bizarre rule at the time both clubs progressed to the 2nd Round.

First clubs to scratch from the competition, Reigate Priory and Harrow Chequers, leading to the first ever walkovers for Royal Engineers and The Wanderers respectively.

First bye awarded in the FA Cup for Hampstead Heathens in the 1st Round.

Royal Engineers were the first club to score four and five goals in one FA Cup game, winning 5-0 at Hitchin in the 2nd Round. The goal-scorers have not been identified.

First Scottish club to compete in FA Cup, Queen's Park, who ended up playing just one game across four rounds, reaching the semi-finals, scoring no goals and remaining unbeaten in the campaign.

First FA Cup replay after Barnes drew one apiece with Hampstead Heathens in the 2nd Round, before the Heathens went on to win 1-0 in the replay.

First ever FA Cup winners, The Wanderers, beating Royal Engineers 1-0 at The Kennington Oval.

1872/73 First and only time FA Cup was run as an FA Challenge Cup with the holders playing in the Final against the Challenger who won through the knockout stage of the competition.

First and only time the holders could choose where the following year's FA Cup Final took place. The Wanderers chose a ground at Lillie Bridge, not far from where Stamford Bridge is today.

By beating Marlow 1-0 in the 1st Round Maidenhead became the first club to defeat the same opponents twice in the FA Cup.

First ever voided match in FA Cup after South Norwood won 1-0 against Windsor Home Park in the 2nd Round. The defeated side complained that the match had ended before the 90 minutes were up. The FA agreed and ordered the game to be re-played at Windsor Home Park, who won 3-0 to go through.

'72/'73 cont. First and only time no semi-final games were actually played. The Wanderers had a bye and Queen's Park scratched before playing Oxford University despite having had a bye themselves through to this round.

The first time the FA Cup Final kicked off in the morning, owing to the Varsity Boat Race taking place on the same day.

Oxford University were the first and only club to reach an FA Cup final the first time they entered the competition (aside from the very first Final).

1874/75 The Wanderers became the first club to score double figures in one FA Cup game, winning 16-0 against Farningham in the 1st Round.

Robert Kingsford became the first player to score five goals in one FA Cup game during that record win over Farningham. Charles Wollaston scored four goals in the same match.

Along with Edward H Parry of Oxford University, in their 1st Round 6-0 win over Brondesbury, these are the first recorded hat-tricks in the FA Cup (although hat-tricks could have been scored in Royal Engineers' earlier big wins, but goal-scorers have not been identified for those games).

First instance of a revenge FA Cup win, of sorts, when Shropshire Wanderers progressed to the 2nd Round courtesy of Sheffield FC scratching.

First time it is known that a game played extra time, when Shropshire Wanderers and Woodford Wells played out a one-one draw in the quarter-finals (3rd Round). Shropshire Wanderers won 2-0 in the replay.

First time a tie was settled in extra time as Royal Engineers beat Oxford University 1-0 in their semi-final.

Cuthbert John Ottaway of Old Etonians became the first player to not complete the full 90 minutes in an FA Cup Final when leaving the field of play on 37 minutes with a sprained ankle. Nb. Edmund William Cresswell broke his collar bone in the tenth minute when playing for Royal Engineers against The Wanderers in the 1872 Final, but played on to the end of that game.

First FA Cup Final to require extra time and a replay.

Rank	Midland Football League	R1	Q4	Q3	Q2	Q1	PR	EP
1	Westfields	1			1	1	1	1
2	Sporting Khalsa		1				5	
3	Coleshill Town			1		3		
4	Shepshed Dynamo				1	2		2
5	Highgate United				1	1		3

Top Five FA Cup Clubs whilst Members of MFL.

Nb. Chart shows number of exits per Round

1875/76 First time the same two clubs were drawn together in three successive seasons. Hardly surprising really as Sheffield FC and Shropshire Wanderers were the only two clubs from the Sheffield FA involved. This time it was Shropshire Wanderers turn to withdraw.

First instance of two players scoring five goals apiece in the same FA Cup game, achieved by Herbert Rawson and James Middlemiss when Royal Engineer won 15-0 at home to High Wycombe.

First ever 'varsity' FA Cup match when the dark blues of Oxford University won 4-0 against the light blues of Cambridge University in the quarter-finals (3rd Round).

1876/77 First time two clubs with names that start with a number played each other in the FA Cup. 105th Regiment beat 1st Surrey Rifles 3-0 in the 1st Round.

First time the FA Cup Final was settled in extra time in the first game.

1877/78 First appearance of future Football League clubs in the FA Cup as Notts County lost 3-0 to Sheffield FC in a replay and Reading FC won 2-0 against South Norwood to become the first current Football League club to win an FA Cup game.

Druids became the first Welsh club to participate in the FA Cup, beating Manchester 3-0 in the 1st Round before setting up the first all non-English tie against Queen's Park in the 2nd Round. Unfortunately, as Queen's Park scratched it wasn't to become the first all non-English FA Cup tie between two clubs from different countries as well.

The Wanderers became the first club to receive a bye in the semi-finals for the second time.

1878/79 The first ever Nottingham derby took place as Nottingham Forest won 3-1 after extra time at Notts County in the 1st Round.

The Wanderers became the first holders to exit the following year's competition in the 1st Round, losing 7-2 at home to Old Etonians.

Old Etonians and Darwen played out the first ever five-five score draw in their first quarter-final (4th Round) game, with the southern amateur side eventually progressing 6-2 in a third match.

Nottingham Forest became the first northern English club to reach the FA Cup semi-finals, in what was the club's debut campaign.

1879/80 First appearance in the FA Cup of two future 'best FA Cup club of all time' teams, Aston Villa and Blackburn Rovers.

Hanover United became the first club with that suffix to participate in the FA Cup.

'79/'80 cont. Sheffield FC became the first club to be disqualified from the FA Cup after refusing to play extra time after their 2-2 draw at Nottingham forest in the 4th Round.

This was the first time that the quarter-finals didn't occur until the 5th Round.

Clapham Rovers became the first club to receive a bye in successive semi-finals.

The first FA Cup Final played in the month of April.

1880/81 Darwen became the first club to score double figures in a quarter-final, winning 15-0 against the original Romford FC.

Four different players scored hat-tricks in that comprehensive quarter-final win – Kirkham, Marshall, Mellor and Rostron – the first time that feat was recorded in the FA Cup.

First FA Cup Final to be contested by two clubs whose names both began with the same letter: Old Carthusians 3-0 Old Etonians.

1881/82 First instance of an FA Cup tie requiring four matches to resolve it when Turton finally beat Astley Bridge 2-0 in their 3rd replay in the 1st Round.

Notts County became the first club to score double figures in a re-played game after having their initial 2nd Round 5-3 win over Wednesbury Strollers voided by the FA. The Magpies won 11-1 in the second game.

Henry Cursham of Notts County became the first player to score six goals in one FA Cup game during that victory over Wednesbury Strollers. He had scored a brace in the original match.

Derby Town becomes the first club with that popular suffix to participate in the FA Cup. Their 4-1 defeat at Small Heath Alliance (now Birmingham City) would be their only match in the competition.

Blackburn Rovers versus The Wednesday (Sheffield Wednesday) becomes the first FA Cup semi-final contested by two northern based clubs.

Blackburn Rovers became the first northern club to appear in an FA Cup Final.

This was the first instance of the Cup Winners (Old Etonians) beginning with the same letter as a different club which had lifted the Trophy the previous season (Old Carthusians).

1882/83 This was the first season that the quarter-finals (5th round) actually involved eight clubs.

Druids became the first Welsh club to reach the quarter-finals.

Blackburn Olympic became the first northern (and first professional) club to lift the FA Cup.

1883/84 This was the first season when one hundred clubs participated in the FA Cup.

Queen's Park became the first club to score double figures in two successive rounds, winning 10-0 at Crewe Alexandra in the 1st Round, and 15-0 against Manchester FC in the second. They would go on to become the first club to score over 40 goals (44) in one FA Cup campaign, and be the first Scottish (and non-English) side in an FA Cup Final.

Queen's Park and Old Carthusians became the first clubs to score double figures away from home in the FA Cup.

Rossendale became the first club to be disqualified for 'professionalism' after winning 6-2 against Irwell Springs (now Bacup Borough), meaning their opponents became the first club to be reinstated in the FA Cup. Irwell Springs would also become the first club to advance thanks to two successive voided games, protesting a 3-2 defeat at Hurst FC (now Ashton united) in the second round and progressing when their opponents scratched.

This was the first instance when two successive FA Cup finals were won by two different clubs from the same town or city.

1884/85 First instance of both clubs due to play each other scratching as Bolton Wanderers and Preston Zingari both withdrew before their 1st round game.

Lincoln City become the first club with that common suffix to participate in the FA Cup.

Blackburn Olympic became the first club to score a dozen goals away from home in the FA Cup in their 12-0 victory in the 1st Round at Oswaldtwistle Rovers.

This was the first season when the quarter-finals weren't until the 6th Round.

Merchiston Castle School in Edinburgh became the first venue in Scotland and the first outside of England to host an FA Cup semi-final, witnessing Queen's Park winning 3-0 against Nottingham Forest in a replay. As a consequence of that defeat Nottingham forest became the first club to appear in three semi-finals without reaching the Final.

The first, and only to date, FA Cup Final to be contested by the same two clubs in the previous season's Final.

Blackburn Rovers became the first club to win through eight rounds in the same FA Cup campaign. The run includes the FA Cup Final itself, but only required seven victories as Rovers received a bye in the 5th Round.

1885/86 The 1st Round tie between Hurst FC (now Ashton United) and Bradshaw FC became the first to be voided twice. Hurst won the first game 2-1, the teams played out a one-one draw in the second game, before Hurst won 3-2 in the third. Hurst's next round 3-1 win over Halliwell FC was also voided and then they scratched before the re-played game.

The first FA Cup 'Black Country' Derby took place this season as West Bromwich Albion won 3-1 against Wolverhampton Wanderers in the 4th Round

Swifts become the first club to appear in three FA Cup semi-finals who would never go on to appear in a Cup Final itself.

Blackburn Rovers become the first, and to date the only, club to win 20 successive FA Cup matches played.

1886/87 Cliftonville become the first Irish club to participate in the FA Cup, and the first to host an FA Cup game outside of the mainland of Great Britain in their 7-2 replay victory over Blackburn Park Road in the 1st Round.

Cliftonville versus Partick Thistle in the 2nd Round becomes the first, and to date the only, FA Cup tie to involve two non-English sides from two different countries.

1887/88 Preston North End become the first, and to date the only club to score more than 20 goals in an FA Cup game in their famous 26-0 defeat of Hyde FC in the 1st Round.

Jimmy Ross became the first player to score eight goals in one FA Cup game during that record victory over Hyde FC. Jack Gordon and Sam Thompson both netted five times in the game, making it the first time three players had scored five or more goals for the same club in one FA Cup game.

Jimmy Ross would go on to become the first player to score as many as 19 goals in one FA Cup campaign.

The first FA Cup 'second city' Derby took place this season with Aston Villa winning 4-0 at Small Heath Alliance (Birmingham City) in the 2nd Round.

The first Potteries Derby in the FA Cup also occurred this season when Stoke (City) won 1-0 at home to (Burslem) Port Vale.

1888/89 This was the first season that Qualifying Rounds were used in the FA Cup, introduced as a consequence of results such as Preston's win over Hyde, coinciding with the first season of the Football League.

Warwick County became the first non-league club to defeat League and top-flight opposition winning 2-1 at Stoke (City) in the 1st Qualifying Round.

'88/'89 cont. Blackburn Olympic, Old Etonians and Royal Engineers became the first former winners of the FA Cup to have to start a future campaign in the Qualifying Rounds.

Chatham (Town) became the first, and so far only, club to start in the earliest possible Qualifying round and go as far as the quarter-finals.

Linfield Athletic and Cliftonville play the first, and to date the only, FA Cup tie contested on Christmas Day in their 4th Qualifying Round second replay, won 7-0 by Linfield Athletic.

The Wednesday (Sheffield Wednesday) become the first non-league club to defeat League opposition in the 'Proper' Rounds of the competition, winning 3-2 against Notts County in the 2nd Round.

West Bromwich Albion become the first, and to date the only, club to score double figures away in the quarter-finals (3rd Round), winning 10-1 at Chatham (Town).

1889/90 First appearance of the current record FA Cup winners, Arsenal, in the FA Cup (as Royal Arsenal) becoming the first club to score double figures in their first FA Cup match (11-0 versus Lyndhurst).

The Wednesday (Sheffield Wednesday) are first non-league club to reach both the FA Cup semi-finals and the FA Cup Final.

1890/91 The first season in which the Preliminary Round was used in the FA Cup with just one game: Crusaders 5-0 Rochester, which was also the first FA Cup game played in September.

The original Stockton FC become the first club to score the record 14 goals away from home in their 14-0 win at Hurworth in the 1st Qualifying Round.

Nottingham Forest become the first club to score the record 14 goals away from home in the 'Proper' rounds of the competition when winning 14-0 at Clapton.

1891/92 The first FA Cup Manchester Derby took place this season, although recent research suggests that Ardwick and Newton Heath are not the same clubs as Manchester City and Manchester United. This 1st qualifying Round game was won 5-1 by Newton Heath, whilst the two clubs met in the FA Cup under their current names for the first time in the 1926 semi-finals, won 3-0 by Manchester City.

1894/95 This was the first of only five occasions when all eight clubs involved in the quarter-finals were members of the top-flight.

1895/96 This was the first season when two hundred plus clubs participated in the FA Cup.

'95/'96 cont. This was the first of only three seasons when FA Cup games were scheduled for 29th February. The other two seasons were 1935/36 and 1963/64.

1896/97 This was the first season that included a 5th Qualifying Round.

Bury FC became the first club to score double figures in an FA Cup replay when winning 12-1 against the original Stockton in the 1st Round.

1899/00 First instance of an FA Cup tie requiring five matches to resolve it when New Brompton (now Gillingham) finally beat (Woolwich) Arsenal in their 4th replay in the 3rd Qualifying Round.

The first FA Cup Steel City Derby took place in the 2nd Round this season with Sheffield United winning 2-0 in a replay against The Wednesday.

Southampton beat Millwall in the first, and so far only, semi-final involving two non-league clubs. Both were members of the Southern League.

1900/01 This was the first season that included an Intermediary Round between the Qualifying Rounds and the 'Proper' Rounds. This round was only utilised for five consecutive seasons.

Woodford became the first club to score double figures in a 20th Century FA Cup campaign when wining 10-1 away at Leytonstone in a Preliminary Round replay.

Bury FC became the first FA Cup holders to be knocked out by a non-league side, losing 2-1 at Southern League side Tottenham Hotspur in the 2nd Round.

1901/02 Tottenham hotspur became the first FA Cup holders to be knocked out by a non-league club in the 1st Round, losing 2-1 against fellow Southern League side Southampton in a second replay.

The first FA Cup Merseyside Derby occurred this season when Everton and Liverpool played out a two-two draw in the 1st Round. Liverpool won the replay in what is now the most common 'Proper' Round fixture.

The first FA Cup clash between Bristol City and Bristol Rovers took place this season when they played out a one-one draw in the 4th Qualifying Round Rovers won the replay, but Bristol City winning 5-1 against Bristol East in the earlier 3rd Qualifying round was the first FA Cup game between two clubs from the city.

The first FA Cup game between Sunderland and Newcastle United happened this season, too. Newcastle United won their 2nd Round tie 2-0, but Sunderland had already faced both Newcastle East End and Newcastle West End in the FA Cup in the seasons leading up to the formation of Newcastle United.

1903/04 This was the first season which started off with the Extra Preliminary Round with 13 matches scheduled, twelve of which were played.

1904/05 This was the first season which included a 6th Qualifying Round.

1905/06 Crystal Palace became the first, and so far only, non-league club to score seven goals against a Football League side, winning 7-1 against Chelsea in the 3rd Qualifying Round.

The first FA Cup South Coast Derby happened in the 1st Round this season when Southampton won 5-1 against Portsmouth.

1906/07 This was the first season when three hundred plus clubs participated in the FA Cup.

The first ever six-all draw occurred this season between Page Green Old Boys and Crouch End Vampires in the Preliminary Round. Page Green won 6-2 in the replay.

1907/08 The Wednesday (Sheffield Wednesday) became the first FA Cup holders to be knocked out by a non-league side in their very next FA Cup match, losing 2-0 to Southern league side Norwich City.

1909/10 This was the first season when four hundred plus clubs participated in the FA Cup.

1911/12 The first FA Cup Bradford 'Derby' took place this season when Cup holders Bradford City won 1-0 at the original Bradford (Park Avenue) in the 3rd Round.

1913/14 The first time a reigning monarch, King George V, attended the FA Cup Final.

1914/15 Harold Halse of Chelsea became the first player to appear in three FA Cup finals with three different clubs having won the Cup with Manchester United in 1909 and Aston Villa in 1913.

1919/20 Hednesford Town FC and Thornycrofts (Woolston) FC became the first two clubs to win eight FA Cup matches in the same season, and compete in nine rounds in the same campaign. Both clubs began in the Extra Preliminary Round, both clubs' eighth win came in the 6th Qualifying round, and both clubs appeared in the 1st Round 'Proper'.

1920/21 This was the first season when five hundred plus clubs participated in the FA Cup.

1921/22 This was the first season when six hundred plus clubs participated in the FA Cup.

1925/26 This was the first season whereby clubs from the top two divisions were exempted until the 3rd Round 'Proper', more or less the same structure that exists to this day.

1929/30 The first and only instance of a seven-all score draw occurred this season between Dulwich Hamlet and Wealdstone in their 4th Qualifying Round tie. Dulwich Hamlet won 2-1 in the replay.

1931/32 The first time five non-league clubs all appeared the FA Cup 3rd Round in the same season in the competition's current structure: Bath City, Burton Town, Corinthians, Crook Town and Darwen.

1933/34 In the current competition structure, Cheltenham Town became the first club to reach the 3rd Round 'Proper' having started their campaign in the Extra Preliminary Round.

1936/37 The first time the FA Cup Final took place in the month of May.

1938/39 Folkestone FC became the first non-league club to appear in FA Cup 1st Round in ten consecutive seasons in the competition's current structure.

1947/48 Chris Marron became the first player to score ten goals in one FA Cup match doing so for original South Shields in their 13-0 victory over Radcliffe Welfare United in the Preliminary Round.

Colchester United became the first non-league club to knock out a top-flight club in the current FA Cup structure when winning 1-0 against Huddersfield Town whilst members of the Southern League.

1948/49 The first FA Cup North London Derby took place this season with Arsenal winning 3-0 against Tottenham Hotspur.

1950/51 The first of only two times in the current FA Cup structure that there was no non-league presence in the 3rd Round. The second time was in the 2017/18 season.

1953/54 Blackpool FC became the first FA Cup holders to be knocked out by another Football league club from the third tier, when losing 2-0 at Port Vale in the 5th Round.

1954/55 The oldest Derby, a match between Sheffield FC and Hallam FC, first occurred in the FA Cup in this season, 94 years after their first ever meeting, with Sheffield FC winning 3-1 in their 1st Qualifying round game.

1960/61 This was the first season when the FA Cup began in the month of August.

1961/62 The first time two non-league clubs met in the FA Cup 3rd Round. Southern League Premier Division side Weymouth won 1-0 at Lancashire Combination Division One club Morecambe.

The first FA Cup East Anglian Derby between Norwich city and Ipswich Town occurred in the 4th Round this season with the Canaries winning 2-1 in a replay.

1962/63	Rhyl became the first non-league club to appear in the FA Cup 1st Round 'Proper' in 15 consecutive seasons.
	Falmouth Town became the first Cornish club to appear in the 1st Round 'Proper', doing so in the club's first campaign, eventually losing 2-1 to Oxford United.
1963/64	Oxford United became the first club from the 4th Division of the Football League to reach the FA Cup quarter-finals. It was only their second season as a Football League side.
1968/69	Alvechurch became the first club to participate in the FA Cup whilst members of the Midland Combination.
1969/70	This was the first season the third/fourth place play-off occurred between the two beaten semi-finalists. Manchester United defeated Watford 2-0 at Highbury on the eve of the FA Cup Final.
1971/72	First and only instance of an FA Cup tie requiring six matches to resolve it when Alvechurch finally beat Oxford City 1-0 in their 5th replay in the 4th Qualifying Round.
	Hereford United became the first non-league club to appear in the 1st Round 'proper' for 17 consecutive seasons.
	Ted MacDougall became the first player to score nine goals in an FA Cup 'Proper' Round match, doing so for AFC Bournemouth in their 11-0 victory over Margate in the 1st Round.
	The first time an official FA Cup match was settled on penalties when Stoke City won 4-3 against Birmingham City from spot kicks after the two sides had played out a goal-less draw in this season's third/fourth play-off match.
1974/75	Wimbledon FC became the first non-league club to knock out a top-flight club in the current FA Cup structure away from home when winning 1-0 at Burnley whilst members of the Southern League.
1975/76	For the first time since the current FA Cup structure was put in place a record 14 non-league clubs appeared in the 2nd Round, a level that has subsequently only been matched twice since then, most latterly in the 2020/21 season.
1977/78	The first time as many as six non-league clubs reached the FA Cup 3rd Round in the same season: Blyth Spartans, Enfield, Scarborough, Tilbury, Wealdstone and Wigan Athletic.
1979/80	Basildon United became the first club to participate in the FA Cup whilst members of the Essex Senior League.

1981/82	The 3rd Round tie between Queens Park Rangers and Middlesbrough was the first in the competition's history to be played on an artificial surface. The game ended in a one-one draw.
1983/84	Manchester United became the first FA Cup holders to be knocked out by another Football League club from the third tier in their very next match, losing 2-0 to AFC Bournemouth in the 3rd Round.
1984/85	Telford United became the first non-league team to face five Football League clubs in the same FA Cup campaign, eventually losing 3-0 at Everton in the 5th Round.
1991/92	Rotherham United became the first club to progress in the FA Cup as a consequence of a penalty shoot-out, winning 7-6 on penalties after playing out a 3-3 draw with Scunthorpe United in their 1st Round replay.
1995/96	Fourth tier Fulham FC record the biggest margin of victory over a higher league side in FA Cup 'Proper' Round history with a 7-0 win against third tier Swansea City.
2000/01	Oxford City became the first club in a 21st Century FA Cup campaign to score double figures when winning 10-1 at Shoreham in the Preliminary Round.
2001/02	Tony Roberts became the first goalkeeper to score an FA Cup goal from open play, doing so for Dagenham and Redbridge in their 4th Qualifying Round 2-2 draw at Basingstoke Town.
2007/08	This was the first season when seven hundred plus clubs participated in the FA Cup.
2008/09	The first time as many as seven and eight non-league clubs reached the FA Cup 3rd Round in the same season: Barrow, Blyth Spartans, Eastwood Town, Forest Green Rovers, Histon, Kettering Town, Kidderminster Harriers and Torquay United.
2012/13	Ashford United became the first club to participate in the FA Cup whilst members of the Kent Invicta League.
2014/15	The first FA Cup 'Proper' Round tie to require a record 32 spot kicks to resolve it happened when Scunthorpe United won 14-13 on penalties against Worcester City in their 2nd Round replay after a one-one draw.
2016/17	Lincoln City became the first non-league club to reach the FA Cup quarter-finals since the current structure was put in place, 103 years after the last non-league side achieved the feat, and also became the first non-league club to defeat five League clubs in the same campaign.
	Burnley became the first team to be beaten twice at home by a non-league side whilst a top-flight club, one of the victims of Lincoln City's run.

2018/19 This season ended the first ever decade where all ten FA Cup runners-up were different clubs; Portsmouth, Stoke City, Liverpool, Manchester City, Hull City, Aston Villa, Crystal Palace, Chelsea, Manchester United and Watford.

2019/20 For the first time ever, all four FA Cup semi-finalists were the four previous winners; Manchester United, Arsenal, Chelsea and Manchester City.

2020/21 This season witnessed the first instance of the opening game of the campaign, Woodford Town versus Colney Heath in the Extra Preliminary Round, occurring in same month (August) as the previous season's Cup Final.

For the first time, draws for both 4th and 5th Rounds were made at same time.

Marine FC of Northern Premier League Division One North West versus Premier League Tottenham Hotspur in the 3rd Round is the first FA Cup game with seven levels of the football pyramid separating the two competing clubs.

Torquay United 5-6 Crawley Town is the first time as many as eleven goals are scored in a one-goal margin of victory in 'Proper' Rounds of the FA Cup.

Due to Covid_19 restrictions this was the first FA Cup campaign to not have any replays.

Rank	Birmingham and District League / West Midlands Regional League	R3	R2	R1	IR	Q6	Q5	Q4	Q3
1	Burton Town	1		1				6	
2	Burton Albion	1		1				2	1
3	Alvechurch	1						1	
4	Kidderminster Harriers		1	8	1		1	8	5
5	Telford United		1	6			1	2	3
6	Tamworth		1	3				1	3
7	Crewe Alexandra		1	2			3	1	3
8	Nuneaton Borough		1	1				2	
9	Bilston Town		1	1					2
10	Brierley Hill Alliance		1					5	10
11	Hinckley Athletic		1					2	5
12	Boston United		1					1	
13	Coventry Sporting		1						
14	Worcester City			3				5	2
15	Stoke City			3					
16	Oswestry Town			2				1	2
17	Halesowen Town			2					4
18	Shrewsbury Town			1	1	1	2	5	5
19	Hednesford Town			1		1		4	3
20	Walsall			1			4	1	

Top 20 FA Cup Clubs whilst Members of WMRL.

Nb. Chart shows number of exits per Round

150 Repeated Names Used in FA Cup

One of the major challenges of compiling statistics for a competition such as the FA Cup that has been running for 150 years is that different clubs have competed in it over the years using the same name. For example, there have been two 'Coalville Towns', three 'Kirkleys' and four 'Jarrows'! Some duplicated names are directly linked to each other often through a merger. For example Barking FC merged with East Ham United in 2001 to form Barking and East Ham United, but that new club changed its name to Barking FC five years later. Other clubs are linked through re-formations and can often be regarded by fans and club officials as one continuous club. Newport County and Darlington fall into this camp, taking on the original club's name a few years after the re-formed club had become founded.

Two current clubs have even faced opponents in the FA Cup who had the future name that they themselves would eventually adopt. Kendal Town's first ever FA Cup game in 1925/26 was played under the name Netherfield (Kendal) and they lost 2-1 at the original Kendal Town. Similarly, for 20 years between 1981 and 2002 Hastings United were known as Hastings Town, and they were also beaten 2-1 in the FA Cup in 1984/85 by the original Hastings United. So to follow are the 150 or so names that more than one club has used at some point in their history to enter the FA Cup, alongside their best Cup runs when using those names.

Aberdare	1912–1914	2 campaigns	3rd qualifying round
	1938–1939	1 campaign	2nd qualifying round
Accrington	1881–1896	15 campaigns	3rd Round 'Proper'
	1964–1965	1 campaign	preliminary round
Accrington Stanley	1896–1962	55 campaigns	4th Round 'Proper'
	1971–2021	50 campaigns	4th Round 'Proper
Acton	1879–1886	7 campaigns	2nd Round 'Proper'
	1934–1935	1 campaign	1st qualifying round
Aldershot Town	1927–1932	5 campaigns*	3rd Round 'Proper'*
	1994–2021	27 campaigns	4th round 'Proper'
Alfreton Town	1910–1929	8 campaigns	6th qualifying round
	1960–2021	61 campaigns	2nd Round 'Proper'
Arnold	1903–1908	4 campaigns	1st qualifying round
	1964–1989	25 campaigns	1st Round 'Proper'
Arnold Town	1925–1927	2 campaigns	preliminary round
	1989–2015	26 campaigns	4th qualifying round
Ashford Town	1912–1913	1 campaign*	preliminary round*
(*Kent*)	1948–2011	63 campaigns	2nd Round 'Proper'
Ashford United	1891–1908	15 campaigns	4th qualifying round
	2012–2021	9 campaigns	1st qualifying round

Ashton Town	1903–1910	4 campaigns	2nd qualifying round
	2007–2014	4 campaigns	preliminary round
Atherstone Town	1908–1980	52 campaigns*	4th qualifying round*
	2006–2019	11 campaigns*	3rd qualifying round*
Baldock Town	1923–2001	39 campaigns	4th qualifying round
	2014–2021	6 campaigns	2nd qualifying round
Barking	1905–1915 & 1932–2001	71 campaigns*	2nd Round 'Proper'*
	2006–2021	15 campaigns*	3rd qualifying round*
Barnet	1898–1899	1 campaign	preliminary round
	1911–1912	1 campaign	preliminary round
	1919–2021	96 campaigns*	4th Round 'Proper'*
Barrow	1891–1893	2 campaigns	2nd qualifying round
	1901–2021	110 campaigns	3rd Round 'Proper'
Barton Town	1920–1982	45 campaigns	3rd qualifying round
	2017–2021	4 campaigns*	preliminary round*
Bedford Town	1910–1963	63 campaigns	4th Round 'Proper'
	1995–2021	26 campaigns	1st Round 'Proper'
Belper Town	1887–1911	23 campaigns	1st Round 'Proper'
	1956–2021	65 campaigns	4th qualifying round
Berkhamsted	1902–1903	1 campaign*	preliminary round*
	2011–2021	10 campaigns	2nd qualifying round
Biggleswade United	1935–1938	3 campaigns	preliminary round
	2005–2021	16 campaigns	1st qualifying round
Birmingham	1879–1880	1 campaign	2nd Round 'Proper'
	1905–1939	29 campaigns*	RUNNERS-UP*
Bletchley Town	1931–1933	2 campaigns	extra preliminary round
	1963–1974	11 campaigns*	4th qualifying round*
Bloxwich United	2001–2002	1 campaign	preliminary round
	2011–2013	2 campaigns	extra preliminary round
Blyth	1892–1898	6 campaigns	3rd qualifying round
	2018–2019	1 campaign	preliminary round
Bootle	1881–1894	10 campaigns	QUARTER-FINALS
	1927–1928	1 campaign	1st qualifying round
	1980–2021	34 campaigns	3rd qualifying round

Boston	1887–1906 &1919–1934	26 campaigns*	3rd Round 'Proper'*
	1965–1994	27 campaigns*	1st Round 'Proper'*
Boston Town	1906–1915	5 campaigns*	1st qualifying round*
	1994–2021	27 campaigns*	3rd qualifying round*
Bradford	1908–1974	56 campaigns	QUARTER-FINALS
(Park Avenue)	1992–2018	26 campaigns*	1st Round 'Proper'*
Brentwood	1878–1886	8 campaigns*	QUARTER-FINALS*
	2000–2004	4 campaigns*	preliminary round*
Brentwood Town	1965–1970	5 campaigns*	3rd Round 'Proper'*
	2004–2021	17 campaigns*	4th qualifying round*
Bridgend Town	1921–1922	1 campaign	2nd qualifying round
	1976–1992	16 campaigns*	4th qualifying round*
Bridgwater Town	1949–1985	34 campaigns	2nd Round 'Proper'
	1996–2021	25 campaigns	3rd qualifying round
Bridlington Town	1920–1939	14 campaigns	4th qualifying round
	1959–1994	32 campaigns*	1st Round 'Proper'*
	2000–2021	21 campaigns	4th qualifying round
Brislington	1904–1906	2 campaigns	2nd qualifying round
	1996–2021	25 campaigns	4th qualifying round
Burnham	1974–1986	12 campaigns	2nd qualifying round
	1987–2021	34 campaigns*	1st Round 'Proper'*
Cambridge United	1910–1914	4 campaigns	4th qualifying round
	1951–2021	70 campaigns*	QUARTER-FINALS*
Canterbury City	1948–2000	52 campaigns	1st Round 'Proper'
	2013–2021	8 campaigns	preliminary round
Carlisle City	1895–1908	5 campaigns	preliminary round
	1976–1981	5 campaigns	1st qualifying round
Cheshunt	1904–1930	14 campaigns	4th qualifying round
	1950–2021	64 campaigns	4th qualifying round
Chester	1886–1983	79 campaigns*	5th Round 'Proper'*
	2013–2021	9 campaigns	2nd Round 'Proper'
Chichester City	1948–2000	44 campaigns*	1st Round 'Proper'*
	2009–2021	12 campaigns*	2nd Round 'proper'*
Clay Cross Town	1893–1896	3 campaigns	2nd qualifying round
	1909–1923	6 campaigns	3rd qualifying round

Cleethorpes Town	1886–1931	19 campaigns	2nd Round 'Proper'
	2014–2021	7 campaigns	3rd qualifying round
Close Works	1919–1922	3 campaigns*	4th qualifying round*
	1937–1939	2 campaigns	extra preliminary round
Coalville Town	1893–1955	39 campaigns	4th qualifying round
	2004–2021	17 campaigns	1st qualifying round
Colne	1903–1913	10 campaigns*	3rd qualifying round*
	2002–2021	19 campaigns	4th qualifying round
Cowes	1892–1900	8 campaigns	4th qualifying round
	1904–1979	61 campaigns	4th qualifying round
Crook Town	1936–1939	3 campaigns*	preliminary round*
	1949–2021	68 campaigns*	2nd Round 'Proper'*
Croydon	1903–1923	14 campaigns	1st qualifying round
	1973–2020	47 campaigns*	2nd Round 'Proper'*
Crystal Palace	1871–1876	5 campaigns	SEMI-FINALS
	1905–2021	106 campaigns	RUNNERS-UP
Darlington	1885–2012	117 campaigns	5th Round 'Proper'
	2017–2021	4 campaigns*	2nd Round 'Proper'*
Darlington	1919–1926	7 campaigns	1st qualifying round
Railway Athletic	2006–2014	5 campaigns	preliminary round
Daventry United	1909–1914	4 campaigns	preliminary round
	2007–2012	5 campaigns*	1st qualifying round*
Dorking	1906–1910	42 campaigns*	3rd qualifying round*
	& 1921–1974		
	1983–2014	31 campaigns*	1st Round 'Proper'*
Dorking Town	1910–1915	5 campaigns*	2nd qualifying round*
	1978–1983	5 campaigns*	2nd qualifying round*
Dunstable Town	1950–1976	21 campaigns	1st Round 'Proper'
	2001–2021	20 campaigns	3rd qualifying round
Earlestown	1900–1912	12 campaigns	4th qualifying round
	1947–1964	15 campaigns	2nd qualifying round
Eastwood Town	1896–1898	2 campaigns	3rd qualifying round
	1968–2014	46 campaigns	3rd Round 'Proper'
Edmonton	1921–1928	7 campaigns	4th qualifying round
	1968–1973	4 campaigns*	3rd qualifying round*

Enfield	1896–1897	1 campaign	preliminary round
	1904–2007	93 campaigns	4th Round 'Proper'
	2009–2021	12 campaigns	2nd qualifying round
Epsom Town	1925–1935	10 campaigns*	1st Round 'Proper'*
	1945–1947	2 campaigns	1st qualifying round
Esh Winning	1914–1931	13 campaigns*	4th qualifying round*
	1984–2013	26 campaigns	2nd qualifying round
Exmouth Town	1934–2006	19 campaigns	4th qualifying round
	2017–2021	3 campaigns	1st qualifying round
Farsley Celtic	1928–2010	69 campaigns	1st Round 'Proper'
	2015–2021	6 campaigns*	3rd qualifying round*
Feltham	1966–1991	20 campaigns	3rd qualifying round
	2009–2010	1 campaign*	extra preliminary round*
Fisher	1994–1996	2 campaigns*	2nd qualifying round*
	2011–2021	8 campaigns	1st qualifying round
Fleetwood	1908–1928	11 campaigns	4th qualifying round
	1947–1976	29 campaigns	1st Round 'Proper'
	1994–1996	2 campaigns*	preliminary round*
Fleetwood Town	1978–1994	16 campaigns*	1st Round 'Proper'*
	2002–2021	19 campaigns*	3rd Round 'Proper'*
Frizington United	1901–1903	2 campaigns	preliminary round
	1947–1951	4 campaigns	2nd qualifying round
Gateshead	1912–1915	3 campaigns	1st qualifying round
	1930–1974	38 campaigns*	QUARTER-FINALS*
	1978–2021	43 campaigns	3rd Round 'Proper'
Gateshead Town	1905–1909	4 campaigns	1st qualifying round
	1922–1923	1 campaign	preliminary round
Gresley Rovers	1895–2009	99 campaigns	1st Round 'Proper'
	2020–2021	1 campaign*	preliminary round*
Guildford City	1927–1974	41 campaigns*	2nd round 'Proper'*
	2006–2021	15 campaigns	2nd qualifying round
Hampstead	1898–1908	10 campaigns	1st qualifying round
	1926–1933	7 campaigns*	4th qualifying round*
Handsworth	1921–1922	1 campaign	preliminary round
	2019–2021	2 campaigns*	preliminary round*

Hastings and St Leonards	1901–1906	5 campaigns	4th qualifying round
	1921–1948	18 campaigns*	4th qualifying round*
Hastings United	1948–1986	38 campaigns	3rd Round 'Proper'
	2002–2021	19 campaigns*	3rd Round 'Proper'*
Hatfield Main	1929–1933	4 campaigns	2nd qualifying round
	1968–2004	11 campaigns	2nd qualifying round
Hatfield Town	1949–1978	14 campaigns*	2nd qualifying round*
	2008–2015	7 campaigns	2nd qualifying round
Hendon	1877–1889	12 campaigns	QUARTER-FINALS
	1946–2021	74 campaigns*	3rd Round 'Proper'*
Hereford	1891–1895	4 campaigns*	2nd qualifying round
	2016–2021	5 campaigns	2nd Round 'Proper'
Hillingdon Borough	1964–1984	20 campaigns*	3rd Round 'Proper'*
	1994–2016	22 campaigns	3rd qualifying round
Hinckley	1991–1992	1 campaign	preliminary round
	2010–2011	1 campaign*	extra preliminary round*
	2015–2019	4 campaigns	2nd qualifying round
Hinckley Town	1895–1905	10 campaigns*	4th qualifying round*
	1987–1997	10 campaigns	4th qualifying round
Hinckley United	1909–1939	24 campaigns*	5th qualifying round*
	1997–2014	17 campaigns	2nd round 'Proper'
Hitchin Town	1903–1908	5 campaigns*	5th qualifying round*
	1930–2021	84 campaigns	2nd Round 'Proper'
Hornchurch	1882–1884	2 campaigns	1st Round 'Proper'
	1961–2005	44 campaigns*	2nd round 'Proper'*
	2019–2021	2 campaigns*	3rd qualifying round*
Hove	1902–1905	2 campaigns*	1st qualifying round*
	1924–1950	17 campaigns*	3rd qualifying round*
Hucknall Town	1901–1902	1 campaign	2nd qualifying round
	1992–2014	22 campaigns	4th qualifying round
Hyde	1887–1915	9 campaigns	1st Round 'Proper'
	2010–2015	5 campaigns*	4th qualifying round*
Hythe Town	1985–1993	8 campaigns	4th qualifying round
	2001–2021	20 campaigns*	1st Round 'Proper'*
Ilford	1890–1979	78 campaigns	2nd Round 'Proper'
	1999–2021	22 campaigns	1st qualifying round

Ilkeston	1934–1938	4 campaigns	2nd qualifying round
	2012–2017	5 campaigns	4th qualifying round
Ilkeston Town	1893–1903	10 campaigns	5th qualifying round
	1947–2011	62 campaigns	2nd Round 'Proper'
	2019–2021	2 campaigns	4th qualifying round
Jarrow	1895–1909	10 campaigns	1st Round 'Proper'
	1912–1913	1 campaign*	preliminary round*
	1913–1915	2 campaigns*	3rd qualifying round*
	1920–1950	21 campaigns*	1st Round 'Proper'*
Kendal Town	1922–1930	7 campaigns	1st qualifying round
	2000–2021	21 campaigns*	4th qualifying round*
Kirkby Town	1966–1972	6 campaigns	1st Round 'Proper'
(*Merseyside*)	1986–1988	2 campaigns*	preliminary round*
Kirkley	1899–1929	18 campaigns	3rd qualifying round
	1932–1936	4 campaigns*	1st qualifying round*
	2005–2007	2 campaigns	extra preliminary round
Langley Park	1912–1930	12 campaigns	1st qualifying round
	1990–1993	3 campaigns*	2nd qualifying round*
Leatherhead	1909–1910	1 campaign	preliminary round
	1947–2021	66 campaigns	4th Round 'Proper'
Leeds United	1911–1912	1 campaign	preliminary round
	1920–2021	95 campaigns	WINNERS
Leyton	1896–1995	66 campaigns	3rd Round 'Proper'
	2001–2009	8 campaigns	4th qualifying round
Louth Town	1920–1938	13 campaigns	4th qualifying round
	2011–2014	3 campaigns	1st qualifying round
Maidstone United	1898–1993	80 campaigns	3rd Round 'Proper'
	2002–2021	19 campaigns	2nd Round 'Proper'
Maltby Main	1946–1951	5 campaigns*	preliminary round*
	1997–2021	20 campaigns*	2nd qualifying round*
Mansfield Town	1890–1894	4 campaigns	4th qualifying round
	1910–2021	101 campaigns*	QUARTER-FINALS*
Merthyr Town	1910–1935	21 campaigns	2nd Round 'Proper'
	2010–2021	11 campaigns	3rd qualifying round
Mexborough	1885–1900	8 campaigns	1st Round 'Proper'
	1919–1930	11 campaigns*	1st Round 'Proper'*

Mexborough Town	1903–1915	11 campaigns	5th qualifying round
	1964–1974	10 campaigns*	2nd qualifying round*
Milton Keynes City	1974–1985	11 campaigns*	3rd qualifying round*
	1999–2004	5 campaigns	1st qualifying round
Moss Bay	1891–1892	1 campaign	1st qualifying round
	1946–1951	4 campaigns	1st qualifying round
New Mills	1923–1983	19 campaigns	2nd qualifying round
	2005–2018	13 campaigns	2nd qualifying round
Newark	1884–1908	20 campaigns	2nd Round 'Proper'
	2020–2021	1 campaign	2nd qualifying round
Newbury	1891–1899	8 campaigns*	2nd qualifying round*
	2011–2015	4 campaigns	preliminary round
Newcastle East End	1887–1892	5 campaigns	1st Round 'Proper'
	1895–1896, 1906-1915 & 1932–1934	10 campaigns*	2nd qualifying round*
Newcastle West End	1886–1892	6 campaigns	2nd Round 'Proper'
	1936–1939	2 campaigns	1st qualifying round
Newport County	1913–1989	65 campaigns	5th Round 'Proper'
	1999–2021	22 campaigns*	5th Round 'Proper'*
Nuneaton Borough	1945–2008	63 campaigns	3rd Round 'Proper'
	2018–2021	3 campaigns*	3rd qualifying round*
Nuneaton Town	1899–1937	26 campaigns	4th qualifying round
	2008–2018	10 campaigns*	1st Round 'Proper'*
Ormskirk	1914–1915	1 campaign	1st qualifying round
	1971–1975	4 campaigns*	3rd qualifying round*
Padiham	1883–1915	14 campaigns	3rd Round 'Proper'
	2004–2021	17 campaigns	1st qualifying round
Peterborough City	1907–1924	9 campaigns	4th qualifying round
	1992–1993	1 campaign*	preliminary round*
Ramsgate	1911–1925	8 campaigns	3rd qualifying round
	1972–2021	41 campaigns*	1st Round 'Proper'*
Raunds Town	1902–1922	11 campaigns	3rd qualifying round
	1991–2019	24 campaigns	4th qualifying round
Ripley Town	1908–1910	2 campaigns	1st qualifying round
	1927–1938	11 campaigns	4th qualifying round

Rochdale	1897–1901	4 campaigns*	3rd qualifying round*
	1908–2021	103 campaigns	5th Round 'Proper'
Rochdale Town	1901–1903	2 campaigns*	3rd qualifying round*
	2014–2015	1 campaign*	extra preliminary round*
Rock-A-Nore	1904–1909	5 campaigns*	2nd qualifying round*
	1924–1928	4 campaigns	2nd qualifying round
Romford	1878–1910	20 campaigns*	QUARTER-FINALS*
	1929–1978	42 campaigns	2nd Round 'Proper'
	1994–1996	2 campaigns	3rd qualifying round
	1997–2021	24 campaigns*	4th qualifying round*
Rotherham Town	1883–1896	13 campaigns	2nd Round 'Proper'
	1905–1925	16 campaigns*	1st Round 'Proper'*
Rugby Town	1912–1973	33 campaigns	4th qualifying round
	2005–2021	16 campaigns*	3rd qualifying round*
Rushall Olympic	1921–1922	1 campaign	preliminary round
	1981–2021	40 campaigns	4th qualifying round
Salisbury	1905–1928	16 campaigns*	4th qualifying round*
	1947–1993	46 campaigns*	2nd Round 'Proper'*
	2016–2021	5 campaigns	3rd qualifying round
Salisbury City	1928–1939	11 campaigns*	4th qualifying round*
	1993–2015	22 campaigns*	3rd Round 'Proper'*
Sheppey United	1892–2001	97 campaigns	6th qualifying round
	2016–2021	5 campaigns	3rd qualifying round
Shepshed Albion	1909–1927	11 campaigns	1st qualifying round
	1949–1950	2 campaigns*	3rd qualifying round*
	& 1992–1993		
Sherwood Colliery	1948–1951	3 campaigns	preliminary round
	2019–2021	2 campaigns	preliminary round
South Liverpool	1898–1921	8 campaigns*	6th qualifying round*
	1935–1991	49 campaigns	2nd Round 'Proper'
South Shields	1898–1901	3 campaigns	2nd qualifying round
	1911–1930	15 campaigns*	5th Round 'Proper'*
	1937–1974	30 campaigns*	3rd Round 'Proper'*
	1993–2021	26 campaigns	1st Round 'Proper'
St Helens Town	1901–1929	16 campaigns	3rd qualifying round
	1946-2021	68 campaigns	4th qualifying round

St Leonards	1901–1905	4 campaigns*	1st qualifying round*
	1998–2004	6 campaigns*	2nd qualifying round*
Staines Town	1925–1935	10 campaigns*	2nd qualifying round*
	1958–2021	57 campaigns	2nd Round 'Proper'
Stevenage	1956–1960	4 campaigns*	2nd qualifying round*
	2010–2021	11 campaigns*	5th Round 'Proper'*
Stevenage Town	1927–1956	18 campaigns*	2nd qualifying round*
	1960–1968	7 campaigns*	3rd qualifying round*
Stewarts and Lloyds	1936–1948	4 campaigns*	2nd qualifying round*
	1948–2014	19 campaigns	2nd qualifying round
Stockton	1888–1975	75 campaigns	3rd Round 'Proper'
	1987–1999	12 campaigns*	4th qualifying round*
Stowmarket	1931–1938	5 campaigns	1st qualifying round
	1951–1983	19 campaigns*	4th qualifying round*
Sutton Town	1892–1957	46 campaigns*	2nd Round 'Proper'*
(*Nottinghamshire*)	2003–2007	4 campaigns	1st qualifying round
Taunton Town	1928–1936	7 campaigns*	1st Round 'Proper'*
	1969–2021	52 campaigns*	1st Round 'Proper'*
Thornaby	1898–1937	5 campaigns	3rd qualifying round
	2001–2021	12 campaigns*	3rd qualifying round*
Thorne Colliery	1927–1929	2 campaigns	3rd qualifying round
	1933–1968	13 campaigns	2nd qualifying round
Ton Pentre	1909–1923	5 campaigns	4th qualifying round
	1968–1992	24 campaigns	1st Round 'Proper'
Tower Hamlets	1994–1995	1 campaign	preliminary round
	2013–2021	8 campaigns*	preliminary round*
Tufnell Park	1908–1950	32 campaigns	6th qualifying round
	1995–1996	1 campaign*	1st qualifying round*
Tunbridge Wells	1902–1915	9 campaigns	3rd qualifying round
	1969–2021	52 campaigns	2nd qualifying round
Tunbridge	1904–1939	31 campaigns	2nd Round 'Proper'
Wells Rangers	1963–1967	4 campaigns*	2nd qualifying round*
Wakefield	1892–1893	1 campaign	1st qualifying round
	2006–2014	8 campaigns*	2nd qualifying round*

Walsall Wood	1920–1982	3 campaigns	1st qualifying round
	1986–2021	19 campaigns*	2nd qualifying round*
Walthamstow Town	1922–1923	1 campaign	preliminary round
	1923–1925	2 campaigns*	1st qualifying round*
Wednesbury	1881–1893	12 campaigns	QUARTER-FINALS
Old Athletic	1909–1925	12 campaigns	1st qualifying round
Wellingborough	1919–2002	74 campaigns*	1st round 'Proper'*
Town	2007–2021	14 campaigns	1st qualifying round
Witney Town	1923–2002	49 campaigns	1st Round 'Proper'
	2011–2013	2 campaigns*	extra preliminary round*
Wood Green Town	1909–1914	5 campaigns	2nd qualifying round
	1920–1951	22 campaigns*	3rd qualifying round*
Woodford Town	1946–1988	31 campaigns	1st Round 'Proper'
	2019–2021	2 campaigns*	preliminary round*
Workington	1887–1912	23 campaigns	1st round 'Proper'
	1921–2021	94 campaigns	4th Round 'Proper'
Yeovil Town	1907–1915	8 campaigns*	4th qualifying round*
	1946–2021	75 campaigns*	5th Round 'Proper'*
York City	1909–1915	6 campaigns	4th qualifying round
	1923–2021	92 campaigns	SEMI-FINALS

**Participated in the FA Cup under other name(s) as well and may have progressed further in the competition under a different name.*

Rank	Hellenic League	R1	Q4	Q3	Q2	Q1	PR	EP
1	Witney Town (1)	1		2		5	4	
2	Bishop's Cleeve		1	1		1	1	1
3	Hungerford Town		1		2	3	2	3
4	Abingdon Town		1		1	9	11	5
5	Moreton Town		1			4	2	
6	Thame United			1	5	5	4	5
7	Newbury Town			1	4	4	1	
8	Shortwood United			1	3	6	11	1
9	Highworth Town			1	2	5	3	5
10	Banbury United			1	2	1	6	

Top Ten FA Cup Clubs whilst Members of Hellenic League.

Nb. Chart shows number of exits per Round

Top 150 FA Cup Clubs During the 21st Century (2000/01 – 2020/21)

Over 1,150 clubs have participated in the FA Cup so far in the 21st Century, a boom in entrants facilitated by a change of rules on entry criteria that has expanded the access to the competition to village and small town clubs across the length and breadth of the country, resulting in a record 763 entrants competing in the 2011/12 season. The Century has also witnessed a concentration of clubs appearing in and winning FA Cup finals, with either Arsenal or Chelsea lifting the Trophy on almost 60% of occasions. The FA Cup is no longer regarded by many as the pinnacle of the season, but recent first-time victories by Wigan Athletic and Leicester City have shown it still has high affection amongst football fans across the spectrum.

Best Performance - Winners

1	Arsenal	7x Winners
2	Chelsea	5x Winners
3	Manchester United	2x Winners, 5x Finalists
4	Manchester City	2x Winners, 3x Finalists, 6x SF
5	Liverpool	2x Winners, 3x Finalists, 4x SF
6	Portsmouth	1x Winners, 2x Finalists
7	Wigan Athletic	1x Winners, 1x Finalists, 2x SF
8	Leicester City	1x Winners, 1x Finalists, 1x SF

Best Performance - Finalists

9	Watford	1x Finalists, 4x SF
10	Everton	1x Finalists, 3x SF, 7x QF
11	Southampton	1x Finalists, 3x SF, 4x QF
12	Millwall	1x Finalists, 2x SF, 4x QF
13	Aston Villa	1x Finalists, 2x SF, 2x QF
14	West Ham United	1x Finalists, 1x SF, 4x QF
15	Stoke City	1x Finalists, 1x SF, 3x QF
16	Crystal Palace	1x Finalists, 1x SF, 2x QF, 5x R5
17	Hull City	1x Finalists, 1x SF, 2x QF, 4x R5
18	Cardiff City	1x Finalists, 1x SF, 1x QF

Best Performance – Semi-Finalists

19	Tottenham Hotspur	5x SF
20	Middlesbrough	2x SF, 6x QF
21	Sheffield United	2x SF, 5x QF, 9x R5, 14x R4
22	Blackburn Rovers	2x SF, 5x QF, 9x R5, 12x R4
23	Fulham	1x SF, 4x QF, 9x R5
24	Reading	1x SF, 4x QF, 7x R5
25	Newcastle United	1x SF, 4x QF, 4x R5
26	West Bromwich Albion	1x SF, 3x QF, 8x R5
27	Bolton Wanderers	1x SF, 3x QF, 6x R5, 13x R4
28	Sunderland	1x SF, 3x QF, 6x R5, 10x R4

29	Brighton and Hove Albion	1x SF, 2x QF, 6x R5
30	Wolverhampton Wanderers	1x SF, 2x QF, 5x R5
31	Barnsley	1x SF, 2x QF, 3x R5
32	Wycombe Wanderers	1x SF, 1x QF

Best Performance – Quarter-Finalists

33	Birmingham City	3x QF
34	Swansea City	2x QF, 6x R5
35	Charlton Athletic	2x QF, 3x R5, 7x R4
36	Tranmere Rovers	2x QF, 3x R5, 4x R4
37	Burnley	1x QF, 7x R5
38	Norwich City	1x QF, 4x R5
39	Coventry City	1x QF, 3x R5, 11x R4
40	Leeds United	1x QF, 3x R5, 6x R4
41	AFC Bournemouth	1x QF, 2x R5
42	Plymouth Argyle	1x QF, 1x R5, 3x R4, 10x R3
43	Bristol Rovers	1x QF, 1x R5, 3x R4, 7x R3
44	Bradford City	1x QF, 1x R5, 1x R4, 8x R3
45	Lincoln City	1x QF, 1x R5, 1x R4, 3x R3

Best Performance – 5th Round

46	Derby County	6x R5
47	Preston North End	5x R5
48	Sheffield Wednesday	4x R5, 9x R4
49	Huddersfield Town	4x R5, 6x R4
50	Brentford	3x R5, 8x R4
51	Bristol City	3x R5, 6x R4
52	Nottingham Forest	2x R5, 9x R4
53	Rochdale	2x R5, 5x R4
54	Colchester United	2x R5, 4x R4, 9x R3
55	Walsall	2x R5, 4x R4, 8x R3
56	Crawley Town	2x R5, 3x R4
57	Ipswich Town	1x R5, 7x R4
58	Queens Park Rangers	1x R5, 5x R5, 18x R3
59	Gillingham	1x R5, 5x R4, 10x R3
60	Blackpool	1x R5, 4x R4, 17x R3
61	Luton Town	1x R5, 4x R4, 14x R3
62	Doncaster Rovers	1x R5, 4x R4, 12x R3
63	Oldham Athletic	1x R5, 4x R4, 9x R3
64	Notts County	1x R5, 4x R4, 7x R3, 14x R2
65	Shrewsbury Town	1x R5, 4x R4, 7x R3, 10x R2
66	Milton Keynes Dons	1x R5, 3x R4, 10x R3
67	Cheltenham Town	1x R5, 3x R4, 8x R3
68	Oxford United	1x R5, 3x R4, 7x R3, 13x R2
69	Leyton Orient	1x R5, 3x R4, 7x R3, 10x R2

70	Stevenage (Borough)	1x R5, 3x R4, 5x R3
71	Wimbledon	1x R5, 3x R4, 4x R3
72	Crewe Alexandra	1x R5, 2x R4, 8x R3
73	Newport County	1x R5, 2x R4, 5x R3
74	Stockport County	1x R5, 1x R4, 5x R3
75	AFC Wimbledon	1x R5, 1x R4, 4x R3
76	Sutton United	1x R5, 1x R4, 1x R3

Best Performance – 4th Round

77	Peterborough United	5x R4
78	Scunthorpe United	3x R4, 12x R3
79	Southend United	3x R4, 8x R3
80	Yeovil Town	3x R4, 7x R3
81	Accrington Stanley	3x R4, 4x R3
82	Barnet	3x R4, 3x R3
83	Port Vale	2x R4, 6x R3, 16x R2
84	Hartlepool United	2x R4, 6x R3, 12x R2
85	Northampton Town	2x R4, 5x R3, 14x R2
86	Torquay United	2x R4, 5x R3, 8x R2
87	Hereford United	2x R4, 3x R3
88	Bury	2x R4, 2x R3
89	Rotherham United	1x R4, 12x R3
90	Macclesfield Town	1x R4, 8x R3
91	Carlisle United	1x R4, 7x R3, 16x R2
92	Mansfield Town	1x R4, 7x R3, 12x R2
93	Burton Albion	1x R4, 7x R3, 10x R2
94	Swindon Town	1x R4, 6x R3, 11x R2
95	Dagenham and Redbridge ...	1x R4, 6x R3, 8x R2
96	Cambridge United	1x R4, 4x R3, 10x R2
97	York City	1x R4, 4x R3, 5x R2
98	Kidderminster Harriers	1x R4, 3x R3
99	Aldershot Town	1x R4, 2x R3, 10x R2
100	Chesterfield	1x R4, 2x R3, 9x R2
101	Kettering Town	1x R4, 1x R3, 3x R2
102	Havant and Waterlooville	1x R4, 1x R3, 2x R2, 8x R1
103	Kingstonian	1x R4, 1x R3, 2x R2, 2x R1
104	Chorley	1x R4, 1x R3, 1x R2, 4x R1
105	Farnborough Town	1x R4, 1x R3, 1x R2, 2x R1
106	Scarborough	1x R4, 1x R3, 1x R2, 2x R1, (plus 5x q4)
107	Telford United	1x R4, 1x R3, 1x R2, 2x R1, (plus 2x q4)

Best Performance – 3rd Round

108=	Exeter City	5x R3, 9x R2
108=	Grimsby Town	5x R3, 9x R2
110	Fleetwood Town / Freeport	5x R3, 8x R2

111	Chester City	4x R3
112	Morecambe	3x R3, 7x R2, 20x R1
113	Wrexham	3x R3, 7x R2, 15x R1
114	Barrow	3x R3, 5x R2, 11x R1
115	Tamworth	3x R3, 5x R2, 7x R1
116	Forest Green Rovers	2x R3, 6x R2
117	Darlington*	2x R3, 5x R2
118	Dover Athletic	2x R3, 4x R2, 8x R1
119	Eastleigh	2x R3, 4x R2, 6x R1
120	Blyth Spartans	2x R3, 2x R2
121	Woking	1x R3, 5x R2
122	Southport	1x R3, 4x R2, 11x R1
123	Gateshead	1x R3, 4x R2, 9x R1, (plus 4x q4)
124	Northwich Victoria	1x R3, 4x R2, 9x R1, (plus 2x q4)
125	Stourbridge	1x R3, 4x R2, 6x R1
126	Boston United	1x R3, 3x R2, 6x R1
127	Salisbury City	1x R3, 3x R2, 5x R1, (plus 4x q4, 3x q3)
128	Canvey Island	1x R3, 3x R2, 5x R1, (plus 4x q4, 2x q3)
129	Histon	1x R3, 3x R2, 5x R1, (plus 2x q4)
130	Boreham Wood	1x R3, 2x R2, 9x R1
131	AFC Fylde	1x R3, 2x R2, 6x R1
132	Nuneaton Borough*	1x R3, 2x R2, 2x R1
133	Yeading	1x R3, 1x R2, 2x R1, (plus 1x q4)
134	Hastings United	1x R3, 1x R2, 2x R1, (plus 5x q3)
135	Chasetown	1x R3, 1x R2, 2x R1, (plus 2x q3, 7x q2)
136	Eastwood Town	1x R3, 1x R2, 2x R1, (plus 2x q3, 4x q2)
137	Marine	1x R3, 1x R2, 1x R1

Best Performance – 2nd Round

138	Rushden and Diamonds	7x R2
139	Maidstone United	4x R2, 6x R1
140	Solihull Moors	4x R2, 5x R1
141	Altrincham	3x R2, 8x R1
142	Brackley Town	3x R2, 5x R1, (plus 3x q4)
143	Chelmsford City	3x R2, 5x R1, (plus 2x q4)
144	Slough Town	3x R2, 5x R1, (plus 5x q3)
145	Alfreton Town	2x R2, 7x R1
146	FC Halifax Town	2x R2, 6x R1, (plus 6x q4)
147	Oxford City	2x R2, 6x R1, (plus 2x q4)
148	Harrogate Town	2x R2, 5x R1, (plus 6x q4)
149	Guiseley	2x R2, 5x R1, (plus 4x q4)
150	Halifax Town	2x R2, 5x R1, (plus 3x q4)

**Different from current/later club with same/similar name*

150 Top Scoring Clubs in FA Cup

(Excluding void games and games where club(s) disqualified)

1. Overall Top scorers

Pos.	Team Name	Overall	Proper	Qualifying
1	Tottenham Hotspur	900	844	56
2	Kettering Town	893	117	776
3	Arsenal	882	777	105
4	Manchester United	876	819	57
5	Aston Villa	847	847	n/a
6	Gainsborough Trinity	836	96	740
7	Everton	786	786	0
8	Blackburn Rovers	764	764	n/a
9	Chelsea	761	753	8
10	King’s Lynn	748	31	717
11	Hendon	745	39	706
12	Luton Town	734	490	244
13=	Bishop Auckland	730	67	663
13=	Worksop Town	730	13	717
15	Liverpool	728	714	14
16	Bath City	720	99	621
17=	Sheffield Wednesday	707	707	n/a
17=	West Bromwich Albion	707	705	2
19	Wycombe Wanderers	706	192	514
20	Manchester City	701	687	14
21	Grantham Town	695	71	624
22=	Enfield*	684	105	579
22=	Preston North End	684	679	5
24	Bolton Wanderers	681	672	9
25	Wolverhampton Wanderers	680	680	n/a
26	Newcastle United	679	646	33

27	Lowestoft Town	672	2	670
28	Swindon Town	669	523	146
29	Kidderminster Harriers	667	74	593
30	Maidenhead United	661	52	609
31	Wrexham	660	414	246
32	Yeovil Town	656	206	450
33	Cambridge City	651	7	644
34	Weymouth	650	77	573
35=	Chorley	649	22	627
35=	Northwich Victoria	649	102	547
37	Reading	644	524	120
38	Barnet	643	151	492
39	Notts County	641	626	15
40	Worthing	640	6	634
41	Southampton	634	544	90
42=	Spennymoor United	630	31	599
42=	Worcester City	630	40	590
44	Nottingham Forest	629	623	6
45=	Cheltenham Town	628	126	502
45=	Stourbridge	628	19	609
47=	Altrincham	627	97	530
47=	Derby County	627	627	n/a
49	Oxford City	625	25	600
50	Trowbridge Town	624	5	619
51=	Blyth Spartans	621	95	526
51=	Dartford	621	76	545
53	Watford	619	469	150
54	Sutton United	618	60	558
55	Scunthorpe United	617	318	299

56	Frickley Athletic	615	14	601
57	Macclesfield Town	614	133	481
58=	Boston United	612	90	522
58=	Leicester City	612	468	144
60	Southport	609	225	384
61	Birmingham City	606	504	102
62	Bromley	603	31	572
63	Sheffield United	601	570	31
64	Woking	600	96	504
65	Burnley	597	583	14
66	Telford United	594	81	513
67	Middlesbrough	591	511	82
68	Barrow	587	173	414
69	Chesham United	586	8	578
70	Wealdstone	584	21	563
71	Walsall	583	408	175
72	Shrewsbury Town	582	328	254
73=	Brighton and Hove Albion	579	480	99
73=	Shildon	579	13	566
75	Peterborough United	576	430	146
76	Hitchin Town	570	30	540
77	Sunderland	569	562	7
78	AFC Bournemouth	568	455	113
79	Kingstonian	565	30	535
80=	Carlisle United	559	378	181
80=	West Ham United	559	502	57
82=	Lancaster City	557	15	542
82=	Port Vale	557	422	135
84	Slough Town	556	47	509

85	Grimsby Town	554	395	159
86=	Kendal Town	552	20	532
86=	Witton Albion	552	21	531
88	Tooting and Mitcham United	550	26	524
89=	Bristol Rovers	549	445	104
89=	Gillingham	549	381	168
89=	Uxbridge	549	6	543
92	St Albans City	546	20	526
93	Denaby United	544	2	542
94=	Millwall	542	455	87
94=	Stalybridge Celtic	542	27	515
96	Hednesford Town	537	17	520
97	Bideford	534	6	528
98	Goole Town	533	19	514
99	Aylesbury United	532	21	511
100=	Mansfield Town	528	368	160
100=	Southall	528	20	508
102	Wisbech Town	527	13	514
103	Hayes	526	27	499
104=	Margate	525	50	475
104=	Poole Town	525	14	511
104=	Stafford Rangers	525	30	495
107	Marine	524	36	488
108	Darwen	520	155	365
109	Lincoln City	519	347	172
110	Tranmere Rovers	518	420	98
111=	Crewe Alexandra	515	369	146
111=	Stoke City	515	476	39
113	Consett	514	0	514

114	Salisbury City	513	27	486
115=	Darlington*	512	303	209
115=	Southend United	512	407	105
117	Chesterfield	507	321	186
118	Brentford	506	420	86
119=	Bristol City	505	454	51
119=	North Shields	505	18	487
119=	Sittingbourne	505	10	495
122	Queens Park Rangers	500	432	68
123	Fulham	497	439	58
124	Ashington	493	16	477
125	Chelmsford City	492	76	416
126	Buxton	491	16	475
127=	Bedford Town*	490	44	446
127=	Workington AFC	490	141	349
129	Folkestone	485	44	441
130	Bradford City	484	455	29
131	Carshalton Athletic	482	12	470
132	Whitby Town	481	17	464
133	Runcorn FC Halton	479	50	429
134=	Harwich and Parkeston	475	6	469
134=	Horsham	475	8	467
134=	Newport (IOW)	475	12	463
137=	Blackpool	473	378	95
137=	Grays Athletic	473	6	467
137=	Wigan Athletic	473	248	225
137=	Wimbledon	473	163	310
141=	Basingstoke Town	471	17	454
141=	Coventry City	471	383	88

141=	Hyde United	471	2	469
144	Morecambe	470	56	414
145	Hemel Hempstead Town	469	2	467
146	Oldham Athletic	468	419	49
147=	Barry	467	4	463
147=	Chippenham Town	467	1	466
147=	Huddersfield Town	467	421	46
147=	Merthyr Tydfil	467	39	428
147=	Northampton Town	467	407	60
147=	Nuneaton Borough*	467	52	415

**Different from current / later club with same/similar name*

Rank	Northamptonshire League / United Counties League	R1	Q5	Q4	Q3	Q2	Q1	PR	EP
1	Kettering Town	4	1	1	2	1	2		
2	Wellingborough Town (1)	2			2	7	24	22	
3	Desborough Town	1		2	5	20	39	23	10
4	Bedford Town (1)	1		2	2	2	8	8	1
5	Wisbech Town	1		1	2		4	4	1
6	Irthlingborough Town	1		1	1	5	4	6	
7	Buckingham Town	1			2	3	6	4	5
8	Holbeach United	1				10	19	27	7
9	Stamford		1	1	5	9	23	14	3
10	Higham Ferrers Town		1		1	3	4	5	
11	Rushden Town			2	6	10	29	8	
12	Milton Keynes City (1)			2		1	2		
13	Loughborough United			2					
14	Spalding United			1	5	7	18	13	2
15	Biggleswade Town			1	4	8	16	6	
16	Irthlingborough Diamonds			1	4	7	7	4	
17	St Neots Town			1	3	7	14	6	2
18	Kempston Rovers			1	1	2	6	9	4
19	Corby Town			1	1	1	1	1	
20	Kettering Working Mens Club			1	1		1	1	

Top 20 FA Cup Clubs whilst Members of UCL.

Nb. Chart shows number of exits per Round

150 Top Scoring Clubs in FA Cup

(Excluding void games and games where club(s) disqualified)

2. Top scorers by Section of Competition

Pos.	Proper Rounds	Total	Pos.	Qualifying Rounds	Total
1	Aston Villa	847	1	Kettering Town	776
2	Tottenham Hotspur	844	2	Gainsborough Trinity	740
3	Manchester United	819	3=	King's Lynn	717
4	Everton	786	3=	Worksop Town	717
5	Arsenal	777	5	Hendon	706
6	Blackburn Rovers	764	6	Lowestoft Town	670
7	Chelsea	753	7	Bishop Auckland	663
8	Liverpool	714	8	Cambridge City	644
9	Sheffield Wednesday	707	9	Worthing	634
10	West Bromwich Albion	705	10	Chorley	627
11	Manchester City	687	11	Grantham Town	624
12	Wolverhampton Wanderers	680	12	Bath City	621
13	Preston North End	679	13	Trowbridge Town	619
14	Bolton Wanderers	672	14=	Maidenhead United	609
15	Newcastle United	646	14=	Stourbridge	609
16	Derby County	627	16	Frickley Athletic	601
17	Notts County	626	17	Oxford City	600
18	Nottingham Forest	623	18	Spennymoor United	599
19	Burnley	583	19	Kidderminster H.	593
20	Sheffield United	570	20	Worcester City	590
21	Sunderland	562	21	Enfield*	579
22	Southampton	544	22	Chesham United	578
23	Reading	524	23	Weymouth	573
24	Swindon Town	523	24	Bromley	572
25	Middlesbrough	511	25	Shildon	566

Pos.	Proper Rounds	Total	Pos.	Qualifying Rounds	Total
26	Birmingham City	504	26	Wealdstone	563
27	West Ham United	502	27	Sutton United	558
28	Luton Town	490	28	Northwich Victoria	547
29	Brighton & Hove Albion	480	29	Dartford	545
30	Stoke City	476	30	Uxbridge	543
31	Watford	469	31=	Denaby United	542
32	Leicester City	468	31=	Lancaster City	542
33=	AFC Bournemouth	455	33	Hitchin Town	540
33=	Bradford City	455	34	Kingstonian	535
33=	Millwall	455	35	Kendal Town	532
36	Bristol City	454	36	Witton Albion	531
37	Bristol Rovers	445	37	Altrincham	530
38	Fulham	439	38	Bideford	528
39	Queens Park Rangers	432	39=	Blyth Spartans	526
40	Peterborough United	430	39=	St Albans City	526
41	Hull City	429	41	Tooting & Mitcham U	524
42=	Bury	422	42	Boston United	522
42=	Port Vale	422	43	Hednesford Town	520
44	Huddersfield Town	421	44	Stalybridge Celtic	515
45=	Brentford	420	45=	Consett	514
45=	Tranmere Rovers	420	45=	Goole Town	514
47	Oldham Athletic	419	45=	Wisbech Town	514
48	Portsmouth	415	45=	Wycombe Wanderers	514
49	Wrexham	414	49	Telford United	513
50	Walsall	408	50=	Aylesbury United	511
51=	Northampton Town	407	50=	Poole Town	511
51=	Southend United	407	52	Slough Town	509
53	Swansea City	401	53	Southall	508

Pos.	Proper Rounds	Total	Pos.	Qualifying Rounds	Total
54=	Grimsby Town	395	54	Woking	504
54=	Leeds United	395	55	Cheltenham Town	502
56	Norwich City	389	56	Hayes	499
57	Barnsley	384	57=	Sittingbourne	495
58	Coventry City	383	57=	Stafford Rangers	495
59=	Gillingham	381	59	Barnet	492
59=	Leyton Orient	381	60	Marine	488
61=	Blackpool	378	61	North Shields	487
61=	Carlisle United	378	62	Salisbury City	486
61=	Crystal Palace	378	63	Macclesfield Town	481
64	Crewe Alexandra	369	64	Ashington	477
65	Mansfield Town	368	65=	Buxton	475
66	Rotherham United	361	65=	Margate	475
67	Cardiff City	348	67	Carshalton Athletic	470
68	Lincoln City	347	68=	Harwich & Parkeston	469
69	York City	343	68=	Hyde United	469
70	Exeter City	340	70=	Grays Athletic	467
71	Ipswich Town**	332	70=	Hemel Hempstead T.	467
72	Charlton Athletic	331	70=	Horsham	467
73	Shrewsbury Town	328	73	Chippenham Town	466
74	Plymouth Argyle	327	74	Whitby Town	464
75	Chesterfield	321	75=	Barry	463
76	Stockport County	319	75=	Newport (IOW)	463
77	Scunthorpe United	318	77	Great Yarmouth T.	456
78	Torquay United	316	78=	Barking*	455
79	Doncaster Rovers	313	78=	Redhill	455
80	Hartlepool United	311	80	Basingstoke Town	454
81=	Colchester United	303	81	Yeovil Town	450

Pos.	Proper Rounds	Total	Pos.	Qualifying Rounds	Total
81=	Darlington*	303	82	Bedford Town*	446
81=	Rochdale	303	83	Tonbridge Angels	445
84	Aldershot	277	84	Gresley Rovers*	442
85	Chester City	269	85	Folkestone	441
86	Oxford United	259	86	Sutton Town	440
87	Wigan Athletic	248	87	Hinckley Athletic	437
88	Newport County*	243	88	Winsford United	436
89	Halifax Town	231	89	Runcorn FC Halton	429
90	Southport	225	90=	Chatham Town	428
91	Yeovil Town	206	90=	Merthyr Tydfil	428
92	Bradford (Park Avenue)*	203	92	Windsor and Eton	427
93	Hereford United	202	93	Gloucester City	424
94	Wycombe Wanderers	194	94	Horden Colliery Welf.	422
95	Barrow	173	95	Ashford Town (Kent)	420
96	Wimbledon	163	96=	Bromsgrove Rovers	417
97	Cambridge United	162	96=	Dulwich Hamlet	417
98	Old Etonians	161	98=	Chelmsford City	416
99	Gateshead*	160	98=	Metropolitan Police	416
100	Darwen	155	98=	South Bank	416
101	Barnet	151	101	Nuneaton Borough*	415
102	Clapham Rovers	150	102=	Barrow	414
103	Accrington Stanley*	148	102=	Morecambe	414
104	Royal Engineers	143	104	Ebbsfleet United	410
105	Workington AFC	141	105	Rhyl	407
106	Old Carthusians	136	106	Bury Town	406
107	Macclesfield Town	133	107	Tow Law Town	404
108	Cheltenham Town	126	108	Walton and Hersham	399
109	Swifts	123	109	Corby Town	398

Pos.	Proper Rounds	Total	Pos.	Qualifying Rounds	Total
110	Kettering Town	117	110=	Banbury United	396
111	Enfield*	105	110=	Clapton	396
112	Northwich Victoria	102	112	Penrith	394
113=	Bath City	99	113	Rossendale United	392
113=	Oxford University	99	114=	Leigh Genesis	384
113=	Scarborough	99	114=	Southport	384
116	Altrincham	97	116	Ashton United	383
117=	Gainsborough Trinity	96	117	Heanor Town	381
117=	The Wanderers	96	118=	Leytonstone	380
117=	Woking	96	118=	Sheppey United*	380
120	Blyth Spartans	95	118=	Stamford	380
121=	Marlow	92	121	Stockton*	377
121=	Upton Park	92	122=	Nantwich Town	376
123	Boston United	90	122=	Prescot Cables	376
124	Milton Keynes Dons	83	122=	Taunton Town	376
125	New Brighton	82	125	Tamworth	374
126=	Blackburn Olympic	81	126=	Billingham Synthonia	372
126=	Telford United	81	126=	Matlock Town	372
128	Stevenage	78	128	Hastings United	371
129	Weymouth	77	129=	Frome Town	369
130=	Chelmsford City	76	129=	Skelmersdale United	369
130=	Dartford	76	131=	Bognor Regis Town	367
132=	Kidderminster Harriers	74	131=	Burscough	367
132=	Old Westminsters	74	131=	Halesowen Town	367
134=	Crawley Town	73	131=	Marlow	367
134=	Walthamstow Avenue	73	135	Darwen	365
136	Grantham Town	71	136	Scarborough	363
137	Queen's Park (Glasgow)	69	137	Oswestry Town	361

Pos.	**Proper Rounds**	Total	Pos.	**Qualifying Rounds**	Total
138=	Bishop Auckland	67	138	Desborough Town	356
138=	Burton Albion	67	139	Biggleswade Town	353
140=	Crusaders / Brentwood*	65	140	Welton Rovers	350
140=	Dagenham and Redbridge	65	141	Workington AFC	349
142=	Maidstone United*	60	142	Willington	348
142=	Old Foresters	60	143	Bangor City	345
142=	Sutton United	60	144	Spalding United	343
145	Hendon*	58	145	Dorchester Town	342
146	Morecambe	56	146=	Durham City	340
147	Wednesbury Old Athletic*	53	146=	Rushden Town	340
148=	Aldershot Town	52	148	Cowes	339
148=	Maidenhead United	52	149=	Barnstaple Town	338
148=	Nuneaton Borough	52	149=	West Auckland Town	338

**Different from current / later club with same/similar name*

*** Ipswich Town tally includes one goal from a win where the score is not known*

Rank	Wessex League	Q4	Q3	Q2	Q1	PR	EP
1	New Milton Town	3	1		2	2	6
2	Thatcham Town	1	1	3	8	5	1
3	Blackfield and Langley	1	1	1	1	5	4
4	Romsey Town	1	1	1	1	3	6
5	Poole Town	1		1	1	1	1
6	Brockenhurst		4	1	10	9	7
7	Newport (IOW)		3	2	3	3	4
8	Wimborne Town		2	5	12	3	1
9	AFC Totton		2	5	6	6	
10	Andover		2	2	1	6	1

Top Ten FA Cup Clubs whilst Members of Wessex League.

Nb. Chart shows number of exits per Round

150 years of FA Cup Disqualifications

It's hard enough trying to win FA Cup matches on the pitch without having to concern yourself with whether or not you've fallen foul of the latest FA Rules and Regulations. Over the 140 seasons that the FA Cup has taken place a total of 144 clubs have been disqualified from the competition, an average of just one club per season. Not too bad a number given the amount of matches that have been played since the FA Cup started in the 1871/72 season, but obviously some periods in its history warranted more disqualifications than others. Reasons for disqualifications range from refusal to play extra time at the end of a drawn match after 90 minutes (Sheffield were the first club to fall foul of this rule in 1879/80), paying players (a major transgression in the 19th Century), playing an ineligible player (the most common reason for expulsion) and not having a ground meeting the FA Cup standards (Glebe FC fell afoul of this rule as recently as this 2015/16 season).

The FA Cup had been running for eight seasons without a single club being disqualified (although many had scratched and/or refused to travel), but the variations in rules and conflicting views on professionalism between northern clubs and southern clubs soon caused the FA a whole host of problems, with southern based clubs in particular complaining that their opponents were flouting the rules. These protests often led to matches being re-played rather than to expulsions. However, the first instance of a club being disqualified came about after a match in 1879/80 involving two northern based clubs, Nottingham Forest and Sheffield FC. The two clubs drew 2-2 in their fourth-round tie and Sheffield expected that to mean there would be a need for a replay. However, the FA rules at the time indicated that a replay would only be necessary if the two clubs were still level after extra time. Sheffield refused to play the extra 30 minutes and were subsequently booted out of the competition. Bizarrely, Sheffield had been the beneficiary of an older rule in the 1873/74 season when after two draws with Shropshire Wanderers in the first round of that year's competition, Sheffield progressed on the toss of a coin, the first and only time this method of determining the winner of an FA Cup tie was ever used.

Reading was the next club to be disqualified, two seasons after Sheffield, following a second round 1-1 draw with West End, probably for the same reasons of not playing the extra half hour. More substantial reasons for disqualification came about two further seasons on, as in 1883/84 the unstoppable momentum of professionalism came more and more to the fore. Rossendale, later Rossendale United, was the first club to be disqualified for paying some or all of their players in an FA Cup match in their 6-2 first round win over Irwell Springs. Preston North End were notorious at the time in tempting the best players from Scotland to join them using a whole myriad of enticements designed to hoodwink the FA so as not to fall foul of their anti-professionalism stance. However, the FA became wise to their methods and Preston were disqualified from the 1883/84 competition following a 1-1 home draw with Upton Park. The Lilywhites would go on to become one of nine clubs to be expelled from the FA Cup twice by the FA, although to avoid this likely punishment the following season they just refused to enter the competition.

Another club to be kicked out due to professionalism in 1883/84 was Accrington FC (and again the following season). The club had won its second round match at Blackburn Park Road 3-2 but were found by the FA to have paid some of their players. Blackburn Park Road however refused to be reinstated and withdrew from the competition. They themselves would be disqualified for the same reason in the 1887/88 season after a 2-1 first round win over Northern Irish club Distillery. Chaos reigned in the FA Cup throughout the next four seasons because of the FA's stance on professionalism and clubs' variety of attempts to disguise that they were paying players. Lots of matches would be voided following protests and 21 times the FA decided that there was enough evidence to disqualify clubs, on several occasions kicking out both sides. This chaos eventually led to farce in the 1887/88 season. Everton took four attempts to defeat Bolton Wanderers in the first round before going on to lose 6-1 to Preston North End in the second round. However, following this second-round match, the FA discovered Everton had paid players in more than one of their matches against Bolton and disqualified them, reinstating Bolton in the process and making Preston have to play Bolton despite having already made it to the third round. Preston had no trouble defeating Bolton as well, winning 9-1 to make the third round for the second time in the same season!

This reprieve for Bolton Wanderers was the third time the club had progressed in the FA Cup thanks to their opponents being disqualified (the other two were Rawtenstall and Preston North End both in 1885/86), and the club hold the record for most times making the next round due to opponent's disqualifications. Eventually the FA bowed to the inevitable and clubs were allowed to pay their players in FA Cup matches. This culminated with the formation of the Football League, but the number of clubs being disqualified didn't diminish too much over the next few seasons. A record high number of nine clubs had been disqualified in the 1885/86 season, but six seasons later there were still six teams disqualified, the second highest total in one season. Amongst those to be ejected from the competition that year were clubs called Royton and Spennymoor (who beat Halliwell 6-3 and Whitby 4-3 respectively), notable in that those games were both clubs' only ever match played in the FA Cup.

As the nineteenth century became the twentieth the number of clubs per season being disqualified numbered no more than two per season, and this was the case right up until the outbreak of the First World War. Following the cessation of hostilities, however, there was a sudden spike in clubs being expelled based mainly on issues with registrations, physical availability of enough valid players, and a mix of local people and stationed / demobilised armed forces personnel. The 1920/21 season saw six clubs ejected and the 1922/23 season saw five clubs kicked out of the competition. However, things soon calmed down again; until the Second World War broke out, that is. The problems that had dogged clubs after the Great War resurfaced in the immediate years following World War II, with six clubs once again being removed in the 1945/46 season. Unlike the previous post war period, however, player availability issues were resolved within a season and Runcorn, in the 1953/54 season, were to be the last club to be disqualified (strangely ejected after losing their game 2-0 at Witton Albion) for 27 years when Marine were expelled in 1980/81 after a 1-0 win over Gateshead.

Since the mid-1980s it has been quite unusual for clubs to be ejected from the competition, mainly doing so due to ineligible players, with three clubs in both 1998/99 and 2004/05 the highest single season total since the 1950s. Greenwich Borough are the only club so far to be kicked out twice in the 21st Century (in 2000/01 after a 1-0 win over Hythe United and in 2004/05 after a 6-3 victory over Eastbourne United Association). Calne Town became the latest club to be disqualified for a second time in 2010/11 (the first time as Calne and Harris United 80 years earlier). Bury FC became the first club in almost 120 years to be disqualified in the 'Proper' Rounds after fielding an ineligible player in their 3-1 second-round replay victory over Chester City in 2006/07. Kent based club Glebe were expelled from the competition in 2015/16 after the FA deemed their ground was not up to the correct standard and put Tunbridge Wells through to the Preliminary Round at their expense.

In 2016/17 season Shropshire based Shawbury United were expelled from the competition after someone switched off their floodlights with eight minutes remaining in their Extra Preliminary Round replay with Coventry United after there had been a lengthy delay awaiting for an ambulance to treat an injured player. Coventry United were 1-0 up at the time. In 2017/18 season Blaby and Whetstone Athletic were disqualified after having won 4-2 against Kimberley Miners Welfare and their opponents were awarded the tie. In 2018/19 season Litherland REMYCA were disqualified after being adjudged to have fielded an ineligible player in their Extra Preliminary Round tie against Charnock Richard. Similarly, Whyteleafe were disqualified after playing an ineligible player in the Preliminary Round against Saltdean United but it was their 1st Qualifying Round opponents, Corinthian-Casuals, who were reinstated. Phoenix Sports suffered the same fate after having played an ineligible player against Lancing in the 1st Qualifying Round who were reinstated.

In the 2019/20 season Dunkirk were disqualified in the Extra Preliminary Round following their 1-1 draw with Gresley due to fielding an ineligible player. Grays Athletic were also disqualified for playing an ineligible player against Heybridge Swifts, but they had already played and won their next match against March Town United before the club was removed from the competition. And in 2020/21 Peacehaven and Telscombe were disqualified for fielding an ineligible player in their 5-3 win at Bearsted in the Extra Preliminary Round.

Rank	Kent League / Southern Counties East League	R1	Q4	Q3	Q2	Q1	PR	EP
1	Hythe Town	1		1	3	4	4	1
2	Herne Bay		1	3	3	18	10	3
3	Greenwich Borough		1	1		3	4	5
4	Tonbridge Angels		1	1		2		
5	Chatham Town			6	3	12	9	2
6	Ramsgate			4	4	6	5	2
7	Deal Town			3	5	15	12	6
8	Sittingbourne			3	3	12	5	
9	Whitstable Town			2	6	14	16	1
10	Maidstone United			2	1	2		

Top Ten FA Cup Clubs whilst Members of SCEL.

Nb. Chart shows number of exits per Round

Top 150 FA Cup Clubs of All Time
(1871/72 to 2020/21)

Arsenal has won 10% of all the FA Cup finals ever contested, an amazing achievement given there had already been 54 winners before the Gunners even lifted the Trophy for the first time. They are the only club to twice appear in three successive finals, and the only one to win the 'Double' in three separate decades. The first ever FA Cup winners, the Wanderers, are still ranked in the Top 12 of all-time despite last lifting the Trophy 143 years ago. Leicester City is the latest new name to be etched on to the plinth, their victory in the most recent FA Cup Final moving the club up 20 places in the overall rankings.

Best Performance - Winners

1	Royal / Woolwich / Arsenal	14x Winners
2	N. Heath / Manchester Utd.	12x Winners
3	Chelsea	8x Winners, 15x Finalists
4	Tottenham Hotspur	8x Winners, 9x Finalists
5	Liverpool	7x Winners, 14x Finalists
6	Aston Villa	7x Winners, 11x Finalists
7	Newcastle United	6x Winners, 13x Finalists
8	Ardwick / Manchester City	6x Winners, 11x Finalists
9	Blackburn Rovers	6x Winners, 8x Finalists
10	Everton	5x Winners, 13x Finalists
11	West Bromwich Albion	5x Winners, 10x Finalists
12	The Wanderers	5x Winners, 5x Finalists
13	Wolverhampton Wanderers	4x Winners, 8x Finalists
14	Bolton Wanderers	4x Winners, 7x Finalists
15	Sheffield United	4x Winners, 6x Finalists
16	The / Sheffield Wednesday	3x Winners, 6x Finalists
17	Thames Iron. / West Ham U.	3x Winners, 5x Finalists
18	Preston North End	2x Winners, 7x Finalists
19	Old Etonians	2x Winners, 6x Finalists
20	Portsmouth	2x Winners, 5x Finalists
21	Sunderland	2x Winners, 4x Finalists
22	Nottingham Forest	2x Winners, 3x Finalists
23	Bury	2x Winners, 2x Finalists
24	Leicester City / Fosse	1x Winners, 5x Finalists, 8x SF
25	Huddersfield Town	1x Winners, 5x Finalists, 7x SF
26	Derby County	1x Winners, 4x Finalists, 13x SF, 24x QF
27	Southampton / St Mary's	1x Winners, 4x Finalists, 13x SF, 22x QF
28	Leeds United	1x Winners, 4x Finalists, 8x SF
29	Oxford University	1x Winners, 4x Finalists, 6x SF
30	Royal Engineers	1x Winners, 4x Finalists, 4x SF
31	Burnley	1x Winners, 3x Finalists, 8x SF
32	Cardiff City	1x Winners, 3x Finalists, 4x SF

33	Blackpool	1x Winners, 3x Finalists, 3x SF
34	Notts County	1x Winners, 2x Finalists, 5x SF
35	Barnsley / St Peter's	1x Winners, 2x Finalists, 3x SF, 10x QF
36	Clapham Rovers	1x Winners, 2x Finalists, 3x SF, 7x QF
37	Charlton Athletic	1x Winners, 2x Finalists, 2x SF
38	Ipswich Town	1x Winners, 1x Finalists, 3x SF, 7x QF
39	Old Carthusians	1x Winners, 1x Finalists, 3x SF, 5x QF
40	Wimbledon	1x Winners, 1x Finalists, 2x SF, 5x QF
41	Wigan Athletic	1x Winners, 1x Finalists, 2x SF, 4x QF
42	Blackburn Olympic	1x Winners, 1x Finalists, 2x SF, 2x QF
43	Singers / Coventry City	1x Winners, 1x Finalists, 1x SF, 6x QF
44	Bradford City	1x Winners, 1x Finalists, 1x SF, 5x QF

Best Performance - Finalists

45	Small Heath/Birmingham C.	2x Finalists, 9x SF
46	Watford / Rovs. / W. Herts	2x Finalists, 7x SF
47	Crystal Palace	2x Finalists, 4x SF, 8x QF
48	Queen's Park	2x Finalists, 4x SF, 4x QF
49	Fulham	1x Finalists, 6x SF
50	Millwall / Athletic	1x Finalists, 5x SF
51	Stoke / City	1x Finalists, 4x SF, 16x QF
52	Luton Town	1x Finalists, 4x SF, 8x QF
53	Middlesbrough	1x Finalists, 3x SF
54	Hull City	1x Finalists, 2x SF, 8x QF
55	Brighton and Hove Albion	1x Finalists, 2x SF, 4x QF
56	Bristol City / South End	1x Finalists, 2x SF, 3x QF
57	Queens Park Rangers	1x Finalists, 1x SF

Best Performance – Semi-Finalists

58	Norwich City	3x SF, 7x QF
59	Swifts	3x SF, 5x QF
60	Oldham Athletic	3x SF, 4x QF
61	Reading	2x SF, 6x QF
62	Swansea Town / City	2x SF, 5x QF, 16x R5
63	Swindon Town	2x SF, 5x QF, 12x R5
64	Grimsby Town	2x SF, 3x QF
65	Leyton / Clapton / Orient	1x SF, 4x QF, 9x R5
66	Darwen	1x SF, 4x QF, 5x R5
67	Plymouth Argyle	1x SF, 2x QF, 4x R5, 21x R4
68	York City	1x SF, 2x QF, 4x R5, 13x R4
69	Cambridge University	1x SF, 2x QF, 4x R3
70	Burslem / Port Vale	1x SF, 1x QF, 8x R5
71	Chesterfield	1x SF, 1x QF, 4x R5
72	Crewe Alexandra	1x SF, 1x QF, 3x R5
73	Marlow	1x SF, 1x QF, 2x R5

74	Wycombe Wanderers	1x SF, 1x QF, 1x R5, 3x R4
75	Old Harrovians	1x SF, 1x QF, 4x R3
76	Derby Junction	1x SF, 1x QF, 1x R3, 2x R2, 5x R1, (plus 1x q3)
77=	Crystal Palace*	1x SF, 1x QF, 1x R3, 2x R2, 5x R1
77=	Shropshire Wanderers	1x SF, 1x QF, 1x R3, 2x R2, 5x R1
79	Rangers (Glasgow)	1x SF, 1x QF, 1x R3, 1x R2

Best Performance – Quarter-Finalists

80	Brentford	4x QF, 9x R5
81	Upton Park	4x QF, 5x R4
82	Bradford (Park Avenue)*	3x QF, 9x R5
83	Eastville / Bristol Rovers	3x QF, 7x R5
84	Tranmere Rovers	3x QF, 6x R5
85	Wrexham / Olympic	3x QF, 5x R5
86	Maidenhead / United	3x QF, 5x R4
87	Sheffield	3x QF, 4x R4
88	Old Westminsters	3x QF, 6x R3
89	Shrewsbury Town	2x QF, 7x R5
90	AFC Bournemouth / & Bosc.	2x QF, 5x R5
91	Abbey / Cambridge United	2x QF, 4x R5
92	Exeter City	2x QF, 3x R5
93	Headington / Oxford United	1x QF, 6x R5
94	Colchester United	1x QF, 5x R5
95	Peterborough United	1x QF, 4x R5, 19x R4
96	Shaddongate / Carlisle Utd	1x QF, 4x R5, 16x R4
97	Mansfield Town / Wesley ...	1x QF, 4x R5, 9x R4
98	New Brompton / Gillingham	1x QF, 3x R5, 10x R4
99	South Shields* / Gateshead*	1x QF, 3x R5, 5x R4
100	Old Foresters	1x QF, 3x R5, 4x R4
101	Lincoln City	1x QF, 2x R5, 5x R4, 34x R3
102	Southport / Central	1x QF, 2x R5, 5x R4, 16x R3
103	Church	1x QF, 2x R5, 3x R4
104	Chatham / Town	1x QF, 2x R5, 2x R4, 4x R3
105	Bootle*	1x QF, 2x R5, 3x R2
106	Brentwood* / Crusaders	1x QF, 3x R4
107	Romford / Town*	1x QF, 2x R4, 4x R3
108	Northwich Victoria	1x QF, 2x R4, 3x R3, 15x R2
109	Birmingham St George's	1x QF, 2x R4, 3x R3, 6x R2
110	Druids	1x QF, 2x R4, 3x R3, 4x R2
111	Hendon*	1x QF, 2x R4, 2x R3
112	Wednesbury Old Athletic*	1x QF, 2x R3
113	Stafford Road Works	1x QF, 1x R3, 5x R2
114	South Shore	1x QF, 1x R3, 4x R2
115	Redcar and Coatham	1x QF, 1x R3, 3x R2

116	Glossop / North End	1x QF, 1x R3, 2x R2, 13x R1
117	Middlesbrough Ironopolis ...	1x QF, 1x R3, 2x R2, 4x R1
118	Woodford Wells	1x QF, 1x R3, 2x R2, 3x R1
119	Hampstead Heathens	1x QF, 1x R3, 1x R2

Best Performance – 5th Round

120	Walsall / Town Swifts	6x R5
121	Doncaster Rovers	5x R5
122	Southend United	4x R5
123	Stockport County	3x R5, 13x R4
124	Northampton Town	3x R5, 9x R4
125	Rochdale	3x R5, 7x R4
126	Rotherham United	2x R5, 18x R4
127	Scunthorpe / & Lyndsey Utd.	2x R5, 11x R4
128	Chester / City*	2x R5, 9x R4
129	Aldershot / Town*	2x R5, 7x R4
130	Halifax Town	2x R5, 4x R4
131	Crawley Town	2x R5, 3x R4
132	Chirk / AAA	2x R5, 3x R3
133	Darlington*	1x R5, 6x R4, 23x R3
134	Newport County*	1x R5, 6x R4, 21x R3
135	Yeovil Town / & Petters Utd.	1x R5, 4x R4, 19x R3
136	Stevenage (Borough)	1x R5, 4x R4, 7x R3
137	Cheltenham Town	1x R5, 3x R4, 10x R3, 18x R2
138	Milton Keynes Dons	1x R5, 3x R4, 10x R3, 12x R2
139	Sutton United	1x R5, 3x R4, 5x R3
140	Telford Utd. / Wellington T.	1x R5, 3x R4, 4x R3
141	Newport County	1x R5, 2x R4, 5x R3
142	Kidderminster Harriers	1x R5, 2x R4, 4x R3, 8x R2
143	Staveley	1x R5, 2x R4, 4x R3, 5x R2
144	Blyth Spartans	1x R5, 1x R4, 4x R3, 14x R2
145	AFC Wimbledon	1x R5, 1x R4, 4x R3, 8x R2
146	Lockwood Brothers	1x R5, 3x R3, 4x R2
147	Leek	1x R5, 3x R3, 3x R2
148	Davenham	1x R5, 2x R3
149	Horncastle*	1x R5, 1x R3, 1x R2, 3x R1
150	Partick Thistle	1x R5, 1x R3, 1x R2, 2x R1

**Different from current / later club with same/similar name*

When the Class of 2020/21 First Entered the FA Cup

1871/72 **Maidenhead United** *(as Maidenhead)* and **Marlow** *(AKA Great Marlow)*

1873/74 **Sheffield**, **Southall** *(as Southall Park)* and **Uxbridge**

1876/77 **Saffron Walden Town** *(as Saffron Walden)*

1877/78 **Grantham Town** *(as Grantham)*, **Notts County** and **Reading**

1878/79 **Nottingham Forest**

1879/80 **Aston Villa** and **Blackburn Rovers**

1880/81 **Sheffield Wednesday** *(as The Wednesday)*

1881/82 **Birmingham City** *(as Small Heath Alliance)* and **Bolton Wanderers**

1882/83 **Chatham Town** *(as Chatham United)*, **Clitheroe** *(as Clitheroe Central)*, **Grimsby Town**, **Macclesfield Town** *(as Macclesfield)*, **Northwich Victoria** and **Southport**

1883/84 **Ashton United** *(as Hurst)*, **Crewe Alexandra**, **Middlesbrough**, **Preston North End**, **Stoke City** *(as Stoke)*, **West Bromwich Albion**, Wolverhampton **Wanderers** and **Wrexham**

1884/85 **Bournemouth** *(as Bournemouth Rovers)*, **Clapton**, **Derby County**, **Hoddesdon Town** *(as Hoddesdon)*, **Lincoln City**, **Stafford Rangers** and **Sunderland**

1885/86 **Burnley**, **Gainsborough Trinity**, **Luton Town**, **Matlock Town** *(as Matlock)*, **Port Vale** *(as Burslem Port Vale)*

1886/87 **Everton**, **Manchester United** *(as Newton Heath LYR)*, **Swindon Town** and **Watford** *(as Watford Rovers)*

1887/88 **Millwall** *(as Millwall Rovers)*, **Shrewsbury Town** and **Winsford United** *(as Over Wanderers)*

1888/89 **Ashington**, **Doncaster Rovers**, **Kettering Town** *(as Kettering)*, **Nantwich Town** *(as Nantwich)* and **Walsall** *(as Walsall Town Swifts)*

1889/90 **Arsenal** *(as Royal Arsenal)*, **Bishop Auckland** and **Sheffield United**

1890/91 **Bath City** *(as Bath AFC)*, **Hednesford Town** *(as Hednesford)*, **Ipswich Town**, **Kidderminster Harriers** *(as Kidderminster Rovers)*, **Leicester City** *(as Leicester Fosse)* and **Manchester City** *(as Ardwick)*

1891/92 **Blackpool**, **Buxton**, **Poole Town** *(as Poole)*, **Prescot Cables** *(as Prescot)*, **Roman Glass St George** *(as Bristol St George)*, **Southampton** *(as Southampton St Mary's)*, **Stourbridge** and **Tranmere Rovers**

1892/93 **Chesterfield**, **Coventry City** *(as Singers FC)*, **Liverpool**, **Newcastle United** and **Stockport County**

1893/94 **Barnsley** *(as Barnsley St Peter's)*, **Gillingham** *(as New Brompton)*, **Redditch United** *(as Redditch Town)*, **Sittingbourne**, **Weymouth** and **Worksop Town**

1894/95 **Chorley**, **Eastbourne Town** *(as Eastbourne)*, **Glossop North End** and **Tottenham Hotspur**

1895/96 **Bristol City** *(as Bristol South End)*, **Bristol Rovers** *(as Eastville Rovers)*, **Dartford**, **Faversham Town** *(as Faversham)*, **Oxford City**, **Queens Park Rangers**, **West Ham United** *(as Thames Ironworks)* and **Wycombe Wanderers**

1896/97 **Fulham**

1897/98 **Aylesbury United**, **Brentford** and **Redhill**

1898/99 **Bromley**, **Chippenham Town**, **Halesowen Town** *(AKA Halesowen)*, **Lowestoft Town**, **Northampton Town** and **Shildon** *(as Shildon United)*

1899/1900 **Desborough Town**, **Portsmouth**, **Street** and **Worthing**

1900/01 **Bury Town** *(as Bury St Edmunds)*

1901/02 **Barrow**, **Brighton and Hove Albion**, **Carlisle United** *(as Shaddongate United)* and **Hemel Hempstead Town** *(as Apsley)*

1902/03 **Basingstoke Town** *(AKA Basingstoke)*, **Cray Wanderers**, **Norwich City** and **Shoreham**

1903/04 **Bradford City**, **Horsham**, **Plymouth Argyle**, **Wells City** and **Woking**

1904/05 **Biggleswade Town** *(as Biggleswade and District)*, **Hastings United** *(as Rock-A-Nore)*, **Hull City**, **Leyton Orient** *(as Clapton Orient)*, **Paulton Rovers** and **Steyning Town Community** *(as Steyning)*

1905/06 **Chelsea**, **Crystal Palace**, **Newhaven**. **North Shields** *(as North Shields Athletic)*, **Oldham Athletic**, **Skelmersdale United**, **West Auckland Town** *(as West Auckland)* and **Worcester City**

1906/07 **Altrincham**, **Bridport**, **Frome Town**, **Penrith** and **Winchester City**

1907/08 **Carlton Town** *(as Sneinton)*, **Southend United**, **St Ives Town**, **Witton Albion**

1908/09 **Basford United**, **Bognor Regis Town** (as Bognor), **Exeter City**, **Hartlepool United** (as Hartlepools United), **Rochdale** and **St Albans City**

1909/10 **AFC Bournemouth** *(as Boscombe)*, **Blyth Spartans**, **Clevedon Town** *(as Clevedon)*, **Farnham Town** *(as Farnham)*, **Gorleston**, **Huddersfield Town**, **Leighton Town**, **Mansfield Town** *(as Mansfield Wesley)*, **Melksham Town** *(as Melksham)*, **Scunthorpe United** *(as Scunthorpe and Lindsey United)* and **Shaftesbury** *(AKA Shaftesbury Town)*

1910/11 **Cardiff City**, **Frickley Athletic** *(as Frickley Colliery)*, **Kempston Rovers**, **Knaresborough Town** *(as Knaresborough)* and **Whitstable Town** *(AKA Whitstable)*

1911/12 **East Grinstead Town** *(as East Grinstead)*, **Grays Athletic**, **Stamford** *(as Stamford Town)*, **Sutton United** and **Weston-super-Mare**

1912/13 **Barnet** *(as Barnet and Alston)*, **Hendon** *(as Hampstead Town)*, **Lewes** and **Stalybridge Celtic**

1913/14 **AFC St Austell** *(as St Austell)*, **Camberley Town** *(as Camberley and Yorktown)*, **Christchurch**, **Harpenden Town**, **Lancaster City** *(as Lancaster Town)*, **Margate**, **Swansea City** *(as Swansea Town)* and **Wealdstone**

1914/15 **Cambridge City** *(as Cambridge Town)*, **Charlton Athletic** and **Cheltenham Town**

1919/20 **Chesham United**, **Congleton Town**, **Deal Town** *(as Deal Cinque Ports)*, **Dulwich Hamlet**, **Durham City**, **Kingstonian**, **Leiston** *(as Leiston Works Athletic)*, **Peterborough Sports** *(as Brotherhoods Engineering Works)* and **Yeovil Town** *(as Yeovil and Petters United)*

1920/21 **Consett** *(as Consett Celtic)*, **Heaton Stannington**, **Leeds United**, **Liversedge**, **Marine** and **Morecambe**

1921/22 **Calne Town** *(as Calne and Harris United)*, **Eastbourne United Association** *(as Eastbourne Royal Engineers Old Comrades)*, **Guiseley**, **Hertford Town**, **Portland United**, **Spalding United**, **Torquay United**, **Westbury United** and **Workington AFC**

1922/23 **Arlesey Town**, **Boldmere St Michaels**, **Carshalton Athletic**, **Erith and Belvedere**, **Newmarket Town**, **St Neots Town** *(as St Neots and District)*

1923/24 **Wisbech Town** and **York City**

1924/25 **Bishop's Stortford**, **Hanwell Town**, **Metropolitan Police**, **Truro City** and **Wimborne Town** *(as Wimborne)*

1925/26 **Braintree Town** *(as Crittall Athletic)*, **Kendal town** *(as Netherfield)*, **Rotherham United** and **Yorkshire Amateur**

1926/27 **Dorchester Town**, **Keynsham Town** *(as Keynsham)*, **Ware** and **Whitby Town** *(as Whitby United)*

1927/28 **Cambridge United** *(as Abbey United)*, **Tilbury** and **Welwyn Garden City**

1928/29 **Gloucester City** and **Thetford Town**

1929/30 **Thatcham Town** *(as Thatcham)*

1930/31 **Hitchin Town**

1931/32	**Cadbury Heath** *(AKA Cadbury Heath YMCA)*, **Droylsden**, **Oxford United** *(as Headington United)* and **Thame United** *(as Thame)*
1932/33	**Histon** *(as Histon Institute)* and **Tooting and Mitcham United**
1933/34	**Haywards Heath Town** *(as Haywards Heath)*, **Tiverton Town** and **Wigan Athletic**
1934/35	**Banbury United** *(as Banbury Spencer)*, **Boston United** and **Tamworth**
1935/36	**Ely City**, **Eynesbury Rovers**, **Hyde United**, **Peterborough United** and **Sutton Coldfield Town** *(as Sutton Town)*
1936/37	**Sherborne Town** *(AKA Sherborne)*
1937/38	**Harlow Town**
1938/39	**Brantham Athletic**, **Chelmsford City**, **Cobham**, **Colchester United**, **Holbeach United** and **Royal Wootton Bassett Town** *(as Wootton Bassett Town)*
1945/46	**Edgware Town**, **Gosport Borough** *(as Gosport Borough Athletic)*, **Harrow Borough** *(as Harrow Town)*, **Kings Langley**, **Ramsgate** *(as Ramsgate Athletic)* and **Slough Town** *(as Slough United)*
1946/47	**Crook Town** *(as Crook Colliery Welfare)*, **Ebbsfleet United** *(as Gravesend and Northfleet)*, **Odd Down** and **St Helens Town**
1947/48	**Burscough**, **Leatherhead**, **Newton Abbot Spurs**, **Royston Town**, **Sawbridgeworth Town** *(as Sawbridgeworth)* and **Whitton United**
1949/49	**Atherton Collieries**, **Barnstaple Town**, **Bedworth United** *(as Bedworth Town)*, **Bideford**, **Cinderford Town**, **Harrogate Town** *(as Harrogate Hotspurs)*, **Lancing** *(as Lancing Athletic)*, **Leamington** *(as Lockheed Leamington)*, **Lye Town**, **Morpeth Town**, **Mossley**, **Potton United**, **Stowmarket Town** *(as Stowmarket Corinthians)*, **Taunton Town** *(as Taunton)*, **Tavistock** and **Tonbridge Angels** *(as Tonbridge)*
1949/50	**Corby Town** *(as Stewarts and Lloyds)*, **Stansted** and **Wembley**
1950/51	**Banstead Athletic**, **Chertsey Town**, **Cheshunt**, **Corsham Town**, **Diss Town**, **Haverhill Rovers** and **Kidlington**
1951/52	**Burton Albion**
1954/55	**Aveley** and **Bodmin Town**
1955/56	**Fareham Town**
1956/57	**Belper Town**, **Leek Town**, **Long Eaton United**, **Warrington Town** *(as Stockton Heath)* and **Whitley Bay** *(as Whitley Bay Athletic)*
1957/58	**Long Melford** and **Soham Town Rangers**

1958/59 **Crawley Town**, **Evesham United** and **Staines Town**

1959/60 **Redbridge** *(as Ford United)*

1960/61 **Alfreton Town**

1964/65 **Corinthian-Casuals**

1965/66 **Boston Town** *(as Boston)*, **Bracknell Town** and **Herne Bay**

1966/67 **Egham Town**, **Fleet Town**, **Hampton and Richmond Borough** *(as Hampton)* and **Stratford Town** *(as Stratford Town Amateurs)*

1968/69 **Alvechurch** and **Molesey**

1969/70 **Canvey Island**, **Highgate United**, **Thackley**, **Tunbridge Wells** and **Whyteleafe**

1970/71 **Boreham Wood**, **Lincoln United** and **Saltash United**

1971/72 **Accrington Stanley**, **Burgess Hill Town** and **Radcliffe** *(as Radcliffe Borough)*

1972/73 **Pagham** and **Peacehaven and Telscombe**

1973/74 **Haringey Borough** *(as Edmonton and Haringey)*, **Hungerford Town** and **Mangotsfield United**

1975/76 **Curzon Ashton**, **Didcot Town**, **Eastleigh** *(as Swaythling)* and **Tividale**

1976/77 **Barton Rovers**, **Horsham YMCA**, **Racing Club Warwick**, **Rugby Town** *(as VS Rugby)* and **Three Bridges**

1977/78 **Billericay Town**, **Chalfont St Peter**, **Forest Green Rovers** and **Larkhall Athletic**

1978/79 **Gateshead**, **Guisborough Town** and **Welling United**

1979/80 **Basildon United** and **Harefield United**

1980/81 **Bootle**

1981/82 **Heybridge Swifts**, **Horndean**, **Rushall Olympic**, **Seaham Rad Star** *(as Seaham Colliery Welfare Red Star)*, **Shifnal Town**, **Torrington** and **Wellington** (Somerset)

1982/83 **AFC Totton**, **Bristol Manor Farm**, **Brockenhurst**, **Flackwell Heath**, **Horley Town**, **Merstham**, **Walsall Wood** *(as Walsall Borough)* and **Whitehawk**

1983/84 **Beckenham Town**, **Coleshill Town**, **Dover Athletic** and **Stevenage** *(as Stevenage Borough)*

1984/85 **Billingham Town** and **Garforth Town** *(as Garforth Miners)*

1985/86 **Burnham** *(as Burnham and Hillingdon)* and **Northallerton Town**

1986/87 **Abingdon United**, **Witham Town** and **Yate Town**

1987/88 **Brackley Town**, **Chasetown** and **Thornaby** *(as Stockton)*

1988/89 **Bashley**, **Corinthian** and **Halstead Town**

1989/90 **Chipstead**, **East Thurrock United**, **Hebburn Town** *(as Hebburn)*, **Maine Road**, **Northwood** and **Whickham**

1990/91 **Blackstones** *(as Mirrlees Blackstone)*, **Eastbourne Borough** *(as Langney Sports)*, **Oakwood**, **Salford City** and **Waltham Abbey**

1991/92 **Dunston** *(as Dunston Federation Brewery)*, **Eccleshill United**, **Maltby Main** *(as Maltby Miners Welfare)*, **Newcastle Town** and **Wingate and Finchley**

1992/93 **Ashford Town** (Middlesex), **Bamber Bridge**, **Barwell**, **Bemerton Heath Harlequins**, **Bradford (Park Avenue) AFC** *(as Bradford (Park Avenue))*, **Dagenham and Redbridge**, **Newport County** *(as Newport AFC)*, **Norwich United**, **Stocksbridge Park Steels** and **Stourport Swifts**

1993/94 **Daventry Town**, **Glasshoughton Welfare**, **Pickering Town** and **South Shields**

1994/95 **Aldershot Town**, **Cogenhoe United**, **Concord Rangers**, **Crowborough Athletic**, **Folkestone Invicta**, **Newport Pagnell Town**, **Pontefract Collieries** and **Westfields**

1995/96 **Bedford Town**, **Hadleigh United**, **Kidsgrove Athletic**, **Potters Bar Town**, **Raynes Park Vale**, **Shepshed Dynamo**, **Tadcaster Albion**, **Totton and Eling** *(as BAT Sports)*, **Trafford**, **Tuffley Rovers**, **Walthamstow** *(as Leyton Pennant)*, **Woodbridge Town** and **Wroxham**

1996/97 **Bridgwater Town**, **Brislington**, **Cirencester Town**, **Great Wakering Rovers**, **Hassocks**, **London Colney**, **Maldon and Tiptree** *(as Maldon Town)*, **Mile Oak**, **Romford** *(as Collier Row and Romford)* and **Southend Manor**

1997/98 **Beaconsfield Town** *(as Beaconsfield SYCOB)*, **Erith Town**, **Hythe Town** *(as Hythe United)*, **Saltdean United** and **Staveley Miners Welfare**

1998/99 **Cowes Sports**, **East Preston**, **Havant and Waterlooville**, **Marske United**, **Ramsbottom United**, **Sandhurst Town** and **Yaxley**

1999/2000 **AFC Sudbury**, **Fleetwood Town** *(as Fleetwood Freeport)*, **Goole AFC**, **Hullbridge Sports**, **Ilford**, **Lordswood**, **Mickleover** *(as Mickleover Sports)*, **North Leigh**, **Oadby Town** and **Sunderland Ryhope Community Association** *(as Kennek Ryhope Community Association)*

2000/01 **Brentwood Town** *(as Brentwood)*, **Bridlington Town**, **Chichester City** *(as Chichester City United)*, **Felixstowe and Walton United**, **Holmer Green**, **Ipswich Wanderers**, **Mildenhall Town**, **Moneyfields**, **Squires Gate**, **St Margaretsbury**, **VCD Athletic**, **Walton Casuals** and **Whitchurch United**

2001/02 **Barking** *(as Barking and East Ham United)*, **Blackfield and Langley**, **Dunstable Town**, **Fairford Town**, **Highworth Town**, **Shepton Mallet** and **Swindon Supermarine**

2002/03	**Bitton, Colne, Deeping Rangers, Dereham Town, Hall Road Rangers, Hallen, Maidstone United, Quorn, Wantage Town, Westfield** and **Willand Rovers**
2003/04	**Enfield Town, Hartley Wintney, Needham Market** and **Stanway Rovers**
2004/05	**AFC Telford United, AFC Wimbledon, Bishop's Cleeve, Bowers and Pitsea, Broadbridge Heath, Cammell Laird 1907** *(as Cammell Laird)*, **Coalville Town, Frimley Green, Godmanchester Rovers, Hamworthy United, Leverstock Green, Milton Keynes Dons, Newcastle Benfield** *(as Newcastle Benfield Saints)*, **North Greenford United, Padiham** and **Silsden**
2005/06	**Biggleswade United, Hornchurch** *(as AFC Hornchurch)*, **Loughborough Dynamo, Oxhey Jets, Romulus, Sevenoaks Town, Slimbridge, Spennymoor Town, Sporting Bengal United, Tring Athletic** and **West Allotment Celtic**
2006/07	**Ardley United, Colliers Wood United, Colney Heath, Daisy Hill, Guildford City, Lymington Town, Sholing** *(as VT FC)* and **Walsham-le-Willows**
2007/08	**Bottesford Town, Cockfosters, Coventry Sphinx, Farnborough, FC Clacton, FC United of Manchester, Hayes and Yeading United, Kirkley and Pakefield, Market Drayton Town, Shrivenham, Solihull Moors, Wellingborough Town, Wellington** (Herefordshire)
2008/09	**AFC Fylde, AFC Wulfrunians, Alresford Town, Amesbury Town, Ashton Athletic, Barton Town** *(as Barton Town Old Boys)*, **Brocton, Crawley Down Gatwick** *(as Crawley Down)*, **Dunkirk, FC Halifax Town, Heather St Johns, Lingfield, Nuneaton Borough** *(as Nuneaton Town)*, **Rothwell Corinthians, Runcorn Linnets** and **Sleaford Town**
2009/10	**Badshot Lea, Bewdley Town, Binfield, Buckland Athletic, Crawley Green, Enfield (1893), Gresley Rovers** *(as Gresley)*, **Kirby Muxloe, Loughborough University, Lydney Town, Radford** and **Scarborough Athletic**
2010/11	**Bradford Town, Brighouse Town, Clanfield 85, Hadley, Hemsworth Miners Welfare, Irlam, Merthyr Town, South Park, Sutton Common Rovers** *(as Mole Valley SCR)*, **Takeley, Tower Hamlets** *(as Bethnal Green United)* and **Woodford Town** *(as Mauritius Sports Association)*
2011/12	**AFC Dunstable, AFC Portchester, Anstey Nomads, Ascot United, Barnoldswick Town, Bedfont Sports, Berkhamsted, Fisher, Grimsby Borough, Hanworth Villa, King's Lynn Town, Leicester Nirvana** *(as Thurnby Nirvana)*, **Newton Aycliffe** and **Runcorn Town**
2012/13	**Ashford United, Chester, Farsley Celtic** *(as Farsley)*, **Fawley, London Lions, Peterborough Northern Star, Plymouth Parkway, Sporting Khalsa, Wellingborough Whitworth** and **Windsor**
2013/14	**AFC Croydon Athletic, AFC Rushden and Diamonds, Albion Sports, Brightlingsea Regent, Canterbury City, Cheltenham Saracens, Cray Valley**

Paper Mills, Dorking Wanderers, Harborough Town, OJM Black Country *(as Black Country Rangers)*, **Reading City** *(as Highmoor-Ibis)*, **Swaffham Town** and **Tadley Calleva**

2014/15 **1874 Northwich, Athersley Recreation, Baldock Town, Brimscombe and Thrupp, Bromsgrove Sporting, Cleethorpes Town, Cribbs, Darlington** *(as Darlington 1883)*, **FC Romania, Handsworth** *(as Handsworth Parramore)*, **Knaphill** and **Phoenix Sports**

2015/16 **AFC Bridgnorth, AFC Darwen, AFC Mansfield, Glebe, Hanley Town, Loxwood, Penistone Church, Risborough Rangers, Spelthorne Sports, Sunderland Ryhope Colliery Welfare** *(AKA Ryhope Colliery Welfare)*

2016/17 **Abbey Rangers, AFC Uckfield Town, CB Hounslow United, Coventry United, Haughmond, Hereford, Hollands and Blair, Longlevens, Northampton ON Chenecks, Salisbury** and **Sheppey United**

2017/18 **Bearsted, Biggleswade, Charnock Richard, Chipping Sodbury Town, City of Liverpool,** Exmouth Town, **Framlingham Town, Litherland REMYCA, Little Common, Stockton Town, West Bridgford, West Essex, Whitchurch Alport** and **Widnes**

2018/19 **AFC Stoneham, Baffins Milton Rovers, Balham, Broadfields United, Coggeshall Town, Easington Sports, Hamble Club, K Sports, Langney Wanderers, Lutterworth Town, Ossett United, Pinchbeck United** and **Winslow United**

2019/20 **Avro, Aylesbury Vale Dynamos, Campion, Ilkeston Town, Longridge Town, Melton Town, Punjab United** (Gravesend), **Selston, Sheerwater, Sherwood Colliery, Stone Old Alleynians, Sutton Athletic, Thame Rangers, Virginia Water, Warrington Rylands** *(as Rylands)* and **Welling Town**

2020/21 **Alfold, Benfleet, Billingshurst, Bovey Tracey, Burton Park Wanderers, Chelmsley Town, Hashtag United, Helston Athletic, Kennington, Little Oakey, Long Crendon, Millbrook, New Salamis, Newark, Newent Town, Park View, Shelley Community, Stansfeld, Westside** and **Wythenshawe Amateurs**

Rank	Eastern Counties League / Eastern League	R2	R1	Q4	Q3	Q2	Q1	PR	EP
1	Great Yarmouth Town	2	1	6	8	17	20	16	8
2	Cambridge United	1	1		1	1	2	1	
3	Lowestoft Town		4	9	10	22	10	10	2
4	Harwich and Parkeston		4	1	3	6	16	15	2
5	King's Lynn		3	3	1	2	1		
6	Gorleston		2	5	1	7	21	23	8
7	Wisbech Town		2	3	3	9	15	6	2
8	March Town United		2	1	7	9	19	11	5

Top Eight FA Cup Clubs whilst Members of ECL.

Nb. Chart shows number of exits per Round

All 737 FA Cup Entrants 2020-21 (© @FACupFactfile)

ROW 01: 1874 Northwich, Abbey Rangers, Abingdon United, Accrington Stanley, AFC Bournemouth, AFC Bridgnorth, AFC Croydon Athletic, AFC Darwen, AFC Dunstable, AFC Fylde, AFC Mansfield, AFC Portchester, AFC Rushden and Diamonds, AFC St Austell, AFC Stoneham, AFC Sudbury, AFC Telford United, AFC Totton, AFC Uckfield Town, AFC Wimbledon, AFC Wulfrunians, Albion Sports, Aldershot Town, Alfold, Alfreton Town, Alresford Town, Altrincham, Alvechurch, Amesbury Town, Anstey Nomads, Ardley United, Arlesey Town, Arsenal, Ascot United, Ashford Town (Mdx), Ashford United

ROW 02: Ashington, Ashton Athletic, Ashton United, Aston Villa, Athersley Recreation, Atherton Collieries, Aveley, Avro, Aylesbury United, Aylesbury Vale Dynamos, Badshot Lea, Baffins Milton Rovers, Baldock Town, Balham, Bamber Bridge, Banbury United, Banstead, Athletic, Barking, Barnet, Barnoldswick Town, Barnsley, Barnstaple Town, Barrow, Barton Rovers, Barton Town, Barwell, Basford United, Bashley, Basildon United, Basingstoke Town, Bath City, Beaconsfield Town, Bearsted, Beckenham Town, Bedfont Sports

ROW 03: Bedford Town, Bedworth United, Belper Town, Bemerton Heath Harlequins, Benfleet, Berkhamsted, Bewdley Town, Bideford, Biggleswade, Biggleswade Town, Biggleswade United, Billericay Town, Billingham Town, Billingshurst, Binfield, Birmingham City, Bishop Auckland, Bishop's Cleeve, Bishop's Stortford, Bitton, Blackburn Rovers, Blackfield and Langley, Blackpool, Blackstones, Blyth Spartans, Bodmin Town, Bognor Regis Town, Boldmere St Michaels, Bolton Wanderers, Bootle, Boreham Wood, Boston Town, Boston United, Bottesford Town, Bournemouth (Ams)

ROW 04: Bovey Tracey, Bowers and Pitsea, Brackley Town, Bracknell Town, Bradford (Park Avenue) AFC, Bradford City, Bradford Town, Braintree Town, Brantham Athletic, Brentford, Brentwood Town, Bridgwater Town, Bridlington Town, Bridport, Brighouse Town, Brightlingsea Regent, Brighton and Hove Albion, Brimscombe and Thrupp, Brislington, Bristol City, Bristol Manor Farm, Bristol Rovers, Broadbridge Heath, Broadfields United, Brockenhurst, Brocton, Bromley, Bromsgrove Sporting, Buckland Athletic, Burgess Hill Town, Burnham, Burnley, Burscough, Burton Albion, Burton Park Wanderers, Bury Town

ROW 05: Buxton, Cadbury Heath, Calne Town, Camberley Town, Cambridge City, Cambridge United, Cammell Laird 1907, Campion, Canterbury City, Canvey Island, Cardiff City, Carlisle United, Carlton Town, Carshalton Athletic, CB Hounslow United, Chalfont St Peter, Charlton Athletic, Charnock Richard, Chasetown, Chatham Town, Chelmsford City, Chelmsley Town, Chelsea, Cheltenham Saracens, Cheltenham Town, Chertsey Town, Chesham United, Cheshunt, Chester, Chesterfield, Chichester City, Chippenham Town, Chipping Sodbury Town, Chipstead, Chorley, Christchurch

ROW 06: Cinderford Town, Cirencester Town, City Of Liverpool, Clanfield 85, Clapton, Cleethorpes Town, Clevedon Town, Clitheroe, Coalville Town, Cobham, Cockfosters, Cogenhoe United, Coggeshall Town, Colchester United, Coleshill Town, Colliers Wood United, Colne, Colney Heath, Concord Rangers, Congleton Town, Consett, Corby Town, Corinthian, Corinthian-Casuals, Corsham Town, Coventry City, Coventry Sphinx, Coventry United, Cowes Sports, Crawley Down Gatwick, Crawley Green, Crawley Town, Cray Valley Paper Mills, Cray Wanderers, Crewe Alexandra, Cribbs

ROW 07: Crook Town, Crowborough Athletic, Crystal Palace, Curzon Ashton, Dagenham and Redbridge, Daisy Hill, Darlington, Dartford, Daventry Town, Deal Town, Deeping Rangers, Derby County, Dereham Town, Desborough Town, Didcot Town, Diss Town, Doncaster Rovers, Dorchester Town, Dorking Wanderers, Dover Athletic, Droylsden, Dulwich Hamlet, Dunkirk, Dunstable Town, Dunston, Durham City, Easington Sports, East Grinstead Town, East Preston, East Thurrock United, Eastbourne Borough, Eastbourne Town, Eastbourne United Association, Eastleigh

ROW 08: Ebbsfleet United, Eccleshill United, Edgware Town, Egham Town, Ely City, Enfield (1893), Enfield Town, Erith and Belvedere, Erith Town, Everton, Evesham United, Exeter City, Exmouth Town, Eynesbury Rovers, Fairford Town, Fareham Town, Farnborough, Farnham Town, Farsley Celtic, Faversham Town, Fawley, FC Clacton, FC Halifax Town, FC Romania, FC United of Manchester, Felixstowe and Walton United, Fisher, Flackwell Heath, Fleet Town, Fleetwood Town, Folkestone Invicta, Forest Green Rovers, Framlingham Town, Frickley Athletic, Frimley Green, Frome Town

ROW 09: Fulham, Gainsborough Trinity, Garforth Town, Gateshead, Gillingham, Glasshoughton Welfare, Glebe, Glossop North End, Gloucester City, Godmanchester Rovers, Goole, Gorleston, Gosport Borough, Grantham Town, Grays Athletic, Great Wakering Rovers, Gresley Rovers, Grimsby Borough, Grimsby Town, Guildford City, Guisborough Town, Guiseley, Hadleigh United, Hadley, Halesowen Town, Hall Road Rangers, Hallen, Halstead Town, Hamble Club, Hampton and Richmond Borough, Hamworthy United, Handsworth, Hanley Town, Hanwell Town, Hanworth Villa, Harborough Town, Harefield United

ROW 10: Haringey Borough, Harlow Town, Harpenden Town, Harrogate Town, Harrow Borough, Hartlepool United, Hartley Wintney, Hashtag United, Hassocks, Hastings United, Haughmond, Havant and Waterlooville, Haverhill Rovers, Hayes and Yeading United, Haywards Heath Town, Heather St Johns, Heaton Stannington, Hebburn Town, Hednesford Town, Helston Athletic, Hemel Hempstead Town, Hemsworth MW, Hendon, Hereford, Herne Bay, Hertford Town, Heybridge Swifts, Highgate United, Highworth Town, Histon, Hitchin Town

ROW 11: Hoddesdon Town, Holbeach United, Hollands and Blair, Holmer Green, Horley Town, Hornchurch, Horndean, Horsham, Horsham YMCA, Huddersfield Town, Hull City, Hullbridge Sports, Hungerford Town, Hyde United, Hythe Town, Ilford, Ilkeston Town, Ipswich Town, Ipswich Wanderers, Irlam, K Sports, Kempston Rovers, Kendal Town, Kennington, Kettering Town, Keynsham Town, Kidderminster Harriers, Kidlington, Kidsgrove Athletic, Kings Langley, King's Lynn Town, Kingstonian

ROW 12: Kirby Muxloe, Kirkley and Pakefield, Knaphill, Knaresborough Town, Lancaster City, Lancing, Langney Wanderers, Larkhall Athletic, Leamington, Leatherhead, Leeds United, Leek Town, Leicester City, Leicester Nirvana, Leighton Town, Leiston, Leverstock Green, Lewes, Leyton Orient, Lincoln City, Lincoln United, Lingfield, Litherland REMYCA, Little Common, Little Oakley, Liverpool, Liversedge, London Colney, London Lions, Long Crendon, Long Eaton United

ROW 13: Long Melford, Longlevens, Longridge Town, Lordswood, Loughborough Dynamo, Loughborough University, Lowestoft Town, Loxwood, Luton Town, Lutterworth Town, Lydney Town, Lye Town, Lymington Town, Macclesfield Town, Maidenhead United, Maidstone United, Maine Road, Maldon and Tiptree, Maltby Main, Manchester City, Manchester United, Mangotsfield United, Mansfield Town, Margate, Marine, Market Drayton Town, Marlow, Marske United, Matlock Town, Melksham Town, Melton Town

ROW 14: Merstham, Merthyr Town, Metropolitan Police, Mickleover, Middlesbrough, Mildenhall Town, Mile Oak, Millbrook, Millwall, Milton Keynes Dons, Molesey, Moneyfields, Morecambe, Morpeth Town, Mossley, Nantwich Town, Needham Market, New Salamis, Newark, Newcastle Benfield, Newcastle Town, Newcastle United, Newent Town, Newhaven, Newmarket Town, Newport County, Newport Pagnell Town, Newton Abbot Spurs, Newton Aycliffe, North Greenford United, North Leigh, North Shields, Northallerton Town, Northampton ON Chenecks

ROW 15: Northampton Town, Northwich Victoria, Northwood, Norwich City, Norwich United, Nottingham Forest, Notts County, Nuneaton Borough, Oadby Town, Oakwood, Odd Down, O/M Black Country Rangers, Oldham Athletic, Ossett United, Oxford City, Oxford United, Oxhey Jets, Padiham, Pagham, Park View, Paulton Rovers, Peacehaven and Telscombe, Penistone Church, Penrith, Peterborough Northern Star, Peterborough Sports, Peterborough United, Phoenix Sports, Pickering Town, Pinchbeck United, Plymouth Argyle, Plymouth Parkway, Pontefract Collieries, Poole Town, Port Vale

ROW 16: Portland United, Portsmouth, Potters Bar Town, Potton United, Prescot Cables, Preston North End, Punjab United (Gravesend), Queens Park Rangers, Quorn, Racing Club Warwick, Radcliffe, Radford, Ramsbottom United, Ramsgate, Raynes Park Vale, Reading, Reading City, Redbridge, Redditch United, Redhill, Risborough Rangers, Rochdale, Roman Glass St George, Romford, Romulus, Rotherham United, Rothwell Corinthians, Royal Wootton Bassett Town, Royston Town, Rugby Town, Runcorn Linnets, Runcorn Town, Rushall Olympic, Saffron Walden Town, Salford City, Salisbury

ROW 17: Saltash United, Saltdean United, Sandhurst Town, Sawbridgeworth Town, Scarborough Athletic, Scunthorpe United, Seaham Red Star, Selston, Sevenoaks Town, Shaftesbury, Sheerwater, Sheffield, Sheffield United, Sheffield Wednesday, Shelley Community, Sheppey United, Shepshed Dynamo, Shepton Mallet, Sherborne Town, Sherwood Colliery, Shifnal Town, Shildon, Sholing, Shoreham, Shrewsbury Town, Shrivenham, Silsden, Sittingbourne, Skelmersdale United, Sleaford Town, Slimbridge, Slough Town, Soham Town Rangers, Solihull Moors, South Park

ROW 18: South Shields, Southall, Southampton, Southend Manor, Southend United, Southport, Spalding United, Spelthorne Sports, Spennymoor Town, Sporting Bengal United, Sporting Khalsa, Squires Gate, St Albans City, St Helens Town, St Ives Town, St Margaretsbury, St Neots Town, Stafford Rangers, Staines Town, Stalybridge Celtic, Stamford, Stansfeld, Stansted, Stanway Rovers, Staveley Miners Welfare, Stevenage, Steyning Town Community, Stockport County, Stocksbridge Park Steels, Stockton Town, Stoke City, Stone Old Alleynians, Stourbridge, Stourport Swifts, Stowmarket Town, Stratford Town

ROW 19: Street, Sunderland, Sunderland Ryhope Colliery Welfare, Sunderland Ryhope Community Association, Sutton Athletic, Sutton Coldfield Town, Sutton Common Rovers, Sutton United, Swaffham Town, Swansea City, Swindon Supermarine, Swindon Town, Tadcaster Albion, Tadley Calleva, Takeley, Tamworth, Taunton Town, Tavistock, Thackley, Thame Rangers, Thame United, Thatcham Town, Thetford Town, Thornaby, Three Bridges, Tilbury, Tiverton Town, Tividale, Tonbridge Angels, Tooting and Mitcham United, Torquay United, Torrington, Tottenham Hotspur, Totton and Eling, Tower Hamlets, Trafford

ROW 20: Tranmere Rovers, Tring Athletic, Truro City, Tuffley Rovers, Tunbridge Wells, Uxbridge, VCD Athletic, Virginia Water, Walsall, Walsall Wood, Walsham-le-Willows, Waltham Abbey, Walthamstow, Walton Casuals, Wantage Town, Ware, Warrington Rylands, Warrington Town, Watford, Wealdstone, Welling Town, Welling United, Wellingborough Town, Wellingborough Whitworth, Wellington (Herefordshire), Wellington (Somerset), Wells City, Welwyn Garden City, Wembley, West Allotment Celtic, West Auckland Town, West Bridgford, West Bromwich Albion, West Essex, West Ham United

ROW 21: Westbury United, Westfield, Westfields, Weston-super-Mare, Westside, Weymouth, Whickham, Whitby Town, Whitchurch Alport, Whitchurch United, Whitehawk, Whitley Bay, Whitstable Town, Whitton United, Whyteleafe, Widnes, Wigan Athletic, Willand Rovers, Wimborne Town, Winchester City, Windsor, Wingate and Finchley, Winsford United, Winslow United, Wisbech Town, Witham Town, Witton Albion, Woking, Wolverhampton Wanderers, Woodbridge Town, Woodford Town, Worcester City, Workington AFC, Worksop Town, Worthing, Wrexham

ROW 22: Wroxham, Wycombe Wanderers, Wythenshawe Amateurs, Yate Town, Yaxley, Yeovil Town, York City, Yorkshire Amateur

All 737 FA Cup Entrants 2020-21 (© @FACupFactfile)

Acknowledgements

A work of research such as this could not be accomplished without three important groups of people. Firstly, all those statisticians and researchers who have gone before me whose works I have referenced, checked, double-checked and in some cases amended. These include, but are not limited to, Tony Brown and his excellent *The FA Challenge Cup Complete Results* books, Mike Collett and his comprehensive *The Complete Record of the FA Cup* books, Richard Rundle and his monumental on-line *Football Club History Database,* Shaun Tyas and his detailed *Dictionary of Football Club Nicknames in Britain and Ireland* book, Keith Warsop and his thorough *The Early F.A. Cup Finals* book, Bob Barton and his ground-breaking *Non-League – A History of League and Cup Football* book, Michael Robinson and his labour of love *Non-League Football Tables* series of books, Tony Pawson and his official *100 Years of the FA Cup* book, and Martin Westby's outstanding *England's Oldest Football Clubs 1815–1889* tome.

Secondly, are all those wonderful people responsible for maintaining club websites, league websites, on-line league table databases, football archives etc. all far too numerous to mention by name, but all critical in providing facts and stats that I have discovered, checked and debated over the years. This raft of data sources is invaluable and has enabled a vast proportion of the research undertaken to be achieved without leaving my home.

The third group of people are those who have provided me with the greatest support since even before the launch of FACupFactfile. Again, there are many, many people to thank and I apologise to those not subsequently mentioned, but be assured I will always be grateful for your support. First and foremost I want to thank Paul Stone and Damon Threadgold who encouraged and supported me as FACupFactfile was on the cusp of being launched. Next are all the champions of what I produce on Twitter, again far too numerous to mention individually, but which include @NonLeagueCrowds, @FootballandWar and @VictoriaGooner. Finally, I want to thank those that have enabled me to bring FACupFactfile to a wider audience namely Caroline Barker and Tim Fuell of *The Non-League Show,* Matt Badcock and Tony Incenzo of the *Non-League Paper,* Nick Judd of Envee Media, Vince Taylor at *Groundtastic Magazine,* and all those in the world of mainstream broadcasting and media who have shared my stats, in particular John Murray, Steve Wilson, Dan Walker and Henry Winter.

All the 'Top 150' ranking lists in this book are obviously extracted from much longer lists not feasible to include in a fixed length format such as a book. However, the full list of clubs for all rankings included in this book (and many more besides) have been collated, and can be requested and purchased by visiting **facupfactfile.co.uk**, *e-mailing* **phil@facupfactfile.co.uk** *or by sending a Direct Message to* **@FACupFactfile** *on Twitter.*

Front cover designed by Paul Windebank of Kingpin Sports Design.

Praise for FACupFactfile on Twitter

"A very informative account that covers the Cup in great detail. Even once out we enjoy following!" – Horsham YMCA FC, *@horshamymcafc*

"No matter who you support I highly recommend following @FACupFactfile. In-depth, accurate coverage of ALL rounds and clubs" – Mark Carruthers, *@MarkCarruthers_*

"Make sure you follow the magnificent @FACupFactfile for everything you never knew you needed to know about the FA Cup" – Stourbridge FC, *@stourbridgeFC*

"If you don't already, please follow @FACupFactfile. Great write-ups and info for all FA Cup matches" – Wimborne Town FC, @WimborneTownFC

"@FACupFactfile – this feed should be followed by all football fans. It's that simple." – Rejected Manager, *@RejectedBook*

"If I'm going to be corrected then who better to do it than the FA Cup oracle. It's almost an honour" – Blyth Spirit, *@BlythSpirit66*

"A really good Twitter account for FA Cup news and stats is @FACupFactfile – worth a follow" – Tony Incenzo, *@TonyIncenzo*

"@FACupFactfile – great service for a competition that embraces so much more than football – it's a social service for local communities" – Ray Stubbs, *@raystubbs*

"The FA Cup is the greatest football competition in the world – @FACupFactfile is the greatest FA Cup fact source in the world. No doubt" – Tim Fuell, *@timfuell*

"Just wanted to say how brilliant your work for the smaller clubs is. Absolutely love what you put out" – Sutton Common Rovers FC, *@official_scr*

"Can't tell you how much I love @FACupFactfile facts" – Caroline Barker, *@carolinebarker*

"A big shout out to @FACupFactfile – the account you need to be following on all things FA Cup" – Greg Johnson, *@gregianjohnson*

"Best thing about FA Cup weekends is a read of the @FACupFactfile blog" – George Northover, *@thenorthover*

"Thanks again for your work. It's truly brilliant" – Sheffieldfootball.com, *@footballsheff*

"10/10 stat here from @FACupFactfile", "Amazing work as always" – Emirates FA Cup, *@EmiratesFACup*

Last Page of Facts

Best FA Cup Clubs Throughout the Decades

Decade	Club	w	f	sf	qf	5	4	3	2	1
1870s	The Wanderers	5			2					1
1880s	Blackburn Rovers	3	1	1	1			1	3	
1890s	Aston Villa	2	1		1				2	4
1900s	Bury	2			1			1	5	1
1910s	Newcastle United	1	1		2					2
1920s	Bolton Wanderers	3				1	1		3	2
1930s	Arsenal	2	1		3	1	1	2		
1940s	Charlton Athletic	1	1			1		1		
1950s	Newcastle United	3			1	1	4	1		
1960s	Tottenham Hotspur	3			1	4		2		
1970s	Arsenal	2	2	1	1	1	1	2		
1980s	Liverpool	2	1	2		2	2	1		
1990s	Manchester United	4	1			3	2			
2000s	Arsenal	3	1	2		2	2			
2010s	Chelsea	3	1	1	1	2	2			
2020s	Leicester City	1			1					

Table shows the rounds reached in each season during each decade.

(E.g. Manchester United during the 1990s - Won FA Cup 4 times, were runners-up on one further occasion, 3 times exited in 5th Rd and twice went out in 4th Round)

Non-league versus Non-League in FA Cup 3rd Round 'Proper'

1961/62	Morecambe	0-1	Weymouth
1965/66	Bedford Town*	2-1	Hereford United
1969/70	Hillingdon Boro'*	0-0	Sutton United
1969/70 Rep	Sutton United	4-1	Hillingdon Borough*
1977/78	Blyth Spartans	1-0	Enfield*
2008/09	Kettering Town	2-1	Eastwood Town

**Different from current/later club with same/similar name*